TECHNOLOGY
AND CHOICE

TECHNOLOGY AND CHOICE

Readings from Technology and Culture

EDITED BY

MARCEL C. LAFOLLETTE
AND JEFFREY K. STINE

The University of Chicago Press
Chicago and London

The essays in this volume originally appeared in various issues of *Technology and Culture*. Acknowledgment of the original publication date may be found on the first page of each essay.

The University of Chicago Press, Chicago 60637
The University of Chicago Press, Ltd., London

95 94 93 92 91   5 4 3 2 1
Library of Congress Cataloging-in-Publication Data

Technology and choice : readings from Technology and culture / edited
  by Marcel C. LaFollette and Jeffrey K. Stine.
     p. cm.
  Includes bibliographical references and index.
  ISBN 0-226-46776-7 (alk. paper) : $30.95 (est.). — ISBN
0-226-46777-5 (pbk. : alk. paper) : $16.95 (est.)
    1. Technology—Social aspects.   2. Technological innovations—
Social aspects.   I. LaFollette, Marcel Chotkowski.   II. Stine,
Jeffrey K.   III. Technology and culture.
T14.5.T44138   1991
303.48'3—dc20   90-15504
                                                                                              CIP

Technology and Choice
A *Technology and Culture* Reader

For Evelyn and Henry
For Dorothy

Proceeds from this book will be donated to the Society for the History of Technology for the support of graduate students.

Contemplating Choice: Historical Perspectives on Innovation and Application of Technology

MARCEL C. LAFOLLETTE AND JEFFREY K. STINE

Routine—the same route, the same techniques, the same results—pushes off the need to make choices. Innovation—the imaginative attempt to introduce something new or to solve some problem—smashes routine and demands choice, even if only the choice to retain the status quo. These essays from *Technology and Culture*, the journal of the Society for the History of Technology, provide a spectrum of historical perspectives on how, when, or why individuals, societies, governments, and industries have made choices regarding the use of technologies. As these essays show, the processes whereby innovative technological solutions are applied to social and industrial problems are rarely linear. Far more often, an idea springs to mind but is used in a technical solution only decades later. Or a technological solution may exist but not be implemented because its use generates other problems.

The push and pull between technology and society is evident throughout these essays: at times, a new technology presents society with new capabilities, accompanied by new moral dilemmas; sometimes, society's desires and dissatisfactions stimulate development of a technical solution; at other times, technologies may be rejected or remaindered. Technological developments represent neither automatically reliable nor necessarily positive outcomes.

These essays offer historical accounts, some recent and some from several centuries ago, of the invention, dissemination, adoption, or rejection of technologies that range in complexity from electrical plugs to nuclear power plants. Arranged in a rough chronological

MARCEL C. LAFOLLETTE is associate research professor of science and technology policy, Center for International Science and Technology Policy, George Washington University, and Editor of the journal *Knowledge*. She is the author of *Making Science Our Own: Public Images of Science, 1910–1955* (Chicago, 1990). JEFFREY K. STINE is curator of engineering, National Museum of American History, Smithsonian Institution, and book review editor of *Technology and Culture*.

1

order, the essays in Part I provide case studies of the variations in choices available. Part II turns the spotlight on the choices scholars make when they conduct research on technologies and frame their debates. Some of the essays rely on unusual, almost whimsical anecdotes. Like fables and folk tales, however, the writings encapsulate sobering insights into human nature and collective sociopolitical behavior. In addition, they reveal that, although technologies may extend variety, alternatives, and flexibility to social systems, ultimately, the choices must depend on human wisdom, in all its depth and all its failings, to guide the decision.

Technology and the Private Sector: Regulation

As the world confronts urban and industrial pollution in the 1990s and as debates continue over the causes of global warming and the greenhouse effect, Carlos Flick's analysis of smoke-abatement efforts in Great Britain during the 19th century takes on new relevance. Before industries expanded into the countryside, most complaints about pollution came from urban centers. Today, of course, one need not live in London or Manchester to find soot on the windowsill, or to breathe somewhat cautiously during a hazy summer inversion. When Flick repeats the grim joke that generations of people in the industrialized regions "had come to believe that in nature the sky was grey and vegetation was black," he anticipates, unintentionally, current reports of the dire pollution in Eastern Europe and elsewhere throughout the world.

It was easy to identify both problem and cause in the 19th century—the smoke billowed from coal-burning furnaces and fireplaces. But local and national governments in search of a solution faced a dilemma. Air pollution could be reduced by changing the behavior of the polluters *or* by altering the technology producing the pollution (or, of course, by some combination of options). Because the English generally found it less controversial and less painful to concentrate reform efforts on machines rather than people, the initial efforts focused in that direction. As environmentalist Barry Commoner has observed, we still exhibit this same tendency today and, as a result, make only halting efforts to solve mutual environmental problems. Many countries have passed extensive environmental legislation since the 1960s, yet the pollution continues. All too frequently, a "technological fix" appears to be more palatable than social change or change in individual behavior.

When political action was taken in England to regulate smokestacks, it began with citizen appeals to local governments and politicians, but few people were sufficiently aroused to support either eliminating the technology or giving up coal. From the perspective of policy, it seemed simpler to regulate commercial and business concerns, which were the largest single source of pollution, than to regulate the thousands of homes that contributed collectively to air pollution through their coal-burning stoves and fireplaces.

The industrial furnace owners naturally resisted attempts to regulate how they carried on their business. They claimed that any regulation would harm industry and argued that smoke should be seen as a "signal" for jobs and profits. It was also hard to gather data on specific pollution levels and hence to identify specific sources of pollution. The polluting factories that were located outside cities, for example, disavowed responsibility for the smoke present in urban areas, and governments lacked sufficient evidence to prove otherwise. Even after reasonably strict laws were passed, local authorities were often loath to enforce them because of industry resistance. Abandoning attempts to curb industrial pollution, the reformers turned to efforts to clean up household chimneys.

This goal proved even more difficult to achieve because the English were quite "addicted to the cheery, open coal fire." Government officials knew it was impossible to supervise 20 million hearths in private homes, let alone to require the installation of expensive filters. Most alternative fuels would double private heating bills, in addition to requiring expensive alterations so hearths could accept other fuels. As a result of these and other problems—and the lack of an effective reform movement—attempts at pollution abatement alternated between policies that regulated technology and large-scale polluters and policies that attempted to regulate human behavior. Flick points out that only after World War II was the drive to control commercial smoke pollution in Britain truly successful.

The 19th-century reformers may in fact have been shooting for a technologically unattainable moon. Even though the Victorian-era "environmentalist" did not really expect pollution-abatement technology to achieve 100 percent efficiency, the technology had such an abysmally poor record that its effectiveness was always in question. Designs had to be adapted to each individual coal furnace, and many of the inventions required frequent repairs, even under normal operating conditions.

The victims of commercially produced smoke pollution in England were also themselves "willing polluters" at home. Talk about the problems caused by factory smoke appeared to have little effect on individual life-styles. When one factory owner presented the choice as "jobs versus murk," Flick reports, "most of the inhabitants reportedly never wavered in their choice of the former." Throughout the political system, participants in this debate (and in many subsequent ones) repeatedly faced "feasible alternatives" accompanied by "formidable

problems" and made collective social compromises that left the original problems unresolved.

Government regulation may limit individual choice, but in itself it
represents a form of collective choice. United States federal regulation of steam boiler construction and operation exemplifies just how
long such changes can take, even when death and injury occur. In the
19th century, the introduction of steam-powered vehicles had transformed American culture, but the benefits of faster and less expensive long-distance transport of goods and people were increasingly
counterbalanced by terrible boiler explosions, especially on steamboats. In 1838 alone, 496 people were killed in fourteen explosions in
the United States. In his essay, "Bursting Boilers and the Federal
Power," the late John G. Burke explored how the attitudes of 19th-
century Americans toward whether and when government should
intervene to protect public health and safety influenced the creation
of federal regulatory agencies. Such regulation, Burke recalled, was
not sanctioned by the Constitution but gained favor as public attitudes
changed.

Burke demonstrated that technical hindsight always appears to be
nearly perfect. Looking back, we can see that many boiler accidents
seemed "almost inevitable": design rules went unheeded during manufacture, and construction materials were often of inferior quality.
Technical ignorance and lack of concern for safety pervaded the
steamboat industry. In retrospect, it also seems remarkable that so
little legislation followed the rash of explosions in England and the
United States. France, Belgium, and Holland did, in fact, pass stringent regulations in the 1820s, and those regulations apparently
helped to reduce the number of explosions on the Continent. Despite
this evidence, however, the United States government delayed regulation, possibly because no vested interests or organized reform groups
pushed for such controls. Instead, pressure eventually came from
"scientific and technically knowledgeable members of society" who
were "from the outset firmly committed to the necessity of federal
intervention and regulation." In the 1830s, the Department of the
Treasury gave "the first research grant of a technological nature
made by the federal government" to the Franklin Institute to investigate the problem.

Strong opposition to scientific investigation, as well as to regulation,
came from owners and masters of steamboats. They argued that
boiler explosions were individual, not systemic, problems and therefore not a government matter. The engineers involved in accidents
had been "ignorant," "careless," or "drunk." These arguments parallel those frequently made today to oppose other forms of government
regulation of science and technology, where problems may be de-

scribed as characteristic not of the technology's design or of the inade-
quacies of the group's rules or procedures, but of deviant or
incompetent individuals. No legislation could ever really "remove the
causes of boiler explosions." "Steam and its application must be left to
the control of intellect and practical science," for the "best safeguard"
against accident is the "intelligent conduct of those engaged in its
use." Such arguments attempt to disassociate the fault from the group
concerned (whether steamboat owners or manufacturers or engineering professionals) and thereby deny collective responsibility.

The steamboat industry succeeded for some time in staving off
regulation, even though explosions, and the accompanying loss of
hundreds of lives, continued. The turning point came after the
Franklin Institute reported that its own experiments "exposed errors
and myths in popular theories on the nature of steam and the causes
of explosions." Congress eventually passed legislation relying on the
study in 1838. By 1845, changes in case law, which held owners of
steam engines responsible for injury caused by their machines, also set
important precedents and provided further pressure for change. Finally, with growing public support for regulation, a strong law passed
in 1852 "had the desired corrective effects," and explosions, deaths,
and injuries began to decline. As Burke skillfully demonstrated, the
"bursting boilers" created choices for all involved about whether lives
and property should be continually jeopardized in order to protect
the autonomy of private enterprise.

Technology and Commercial Innovation

Canning, Patrick O'Bannon writes, "broke with the past." The technique of using heat (or steam) in commercial food processing to sterilize the contents of a can or jar permitted the creation of "entirely new
products" for a mass market and revolutionized food processing
plants. The "waves of mechanization" that swept the Pacific Northwest
fish canneries from the 1860s through the 1910s represented innovation in the factory process and replaced hand operations with machines.

Before fish were canned commercially, the distribution and storage
of such a highly perishable product had limited the fishing industry's
prime markets to coastal communities. The canning process thus
"transformed a complex organic raw material, a freshly caught fish,
into a uniform consumer product packed in identical tin containers"
that could be transported and stored without refrigeration. The canning process itself was not uniform, however. The size and timing of
the fish catch varied considerably, and slow production during a rich
harvest could mean lost profits. Speed on the factory line was limited
by the speed and efficiency of individual workers. Mechanization

could accelerate the process and smooth out some of the manufacturing peaks and valleys caused by variations in the seasonal catch. During lulls in packing, for example, workers could construct and solder cans.

Despite the numerous advantages of the various new machines, their adoption by Pacific canneries proceeded in waves and not as "a steady and continual triumph of technology." O'Bannon offers several explanations. Many factory owners saw the machines as a risk—what if they proved to be less economical or efficient than claimed? Environmental conditions and labor markets also varied widely among the hundreds of canneries located on the West Coast. As long as a small firm could exploit new immigrants as cheap labor, expensive machinery seemed less attractive.

One of the first innovations to be widely adopted was a soldering machine, because it replaced the highest-paid employees on the line. Strikes, protests, and even threatened violence initially stopped some mechanization efforts. Nevertheless, the innovations offered an attractive choice if they allowed a plant to speed up production and take advantage of an unusually large catch.

By the turn of the century, nearly every aspect of the commercial canning industry had been mechanized to some degree. The next wave of innovation aimed at increasing productivity. Finally, one manufacturer developed a machine to perform the last remaining hand operation—butchery. As O'Bannon concludes, we should not assume mechanization of an industry to be linear or smooth. Sometimes, the decision to mechanize may be influenced more by social and environmental conditions than by the efficiency and reliability of the technology.

When it comes to technologies that are adopted (or rejected) by individuals, the choices may be even more complex and ambiguous than those faced by industry. Advertising, for example, attempts to create a demand for a new product. When the product represents an imaginative leap in the repertoire of tools and devices currently available, perhaps eliciting new patterns of behavior from potential customers, the challenge of persuasion may be even greater. In such cases, advertisers often create "concepts" that link an item to some basic human emotion, characteristic, or need, if not to a familiar behavior.

The telephone—now so much a part of our daily lives, portable in briefcases and usable in automobiles—represents just such a device. Today, telephones seem "indispensable" in the abstract; the choices we make regarding them have to do with styles and colors, or how and where we use them, not with whether we accept or reject the device altogether. In the home, the telephone did not replace an existing product or tool (unless, perhaps, the shout over the backyard fence). Moreover, manufacturers originally proposed only rather sober uses for the device: to transmit serious information or conduct business, not to engage in chitchat or gossip or to provide entertainment. Most manufacturing executives at first rejected any suggestion that the telephone should be promoted as an agent of sociability, enabling callers to "reach out and touch someone." Although subscribers indeed adopted the instrument for just such purposes, the telephone industry itself resisted that image until the 1920s.

Claude Fischer, in his essay on the early history of the telephone, explores the development of "nonserious" use of the device and describes how, once the industry saw the commercial potential of "sociability," it exploited the concept aggressively. Advertising began to emphasize not just basic or urgent communication but also how telephone conversations could build or maintain social relationships. The telephone "call" began to supplant the face-to-face encounter and people began to speak of "visiting" with relations by telephone. Comfort, convenience, and privacy all underpinned an individual's decision to install a private phone.

The change in advertising themes described by Fischer reflected not only a crass attempt to create a demand but also changes in "the actual beliefs industry men held about the telephone." Even though Alexander Graham Bell had forecast conversational use, the rest of the industry had regarded such calls as "frivolous" and initially even urged residential customers to forgo "unnecessary" calls. The industry simply did not regard residential customers as a potentially profitable part of their business until the 1920s.

Now the cheerful "voice" at the other end of the line is just as likely to be electronically synthesized or to be a recording on an answering machine; a telephone line may link two fax machines or two computer modems. O'Bannon shows how manufacturers incorporate technology; Fischer shows how consumers *use* technology. The adoption and adaptation of technology does not rest solely on technical and economic considerations. If advertisers did indeed persuade consumers to adopt the telephone as an instrument of sociability, then it was a willing and friendly persuasion, and one related to cultural values and concurrent social change rather than to any particular design of the technology.

The telephone is a commonplace item in most American homes, often noticeable only if it lights up or quacks. Another domestic innovation of the turn of the century, the electrical plug, usually escapes attention altogether. After reading Fred Schroeder's essay, you will see the humble plug in an entirely new light. As he writes, "the commonplace act of plugging an electrical appliance into a wall outlet can be regarded as an act that connects directly into an industrial system—even though in the normal activities of a day, people are no more likely to feel aware that the receptacle connects to a dynamo than they are to think of Canadian forests when turning a newspaper page."

Home appliances depend on quick, easy means of tapping into a power source. If they are vacuum cleaners or typewriters, we also want to be able to move them from room to room, or house to house, while maintaining easy access to power. Imagine the inconvenience if, as was the case in the early 1900s, not all appliance plugs and wall sockets were compatible.

Standardization of plugs and outlets and conversion of existing wiring arrangements took almost two decades in the United States. By the mid-1920s, both plugs and outlets were beginning to be standardized, under the leadership of the National Electric Light Association; by the 1930s, standardization was mostly complete. Today, only the absent-minded world traveler who fails to pack an adapter may notice that uniformity does not extend worldwide.

Schroeder's essay offers an important reminder of how the absence of a crucial technological component, no matter how small, can limit options. In the case of the electrical plug, regularization of the technology helped to broaden consumers' choices. By making uniform the connection to the power grid, manufacturers allowed consumers to concentrate on other characteristics of appliances, such as their efficiency, design, or breadth of function.

Just as Schroeder's "Small Things Forgotten" prompts us to glance anew at the technologies of everyday life, Suellen Hoy's essay, "The Garbage Disposer, the Public Health, and the Good Life," shows how engineers have tackled another perennial problem, waste disposal. Hoy focuses not on variations in design, manufacture, or standardization, but on the social aspects of the introduction, promotion, acceptance, and use of the residential garbage disposer. How, for example, did this particular device evoke post–World War II concerns about the environment, consumerism, and changing roles of women?

Although the garbage disposer may seem the exclusive product of tract housing and suburban living, the General Electric Company actually introduced a version of the device in the mid-1930s. Its initial purpose was to improve public health: If putrescible food wastes could be chopped up sufficiently to pass through a sewage system instead of being stored in pails and buckets, then dangers of vermin, insects, and bacterial contamination might be reduced in urban areas. In the 1940s, engineers reduced the size and number of parts and the overall weight of the device, thereby increasing its capacity. When suburbs began to grow in postwar America, therefore, the basic technology stood ready for widespread adoption at a reasonable price. Such a labor-saving device fitted squarely with the introduction of "all-electric" kitchens in the 1950s.

The disposer's advantages for individuals were apparent, but municipal governments did not immediately seize on the device as either practical or economical. Municipal engineers worried initially about the impact of introducing ground garbage into the sewer system and treatment plants. Public works administrators and city officials seemed convinced, however, that widespread use might alleviate the growing problem of solid waste disposal, especially in urban areas, and further study convinced the engineers that the sewer systems could handle the additional waste. Most cities favored the idea of residential disposers. As the cost per unit dropped, more units were sold, and, finally, in 1950 the first U.S. municipality required that the devices be installed in all new housing.

Twentieth-Century Dilemmas: Technology's Darker Side

Electrical plugs, garbage disposers, telephones, and even canning machines represent seemingly beneficial, positive technologies, ones normally cheered with enthusiasm or, at least, greeted with relief that some odious task has been simplified or eliminated. Not all technology appears so benign, however. In his essay on the federal government and technology during the Great Depression, Carroll Pursell explores the darker side of the social reception of technology. Why did so many artists, journalists, and philosophers express fear of a "Technological Age"? Why did Charlie Chaplin's *Modern Times,* as Pursell asserts, emerge as the quintessential expression of a "struggle against the insane rationality of industrial rhythms"? Why did scholars and writers fear "the full implications of the machine"?

During the 1930s, Pursell tells us, ambivalent attitudes toward technology dominated the American mainstream. Widespread unemployment coexisted with "seeming overproduction." Among supporters of the New Deal were those who hoped to minimize the negative effects of technology as well as those who wanted to maximize the benefits. The timeless suggestion of federal regulation seemed attractive to some Americans but not to all, and few people wanted to suspend the onward march of technology. Should government control the development and manufacturing of technology, or just its use? To control or restrict invention raised even more troubling prospects. Yet, if machine technology threatened to ruin agriculture, for example, why shouldn't the government step in, or at least stop promoting the technology's use?

Technology clearly had another face. From one perspective, it offered hope for "saving the nation," for helping industry dig out of the depression, for providing employment to the millions out of work: "It was a deeply held belief that if such research could turn up just one device such as the radio or automobile the resulting new industry would solve the problem of depression." Certainly, large public works projects such as Hoover Dam, the Tennessee Valley Authority, and rural electrification could pull the country along the road to recovery. The metaphors used by proponents of these projects cast technology in a rosy light, as a positive force. The fault with this approach, Pursell emphasizes, rested not so much with its goals as with its assumption that the social impacts of technology could somehow be measured by cost-benefit analysis, and that the resulting calculation would favor innovation.

Pursell raises many of the difficult issues that continue to surround the planning of large-scale technology projects, especially at the federal level. Because special interests often shape public expectations, and because policy alternatives are rarely clear-cut, some people will benefit while others will suffer from the exact same choice. The federal government could point to examples of both benefit and cost during the 1930s, but fair, equitable, and workable policies did not always result from such analyses. Far too often, "one person's good was another person's bad."

In the post–World War II era, even more complex and ambiguous social choices surrounded the decisions to build domestic nuclear power plants. The reception of this new type of power source reflected a significant change from how society treated electrification and the creation of earlier electrical power systems. Electricity, too, represented a mysterious source of power—one that, unlike the "cheery coal fire," could not be seen. Nevertheless, the introduction of electrification stretched slowly over decades and, accompanied by great promises of benefits, apparently gave ordinary citizens little cause for fear. The organized opposition to electrification that did exist eventually dropped away. Incidents of accidental electrocution were regarded as singular and, like the earlier boiler explosions, were attributed to human failing or faulty manufacture, but not to some intrinsic shortcoming of the technology. The benefits of electrification, like the steamboat and the steam engine, seemed too great to dismiss; society chose to regulate manufacturing and use, and to monitor standards for wiring buildings, but not to dismiss electricity or electrification as too dangerous for widespread adoption. Contemporary controversies over potential biological effects of power transmission lines raise some of these same concerns and same disagreements over how electricity is delivered.

Proposals to use nuclear reactors to generate power were received very differently, largely because the technology (in this case, more a technique for efficiently achieving great quantities of heat) was associated from the beginning with terrifying and horrible destruction. The promoters of domestic nuclear energy technology could not erase that link in the public mind. This type of invisible power—radiation—was an even more mysterious force; it could kill from a distance. The story that George Mazuzan tells about a proposal to build a nuclear power plant in the middle of New York City offers a dramatic but representative example of just how such public images of a technology and their consequent effect on public opinion reshaped government policy.

In this episode, the interests of grass-roots organizations, the commercial power industry, public utilities, and government regulatory agencies intersected and clashed. Even the most basic assumption—that the reactor was needed at all—met with opposition. All parties more or less concurred that the technology could possibly bring some benefit; none agreed on the extent to which building the proposed plant on that particular site could endanger human health and safety. Eventually, the project was stopped, not because of compelling technical arguments, but because those people perceived to be most at risk from the project (or those who perceived themselves to be most at risk) offered major opposition and intervened in the regulatory process.

The controversy began when Consolidated Edison Company, the major power utility for New York City, applied in 1962 for a construction permit to build a 1,000-electrical-megawatt facility in the city borough of Queens. Not only was the reactor one of the largest that had been proposed to date, but its site also lay in one of the most densely populated areas of the country. Nevertheless, New York City needed electricity, and the price of using coal or oil to generate power was rising. Siting generating plants at some distance from the city greatly increased the transmission costs and hence the overall price of electricity. Nuclear power, from a locally sited plant, offered an economical alternative.

A principal objection to the plan to build a New York City reactor concerned not economics but safety. The containment designs then available (primarily large steel or concrete structures) had been tested in theory or in model but never in operation. Although no major accident had yet occurred, preliminary analyses of possible safety hazards were ambiguous enough to cause the regulatory agency in charge, the Atomic Energy Commission (AEC), to adopt a cautious approach to the approval process. Within the AEC, debate therefore centered on how to balance "the agency's initial stress on isolation of reactors" with the industry's "preference for engineered safety features (instead of remote sites)."

Mazuzan's essay provides an interesting comparison to John Burke's description of federal boiler regulation. Both authors attribute a significant role to grass-roots or nongovernmental groups concerned about the safety of a technology and able to develop and use technical arguments to support their positions. Mazuzan notes that the New York City episode in fact "marked the beginning of local protests against nuclear power reactor facilities in the United States." It also demonstrated the increasingly complex problem of regulating potentially dangerous technologies.

Even if a technology operates as safely and efficiently as promised, inadvertent negative side effects may be inherent in its specific design. Nuclear power plants provide examples of just such second-order effects. To ensure that nuclear reactions remain at safe and acceptable levels within the containment vessel, massive amounts of water must pour through a cooling system. The waste heat then escapes to the environment as steam or to some large body of water. In the 1960s, in the wake of general concern about environmental quality, some critics began to focus on how this waste heat might affect aquatic life in the rivers or estuaries into which it was discharged.

The "thermal pollution" question explored in the essay by J. Samuel Walker does not concern risk inherent in the technology itself. Instead, critics focused on a single effect of one commonly accepted design feature. "Thermal pollution resulted from cooling the steam that drove the turbines to produce electricity in fossil fuel plants as well," Walker points out, "but the nuclear plants used steam heat less efficiently and discharged far more waste heat than any comparable fossil fuel plants." Opponents charged that fish and vital plant life would be killed by the artificially raised temperatures. Moreover, the increased temperature would foster the growth of great quantities of blue-green algae, making the water "look, taste, and smell unpleasant."

The technical choices available to solve these second-order effects unfortunately posed additional problems. Artificial cooling ponds, to have any real effect, would have to be several hundred acres in size. The other design choice, cooling towers, blighted the horizon and were invariably even more expensive than the ponds. Walker describes how the environmental protests against nuclear power eventually extended beyond concerns about radiation, incorporating such issues as thermal pollution. "In a period of a few years," he writes, "the image of nuclear power was transformed from being a solution to the dilemma of producing electricity without ravaging the environment to being itself a significant threat to the environment. This perception endured long after the debate over thermal pollution ended, and it played a major role in subsequent controversies over nuclear power and the environment."

Reaching for the Moon and the Stars

The debate over the design of the National Aeronautics and Space Administration's (NASA) space program in the 1960s and 1970s raised still other public technology issues. In her article on the NASA civilian space station proposals, Sylvia Fries shows that, when major technological projects are planned in the public sector, the political and social environment, as well as technical considerations, can "alter the logic of a new technological system."

In addition to federal politics (especially at the congressional level), Fries emphasize three other more subtle influences. First, she describes the prevalent cultural images of the technical possibilities for space travel, many derived from science fiction movies such as *2001: A Space Odyssey.* Her second example incorporates public arguments about the relevance of the space station to national prestige. Third, market forces, in terms of both the availability of commercial products and the push for stations that could launch and service commercial satellites, have steadily influenced the design choices.

To illustrate her argument, Fries chooses three examples from NASA projects. Her first example, the hexagonal design that emerged during the "enthusiastic" first phase of the space program, reflected the political ambiguities of the time. NASA's political situation was dominated by local and congressional constituencies, swayed by exaggerated expectations of success, spurred on by Cold War fears, and maneuvered as a chess piece in presidential politics. In her second example—the project that evolved eventually into Skylab—the scientific community played a prime political role by lobbying NASA for a redesign that would allow more on-board experimentation. NASA officials caved in to the pressure because they were convinced that the scientists might otherwise actively oppose the project; as a consequence, the agency rearticulated its stance on space research so that it formed an integral part of the launch mission and included not just experiments on human biology but also work on astronomy, physics, plant biology, meteorology, and earth resources. These multiple purposes resulted in a submodule design, in which sections of the station would be devoted to specific groups of experiments. In the 1980s, NASA began to consider a third design type, one that emphasized the concept of a "power tower." This design reflected the shift toward a reusable space "shuttle," which would bring supplies and replacement crews from earth. It also permitted the modular construction, in space, of an enormous structure with a separate power system.

Throughout her essay, Fries weaves descriptions of the engineering designs into her accounts of the politics, explaining how factors external to and usually unrelated to the actual design influenced technical decision making at each phase. She argues that "technology cannot be isolated from politics if our picture of the space program is to be complete." The space station shows how public-sector R&D agencies "continuously redefine new technologies in the absence of the market discipline that governs private-sector technological development." Space station design, Fries observes, is thus "as much a product of its political environment as of the engineers who designed it."

Cultural Images of Technology

Many of the essays in this book extend traditional historical methods, combining research in archives, business and government records, and congressional testimony with analysis of popular press coverage, advertising, and personal interviews. Part II includes four essays that use various methodologies and that challenge the history of technology about many of its own assumptions and choices.

The essay by Christine Bose, Philip Bereano, and Mary Malloy blends the insights of history, economics, and sociology in an attempt to understand work that takes place in the home (i.e., "housework"). We have progressed far from the time of primitive hunter-gatherers and fire tenders, the authors remind us; we now depend on tools made by others that contain technological innovations (e.g., the semiconductor chips in new electrical appliances) that we may not understand. The design and intention of household devices can sometimes resemble more the tools used in modern factories than the tools used in households even half a century ago (i.e., such devices are not necessarily derived from other household implements or tools).

The essay offers a framework for examining routine tasks and roles and some standard assumptions about whether the effects of technology on housework have been positive or negative or both. Exploiting a combination of methodological approaches from such disciplines as anthropology, home economics, and marketing, Bose and her co-authors analyze the productivity, efficiency, convenience, and equity of use of such devices. What, for example, are the real costs of performing housework with them? The authors also match popular assertions about technology with experience: Is a particular device really as "labor-saving" as many suggest, for example?

While technology may sometimes reduce the actual physical effort required to accomplish a task, this essay shows that its presence can also create new tasks (e.g., maintenance of appliances) and higher standards (e.g., change the linens more often). Moreover, the new devices do not necessarily decrease household costs overall (e.g., a vacuum cleaner is more expensive than a broom and depends on a reliable source of electricity), and also do not necessarily save time, redistribute tasks, or automatically benefit female members of households, who have traditionally been responsible for housework.

Such "gender-use" questions in the history of technology have always been somewhat problematical. Feminist historians will point out that many crucial issues were completely ignored until quite recently, and that it is the presence of more women in academe and a "critical mass" of feminist historians that has reoriented research and sensitized much of the profession. For that reason in particular, Ruth Schwartz Cowan's talk at a 1975 meeting celebrating the history of technology (which appears in this anthology as her essay "From Virginia Dare to Virginia Slims") was itself an important turning point. Cowan stood up and said what other historians had just admitted quietly—women have used and been affected by technology differently than men have, but the histories themselves have largely ignored this fact. Some differences in use or effect derive from simple (or, depending on your experiences, not so simple) biological differences that led to the development of technologies specific to child rearing, for example. We need go no further than the baby bottle, she points out, to find an example of a technology crucial to modern life (and to the ability of mothers to take jobs outside the home) yet ignored by historians until the 1970s.

The standard histories also ignored how technology specifically affected women workers. The same social attitudes that labeled women economically inferior sometimes placed them in situations where industrial technologies required demeaning (and even dangerous) tasks; in other cases, women were swiftly replaced by technologies at times when male workers' jobs were protected. Cowan challenges many of the most basic assumptions of the history of technology, such as the assertion that technology brought more women into the work force because it allowed them to take on more physically demanding tasks. And in her examination of "women as homemakers," she shows that historians often set up a false model of domestic technological resistance, one based neither on evidence nor on accurate economic models.

Cowan also examines women as "antitechnocrats." How untechnological it must seem to be characterized (as are women in many cultural groups) as irrational, passive, "humanistic," and nature-loving. What role have cultural images of both women and technology played in discouraging young women from becoming engineers? Will the young girls of the 21st century who want to become jackhammer operators or construction workers or computer designers be required, like their foremothers, to "suppress some deeply ingrained notions about their own sexual identity"? As long as women are believed to "experience" technology best as consumers, not as producers, they will be excluded from the hall of technology. They will be looking in, rather than shaping what comes out.

David Billington and Robert Mark also take on the task of comparing two different images—in their case, the high Gothic cathedrals of northern France and the Brooklyn Bridge—to show how historical study from an engineering perspective can illuminate both technical understanding and the intrinsic cultural value of a technological achievement. "While the modern world has properly viewed these cathedrals as Christian monuments which symbolize religious ideas of the medieval world," the authors write, it has often missed the significance of their engineering achievements. Similarly, most historical discussion of the Brooklyn Bridge has tended to emphasize the engineering feat rather than the bridge's extraordinary symbolic value or its powerful aesthetic appeal. Are these symbols of social unity, or disunity? Clarifying those types of questions, Billington and Mark argue, helps in understanding the complete context for modern technology. These were works of both passion and discipline, of aesthetics and engineering.

By moving back and forth between these two remarkable achievements, Billington and Mark disclose a rich texture of common aspects. They show how the cathedrals' flying buttresses exemplify good engineering design and fulfill modern standards for structural soundness. Likewise, the huge cables that string the Brooklyn Bridge not only suspend its weight but also lend it a gracefulness, a sweetness of curve, an attractiveness unavailable to bridges built only of ponderous concrete piles.

Engineering history, like engineering, cannot speak without numbers. Billington and Mark show that adding other dimensions to the analysis can produce a more accurate appreciation of why a structure looks the way it does.

The final essay in this volume, "Elegant Inventions: The Artistic Component of Technology," by Eugene Ferguson, addresses the "inscrutability" of "nonscientific modes of thought." Ferguson wisely does not argue that the scientific mode is always scrutable, but he opens up the aesthetic dimension of the design of even ordinary objects. Thus he exposes the conjunction among innovation, artistic invention, and technological expertise.

Ferguson asserts that sometimes the very lack of a plan, or the spontaneity of an invention (the idea just "springs to mind"), can enhance its elegance. For many reasons, engineering accomplishment may require planning and hard choices, but innovation needs aesthetic elbowroom. Inventiveness demands the freedom to capture the ideas of a moment, the realization that such-and-such a problem exists and could possibly, just possibly, be solved in such-and-such a way.

From Leonardo da Vinci to the work of toy makers, form follows function, but the route to function may often be elegant form. A block of wood is transformed into practical chair or sculpture, into baseball bat or chopstick, but the most successful design is propelled by the inventor's, designer's, manufacturer's, or user's individual search for solution or tool. Science, Ferguson concludes, "will continue to influence technology, but it is art that will choose the specific shape of the future."

Looking Both Ways

Despite the forecasts of science fiction movies in which computers beget computers, technology springs from the inventiveness of human beings, not from itself. The complexity of that creation—and of any subsequent adoption, modification, or rejection—makes the study of the history of technology more than a chronological listing of events. Each technology carries with it human values, biases, and flaws. Each technology presents choices to designers, manufacturers, exploiters, users, and regulators, and their decisions, in turn, are affected by values, biases, and flaws. By baring this complexity for analysis, these essays help us to look forward as well as backward, to see beyond the histories of particular devices or projects toward the greater social and political contexts of technological change.

Part I

The Movement for Smoke Abatement in 19th-Century Britain

CARLOS FLICK

British complaints about atmospheric pollution resulting from the use of coal as a fuel span almost seven centuries. As early as the reign of Edward I there were denunciations of the "smoke nuisance" created by workshops and domestic hearths in London. The problem grew acute with the increase in population and the demand for coal in the capital and other towns, apparently diminished with the decrease following the Black Death, and emerged once more in the 16th century as a major grievance.[1] Until the 19th century, however, only the metropolitan area and parts of several of the older provincial cities were seriously blighted.

With the coming of the Industrial Revolution the problem assumed wholly new dimensions as hundreds of factory chimneys spewed black smoke onto rapidly developing industrial towns. Attention now shifted to the grimy condition of manufacturing cities such as Manchester, Birmingham, Glasgow, and Leeds, as well as to smaller but equally besmirched communities. The minutes of the governing bodies of these towns are filled with grumblings about the adverse effect of smoke upon health, cleanliness, and temperament. Entire regions eventually were affected—the black belt of central and northern England came into being—and grim humor held that generations of people in these regions had come to believe that in nature the sky was gray and vegetation was black. Nevertheless, in the 1880s foreign competition made control of industrial smoke increasingly unlikely, and attention focused once again on the cumulative pollution pro-

CARLOS FLICK is professor of history at Mercer University.

[1]William H. Te Brake, "Air Pollution and Fuel Crises in Preindustrial London, 1250–1650," *Technology and Culture* 16, no. 3 (July 1975): 337–59. See also Peter Brimblecombe, "Attitudes and Responses towards Air Pollution in Medieval England," *Journal of the Air Pollution Control Association* 26, no. 10 (October 1976): 941–45; and John U. Nef, *The Rise of the British Coal Industry*, 2 vols. (London, 1932), 1:7–22, 79–83, 95–109.

This essay originally appeared in *Technology & Culture*, vol. 21, no. 1, January 1980.

duced by square miles of domestic chimneys. The evil assumed a menacing new form before the turn of the century when periodic "black fogs" invested London and some of the cities in the north. Finally, by the 1920s coal-burning electric generating plants with their telltale massive effluvia had been added to the scene, ushering in the present age of smoke pollution.

Literary and artistic depictions of the black shroud enveloping the towns changed little over the decades. The scene is one that is familiar to most people. What is not generally known is that inventors and environmental reformers in Britain made a major effort during the 19th century to develop the technology and to pass the laws needed to control smoke pollution. The movement preceded the equally unsuccessful continental and American ones by a half-century and, unlike them, was national in scope. The history of the drive for smoke abatement in Victorian Britain provides a useful perspective to the current endeavors in Britain and elsewhere to purify the atmosphere.

The Legal Response

The first attention given by Parliament to the smoke nuisance came in 1819 and 1820 when a small, energetic reformer named Michael Angelo Taylor got the House of Commons to appoint two select committees to investigate the possibility of reducing smoke emissions from steam-engine furnaces. Taylor already was well known for his efforts to reform the legal system and for his attacks on defective paving and lighting in London. The committees under his chairmanship summoned a few inventors and manufacturers and quickly concluded that smoke abatement was feasible.[2] In 1821 Taylor introduced a bill to facilitate local prosecutions of owners of steam engines by parties suffering damage from their smoke. The bill permitted justices to impose court costs on convicted defendants and to order action taken to remedy the nuisance. The measure passed, but not until M.P.'s from mining, smelting, and machining industries had these works exempted, beginning a privileged status for them which was to last throughout the drive for abatement.[3]

The law proved ineffectual because private citizens hesitated to litigate against their powerful neighbors and because local justices, some of whom were polluters themselves, did not use the powers given them. By the late 1830s official bodies in several of the large towns had decided to take action against all smoking furnaces in

[2] Great Britain, *Parliamentary Papers*, 1819, VIII, 271–94; 1820, II, 235–51.
[3] Great Britain, *The Public General Statutes*, 1 & 2 Geo. IV. c. 41.

commercial use. In Birmingham in 1839 several shopkeepers on the Board of Street Commissioners complained that smoke from neighboring factories and processing plants was ruining their businesses and homes, and they pressed the board to appoint a steam-engine nuisance committee to enforce abatement. The commissioners complied, and they designated as chairman a brass founder who declared that smoke often made his own house virtually uninhabitable. The members of the committee, however, subsequently found their work frequently impeded by several commissioners who were among the polluters and by other members of the board who disliked to prosecute their fellow members and townsmen.[4] In Manchester, Glasgow, and Bradford street commissioners or other authorities attempted to take similar action against smoking chimneys, acting under old powers given them to remove nuisances in general.

Of more significance, in Derby and Leeds, joined later by Manchester, the new town councils took up the issue and had Parliament pass local improvement acts into which they inserted clauses specifically empowering improvement authorities (the councils themselves or commissioners) to abate smoke. The clause in the Leeds Improvement Act of 1842 resulted from pressure applied to the council by a new citizens' smoke-control association in the city. The dyers of the town, on the other hand, offered vehement opposition and eventually sent a deputation of their own to Parliament and had themselves exempted from the provisions of the clause; they and other manufacturers prevented the appointment by the council of a smoke inspector for almost a year, and afterward they opposed every effort by the nuisance committee of the council to enforce the law.[5]

At Manchester in 1842 J. E. N. Molesworth, vicar of Rochdale, helped establish the Manchester Association for the Prevention of Smoke and began a campaign to persuade manufacturers to sign a resolution pledging themselves voluntarily to abate smoke. Only thirty-five persons signed, and only three of them actually adopted abatement devices. Two years later Molesworth and others used their influence to get a smoke-control clause inserted into the Manchester Improvement Act. The council soon employed an inspector to take

[4]Minutes of the Birmingham Street Commissioners, October 7 and November 4, 1839, and October 5, 1840, Birmingham Reference Library; *Birmingham Journal* (October 10, 1840). There had been a smoke-nuisance committee appointed several years previously at Birmingham, but it had been inactive from the start.

[5]*Parliamentary Papers*, 1843, VII, 387–89, 424; John Wilson to Lord Palmerston, December 22, 1853, Public Record Office, H.O. 45/O.S./4761; *Minutes of Evidence Given on the Smoke Clause in the Leeds Improvement Act* (Leeds, 1857), pamphlet in Leeds Reference Library.

sightings, record excessive smoke according to degrees of blackness, and report offenders to the authorities for prosecution. As was the case at Derby and Leeds, however, efforts to enforce the act encountered heavy opposition from the proprietors of some of the largest factories of the city.[6] The clauses of these local acts at Derby, Leeds, and Manchester attracted much attention from reformers elsewhere because they required owners of furnaces to adopt smoke-control apparatus and to operate them efficiently, thus placing the initiative for remedial measures on the manufacturers and merchants themselves.[7]

A few aroused citizens in these towns had pushed the local governments to take a stance against smoke. Nevertheless, most industrial towns remained without laws on the subject, and in 1843 and 1845 William Alexander Mackinnon moved in Parliament for select committees to consider whether national legislation was needed. Mackinnon was a Scot, a Liberal M.P., and a historian. Like Taylor, he seems to have advocated smoke control because he was shocked at the difference in the atmosphere prevailing at his country seat and that found in London and other large cities. He was resolved, he said, to call the attention of the country gentlemen in Parliament to the ill effects that smoke had upon the health and habits of the inhabitants of the manufacturing districts.

The committees under Mackinnon's chairmanship interviewed numerous inventors, engineers, chemists, manufacturers, reformers, and town officials. They inquired particularly into the effectiveness of the local acts at Derby and Leeds and found that, after some early optimism, these laws already were considered a failure. The chief problem was that owners of furnaces when threatened with prosecution could make inconsequential adjustments and then maintain that they had done their legal best to diminish smoke, throwing the burden of proof back on the authorities. The law also was not clear as to how much smoke was permissible, and town councils in any case were reluctant to press for prosecutions when some of their own members were culprits. Finally, to compound the problem, a procession of mine owners, smelters, and manufacturers of pottery and metallic items appeared before the committees and claimed immunity from legislation on the ground that their industries necessitated heavy loading of furnaces to obtain intense heat or to produce surges of power, render-

[6]*Parliamentary Papers*, 1843, VII, 448–55, 462–65; Benjamin Nicholls to Lord Palmerston, December 10, 1853, H.O. 45/O.S./4761.

[7]6 Geo. IV. c. 132, clause 65; 5 & 6 Vict. c. 104, clause 249; 7 & 8 Vict. c. 40, clause 75. The text of these local acts is not included in the *Public General Statutes* and must be consulted in the local reference libraries.

ing abatement equipment unsuitable. Mackinnon concluded that the only answer was to concede the exemptions and to make it illegal for all other owners of furnaces to create opaque smoke for more than a specified time each day.[8] Abatement equipment thus would be required as a practical matter. Mackinnon introduced bills to this effect in 1844 and 1845, but the government spokesmen refused to be hurried into action. They countered by appointing a commission of two scientists to review the whole matter.

The commission consisted of Sir Henry De la Beche and Dr. Lyon Playfair, both associated with the Museum of Economic Geology in London. In 1846 the two men reported that they had little to add to the select committees' work. The problem was difficult to advise on, they said, for while smoke control was possible it never was a simple matter.[9] The government announced that the inconclusiveness of this assessment did not justify national legislation; Mackinnon made the opposite interpretation and promptly reintroduced his bill. Finally, the government, not wanting to appear indifferent to an admitted evil, included a smoke-control article in the Town Improvement Clauses Act of 1847. The act consolidated older legislation and became operative in a town at the request of the municipal authorities and with the permission of Parliament. A local board of improvement commissioners was empowered to enforce all of the provisions of the measure, including the one dealing with smoke, and to prosecute violators. The smoke clause, however, retained the wording of the Derby, Leeds, and Manchester local acts in that it stipulated that all commercial furnaces were to be constructed so as to abate smoke, and it failed to define offensive emissions.[10]

The act did not apply to London and Scotland. Much to the surprise of reformers, the government on its own moved to legislate separately for these areas. Many officials had been embarrassed by adverse remarks on the smutty metropolis made by foreign visitors during the recent Exhibition of 1851, and the criticism may have led the ministers to sponsor the Smoke Nuisance Abatement (Metropolis) Act of 1853. The act embodied Mackinnon's suggestion that the metropolitan police commissioners serve as the enforcing authority, and it provided for central supervision in that the commissioners were officially responsible to the home secretary. Steamboats plying the Thames were included in the provisions of the measure. The ministers followed previous precedents, however, in requiring abatement

[8]*Parliamentary Papers*, 1843, VII, 379–622; 1845, XIII, 539–602, 621–61.
[9]Ibid., 1846, XLIII, 331–43.
[10]10 & 11 Vict. c. 34, clause 108.

apparatus rather than simply outlawing dark smoke.[11] Government speakers said they doubted whether opaqueness could be legally determined under varying atmospheric conditions, and they believed the law could only compel owners of furnaces to attempt to remedy the nuisance. But to be certain of his ground, Lord Palmerston immediately afterward authorized an inquiry by the General Board of Health into the effectiveness of abatement inventions, and in 1856 as prime minister he sanctioned an amendment act removing the immunity initially granted bathhouses and pottery works.[12] The next year a law similar to that of London was passed for Scotland.[13] In addition, landowners from the start had forced railway companies to use locomotives which burned smokeless fuel or otherwise accomplished smoke control.[14]

Several of the reformers in Parliament were unhappy that the legislation did not go further, and they unsuccessfully introduced new and stronger bills. Mackinnon was joined in these endeavors by Acton Aryton, a brusque and energetic nabob who recently had returned to England, and by the Conservative Lord Redesdale. The environmental cause obviously drew strength from diverse political quarters. All of these parliamentary spokesmen, however, tended to be deferential toward the government and not inclined to press matters very hard, especially in the face of opposition from manufacturing spokesmen such as John Bright, Richard Cobden, Josiah Guest, and Joseph Bailey and in the absence of strong support from other legislators. In any case, the ministers maintained that the initiative was now up to the municipalities.

The ministers' position seemed justified, for in the 1850s and 1860s most of the large towns obtained passage of bills applying the Improvement Clauses Act of 1847 to themselves. Almost all of them accepted the smoke clause, although with some exemptions, and appointed smoke inspectors responsible to the improvement commis-

[11] 16 & 17 Vict. c. 128.

[12] *Parliamentary Papers*, 1854, LXI, 533–61; 19 & 20 Vict. c. 107. Edwin Chadwick at the Board of Health had chided Lord Palmerston with the observation that most manufacturers did not believe that he would enforce the law. Chadwick to Palmerston, May 9, 1854, H.O. 45/O.S./5677.

[13] 20 & 21 Vict. c. 73.

[14] The stipulation for smoke control imposed upon individual companies was retained in the Railway Clauses Consolidation Act of 1845 (8 & 9 Vict. c. 20, clause 114). The railways soon claimed that engines which were constructed on the principle of consuming their own smoke met the requirements of the law without regard to the manner in which they were operated. This gap in the regulations was closed by clause 19 of the Regulation of Railways Act of 1868 (*English and Empire Digest* [London, 1960], 38:347; 31 & 32 Vict. c. 119). Nevertheless, widespread evasions of the law persisted.

sioners. (The Local Government Act of 1858 transferred the enforcement duties to local boards of health for the provincial towns which adopted that reorganization measure, and again excluded the mining, metals, and earthenware industries, but otherwise left the wording of the law unchanged.) The general assessment by the mid-1860s was that London had experienced some improvement since the passage of its act, but that the industrial towns remained, with only temporary respites, as smoky as ever.

Evidence that legislative action could be taken effectually against polluters of the atmosphere meanwhile was provided by the Alkali Works Regulation Act of 1863. Fumes from alkali works and from copper smelters were the foulest and most destructive of all pollutants, so damaging that places such as Liverpool and Swansea early banished the offending manufactories from the boroughs, only to see them set up shop nearby. By the middle of the 19th century copper production was centered in the Swansea region and alkali manufacture in the Glasgow, Tyneside, and Merseyside areas. Despite the use of improved furnaces, relatively little could be done to control the "copper smoke" given off by the South Wales smelters. The development of Gossage towers, however, provided a means for absorbing the hydrochloric acid fumes emitted by the alkali works, and the Alkali Act required producers to suppress 95 percent of the gas.[15] The advocates of smoke control did not fail to point to the success of this act in pressing their own cause.

Sir Robert Peel, the son of the former prime minister, in a lengthy speech in March 1866, called for new exertions to alleviate the "pestilential atmosphere" of the industrial towns. Some of the places which he had visited recently, he said, could hardly be seen for the smoke. The home secretary replied that the existing law was adequate, but he agreed to survey the mayors of the large towns to see why it was not being enforced.[16] The replies to this inquiry, given in a return dated April 1866, were somewhat evasive. They revealed that numerous violations were reported by inspectors in most places, but that the enforcing authorities were lax. In order to make a case, the inspectors had to observe a polluting chimney for as long as four hours a day over a period of several weeks, gathering data on the density of the smoke emitted, usually on a scale of one to ten, and on the duration of each type. In most cases the nuisance committee of the commissioners or of the board of health then decided whether to summon the accused party and, afterward, whether to let him off with a warning or

---

[15] W. A. Damon, "The Alkali Act and the Work of the Alkali Inspectors," *Royal Society of Health Journal* (London) 76, no. 9 (September 1956): 566–75.

[16] Great Britain, *Hansard*, CLXXXI, 1810–28.

refer the case to the magistrates for action. The offenders usually pleaded special circumstances, and frequently they adopted the tactic employed earlier in Derby and Leeds of making minor alterations in their furnaces and claiming thereby to have met the requirements of the law. Some committees permitted the guilty parties to pay a light fine to the commissioners or the board of health to avoid having the cases taken before the justices. Offenders, in short, almost always got a sympathetic hearing.

The result was that many violations were cited but few convictions were made in the courts. From the 1850s (the dates of their adoption of the Improvement Clauses Act) through 1865, for example, Leeds, Newcastle, Derby, Leicester, and Manchester averaged four or fewer convictions per year, and Huddersfield, Stoke-on-Trent, Sunderland, Worcester, and Wolverhampton reported none at all.[17] Typical of the difficulties was the experience of Manchester three years later, in 1868, when the nuisance inspector reported over 4,000 observations and 140 summons issued, but only six cases taken before the magistrates and only five persons convicted.[18] Even where convictions were more common, in places such as Birmingham, Liverpool, and Sheffield, the fines imposed were so low that the offenders readily pleaded guilty and paid rather than contest the charges.[19] As some of the reformers noted, it was cheaper for owners of furnaces to go on sinning than to take remedial measures.

The government admitted on the basis of the replies to its inquiry that further measures were needed, and the home secretary accomplished them by inserting an appropriate provision in the Sanitary Act of 1866. This act stipulated that in all towns a local board (of health or otherwise) must serve as a nuisance authority, and clause 19 gave the authority supervision of all chimneys other than those of private dwelling houses. The clause declared that the creation of black smoke was an offense in itself, without reference to abatement devices. There were no automatic exemptions, although local justices could decide whether abatement was practicable for a particular manufacture or trade. If the authority in any place failed to enforce any of the provisions of the act, including the smoke one, the home secretary could instruct the municipal chief of police to do so. The reformers thus got almost everything they had demanded.[20]

[17]H.O. 45/O.S./7806/3–7, 9, 12, 14, 17–19.
[18]Manchester Council Proceedings, May 6, 1868, p. 477, Manchester Reference Library.
[19]H.O. 45/O.S./7806/ 8, 10–11. The fines at Sheffield in September 1864, for example, averaged less than 10 s. each (Sheffield Council Minutes, October 12, 1864, p. 22, Sheffield Reference Library).
[20]29 & 30 Vict. c. 90.

With the passage of this measure the law pertaining to smoke pollution arrived at substantially the form which it was to retain for the next ninety years. Changes thereafter were largely administrative. Provisions relating directly to smoke control maintained the existing scheme, and in fact the only alterations before 1926 were those in the Public Health Act of 1875 which allowed authorities to bring action against polluters outside their district if the smoke created a nuisance within it, and which once more extended de jure special status to the mining and metals interests.[21]

Despite the powers given the local governments to curtail commercial smoke pollution, the general verdict by the 1880s was that little improvement had resulted. The town archives for this period contain repeated laments by the officers of health that the sooty pall was as oppressive as ever.[22] A few places sought further powers through new local acts, but they had no effect. Most large towns now employed two or more inspectors, yet the number of convictions remained low.[23] The principal causes cited for the failure were the same as before: legal technicalities making prosecutions difficult, and permissiveness on the part of the authorities. It remained difficult to prove to the courts that the smoke complained of was uniformly objectionable at different times and in varying weather. The worst polluters were now located outside the town limits, where they denied responsibility for the canopy of smoke which hung over the adjacent town. Larger fines did no good, for the big manufacturers were indifferent to penalties sufficient to ruin marginal operators. Lax enforcement increasingly was justified by the rapid growth of foreign competition, especially

[21]38 & 39 Vict. c. 55, clauses 108 and 334.

[22]Typical of the reports were those of the medical officers of Leeds, Manchester, and Sheffield who, respectively, complained of the "deep gloom," the "somber tone," and the "great nuisance" still produced by unnecessary smoke in those towns (*Report on the Sanitary Condition of Leeds, 1877*, Committee Reports to the Council of the Borough of Leeds, January 1, 1878, Leeds Reference Library; Report of the Health Committee, Manchester Council Proceedings, May 4, 1881, pp. 238–39, Manchester Reference Library; and *Annual Report on the Health of the Borough of Sheffield, 1886*, pp. 60–61, Reports to the Council of Sheffield, Sheffield Reference Library).

[23]In Sheffield in the decade of the 1890s, for example, the number of observations made each year more than tripled (three inspectors were employed by 1900) and the average number of notices served upon offenders doubled, but the number of convictions per year averaged only nine and the average fine imposed was less than £2 (*Annual Report on the Health of the Borough of Sheffield, 1900*, pp. 80–84, Sheffield Reference Library). In Manchester in 1898, four inspectors made 2,111 half-hour observations and got 157 persons before the magistrates, with 104 being fined, but the fines averaged less than £2 each. The following year the summons and convictions dropped by almost half (Report of the Sanitary Committee, Manchester Council Proceedings, September 6, 1899, p. 1687, and October 3, 1900, p. 1818, Manchester Reference Library).

from Germany and America where the Industrial Revolution was now fully under way and where concern about smoke was just beginning. Many industrialists in Britain no longer apologized for their pollution but instead boasted that smoke signified jobs and profits.

Reformers all but gave up on commercial polluters and turned to the domestic chimneys interlacing the sky with innumerable small columns of coal smoke. Speakers in Parliament and elsewhere now emphasized that private grates contributed immensely to the smoke nuisance, most conspicuously so in the metropolis, and that factory chimneys probably could not be regulated until this collectively larger mischief was dealt with. In 1881 Ernest Hart, a medical journalist and sanitary reformer, and Octavia Hill, a well-known Christian Socialist housing crusader, organized a smoke-abatement committee which in the following year in London and Manchester sponsored an exhibition of smokeless apparatus (furnaces, stoves, and grates) and fuels (gas, coke, and anthracite coal) for use in homes. The committee reorganized itself afterward into a national society, with the duke of Westminster as president.[24] In Parliament the reformers found a new leader in a Liberal Unionist peer, Lord Stratheden and Campbell, who in 1887 chaired a select committee on the problem of smoke from private dwellings, and who from 1884 until his death in 1893 regularly introduced bills to curb domestic smoke in London.

The government politicians took the position that it was ludicrous to suppose that they could supervise 20,000,000 coal fires in private homes. Englishmen, they said, were addicted to the cheery, open coal fire and would never relinquish it. More to the point, alternatives to the cheap coal in domestic use would double the price of heating and cooking, not to mention the cost of alterations of old houses and interference with the construction of new ones.

On the other hand, the ministers expressed a willingness to consider further legislation against commercial smoke. Bills introduced for this purpose in 1913 and 1914 failed to win their approval, and they appointed a departmental committee to look into the question. War soon suspended the committee's work, but in 1920 and 1921 it issued interim and final reports in which it recommended action against both domestic and commercial chimneys.[25] The ministers agreed only to the latter recommendation, and after compromises with the National Union of Manufacturers the Public Health (Smoke Abatement) Act of 1926 was passed. The act, applicable both to Lon-

[24]*Report of the Smoke Abatement Committee, 1882* (London, 1883), British Library.
[25]*Parliamentary Papers*, 1920, XXV, 253–64; Great Britain, *Parliamentary Debates*, 5th ser., House of Lords, L, 371–74, LI, 685–96.

don and to the country, declared that any smoke, black or not, was an offense if it created a nuisance, and that local governments could decide matters of density and color; it prohibited grit as well as "smoke"; it increased the maximum fines; and it allowed authorities to combine their administrative areas if they wished. But it did not apply to private housing, it did not clarify the legal complexities, it left all exemptions intact, and it did not compel greater exertions by local authorities.[26] Reformers regarded the changes as virtually worthless. Afterward, in the 1930s, the depression and rearmament ended the movement for smoke abatement on the national level.

Although a new and more successful drive would begin after World War II, laws to control commercial smoke pollution had now been on the books for more than a century. But was smoke abatement really practicable during this early period?

Smoke-Abatement Technology

There were three categories of 19th-century inventions designed to curtail commercial smoke. The most important was the group which introduced air directly into the hot "carburetted hydrogen" gases (simple hydrocarbons) and "smoke" (soot and ash particles) in the furnace in order to burn them. The theory behind this approach was that the air entering below the fire bars and igniting the fuel was insufficient to burn the large amounts of carbon particles and coal gases which were released when new fuel was added to the fire and which therefore escaped up the chimney. If fresh air could be injected into the furnace in such a way that it mixed thoroughly with these pollutants at a point at which they were still hot enough to burn, but without the new air cooling the fire and the boiler, then in theory more heat would be produced and the amount of smoke reduced.

This conception was an old one which dated back to James Watt and even beyond, to Denis Papin,[27] and the inventions divided generally into those that introduced the air at the front of the furnace and those that supplied it at the rear, in the vicinity of the bridge. In 1785 Watt took out a patent on a furnace with two vents which admitted a converging sheet of air into the smoke and gases above the hot coals.[28] Dozens of similar devices delivering the air by means of perforated bricks, pipes, and plates, by jets of steam, and by fans and pumps were registered during the next century. Some of the patentees heated the air before injecting it, some had valves to regulate the quantity, and

[26] 16 & 17 Geo. V. c . 43.

[27] Royal Society of London, *Philosophical Transactions* (1697), p. 482.

[28] National Reference Library of Science and Invention, *Specifications of Patents*, O.S., no. 1485.

some had deflectors to diffuse it amid the smoke and gases. But other inventors dismissed these refinements as superfluous.

Commercially the two most successful, and therefore perhaps the best examples, of this category of furnaces were those patented by Josiah Parkes and Charles Wye Williams. Parkes perfected his "split bridge" furnace in 1820.[29] His father was a worsted manufacturer at Warwick who had hired the firm of Boulton and Watt to install Watt's "smoke consuming" furnace in order to prevent soot from spoiling the factory's bleaching operation. The alterations worked very imperfectly, and the young Parkes later set out to improve on them. His innovation was to admit air from the ash pit through a slit near the front of the bridge and extending all the way across it, a strategic point within the furnace where the gases and smoke were rising from the grate and were sufficiently hot to suck in a volume of fresh air, mix thoroughly with it, and burn. The plan called for the fireman to observe the process through a sight hole in the furnace and, by means of a chain attached to a pulley and connected to a valve, to open and close the vent leading to the opening in the bridge as he judged whether air was needed to burn the gases and smoke (fig. 1).[30] The process worked best with furnaces which could be fed heavily and infrequently. Parkes zealously promoted the merits of his invention—the select committee of 1820 all but endorsed his plan—and later he made a living as an engineer chiefly engaged in furnace construction.

A mark of Williams's greater success was that he employed Parkes in the 1840s to promote the "argand furnace" patented by Williams in 1839.[31] The inventor, a native of Ireland and a resident of Liverpool, was a pioneer in the development of steam shipping on the Irish Sea, and at this time he was managing director of the Dublin Steam Packet Company.[32] He claimed that his furnace duplicated "in reverse" and on a larger scale the operation of the argand lamp: hollow, perforated boxes or tubes of platinum or fire clay were installed about 9 inches behind a narrow bridge and admitted jets of air into the "atmosphere" of hot gases and smoke rising from the grate. The boxes or tubes in theory restricted the powerful rush of air into the furnace, which

---

[29] Ibid., no. 4455.

[30] This illustration and figs. 3 and 4 were made by combining and photographing photocopied copies of patent specifications. I am grateful to the University of Chicago Press for their photographic services.

[31] *Specifications of Patents,* no. 8118.

[32] J. Foster Petree, "Charles Wye Williams (1779–1866): A Pioneer in Steam Navigation and Fuel Efficiency," Newcomen Society for the Study of the History of Engineering and Technology, London, *Transactions* 39 (1966–67): 35–45.

made Parkes's invention hard to manage, yet the whirling effect of the jets produced a thorough mixture of about 10 volumes of air to one of the combustibles, as in the argand lamp (fig. 2). Some models had deflectors attached to the bottom of the boiler to drive the gases and smoke downward into the pit where the diffusion boxes were placed; in others the boxes reached all the way to the boiler, or if fashioned as horizontal tubes, all the way across the flame bed. A workman observed the combustion through a small window in the furnace and closed the valve to the air inlet when the smoke had almost disappeared. As was the case with Parkes's invention, the plan worked best with furnaces possessing a large boiler space and in which "thick" fires of coal heaped 6–8 inches deep could burn for an extended period.

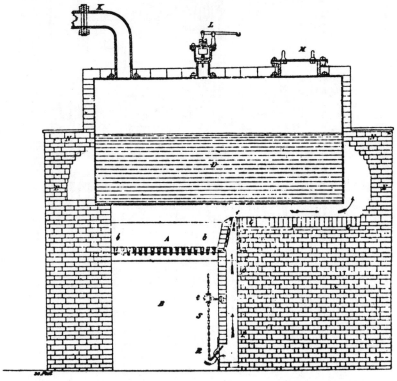

Fig. 1.—Josiah Parkes's split bridge furnace, 1820. Air was admitted from the ash pit (B) through a narrow opening (O) in the bridge (G). The opening extended all the way across the bridge and injected fresh air into the hot gases and smoke arising from the ignited fuel on the grate (A). The fireman could regulate the air admitted into the opening by means of a valve (R) controlled by a chain (S) attached to a pully (t) and extending to the fire door (not shown). The hot exhaust circled the boiler (D) before entering the chimney. (Courtesy of the Patent Office Sales Branch, Orpington, Kent.)

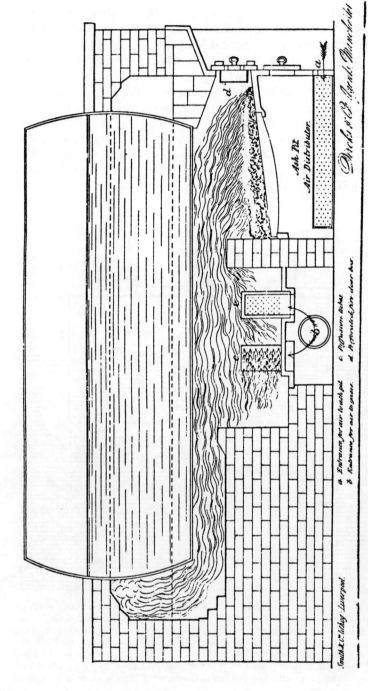

Smith & Withey, Liverpool.

a. *Entrance for air to ash pit.*
b. *Entrance for air to grate.*
c. *Diffusion tubes.*
d. *Perforated fire door box.*

Dyche & Pigott. Manchester.

Ash Pit
Air Distributor.

Fig. 2.—Charles Wye Williams's patent argand furnace, 1839. Air was admitted through an inlet (b) and discharged in jets through perforated boxes or tubes (c) into the hot gases and smoke behind the bridge, as well as separately into the ash pit (a) under the fire. (Courtesy of the British Library.)

In addition to the reduction of smoke, Williams claimed that his argand furnace converted profuse amounts of harmful carbon monoxide into harmless carbon dioxide. Although scientists such as Michael Faraday went on record as doubting (correctly) that the amount of carbon monoxide in furnace emissions was hazardous, Williams garnered and publicized favorable testimonials from other chemists and engineers, and he published his own views in 1841 in a treatise entitled *The Combustion of Coal and the Prevention of Smoke.* He also cultivated contacts with reformers on a local and national level. By the time his patent expired he had installed his argand furnace in hundreds of sites.

A second category of inventions to prevent smoke consisted of devices to ensure a continuous supply of hot coals sufficient to burn the impurities given off by fresh fuel. This approach worked on the same general principle as did those inventions that introduced fresh air to consume the gases and smoke, but here the object was to add fuel continuously to the fire in small quantities so that the ordinary volume of air rising through the grate would burn the impurities. (Banking coal in the furnace was a traditional but inefficient way to accomplish the same purpose.) This approach also had 18th-century scientific antecedents: as early as 1766 Benjamin Franklin had advised Matthew Boulton, Watt's future partner, to construct his furnaces so that the smoke would have to descend through fuel that already was ignited.[33]

In general the 19th-century inventions consisted of hoppers which distributed the new coal evenly upon the fire, in many cases after crushing it through rollers, and grates of various kinds designed to collect the hot coals where the smoke arising from fresh fuel would have to pass over them. Some of the grates were fashioned so that the fire bars moved or vibrated, others were inclined or multileveled, and others consisted simply of dual compartments connected by flues. Some of the patents of course employed a combination of hoppers and grates. All of them were designed to be almost airtight above the grate and thus to avoid the excessive draughts which carried heat away from the boiler and which Parkes and Williams found difficult to control.

Probably the best known of the many inventions in this category were the longitudinal and circular moving grates of John Juckes, patented in 1841 and 1842.[34] The former was the one most often recommended by engineers. It consisted of an endless chain of break-joint fire bars which were driven forward by two cylindrical chain

---

[33]Franklin to Boulton, March 19, 1766, Birmingham Assay Office Papers, box F2, no. 121, Birmingham Reference Library.

[34]*Specifications of Patents,* nos. 9067 and 9476.

wheels at the rate of about a foot every twenty minutes. Fuel was fed from a hopper onto the moving grate, and gases and smoke arising from fresh coals passed over the hot ones farther along the bars and were consumed. Air was admitted through the ash pit beneath the entire length of the grate, about nine-tenths of it, Juckes estimated, finding its way through the hot coals farther along the bars where it was most needed. The frame was mounted upon wheels, which ran on rails, so that the entire apparatus could be moved in and out of the ash pit, facilitating the removal of ashes and clinkers which dropped from the grate at the end of the pit (fig. 3). The grate worked best for large furnaces in which slow combustion of a thin layer of coal was desired. The device clearly had its merits, and Juckes, a former Shropshire-man then resident in London, secured endorsements from chemists and engineers, including among the latter Sir Isambard Brunel, and marketed his furnace successfully for many years.

A third category of improvements was construction of flues so as to trap or wash out impurities discharged by furnaces. These inventions treated the problem as an external, mechanical operation rather than an internal, chemical process relating to the fire itself. Most of the contrivances passed the smoke through sprays of water to remove the particles of soot. But despite the use of fans and pumps all of the devices reduced the draught in the furnace, and none was utilized widely for smoke abatement—although they were used to control noxious fumes emitted by chemical and metal works. A curious foot-note to their failure was the prolonged legal action relating to an early patentee of a spray device, George F. Muntz: twenty-five years after the date of his patent Muntz was cited repeatedly by the street commissioners of Birmingham for permitting smoke from his mill to choke patients at a hospital nearby, and twenty years after that, in 1865, his brother was prosecuted by the sanitary authority of Birmingham for excessive smoke from the same factory.[35]

Perhaps the most elaborate example of these spray inventions was the one patented in 1842 by Thomas Hedley, an ironmaster of New-castle.[36] Hedley sought to overcome the problem of the impeded draught by arranging an extended flue so that the smoke and gases issuing from the furnace descended in showers of water from a tank 10–30 feet high before exiting into the open air. Instead of attempting to drive the smoke through a spray of water, as other inventors

[35]Minutes of the Birmingham Street Commissioners, February 3 and July 6, 1840, June 5, 1843, and April 1 and May 6, 1844; Minutes of the Birmingham Council, no. 5338, November 28, 1865, all in Birmingham Reference Library. Muntz's patent was 1816, no. 3989.

[36]*Specifications of Patents*, no. 9289.

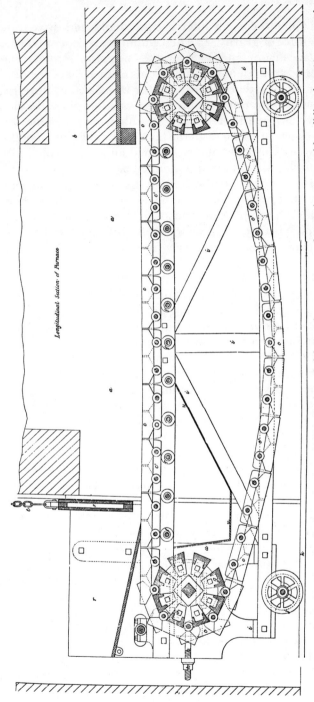

FIG. 3.—John Juckes's longitudinal moving grate, 1841. Fuel was fed from a hopper (r) onto the moving grate, with a sliding door (s) to control the quantity of coal admitted. The grate consisted of a moving chain of fire bars (c), advanced by two chain wheels (g) and moving upon rollers (f), which carried the fuel forward so that smoke and gases had to pass over the hot coals before crossing the bridge (b) and entering the flue. (Courtesy of the Patent Office Sales Branch, Orpington, Kent.)

had done, he had the water intercept the smoke and drive it downward by the force of gravity. The descending water not only removed the particulate matter and soluble gases but also, Hedley claimed, maintained the strength of the draught in the flue. Since the opening at the bottom of each descending chamber was sealed by the escaping water, the smoke ascended into the next one, aided by the natural steam created in the first ascending chamber, and in some models augmented by jets of steam from the boiler. The collected soot floated on the surface of the water after it drained into a reservoir, and thus the water could be drawn off and pumped back to the tank at the top of the apparatus (fig. 4). Hedley sold his invention to a few owners of small engines but had no luck with the large establishments. Even so, his invention and other devices in this category should not be dismissed as unimportant, for they were the forerunners of the scrubbers and separators used extensively for smoke control today.

19th-Century Smoke Abatement: An Assessment

How efficient were these 19th-century British inventions as a whole in abating smoke, and to what degree was their potential utilized? Two qualifications should be noted in assessing their value. First, the Victorian environmentalists did not expect to achieve a pure atmosphere from their abatement technology. Excessive smoke was deemed inevitable during firing and refueling in some industries, and a small amount of smoke from all manufactories was to be endured constantly. In contrast, restrictions today upon coal smoke are stringent. To meet current standards, particulate matter in most instances has to be removed mechanically—by scrubbers, separators, baghouses, and electrostatic precipitators—for it cannot all be burned. Modern requirements also go beyond the Victorian and Edwardian Alkali Acts. Second, there are many factors, legal, economic, social, and political, which advance or limit the application of technology to problems. In the 19th century the tendency to give manufacturers and traders a relatively free hand meant that all of these factors could be more aggressively marshaled against pollution control than in favor of it. Thus both on technological and other grounds a lower level of improvement was anticipated than is considered tolerable today.

The question whether the abatement inventions of the 19th century could substantially reduce smoke emissions received contradictory answers from two groups possessing divergent biases. Reformers pointed to the fact that in test situations most of the inventions reduced smoke considerably, and some of the devices reduced it dramatically. It was true that in everyday operation the performance of

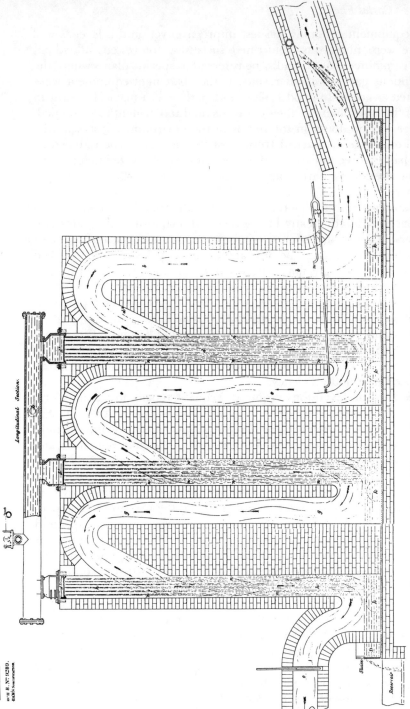

Fig. 4.—Thomas Hedley's apparatus for purifying smoke, 1842. An extended flue was so arranged that the smoke and gases issuing from the furnace descended through several showers of water (d, f, h) from perforated water boxes (d'). Inside the descending parts of the flue ledges or projections (n) prevented the gases and smoke from escaping back up the sides of the chambers. The sludge passed through openings (k) and was run off by a sluice (D) into a reservoir. To strengthen the draught in the ascending parts of the flue, jets of steam (m) sometimes were added. (Courtesy of the Patent Office Sales Branch, Orpington, Kent.)

the equipment generally was less impressive, yet on this level as well there were numerous, confirmed successes. Interested individuals and committees could readily be referred to specific plants where the inventions gave excellent results. If the abatement equipment were treated as an aid to good stoking rather than as a magical answer in itself, the usefulness of the devices seemed too evident to be denied. There was no doubt in the minds of the environmentalists that the level of smoke discharged from most furnaces could be reduced by one half to three fourths. And the reformers emphasized that the cost of the alterations, parts, and fees seldom exceeded £200 or £300 per furnace.

Manufacturers and merchants, on the other hand, pointed out that furnaces differed greatly in the size and shape of their grates and boilers, in the quality of their construction, in the application made of their heat, and in the type of coal they used. A device which worked well in one site might fail entirely in another, and owners of furnaces could be forced to spend heavily in searching for the apparatus, or various combinations thereof, which would perform acceptably in their own situations. Since multiple furnaces in a single operation were common, the cost of the equipment could be multiplied many-fold. Also, despite promises by inventors that fuel economy would offset expenses, most owners who adopted the apparatus reported reduced heat and efficiency.

Most of the inventions required frequent repairs in actual operation: for example, the holes in the diffusion boxes and tubes in Williams's furnaces often became clogged with vitrified ash, and the links in Juckes's endless chain broke repeatedly. Marginal operators and those whose establishments required intense heat consequently maintained that they could not afford to experiment with uncertain, encumbering, and potentially costly inventions. Their fellow owners who could afford to try the equipment cited the pressure of competition as a valid reason for noncompliance. Serving as an example and an incentive to all of these hesitant men were those more fortunate or more powerful interests who had won formal exemption from the law. In testifying before committees most manufacturers contended that the best that they could do was to effect small reductions in smoke through proper firing and refueling of furnaces, plus the erection of higher chimneys to disperse the smoke over a wider area.

The lack of a technology capable of certifying the precise performance of abatement apparatus under differing industrial and atmospheric conditions proved to be a critical weakness for the proponents of smoke control. Enforced hit-or-miss experiments in the adoption of equipment not only went against the capitalist grain, they also went against established legal principles. The local government committees and private societies which provided information on the effectiveness of various devices soon found that their evidence had no status in the courts. Similarly, the absence of sophisticated monitoring mechanisms compelled the local authorities to rely upon inexact visual sightings in prosecuting offenders. It was difficult to produce an airtight legal case against malefactors, particularly before justices who frequently were sympathetic to the protestations of the offenders. The local prosecutors therefore generally limited their indictments to the worst violators and then resorted to prolonged legal harassment in order to force compliance.

The lack of responsiveness on the part of the owners of furnaces was not wholly a matter of indifference to the public welfare, although this facet of it certainly existed. To most producers of goods the generation of steam power was a secondary part of their operations, one in which they had no expertise. Many manufacturers testified before committees that they were virtual strangers to their furnace rooms and were entirely at the mercy of their stokers concerning its procedures. These owners conceded that skillful maintenance and tending of furnaces was essential to the control of smoke, but they knew not how to improve affairs, especially since the stokers resisted the addition of abatement equipment which kept them at the hot furnaces between refuelings. If the question of smoke control had been a simple one and if the technology for it had been unequivocally effective, the owners claimed that they would have been favorable to it. The situation being otherwise, they were discouraged by the faintest prospect of failure and avoidable expenses.

The populace of the grimy towns onto which the commercial furnaces unloaded their smoke were more than hapless victims, they themselves were willing polluters. The forests of private chimneys dotting the urban landscape unfailingly contributed their share of the blight, yet the reformers' talk of stoves and smokeless fuels seemingly made no impression on the inhabitants. Open hearths were customary and bituminous coal was economical, and both therefore were inviolable. Perhaps this participation in the creation of smoke made the workers receptive to the argument that competitive businesses could not afford to control commercial smoke. The options as presented by the owners were jobs versus murk, and most of the inhabitants reportedly never wavered in their choice of the former. Those who dwelt in the dirtiest parts of town were in the worst position to demur. In any case, throughout the century reformers lamented that the public was apathetic to the problem of smoke. A growing number of environmentalists concluded that the movement for smoke abatement, like the steam engines themselves, could not work without sufficient pressure behind it. In the absence of popular alarm and indignation, the legal and economic opposition to abatement by the owners of furnaces seemed insuperable.

It was the politicians who had to decide what to do about the matter. For men who were responsible for the general welfare it was not an easy judgment to make. Almost every investigation during the period concluded that, if used with care, the available technology could significantly reduce the commercial smoke nuisance. In addition, there were feasible alternatives to the open grates and soft coal principally responsible for domestic smoke. But there were also formidable problems. The pollution from domestic chimneys seemed unassailable: the projected cost and difficulty of compelling millions of householders to alter their private hearths and to abandon cheap coal for smokeless fuels was such that the British ministries before World War II made no move at all in that direction. This tolerance left commercial furnaces as the only accepted target for legislation. Under the prodding of environmentalists, local and national, action was taken. Yet all went in vain, for the combined technological, legal, and economic uncertainties of abatement were such that the movement stalled on the question of enforcement. Parliament passed laws giving local authorities the power to act; the local authorities, forced to confront the polluters at close quarters in the councils and courts, wavered and passed the responsibility back to the central government. In the end, little abatement was achieved.

Bursting Boilers and the Federal Power

JOHN G. BURKE

I

When the United States Food and Drug Administration removes thousands of tins of tuna from supermarket shelves to prevent possible food poisoning, when the Civil Aeronautics Board restricts the speed of certain jets until modifications are completed, or when the Interstate Commerce Commission institutes safety checks of interstate motor carriers, the federal government is expressing its power to regulate dangerous processes or products in interstate commerce. Although particular interests may take issue with a regulatory agency about restrictions placed upon certain products or seek to alleviate what they consider to be unjust directives, few citizens would argue that government regulation of this type constitutes a serious invasion of private property rights.[1]

Though federal regulatory agencies may contribute to the general welfare, they are not expressly sanctioned by any provisions of the U.S. Constitution. In fact, their genesis was due to a marked change in the attitude of many early nineteenth-century Americans who insisted that the federal government exercise its power in a positive way in an area that was non-existent when the Constitution was enacted. At the time, commercial, manufacturing, and business interests were willing to seek the aid of government in such matters as patent rights, land grants, or protective tariffs, but they opposed any action that might smack of governmental interference or control of their internal affairs. The government might act benevolently but never restrictively.

The innovation responsible for the changed attitude toward government regulation was the steam engine. The introduction of steam power

At the time this article was originally published, the late JOHN G. BURKE was professor of history at the University of California, Los Angeles.

[1] See, e.g., *Report* on Practices and Procedures of Governmental Control, Sept. 18, 1944 (House of Representatives document 678, ser. 10873 [Washington: 78th Congress, 2d session]), p. 3, where it is stated: "Regulation, seen through modern eyes is not a violent departure from the ways of business to which the nation is both habituated and strongly attached . . . . regulation . . . enjoys, as a system, in large measure the confidence and approval of the parties concerned."

This essay originally appeared in *Technology and Culture*, vol. 7, no. 1, Winter 1966.

was transforming American culture, and while Thoreau despised the belching locomotives that fouled his nest at Walden, the majority of Americans were delighted with the improved modes of transportation and the other benefits accompanying the expanding use of steam. However, while Americans rejoiced over this awesome power that was harnessed in the service of man, tragic events that were apparently concomitant to its use alarmed them—the growing frequency of disastrous boiler explosions, primarily in marine service. At the time, there was not even a governmental agency that could institute a proper investigation of the accidents. Legal definitions of the responsibility or negligence of manufacturers or owners of potentially dangerous equipment were in an embryonic state. The belief existed that the enlightened self-interest of an entrepreneur sufficed to guarantee the public safety. This theory militated against the enactment of any legislation restricting the actions of the manufacturers or users of steam equipment.

Although the Constitution empowered Congress to regulate interstate commerce, there was still some disagreement about the extent of this power even after the decision in *Gibbons* v. *Ogden,* which ruled that the only limitations on this power were those prescribed in the Constitution. In the early years of the republic, Congress passed legislation under the commerce clause designating ports of entry for customs collections, requiring sailing licenses, and specifying procedures for filing cargo manifests. The intent of additional legislation in this area, other than to provide for these normal concomitants of trade, was to promote commerce by building roads, dredging canals, erecting lighthouses, and improving harbors. Congress limited its power under the commerce clause until the toll of death and destruction wrought by bursting steamboat boilers mounted, and some positive regulations concerning the application of steam power seemed necessary. Thomas Jefferson's recommendation that we should have "a wise and frugal Government, which shall restrain men from injuring one another, shall leave them otherwise free to regulate their own pursuits of industry and improvement" took on a new meaning.[2]

Although several historians have noted the steamboat explosions and the resulting federal regulations, the wider significance of the explosions as an important factor in altering the premises concerning the role of government vis à vis private enterprise has been slighted.[3] Further, there has been no analysis of the role of the informed public in this matter.

[2] Thomas Jefferson, "Inaugural Address," *Journal of the Executive Proceedings of the U.S. Senate,* I (Washington, 1828), 393.

[3] The most authoritative work is Louis C. Hunter, *Steamboats on the Western Rivers* (Cambridge, Mass., 1949), pp. 122–33, 271–304, 520–46.

The scientific and technically knowledgeable members of society were —in the absence of a vested interest—from the outset firmly committed to the necessity of federal intervention and regulation. They conducted investigations of the accidents; they proposed detailed legislation which they believed would prevent the disasters. For more than a generation, however, successive Congresses hesitated to take forceful action, weighing the admitted danger to the public safety against the unwanted alternative, the regulation of private enterprise.

The regulatory power of the federal government, then, was not expanded in any authoritarian manner. Rather, it evolved in response to novel conditions emanating from the new machine age, which was clearly seen by that community whose educations or careers encompassed the new technology. In eventually reacting to this danger, Congress passed the first positive regulatory legislation and created the first agency empowered to supervise and direct the internal affairs of a sector of private enterprise in detail. Further, certain congressmen used this precedent later in efforts to protect the public in other areas, notably in proposing legislation that in time created the Interstate Commerce Commission. Marine boiler explosions, then, provoked a crisis in the safe application of steam power, which led to a marked change in American political attitudes. The change, however, was not abrupt but evolved between 1816 and 1852.

II

Throughout most of the eighteenth century, steam engines worked on the atmospheric principle. Steam was piped to the engine cylinder at atmospheric pressure, and a jet of cold water introduced into the cylinder at the top of the stroke created a partial vacuum in the cylinder. The atmospheric pressure on the exterior of the piston caused the power stroke. The central problem in boiler construction, then, was to prevent leakage. Consequently, most eighteenth-century boilers were little more than large wood, copper, or cast-iron containers placed over a hearth and encased with firebrick. In the late eighteenth century, Watt's utilization of the expansive force of steam compelled more careful boiler design. Using a separate condenser in conjunction with steam pressure, Watt operated his engines at about 7 p.s.i. above that of the atmosphere. Riveted wrought-iron boilers were introduced, and safety valves were employed to discharge steam if the boiler pressure exceeded the designed working pressure.

Oliver Evans in the United States and Richard Trevithick in England introduced the relatively high-pressure non-condensing steam engine almost simultaneously at the turn of the nineteenth century. This development led to the vast extension in the use of steam power. The high-pressure engines competed in efficiency with the low-pressure type, while their compactness made them more suitable for land and water vehicular transport. But, simultaneously, the scope of the problem faced even by Watt was increased, that is, the construction of boilers that would safely contain the dangerous expansive force of steam. Evans thoroughly respected the potential destructive force of steam. He relied chiefly on safety valves with ample relieving capacity but encouraged sound boiler design by publishing the first formula for computing the thickness of wrought iron to be used in boilers of various diameters carrying different working pressures.[4]

Despite Evans' prudence, hindsight makes it clear that the rash of boiler explosions from 1816 onward was almost inevitable. Evans' design rules were not heeded. Shell thickness and diameter depended upon available material, which was often of inferior quality.[5] In fabrication, no provision was made for the weakening of the shell occasioned by the rivet holes. The danger inherent in the employment of wrought-iron shells with cast-iron heads affixed because of the different coefficients of expansion was not recognized, and the design of internal stays was often inadequate. The openings in the safety valves were not properly proportioned to give sufficient relieving capacity. Gauge cocks and floats intended to ensure adequate water levels were inaccurate and subject to malfunction by fouling with sediment or rust.

In addition, there were also problems connected with boiler operation and maintenance.[6] The rolling and pitching of steamboats caused

[4] Greville and Dorothy Bathe, *Oliver Evans* (Philadelphia, 1935), pp. 151, 253. Also, see Walter F. Johnson, "On the Strength of Cylindrical Steam Boilers," *Journal of the Franklin Institute* (hereinafter cited as "JFI"), X, N.S. (1832), 149. Evans' formula reveals that he considered that a safe design tensile strength for good quality wrought iron was about 42,000 p.s.i. and that a factor of safety of 10 should be used to arrive at a safe shell thickness.

[5] For reports of defective design and poor quality material see: Charles F. Partington, *An Historical and Descriptive Account of the Steam Engine* (London, 1822), p. 85; Committee on Steamboats *Report*, May 18, 1832 (House of Representatives document 478, ser. 228 [Washington: 22d Congress, 1st session]), pp. 44, 170 (hereinafter cited as "Doc. 478"). Also, *JFI*, VI, N.S. (1830), 44–51; VIII, N.S. (1831), 382; IX, N.S. (1832), 28, 100, 363; X, N.S. (1832), 226–32; XVII, N.S. (1836), 298–302; XX, N.S. (1837), 100, 103.

[6] For operating difficulties see: Partington, *op. cit.*, p. 118; *JFI*, V, N.S. (1830), 402; VI, N.S. (1830), 9; VIII, N.S. (1831), 277, 289–92; VIII, N.S. (1831), 309, 313, 382; IX, N.S. (1832), 20–22. Also, Secretary of the Treasury, *Report on Steam Engines*, Dec. 13, 1838 (House of Representatives document 21, ser. 345 [Washington: 25th Congress, 3d session]), p. 3 (hereinafter cited as "Doc. 21"). The whole number of steam engines in the United States in 1838 was estimated at 3,010: 800

alternate expansion and contraction of the internal flues as they were covered and uncovered by the water, a condition that contributed to their weakening. The boiler feedwater for steamboats was pumped directly from the surroundings without treatment or filtration, which accelerated corrosion of the shell and fittings. The sediment was frequently allowed to accumulate, thus requiring a hotter fire to develop the required steam pressure, which led, in turn, to a rapid weakening of the shell. Feed pumps were shut down at intermediate stops without damping the fires, which aggravated the danger of low water and excessive steam pressure. With the rapid increase in the number of steam engines, there was a concomitant shortage of competent engineers who understood the necessary safety precautions. Sometimes masters employed mere stokers who had only a rudimentary grasp of the operation of steam equipment. Increased competition also led to attempts to gain prestige by arriving first at the destination. The usual practice during a race was to overload or tie down the safety valve, so that excessive steam pressure would not be relieved.

III

The first major boiler disasters occurred on steamboats, and, in fact, the majority of explosions throughout the first half of the nineteenth century took place on board ship.[7] By mid-1817, four explosions had taken five lives in the eastern waters, and twenty-five people had been killed in three accidents on the Ohio and Mississippi rivers.[8] The city council of Philadelphia appears to have been the first legislative body in the United States to take cognizance of the disasters and attempt an investigation. A joint committee was appointed to determine the causes of the accidents and recommend measures that would prevent similar occurrences on steamboats serving Philadelphia. The question was referred to a group of practical engineers who recommended that all boilers should be subjected to an initial hydraulic proof test at twice the intended working pressure and additional monthly proof tests to be conducted by a competent inspector. Also, appreciating the fact that marine engineers were known to overload the safety valve levers, they advocated placing the valve in a locked box. The report of the joint

---

on steamboats, 350 in locomotives, and 1,860 in manufacturing establishments. The majority of these engines were put into service after 1830. The term "practical engineer" was reserved for a designer or builder of engines, while engine-room operatives were called "engineers." The complaints about the incompetence of the latter are very frequent in the literature.

[7] *Doc. 21*, p. 3.   [8] Bathe, *op. cit.*, p. 250.

committee incorporated these recommendations, but it stated that the subject of regulation was outside the competence of municipalities. Any municipal enactment would be inadequate for complete regulation. The matter was referred, therefore, to the state legislature, and there it rested.[9]

Similar studies were being undertaken abroad. In England, a fatal explosion aboard a steamboat near Norwich prompted Parliament to constitute a Select Committee in May 1817 to investigate the conditions surrounding the design, construction, and operation of steam boilers. In its report, the committee noted its aversion to the enactment of any legislation but stated that where the public safety might be endangered by ignorance, avarice, or inattention, it was the duty of Parliament to interpose. Precedents for legislation included laws covering the construction of party walls in buildings, the qualification of physicians, and the regulation of stage coaches. The committee recommended that passenger-carrying steam vessels should be registered, that boiler construction and testing should be supervised, and that two safety valves should be employed with severe penalties for tampering with the weights.[10]

No legislation followed this report, nor were any laws enacted after subsequent reports on the same subject in 1831, 1839, and 1843.[11] The attitude of the British steamboat owners and boiler manufacturers was summarized in a statement that the prominent manufacturer, Sir John Rennie, made to the Select Committee in 1843. There should be, he said, no impediments in the application of steam power. Coroners' juries made such complete investigations of boiler explosions that no respectable manufacturer would risk his reputation in constructing a defective boiler. Constant examination of boilers, he argued, would cause serious inconvenience and would give no guarantee that the public safety would be assured. Admittedly, it would be desirable for steam equipment to be perfect, but with so many varied boiler and engine designs, it would be next to impossible to agree on methods of examination. Besides, he concluded, there were really few accidents.[12]

In this latter remark, Sir John was partially correct. In England, from 1817 to 1839, only 77 deaths resulted from twenty-three explosions.[13] This record was relatively unblemished compared to the slaughter in the United States, where in 1838 alone, 496 lives had been lost as

[9] *Ibid.*, p. 255; *JFI*, VIII, N.S. (1831), 235–43.

[10] Parliamentary Sessional Papers, *Report* (1817), VI, 223.

[11] *Ibid.* (1831), VIII, 1; (1839), XLVII, 1; (1843), IX, 1.

[12] *Ibid.* (1842), IX, 383–84.

[13] *Ibid.* (1839), XLVII, 10.

a result of fourteen explosions.[14] The continued use of low-pressure engines by the British; the fact that by 1836 the total number of U.S. steamboats—approximately 750—was greater than the total afloat in all of Europe; and the fact that the average tonnage of U.S. steamboats was twice that of British vessels, implying the use of larger engines and boilers and more numerous passengers, accounted for the large difference in the casualty figures.[15]

In France, the reaction to the boiler hazard was entirely different than in Great Britain and the United States. Acting under the authority of Napoleonic legislation, the government issued a Royal Ordinance on October 29, 1823 relative to stationary and marine steam engines and boilers.[16] A committee of engineers of mines and civil engineers prepared the regulations, but the scientific talent of such men as Arago, Dulong, and Biot was enlisted to prepare accurate steam tables.[17] By 1830, amendments resulted in the establishment of a comprehensive boiler code. It incorporated stress values for iron and copper and design formulas for these materials. It required the use of hemispherical heads on all boilers operating above 7 p.s.i. and the employment of two safety valves, one of which was enclosed in a locked grating. Boiler shells had to be fabricated with fusible metal plates made of a lead-tin-bismuth alloy and covered with a cast-iron grating to prevent swelling when close to the fusing point. Boilers had to be tested initially at three times the designed working pressure and yearly thereafter. The French engineers of mines and government civil engineers were given detailed instructions on the conduct of the tests and were empowered to remove any apparently defective boiler from service. The proprietors of steamboats or factories employing boilers were liable to criminal prosecution for evasion of the regulations, and the entire hierarchy of French officialdom was enjoined to report any infractions.[18]

Proper statistics proving that this code had a salutary effect in the prevention of boiler explosions are not available. It is certain that some

[14] The number of explosions and the loss of life occasioned thereby, listed throughout this paper, were obtained by a comparison and tabulation of the figures listed in *Doc. 21*, pp. 399–403, and in the Commissioner of Patents, *Report*, Dec. 30, 1848 (Senate document 18, ser. 529 [Washington: 30th Congress, 2d session]), pp. 36–48 (hereinafter cited as "Doc. 18").

[15] Department of the Interior, Census Office, *10th Census* (Washington, 1883), IV, 6–7; *JFI*, IX, N.S. (1832), 350.

[16] *Archives Parlementaires* (Paris, 1864), III, ser. 2, 732; *JFI*, VII, N.S. (1831), 272.

[17] *JFI*, X, N.S. (1832), 106; *Doc. 478*, p. 145.

[18] *JFI*, VII, N.S. (1831), 272, 323, 399; VIII, N.S. (1831), 32; X, N.S. (1832), 105, 181.

explosions occurred despite the tight regulations. Arago, writing in 1830, reported that a fatal explosion on the "Rhone" resulted from the tampering with a safety valve and pointed out that fusion of the fusible metal plates could be prevented by directing a stream of water on them.[19] Undoubtedly, in some instances the laws were evaded, but Thomas P. Haldeman, an experienced Cincinnati steamboat captain said in 1848 that the code had been effective. He wrote: "Since those laws were enforced we have scarcely heard of an explosion in that country. . . . What a misfortune our government did not follow the example of France twenty years ago."[20] Significantly, both Belgium and Holland promulgated boiler laws that were in all essentials duplicates of the French regulations.[21]

IV

From 1818 to 1824 in the United States, the casualty figures in boiler disasters rose, about forty-seven lives being lost in fifteen explosions. In May 1824 the "Aetna," built in 1816 to Evans' specifications, burst one of her three wrought-iron boilers in New York harbor, killing about thirteen persons and causing many injuries. Some experts attributed the accident to a stoppage of feedwater due to incrustations in the inlet pipes, while others believed that the rupture in the shell had started from an old fracture in a riveted joint.[22] The accident had two consequences. Because the majority of steamboats plying New York waters operated at relatively low pressures with copper boilers, the public became convinced that wrought-iron boilers were unsafe. This prejudice forced New York boat builders who were gradually recognizing the superiority of wrought iron to revert to the use of copper even in high-pressure boilers. Some owners recognized the danger of this step, but the outcry was too insistent. One is reported to have said: "We have concluded therefore to give them [the public] a copper boiler, the strongest of its class, and have made up our minds that they have a perfect right to be scalded by copper boilers if they insist upon it."[23] His forecast was correct, for within the next decade, the explosion of copper boilers employing moderate steam pressures became common in eastern waters.[24]

[19] *Ibid.*, V, N.S. (1830), 399, 411.

[20] *Doc. 18*, p. 180.

[21] Parliamentary Sessional Papers, *Report* (1839), XLVII, 180.

[22] Bathe, *op. cit.*, p. 237; *JFI*, II (1826), 147.

[23] *Doc. 21*, p. 425.

[24] *Ibid.*, pp. 105, 424; *JFI*, XIII, N.S. (1834), 55, 126, 289.

The second consequence of the "Aetna" disaster was that it caught the attention of Congress. A resolution was introduced in the House of Representatives in May 1824 calling for an inquiry into the expediency of enacting legislation barring the issuance of a certificate of navigation to any boat operating at high steam pressures. Although a bill was reported out of committee, it was not passed due to lack of time for mature consideration.[25]

In the same year, the Franklin Institute was founded in Philadelphia for the study and promotion of the mechanical arts and applied science.[26] The institute soon issued its *Journal*, and, from the start, much space was devoted to the subject of boiler explosions. The necessity of regulatory legislation dealing with the construction and operation of boilers was discussed, but there was a diversity of opinion as to what should be done. Within a few years, it became apparent that only a complete and careful investigation of the causes of explosions would give sufficient knowledge for suggesting satisfactory regulatory legislation. In June 1830, therefore, the Institute empowered a committee of its members to conduct such an investigation and later authorized it to perform any necessary experiments.

The statement of the purpose of the committee reflects clearly the nature of the problem created by the frequent explosions. The public, it said, would continue to use steamboats, but if there were no regulations, the needless waste of property and life would continue. The committee believed that these were avoidable consequences; the accidents resulted from defective boilers, improper design, or carelessness. The causes, the committee thought, could be removed by salutary regulations, and it affirmed: "That there must be a power in the community lodged somewhere, to protect the people at large against any evil of serious and frequent recurrence, is self-evident. But that such power is to be used with extreme caution, and only when the evil is great, and the remedy certain of success, seems to be equally indisputable."[27]

Here is a statement by a responsible group of technically oriented citizens that public safety should not be endangered by private negligence. It demonstrates the recognition that private enterprise was considered sacrosanct, but it calls for a reassessment of societal values in the light of events. It proposes restrictions while still professing un-

---

[25] *Annals of Congress* (Washington: 18th Congress 1st session), pp. 2670, 2694, 2707, 2708, 2765.

[26] For the history of the Franklin Institute, see S. L. Wright, *The Story of the Franklin Institute* (Philadelphia, 1938).

[27] *JFI*, VI, N.S. (1830), 33.

willingness to fetter private industry. It illustrates a change in attitude that was taking place with respect to the role of government in the affairs of industry, a change that was necessitated by technological innovation. The committee noted that boiler regulation proposals had been before Congress twice without any final action. Congressional committees, it said, appeared unwilling to institute inquiries and elicit evidence from practical men, and therefore they could hardly determine facts based upon twenty years of experience with the use of steam in boats. Since Congress was apparently avoiding action, the committee asserted, it was of paramount importance that a competent body whose motives were above suspicion should shoulder the burden.[28] Thus, the Franklin Institute committee began a six-year investigation of boiler explosions.

From 1825 to 1830, there had been forty-two explosions killing about 273 persons, and in 1830 a particularly serious one aboard the "Helen McGregor" near Memphis which killed 50 or 60 persons, again disturbed Congress. The House requested the Secretary of the Treasury, Samuel D. Ingham of Pennsylvania, to investigate the boiler accidents and submit a report.[29] Ingham had served in Congress from 1813 to 1818, and again from 1822 to 1829. He was a successful manufacturer who owned several paper mills; he was acquainted with the activities of the Franklin Institute and had written to the *Journal* about steam boiler problems.[30] Ingham was thus in a unique position to aid the Franklin Institute committee which had begun its inquiries. Before his resignation from Jackson's cabinet over the Peggy O'Neill Eaton affair, Ingham committed government funds to the Institute to defray the cost of apparatus necessary for the experiments.[31] This was the first research grant of a technological nature made by the federal government.[32]

Ingham attempted to make his own investigation while still secretary of the treasury. His interim report to the House in 1831 revealed that two investigators, one on the Atlantic seaboard and the other in the Mississippi basin, had been employed to gather information on the boiler explosions. They complained that owners and masters of boats

---

[28] *Ibid.*, 34.

[29] *Congressional Debates* (Washington: 21st Congress, 1st session), VI, Part 2, 739.

[30] *Dictionary of American Biography* (New York, 1932), IX, 473; *JFI*, IX, N.S. (1832), 12 (communicated Oct. 21, 1830).

[31] *JFI*, VII, N.S. (1831), 42.

[32] Arthur V. Greene, "The A.S.M.E. Boiler Code," *Mechanical Engineer*, LXXIV (1952), 555; A. Hunter Dupree, *Science in the Federal Government* (Cambridge, Mass., 1957), p. 50.

seemed unwilling to aid the inquiry. They were told repeatedly that the problem was purely individual, a matter beyond the government's right to interfere.[33] In the following year, the new secretary, Louis B. McLane, circulated a questionnaire among the collectors of customs, who furnished information and solicited opinions about the explosions. Their answers formed the basis of McLane's report to Congress. They mentioned the many causes of boiler explosions. One letter noted that steamboat trips from New Orleans to Louisville had been shortened from twenty-five to twelve days since 1818 without increasing the strength of the boilers. A frequent remark was that the engineers in charge of the boilers were ignorant, careless, and usually drunk.[34]

This report prompted a bill proposed in the House in May 1832. It provided for the appointment of inspectors at convenient locations to test the strength of the boilers every three months at three times their working pressure, and the issuance of a license to navigate was made contingent upon this inspection. To avoid possible objections on the score of expense, inspection costs were to be borne by the government. To prevent explosions caused by low water supply, the bill provided that masters and engineers be required under threat of heavy penalties to supply water to the boilers while the boat was not in motion.

The half-hearted tone of the House committee's report on the bill hardly promised positive legislative action. The Constitution gave Congress the power to regulate commerce, the report noted, but the right of Congress to prescribe the mode, manner, or form of construction of the vehicles of conveyance could not be perceived. Whether boats should be propelled by wind, paddles, or steam, and if by steam, whether by low or high pressure, were questions that were not the business of Congress. No legislation was competent to remove the causes of boiler explosions, so that steam and its application must be left to the control of intellect and practical science. The intelligent conduct of those engaged in its use would be the best safeguard against the dangers incident to negligence. Besides, the report concluded, the destruction was much less than had been thought; the whole number of explosions in the United States was only fifty-two, with total casualties of 256 killed and 104 injured.[35] Supporters of the bill could not undo the damage of the

[33] Secretary of the Treasury, *Report*, March 3, 1831 (House of Representatives document 131, ser. 209 [Washington: 21st Congress, 2d session]), p. 1.

[34] *Doc. 478*, p. 44.

[35] *Ibid.*, pp. 1–7. Actually, the committee depended for its statistics upon the estimate of William C. Redfield, agent for the Steam Navigation Company of New York, who could hardly have been expected to be impartial. Comparing Redfield's figures with those listed in *JFI*, IX, N.S. (1832), 24–30 and with the sources listed

watered-down committee report, however. The bill died, and the disasters continued.

In his State of the Union message in December 1833, President Jackson noted that the distressing accidents on steamboats were increasing. He suggested that the disasters often resulted from criminal negligence by masters of the boats and operators of the engines. He urged Congress to pass precautionary and penal legislation to reduce the accidents.[36] A few days later, Senator Daniel Webster proposed that the Committee on Naval Affairs study the problem. He suggested that all boilers be tested at three times their working pressure and that any steamboat found racing be forfeited to the government. Thomas Hart Benton followed Webster, stating that the matter properly was the concern of the Judiciary Committee. The private waters of states were involved, Benton said; interference with their sovereignty might result. In passing, Benton remarked that the masters and owners of steamboats were, with few exceptions, men of the highest integrity. Further, Benton said, *he* had never met with any accident on a steamboat despite the fact that he traveled widely; upon boarding he was always careful to inquire whether the machinery was in good order. Webster still carried the day, since the matter went to the Committee on Naval Affairs; however, Benton's attitude prevailed in the session, for the reported Senate bill failed to pass.[37]

V

A program of experiments carried out by the Franklin Institute from 1831 to 1836 was based largely upon the reports of circumstances surrounding previous boiler explosions, the contemporary design and construction of boilers and their accessories, and methods of ensuring an adequate water supply. The work was done by a committee of volunteers led by Alexander Dallas Bache, later superintendent of the U.S. Coast Survey, who, at the time, was a young professor of natural philosophy at the University of Pennsylvania. A small boiler, one foot in diameter and about three feet long, with heavy glass viewing ports at each end, was used in most of the experiments. In others, the zeal of the workers led them to cause larger boilers to burst at a quarry on the outskirts of Philadelphia.

---

in n. 14, it is clear that he omitted many minor accidents; where the number of casualties were unknown, they were not counted; where they were estimated, Redfield took the lowest estimate.

36 *Congressional Globe,* I (Washington: 23d Congress, 1st session), 7.

37 *Ibid.,* I, 49, 442.

The group's findings overturned a current myth, proving conclusively that water did not decompose into hydrogen and oxygen inside the boiler, with the former gas exploding at some high temperature. The experimenters demonstrated that an explosion could occur without a sudden increase of pressure. Another widely held theory they disproved was that when water was injected into a boiler filled with hot and unsaturated steam, it flashed into an extremely high-pressure vapor, which caused the boiler to rupture. The group proved that the reverse was true: the larger the quantity of water thus introduced, the greater the decrease in the steam pressure.

The Franklin Institute workers also produced some positive findings. They determined that the gauge cocks, commonly used to ascertain the level of water inside the boilers, did not in fact show the true level, and that a glass tube gauge was much more reliable, if kept free from sediment. They found the fusing points of alloys of lead, tin, and bismuth, and recommended that fusible plates be employed with caution, because the more fluid portion of an alloy might be forced out prior to the designated fusion temperature, thus leaving the remainder with a higher temperature of fusion.[38] They investigated the effect of the surface condition of the shell on the temperature and time of vaporization, and they determined that properly weighted safety valves opened at calculated pressures within a small margin of error. The results of their experiments on the relationship of the pressure and temperature of steam showed close correspondence with those of the French, although, at this time, values of the specific heat of steam were erroneous due to the inability to differentiate between constant volume and constant temperature conditions.[39]

Simultaneously, another committee, also headed by Bache, investigated the strength of boiler materials. In these experiments, a sophisticated tensile testing machine was constructed, and corrections were made for friction and stresses producing during the tests. The investigators tested numerous specimens of rolled copper and wrought iron, not only at ambient temperatures but up to 1,300° F. They showed conclusively that there were substantial differences in the quality of domestic wrought irons by the differences in yield and tensile strengths. Of major importance was their finding that there was a rapid decrease in the ultimate strength of copper and wrought iron with increasing

[38] In this series of experiments, the committee was actually investigating the solid solutions of these metals and determining points on what would later be called equilibrium diagrams.

[39] Franklin Institute, *Report,* March 1, 1836 (House of Representatives document 162, ser. 289 [Washington]).

temperature. Further, they determined that the strength of iron parallel to the direction of rolling was about 6 per cent greater than in the direction at right angles to it. They proved that the laminated structure in "piled" iron, forged from separate pieces, yielded much lower tensile values than plate produced from single blooms. Their tests also showed that special precautions should be taken in the design of riveted joints.[40]

Taken as a whole, the Franklin Institute reports demonstrate remarkable experimental technique as well as a thorough methodological approach. They exposed errors and myths in popular theories on the nature of steam and the causes of explosions. They laid down sound guidelines on the choice of materials, on the design and construction of boilers, and on the design and arrangement of appurtenances added for their operation and safety. Further, the reports included sufficient information to emphasize the necessity for good maintenance procedures and frequent proof tests, pointing out that the strength of boilers diminished as the length of service increased.

VI

The Franklin Institute report on steam boiler explosions was presented to the House through the secretary of the treasury in March 1836, and the report on boiler materials was available in 1837. The Franklin Institute committee also made detailed recommendations on provisions that any regulatory legislation should incorporate. It proposed that inspectors be appointed to test all boilers hydraulically every six months; it prohibited the licensing of ships using boilers whose design had proved to be unsafe; and it recommended penalties in cases of explosions resulting from improper maintenance, from the incompetence or negligence of the master or engineer, or from racing. It placed responsibility for injury to life or property on owners who neglected to have the required inspections made, and it recommended that engineers meet certain standards of experience, knowledge, and character. The committee had no doubt of the right of Congress to legislate on these matters.[41]

Congress did not act immediately. In December 1836 the House appointed a committee to investigate the explosions, but there was no action until after President Van Buren urged the passage of legislation

[40] *JFI*, XVIII, N.S. (1836), 217, 289; XIX, N.S. (1837), 73, 157, 241, 325, 409; XX, N.S. (1837), 1, 73.

[41] *JFI*, XVIII, N.S. (1836), 369–75.

in December 1837.[42] That year witnessed a succession of marine disasters. Not all were attributable to boiler explosions, although the loss
of 140 persons in a new ship, the "Pulaski," out of Charleston, was
widely publicized. The Senate responded quickly to Van Buren's appeal, passing a measure on January 24, 1838. The House moved less
rapidly. An explosion aboard the "Moselle" at Cincinnati in April
1838, which killed 151 persons,[43] caused several Congressmen to request
suspension of the rules so that the bill could be brought to the floor,
but in the face of more pressing business the motion was defeated.[44]
The legislation was almost caught in the logjam in the House at the
end of the session, but on June 16 the bill was brought to the floor.
Debate centered principally upon whether the interstate commerce
clause in the Constitution empowered Congress to pass such legislation.
Its proponents argued affirmatively, and the bill was finally approved
and became law on July 7, 1838.[45]

The law incorporated several sections relating to the prevention of
collisions, the control of fires, the inspection of hulls, and the carrying of lifeboats. It provided for the immediate appointment by each
federal judge of a competent boiler inspector having no financial interest in their manufacture. The inspector was to examine every steamboat boiler in his area semiannually, ascertain its age and soundness,
and certify it with a recommended working pressure. For this service
the owner paid the inspector $5.00—his sole remuneration—and a license
to navigate was contingent upon the receipt of this certificate. The law
specified no inspection criteria. It enjoined the owners to employ a
sufficient number of competent and experienced engineers, holding the
owners responsible for loss of life or property damage in the event of

[42] *Congressional Globe*, IV (Washington: 24th Congress, 2d session), 29; VI
(Washington: 25th Congress, 2d session), 7–9.

[43] The *Moselle* disaster was important because of its effect upon marine insurance
policies. The estate of the captain and part owner, Isaac Perrin, sued for recovery
under the policy (*The Administrators of Isaac Perrin v. The Protection Insurance
Co.*, 11 Ohio [1842], 160). The defense gave evidence that Perrin was determined to
outstrip another boat and that when passengers expostulated with him concerning
the dangerous appearance of the boiler fires, he swore that he would be "that night in
Louisville or hell." Despite proof of negligence on the part of the captain, the court
ruled against the insurance company, stating that the explosion of boilers was a risk
insured against. The insurance companies, thereafter, moved to exclude boiler explosions as a covered risk. See *Citizens Insurance Co. v. Glasgow, Shaw, and Larkin*,
9 Missouri (1852), 411, and *Roe and Kercheval v. Columbus Insurance Co.*, 17 Missouri (1852), 301.

[44] *Congressional Globe*, VI, 342.   [45] *Ibid.*, VI, 455.

a boiler explosion for their failure to do so. Further, any steamboat employee whose negligence resulted in the loss of life was to be considered guilty of manslaughter, and upon conviction could be sentenced to not more than ten years imprisonment. Finally, it provided that in suits against owners for damage to persons or property, the fact of the bursting of the boilers should be considered prima facie evidence of negligence until the defendant proved otherwise.[46]

This law raises several questions, because the elimination of inspection criteria and the qualification of engineers rendered the measure ineffectual. Why was this done? Did Congress show restraint because it had insufficient information? Did it yield to the pressure of steamboat interests who feared government interference? Such questions cannot be definitely answered, but there are clues for some tentative conclusions.

The bill, as originally introduced, was similar to the Franklin Institute proposals, so that the Senate committee to which it was referred possessed the most recent informed conclusions as to the causes of boiler explosions and the means of their prevention. The President's plea to frame legislation in the face of the mounting fatalities undoubtedly persuaded the Democratic majority to act. They were unmoved by a memorial from steamboat interests urging the defeat of the bill.[47] But the majority was not as yet prepared to pass such detailed regulations as had originally been proposed. In response to a question as to why the provision for the qualification of engineers had been eliminated, the Senate committee chairman stated that the committee had considered this requirement desirable but foresaw too much difficulty in putting it into effect. Further, the Senate rejected an amendment to levy heavy penalties for racing, as proposed by the Whig, Oliver Smith of Indiana. The Whigs appear to have seen the situation as one in which the federal government should use its powers and interpose firmly. Henry Clay, R. H. Bayard of Delaware, and Samuel Prentiss of Vermont supported Smith's amendment, and John Davis of Massachusetts declared that he would support the strongest measures to make the bill effective. Those who had urged rapid action of the bill in the House were William B. Calhoun and Caleb Cushman of Massachusetts and Elisha Whittlesey of Ohio, all Whigs. But at this time the majority hewed to the doctrine that enlightened self-interest should motivate owners to provide safe operation. The final clause, specifying that the

<hr />

[46] *U.S. Statutes at Large* (Washington: 25th Congress, 2d session, July 7, 1838), V, 304–6.

[47] *Congressional Globe*, VI, 265.

bursting of boilers should be taken as prima facie evidence of negligence until proved otherwise, stressed this idea.

The disappointment of the informed public concerning the law was voiced immediately in letters solicited by the secretary of the treasury, contained in a report that he submitted to Congress in December 1838.[48] There were predictions that the system of appointment and inspection would encourage corruption and graft. There were complaints about the omission of inspection criteria and a provision for the licensing of engineers. One correspondent pointed out that it was impossible legally to determine the experience and skill of an engineer, so that the section of the law that provided penalties for owners who failed to employ experienced and skilful engineers was worthless. One critic who believed that business interests had undue influence upon the government wrote: "We are mostly ruled by corporations and joint-stock companies. . . . If half the citizens of this country should get blown up, and it should be likely to affect injuriously the trade and commerce of the other half by bringing to justice the guilty, no elective officer would risk his popularity by executing the law."[49]

But there also was a pained reaction from the owners of steamboats. A memorial in January 1841 from steamboat interests on the Atlantic seaboard stressed that appropriate remedies for the disasters had not been afforded by the 1838 law as evidenced by the casualty figures for 1839 and 1840. They provided statistics to prove that in *their* geographical area the loss of life per number of lives exposed had decreased by a factor of sixteen from 1828 to 1838, indicating that the troubles centered chiefly in the western waters. But at the same time the memorial emphasized that the 1838 law acted as a deterrent for prudent men to continue in the steamboat business, objecting particularly to the clause that construed a fatal disaster as prime facie evidence of negligence. They argued that if Congress considered steam navigation too hazardous for the public safety, it would be more just and honorable to prohibit it entirely.[50]

However, it not only was the Congress that was reconsidering the concepts of negligence and responsibility in boiler explosions. The common law also searched for precedents to meet the new conditions, to establish guidelines by which to judge legal actions resulting from technological innovation. A key decision, made in Pennsylvania in 1845, involved a boiler explosion at the defendant's flour mill that killed the

---

[48] *Doc. 21.*   [49] *Ibid.*, p. 396.

[50] *Memorial,* Jan. 23, 1841 (House of Representatives document 113, ser. 377 [Washington: 26th Congress, 2d session]).

plaintiff's horse. The defense pleaded that any negligence was on the part of the boiler manufacturer. The court, however, ruled otherwise, stating that the owner of a public trade or business which required the use of a steam engine was responsible for any injury resulting from its deficiency.[51] This case was used as a precedent in future lawsuits involving boiler explosions.

<h2 style="text-align:center">VII</h2>

Experience proved that the 1838 law was not preventing explosions or loss of life. In the period 1841–48, there were some seventy marine explosions that killed about 625 persons. In December 1848 the commissioner of patents, to whom Congress now turned for data, estimated that in the period 1816–48 a total of 233 steamboat explosions had occurred in which 2,563 persons had been killed and 2,097 injured, with property losses in excess of $3 million.[52]

In addition to the former complaints about the lack of proof tests and licenses for engineers, the commissioner's report included testimony that the inspection methods were a mockery. Unqualified inspectors were being appointed by district judges through the agency of highly placed friends. The inspectors regarded the position as a lifetime office. Few even looked at the boilers but merely collected their fees. The inspector at New York City complained that his strict inspection caused many boats to go elsewhere for inspections. He cited the case of the "Niagara," plying between New York City and Albany, whose master declined to take out a certificate from his office because it recommended a working pressure of only 25 p.s.i. on the boiler. A few months later the boiler of the "Niagara," which had been certified in northern New York, exploded while carrying a pressure of 44 p.s.i. and killed two persons.[53]

Only eighteen prosecutions had been made in ten years under the manslaughter section of the 1838 law. In these cases there had been nine convictions, but the penalties had, for the most part, been fines which were remitted. It was difficult to assemble witnesses for a trial, and juries could not be persuaded to convict a man for manslaughter for an act of negligence, to which it seemed impossible to attach this degree of guilt. Also, the commissioner's report pointed out that damages were given in cases of bodily injury but that none were awarded for loss of life in negligence suits. It appeared that exemplary damages might be effective in curbing rashness and negligence.[54]

---

[51] *Spencer* v. *Campbell*, 9 Watts & Sergeants (1845), 32.

[52] *Doc. 18*, p. 2.   [53] *Ibid.*, pp. 18, 78, 80.   [54] *Ibid.*, pp. 29, 52–53.

The toll of life in 1850 was 277 dead from explosions, and in 1851 it rose to 407.[55] By this time Great Britain had joined France in regulatory action, which the Congress noted.[56] As a consequence of legislation passed in 1846 and 1851, a rejuvenated Board of Trade was authorized to inspect steamboats semiannually, to issue or deny certificates of adequacy, and to investigate and report on accidents.[57] The time had come for the Congress to take forceful action, and in 1852 it did.

John Davis, Whig senator from Massachusetts, who had favored stricter legislation in 1838, was the driving force behind the 1852 law. In prefacing his remarks on the general provisions of the bill, he said: "A very extensive correspondence has been carried on with all parts of the country . . . there have been laid before the committee a great multitude of memorials, doings of chambers of commerce, of boards of trade, of conventions, of bodies of engineers; and to a considerable extent of all persons interested, in one form or another, in steamers . . . in one thing . . . they are all . . . agreed—that is, that the present system is erroneous and needs correction."[58]

Thus again, the informed public submitted recommendations on the detailed content of the measure. An outstanding proponent who helped shape the bill was Alfred Guthrie, a practical engineer from Illinois. With personal funds, Guthrie had inspected some two hundred steamboats in the Mississippi valley to ascertain the causes of boiler explosions. Early in the session, Senator Shields of Illinois succeeded in having Guthrie's report printed, distributed, and included in the Senate documents.[59] Guthrie's recommendations were substantially those made by the Franklin Institute in 1836. His reward was the post as first supervisor of the regulatory agency which the law created.

[55] *Congressional Globe* (Washington: 32d Congress, 1st session), Appendix, 287.

[56] *Ibid.,* p. 2426.

[57] Public and General Acts, 9, 10 Victoria (1846), chap. l; 14, 15 Victoria (1851), chap. lxxix.

[58] *Congressional Globe* (32d Congress, 1st session), p. 1669. Organizations of experienced steamboat engineers were formed in many cities during the 1840's to promote safe operation and had attempted on previous occasions to influence Congress to improve the 1838 law, particularly with respect to providing for proof tests, better inspection methods, and the establishment of boards to qualify engineers. See *Relative to Steamboat Explosions* (House of Representatives document 68, ser. 441 [Washington: 28th Congress, 1st session]), which is a petition from a body in the city of Cincinnati.

[59] *Memorial of Alfred Guthrie, a Practical Engineer*, Feb. 6, 1852 (Senate miscellaneous document 32, ser. 629 [Washington: 32d Congress, 1st session]).

After the bill reached the Senate floor, dozens of amendments were proposed, meticulously scrutinized, and disposed of. The measure had been, remarked one senator, "examined and elaborated . . . more patiently, thoroughly, and faithfully than any other bill before in the Senate of the United States."[60] As a result, in place of the 1838 law which embodied thirteen sections and covered barely three pages, there was passed such stringent and restrictive legislation that forty-three sections and fourteen pages were necessary.[61]

The maximum allowable working pressure for any boiler was set at 110 p.s.i., and every boiler had to be tested yearly at one and one-half times its working pressure. Boilers had to be fabricated from suitable quality iron plates, on which the manufacturer's name was stamped. At least two ample safety valves—one in a locked grating—were required, as well as fusible plates. There were provisions relating to adequate supply of boiler feedwater and outlawing designs that might prove dangerous. Inspectors were authorized to order repairs at any time. All engineers had to be licensed by inspectors, and the inspectors themselves issued certificates only under oath. There were stiff monetary penalties for any infractions. The penalty for loading a safety valve excessively was a two hundred dollar fine and eighteen months imprisonment. The fine for manufacturing or using a boiler of unstamped material was five hundred dollars. Fraudulent stamping carried a penalty of five hundred dollars and two years imprisonment. Inspectors falsifying certificates were subject to a five hundred dollar fine and six months imprisonment, and the law expressly prohibited their accepting bribes.

A new feature of the law, which was most indicative of the future, was the establishment of boards of inspectors empowered to investigate infractions or accidents, with the right to summon witnesses, to compel their attendance, and to examine them under oath. Above the local inspectors were nine supervisors appointed by the President. Their duties included the compilation of evidence for the prosecution of those failing to comply with the regulations and the preparation of reports to the secretary of the treasury on the effectiveness of the regulations. Nor did these detailed regulations serve to lift the burden of presumptive negligence from the shoulders of owners in cases of explosion. The explosion of boilers was not made prime facie evidence as in the 1838 law, but owners still bore a legal responsibilty. This was

[60] *Congressional Globe,* (32d Congress 1st session), p. 1742.

[61] *U.S. Statutes at Large* (Washington: 32d Congress, 1st session, Aug. 30, 1852), X, 61–75.

made clear in several court decisions which held that proof of strict compliance with the 1852 law was not a sufficient defense to the allegations of loss by an explosion caused by negligence.[62]

The final Senate debate and the vote on this bill shows how, in thirty years, the public attitude and, in turn, the attitudes of its elected representatives had changed toward the problem of unrestricted private enterprise, mainly as a result of the boiler explosions. The opponents of the bill still argued that the self-interest of the steamboat companies was the best insurance of the safety of the traveling public.[63] But their major argument against passage was the threat to private property rights which they considered the measure entailed. Senator Robert F. Stockton of New Jersey was most emphatic:

> It is this—how far the Federal Government . . . shall be permitted to interfere with the rights of personal property—or the private business of any citizen . . . under the influence of recent calamities, too much sensibility is displayed on this subject . . . I hold it to be my imperative duty not to permit my feelings of humanity and kindness to interfere with the protection which I am bound, as a Senator of the United States, to throw around the liberty of the citizen, and the investment of his property, or the management of his own business . . . what will be left of human liberty if we progress on this course much further? What will be, by and by, the difference between citizens of this far-famed Republic and the serfs of Russia? Can a man's property be said to be his own, when you take it out of his own control and put it into the hands of another, though he may be a Federal officer?[64]

This expression of a belief that Congress should in no circumstances interfere with private enterprise was now supported by only a small minority. One proponent of the bill replied: "I consider that the only question involved in the bill is this: Whether we shall permit a legalized, unquestioned, and peculiar class in the community to go on committing murder at will, or whether we shall make such enactments as will compel them to pay some attention to the value of life."[65] It was, then, a question of the sanctity of private property rights as against the duty of government to act in the public weal. On this question the Senate voted overwhelmingly that the letter course should prevail.[66]

[62] *Curran* v. *Cheeseman*, 1 Cincinnati Rep. (1870), 52.

[63] *Congressional Globe* (32d Congress, 1st session), pp. 1741, 2425.

[64] *Ibid.*, pp. 2426, 2427.   [65] *Ibid.*, p. 2427.

[66] The strength of the vote can be gauged by the defeat, forty-three to eight, of a motion to table the bill by Senator Stockton just prior to its passage. The eight

Though not completely successful, the act of 1852 had the desired corrective effects. During the next eight years prior to the outbreak of the Civil War, the loss of life on steamboats from all types of accidents dropped to 65 per cent of the total in the corresponding period preceding its passage.[67] A decade after the law became effective, John C. Merriam, editor and proprietor of the *American Engineer*, wrote: "Since the passage of this law steamboat explosions on the Atlantic have become almost unknown, and have greatly decreased in the west. With competent inspectors, this law is invaluable, and we hope to hail the day when a similar act is passed in every legislature, touching locomotive and stationary boilers.[68]

There was, of course, hostility and opposition to the law immediately after its passage, particularly among the owners and masters of steamboats.[69] It checked the steady rise in the construction of new boats, which had been characteristic of the earlier years.[70] The effect, however, was chastening rather than emasculating. Associations for the prevention of steam boiler explosions were formed; later, insurance companies were organized to insure steam equipment that was manufactured and operated with the utmost regard for safety. In time, through the agency of the American Society of Mechanical Engineers,

---

were: Bayard (D., Del.), Butler (States Rights D., S.C.), Clemens (D., Ala.), Hale (Antislavery D., N.H.), Hunter (D., Va.), James (Protective Tariff D., R.I.), Pratt (Whig, Md.), and Stockton (D., N.J.). Although these senators represented only states along the eastern seaboard and in the South, it would be difficult to interpret their vote on a geographical basis, since eighteen senators from the same group of states voted against the motion. One might be tempted to ascribe some partisan basis to the vote, since only one Whig joined seven Democrats in supporting the motion. On the other hand, twenty-six Democrats and seventeen Whigs constituted the majority. Of those not voting—seven Democrats and four Whigs —by their comments during prior debates on the measure, Brodhead (D., Pa.) and De Saussure (D., S.C.) appear to have favored the bill, while Gwin (D., Calif.) was against it. The conclusion seems justified that the movement and final step toward positive regulation found support from congressmen of all political postures and from all geographical areas, that it was prompted by the recognition of the inadequacy of the 1838 law as evidenced by the continued severe loss of life, and that congressmen were urged to pass the legislation by constituents who were able to recognize how the problem could be solved.

[67] *10th Census*, IV, 5.

[68] L. Stebbins, pub., *Eighty Years' Progress of the United States* (New York, 1864), p. 243.

[69] Lloyd M. Short, *Steamboat Inspection Service* (New York, 1922), p. 5.

[70] Department of the Interior, *op. cit.*, IV, 5.

uniform boiler codes were promulgated and adopted by states and municipalities.[71]

Thus, the reaction of the informed public, expressed by Congress, to boiler explosions caused the initiation of positive regulation of a sector of private enterprise through a governmental agency. The legislation reflected a definite change of attitude concerning the responsibility of the government to interfere in those affairs of private enterprise where the welfare and safety of the general public was concerned. The implications of this change for the future can be seen by reference to the Windom Committee report of 1874, which was the first exhaustive study of the conditions in the railroad industry that led ultimately to the passage of legislation creating the Interstate Commerce Commission. One section of this report was entitled: "The Constitutional Power of Congress to Regulate Commerce among the Several States." The committee cited the judicial interpretation of the Constitution in *Gibbons* v. *Ogden*, that it was the prerogative of Congress solely to regulate interstate commerce, and also referred to the decision of Chief Justice Taney in *Genesee Chief* v. *Fitzhugh*, wherein it was held that this power was as extensive upon land as upon water. The report pointed out that no decision of the Supreme Court had ever countenanced the view that the power of Congress was purely negative, that it could be constitutionally exercised only by disburdening commerce, by preventing duties and imposts on the trade between the states. It fact, the report argued, Congress had already asserted its power positively. Referring to the acts of 1838 and 1852, it stated that "Congress has passed statutes defining how steamboats shall be constructed and equipped."[72] Thus, the legislation that was provoked by bursting boilers was used as a precedent to justify regulatory legislation in another area where the public interest was threatened.

Bursting steamboat boilers, then, should be viewed not merely as unfortunate and perhaps inevitable consequences of the early age of steam, as occurrences which plagued nineteenth-century engineers and which finally, to a large degree, they were successful in preventing. They should be seen also as creating a dilemma as to how far the lives and property of the general public might be endangered by unrestricted private enterprise. The solution was an important step toward the inauguration of the regulatory and investigative agencies in the federal government.

[71] Greene, *op. cit.*

[72] *Report of the Select Committee on Transportation to the Seaboard* (Senate Report No. 307, Ser. 1588 [Washington: 43d Congress, 1st session]), pp. 79–92.

Waves of Change: Mechanization in the Pacific Coast Canned-Salmon Industry, 1864–1914

PATRICK W. O'BANNON

The processing of agricultural products and other foodstuffs has long interested historians of technology. Oliver Evans's 18th-century flour mill and the "disassembly" lines of 19th-century midwestern meat packers are perhaps the most familiar subjects of this interest, but the historical importance of these developments lies with the innovative manner in which they combined existing technologies into vastly more efficient systems for moving and handling materials, not with any fundamental departure from traditional food-processing technologies.[1]

Canning, however, broke with the past, introducing new food-processing technologies and entirely new food products to society. Developed in Napoleonic France, canned food became popular in the United States about the time of the Civil War. The American canning industry grew rapidly throughout the second half of the 19th century, producing over $63 million worth of goods in 1899. During the first decades of the 20th century it constituted the fastest growing food industry in the country.[2]

PATRICK W. O'BANNON is principal historian with John Milner Associates, a cultural resources consulting firm located in Philadelphia. This research was sponsored in part by NOAA, National Sea Grant College Program, Department of Commerce, under grant NA 80AA-D-00120, Project R/MA-6 through the California Sea Grant College Program. The project principal investigator was Professor Harry N. Scheiber, University of California, Berkeley.

[1]David A. Hounshell, *From the American System to Mass Production 1800–1932: The Development of Manufacturing Technology in the United States* (Baltimore, 1984), pp. 10–11, 241. See Sigfried Giedion, *Mechanization Takes Command: A Contribution to Anonymous History* (Oxford, 1948), pp. 130–251, for evidence of the early interest of historians of technology in the processing of agricultural products and other foodstuffs. More recent works on this subject include Mary Yeager, *Competition and Regulation: The Development of Oligopoly in the Meat Packing Industry* (Greenwich, Conn., 1981) and Margaret Walsh, *The Rise of the Midwestern Meat Packing Industry* (Lexington, Ky., 1982).

[2]Charles B. Kuhlmann, "The Processing of Agricultural Products after 1860," in *The*

This essay originally appeared in *Technology and Culture*, vol. 28, no. 3, July 1987.

Salmon was one of the most important products of American can- neries, the nation's fifth most valuable canned foodstuff at the turn of the century.[3] In the Pacific Northwest the canneries pioneered the settlement of many parts of the coast, and the industry formed, along with mining and lumbering, a cornerstone of the region's extractive, resource-based economy.

The canned-salmon industry had to pay close attention to develop- ments in canning technology. The industry was forced into this posi- tion by the nature of its raw material. The annual spawning runs lasted as few as fifteen days, strictly limiting the length of both the fishing and canning seasons and forcing packers to produce their entire annual output within, at best, a period of three to four months. The shortness of the season placed a heavy emphasis on speed and efficiency in cannery operations, an emphasis further stressed by the unpredictabil- ity of the spawning runs. Unlike fruit and vegetable canners, who could observe the fields and crops and prepare accordingly, salmon canners prepared for the arrival of the annual runs without any notion of their size. Like a gambler, or a general, the salmon canner studied the signs and laid his plans. Then he waited and trusted to luck. Failure of the local run forced canners to scramble for alternative supplies of fish in order to salvage something of their preseason investment in materials and workers. Large runs offered a chance to make a large pack and, in theory, a large profit. During heavy runs the canning lines had to be capable of quickly processing large numbers of fish, since delays meant spoilage and a smaller pack. Mechanization of the can- ning lines offered canners their best opportunity to obtain this capabil- ity. The drive to mechanize the canneries consequently became a chief characteristic of the industry.[4]

Growth of the American Economy, ed. Harold F. Williamson (Englewood Cliffs, N.J., 1951), p. 445; U.S. Bureau of the Census, *Thirteenth Census of the United States—Abstract of the Census* (Washington, D.C., 1913), p. 476. There are no recent scholarly studies of the American canning industry. The standard secondary sources are Earl Chapin May, *The Canning Clan: A Pageant of Pioneering Americans* (New York, 1937), A. W. Biting, *Appertiz- ing or the Art of Canning: Its History and Development* (San Francisco, 1937), and Arthur I. Judge, ed., *A History of the Canning Industry by Its Most Prominent Men* (Baltimore, 1914). All three of these works adopt a worshipful tone toward the industry.

[3]Bureau of the Census, *Abstract of the Thirteenth Census* (n. 2 above), p. 476.

[4]The Pacific Coast canned-salmon industry has received little attention from serious historians. Most secondary accounts were written by individuals connected with the industry and emphasize progress and romance, as exemplified by the steadily increasing size of the industry's annual pack and the sailing vessels that transported cannery workers to Alaskan plants. Some recent works, most notably Courtland L. Smith, *Salmon Fishers of the Columbia* (Corvallis, Ore., 1979), and Jack Masson and Donald Guimary, "Asian Labor Contractors in the Alaskan Canned Salmon Industry: 1880–1937," *Labor*

Between 1864, when a single plant on California's Sacramento River packed 2,000 cases of salmon, and 1914, when over 200 plants scattered along the Pacific rim from California to Alaska (fig. 1) produced over 6.6 million cases, the canning lines became almost wholly mechanized.[5] The canning process, which manipulated fish and cans in turn, complicated efforts to introduce machinery onto the canning lines and imposed a pattern of technological innovation on the industry that remained unbroken for fifty years.

The canning process transformed a complex organic raw material, a freshly caught fish, into a uniform consumer product packed in identical tin containers. Salmon were delivered to the cannery, butchered, cleaned, and cut into can-sized pieces. The cans, fabricated prior to the start of the fishing season, were then filled with these pieces, fitted with tops, and washed, cooked, lacquered, labeled, and boxed for delivery to market.

Butchering and cleaning proved more difficult to mechanize than other steps in the canning process because these operations manipulated individual salmon, rather than identical tin cans. Once the fish had been reduced to fairly uniform pieces, machinery could perform the remaining steps in the canning process with relative ease. Mechanization of those steps that manipulated cans, rather than fish, also benefited from the experiences of eastern canners, who developed most basic canning machinery. The complexities involved in mechanizing the operations that manipulated fish, and the comparative ease with which machines could be used in those operations that manipu-

---

History 22 (1981): 377–97, have examined certain aspects of the industry in a more scholarly fashion. Virtually the only extant business papers relevant to canning are those of the Columbia River Packers Association (CRPA) at the Oregon Historical Society, Portland. The University of Oregon has some of the papers of the industry's pioneer firm, Hume & Hapgood, and the Alaska State Historical Library, Juneau, has miscellaneous Alaska Packers Association papers, but both these collections are incomplete and provide, at best, an impressionistic view of these firms. The CRPA operated in what was perhaps the most technologically backward of all the major canning regions on the Pacific Coast. Consequently, these papers can provide only limited data on questions of mechanization and technological innovation. The lack of extant company records forces the historian to reply on two principal sources: the industry trade journal, *Pacific Fisherman*, and the voluminous and detailed annual reports of the United States Bureau of Fisheries, which administered the Alaskan fisheries until 1959. Both had promotional aims, but, used critically and in conjunction with other material, these permit the compilation of a fairly accurate portrait of the industry.

[5]Bureau of the Census, *Abstract of the Thirteenth Census* (n. 2 above), p. 476; John N. Cobb, "Pacific Salmon Fisheries," 4th ed., Appendix 13 to U.S. Department of Commerce, *Report of the Commissioner of Fisheries: 1930*, Bureau of Fisheries Doc. 1092 (Washington, D.C.,1931), p. 554.

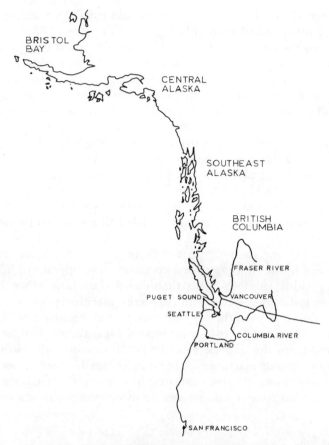

FIG. 1.—The canning regions of the Pacific Coast

lated cans, caused a basic pattern of technological innovation to emerge within the canned-salmon industry.

Innovation expressed itself in two waves of activity. In the first, which lasted from about 1880 to 1900, machinery reached virtually every part of the cannery that manipulated tin cans. The second, which began in 1905, resulted from the perfection of a practical butchering machine. During the next decade machinery appeared on the canning lines that refined, improved, and ultimately replaced the machines of the first wave of innovation.

Both these waves of activity began with the widespread adoption of a device that shattered existing production bottlenecks, creating opportunities and imperatives for a series of subsequent innovations. Adoption of this collection of new machinery, the leading innovation and those that followed, caused a surge in cannery productivity.

The mechanization of the canned-salmon industry did not, however, progress in a steady and continual triumph of technology. The industry entailed a great deal of inherent risk for canners, and few chose to increase that risk by unhesitatingly adopting whatever technological marvel appeared on the horizon. Large firms, better able to absorb the cost of incorporating a new and untried innovation into the canning lines, pioneered the industry's mechanization. Smaller operators proved more than willing to sit back and let others adapt new machinery to the rigors of daily operation. Only when a new machine proved itself economical, efficient, and capable of surviving in the field was it embraced by the industry as a whole. And, even then, the dictates of local conditions precluded adopting some innovations.

The industry operated along thousands of miles of shoreline in virtually hundreds of local environments, and a machine that increased productivity in one was not guaranteed a place in every cannery on the Pacific Coast. Environmental conditions in one locale, economic conditions in another, and labor conditions in a third could cause canners in each to make widely differing decisions concerning the adoption of an innovation. Regional variation characterized and determined the course of mechanization within the industry.

Labor concerns heavily influenced canners' attitudes toward new machinery. The industry depended on a Chinese work force supplied by Chinese labor contractors, but in 1882 Congress implemented the Oriental Exclusion Act, halting the influx of new Chinese laborers into the United States. By about 1890 the contractors began to experience a shortage of able-bodied Chinese workers. They substituted other ethnic workers, first Japanese, then Filipino, and finally Mexican, but none of these proved as satisfactory to the canners as had the Chinese. Skilled Chinese cannery workers took advantage of the situation by demanding, and receiving, greatly increased wages.[6]

In Canada, where Chinese workers continued to enter the country, canners continued to rely on them long after their American counter-

[6]The exact reasons why other ethnic workers were not as satisfactory as the Chinese are unclear. It is very clear, however, that canners ultimately preferred to mechanize their operations rather than replace skilled Chinese with others. Canners viewed the Chinese as "trustworthy," "reliable," and, perhaps most important, "docile." They worked for Chinese foremen and contractors and thus felt some bonds with them, but these bonds of course dissolved when the contractors hired Japanese and other ethnic workers to fill out their cannery gangs. The new workers were much more prone to rebel or protest against low pay, poor conditions, and mistreatment. Their fights and protests irritated canners, who vowed to replace all their highly paid skilled workers with easily replaced machine tenders. For more on this topic, see Patrick W. O'Bannon, "Technological Change in the Pacific Coast Canned Salmon Industry: 1864–1924" (Ph.D. diss., University of California, San Diego, 1983), pp. 181–83, 223–28, 344–53.

parts had replaced them with machinery tended by unskilled workers from other ethnic groups. In the United States, however, the high wages of the skilled Chinese and the growing shortage of Chinese workers impelled canners to resolve their labor problems by mechanizing the canning lines. Still, the contract system endured into the 1930s, largely because it freed canners from the need to negotiate with individual workers and because American and European workers refused to accept the long hours, harsh conditions, and seasonal nature of cannery work.

*   *   *

The industry's first wave of technological innovation began in the mid-1870s with the introduction onto canning lines of the steam retort. Invented in Baltimore, an eastern canning center, the retort amounted to little more than a modified boiler that used pressurized steam to cook and sterilize the contents of the cans.[7] Despite its simplicity, the retort offered important advantages over earlier cooking methods, which for the most part consisted simply in placing trays of cans into open kettles of boiling water. The retort cooked at higher temperatures than the old method, reducing cooking time and speeding production. Temperature and pressure gauges on the retorts gave canners their first opportunity to monitor precisely the cooking process.[8]

Salmon canners rapidly adopted the retort because of its advantages over traditional cooking methods—but only after they modified it to meet the specific needs and conditions of their industry. Vertical retorts imported from the East were designed to be loaded and unloaded using block and tackle. On the Pacific Coast, they were laid on their side so that handcarts stacked with cans could be easily wheeled in and out (fig. 2). This innovation reduced handling time and eliminated the need for some of the workers previously required for loading and unloading, thereby permitting both increased productivity and reduced labor costs.

The increase in productivity associated with the retort, which had become a common fixture in most canneries by 1880, created both opportunities and imperatives for innovation at other points on the canning line.[9] Canners sought to eliminate bottlenecks that restricted the flow of cans to the retorts and prevented their operating at full

[7]See Andrew K. Shriver, U. S. Patent no. 149,256, March 31, 1874.

[8]Duncan A. Stacey, "Technological Change in the Fraser River Salmon Canning Industry: 1871–1912" (master's thesis, University of British Columbia, 1977), p. 15; Alfred S. Eichner, *The Emergence of Oligopoly: Sugar Refining as a Case Study* (Baltimore, 1969), p. 31.

[9]Stacey (n. 8 above), p. 17.

FIG. 2.—A battery of horizontal retorts in a salmon cannery. (*Pacific Fisherman* 10 [November 1912]: 27.)

capacity, thereby limiting gains in productivity. The point on the canning line most directly affected by the adoption of the retort was the soldering bench. Chinese laborers, each capable of soldering a top onto a can in one minute, worked here. Despite the skill of these workers, the average soldering gang could not seal cans quickly enough to keep the retorts operating at full capacity.[10] Because solderers earned among the highest wages of all cannery employees, few canners attempted to increase production at the soldering bench by hiring additional workers. Instead they sought a mechanical solderer that would simultaneously eliminate this production bottleneck and reduce their labor costs.

The first soldering machine in a salmon cannery, put in service in an Oregon plant during the 1877 season, was a Howe "floater," made in the East. As a chain rolled topped cans through a trough filled with molten solder, the solder "floated" onto the seam between the top and the body, sealing the can closed.[11] Salmon canners modified the soldering machine, as they had the retort, in order to increase its reliability and productivity. The shortness and uncertainty of the canning season, combined with the remote location of many salmon canneries,

[10]George B. Goode et al., *The Fisheries and Fishery Industries of the United States*, Sec. 3, "The Fishing Grounds of North America" (Washington, D.C., 1887), p. 41; Stacey (n. 8 above), pp. 16, 25; *The West Shore*, June 1877, p. 160.

[11]W. H. Barker, "Reminiscences of the Salmon Industry," *Pacific Fisherman Yearbook*, January 1920, p. 68; May (n. 2 above), p. 28; Judge (n. 2 above), p. 92.

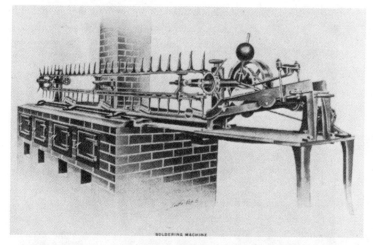

FIG. 3.—This soldering machine used metal fingers to drag the cans through the molten solder. (*Pacific Fisherman Annual* 1 [January 1903]: 5.)

required a machine that could operate at high speed for long periods of time without breaking down. (See fig. 3.)

The soldering machine proved far more efficient and economical than hand soldering. A single machine, tended by two unskilled workers, closed forty-five to fifty cans per minute, about double the output of the average soldering gang. The two machine tenders earned a combined wage of about fifty dollars per month, a fraction of the 900 to 1,000 dollars earned monthly by the average twenty-man soldering gang.[12] Such dramatic increases in productivity and reductions in labor costs should have made the soldering machine almost irresistible to canners, particularly since each one cost only 250 to 300 dollars.[13] Instead, many canners at first balked at purchasing the new device. Some claimed that hand soldering produced fewer leaky cans, but most who resisted the new innovation did so out of a reluctance to antagonize their Chinese work force. In at least one instance an entire Chinese cannery gang refused to work until a soldering machine was removed from the cannery.[14]

Strikes and protests proved effective short-term tactics for workers

[12]*The West Shore*, June 1877, p. 160; *Astoria* (Oregon) *Daily Astorian*, May 24, 1878.

[13]W. S. Van Vleet, "Engineering the Tin Can," *Mechanical Engineering* 47 (August 1923): 612.

[14]J. G. Megler & Co. to John N. Cobb, 1916, John N. Cobb Papers, University of Washington Library, Seattle; Stacey (n. 8 above), p. 16; J. C. Lawrence, "An Historical Account of the Early Salmon Canning Industry in British Columbia" (undergraduate essay, University of British Columbia, 1951), p. 323.

because of the lack of a willing substitute labor force and because these were invariably threatened right in the midst of the fishing season. Few canners opted to hold out against strikers and let the salmon escape upstream to the spawning grounds or into the nets of their competitors. Protests from Chinese workers, and a reluctance to abandon established methods, delayed the widespread adoption of the soldering machine until the mid-1880s, roughly a decade after its introduction.

Among the many other innovations that followed the steam retort onto the canning lines were a series of machines that mechanized the production of tin cans. Previously the Chinese solderers had laboriously fabricated all of the season's cans during the weeks prior to the arrival of the runs. The soldering machine eliminated the need for these workers during the canning season and led canners to seek a means of mechanically fabricating cans so that they could completely free themselves of these highly paid employees.

As with the retort and the soldering machine, canners first imported can-making machinery from the East. In 1883 Edwin and O. W. Norton pioneered its use at their Chicago factory. The Nortons employed a series of machines to fabricate a can body, solder the body seam, fit a bottom to the body, solder that seam, and test the entire assemblage. Their line of machinery produced thirty cans a minute and used one-sixth the number of workers required to hand-fabricate cans at the same rate.[15]

During 1883 a Pacific Coast firm, licensed by the Nortons, produced 3,000 cases of machine-made salmon cans for an Alaskan cannery.[16] Despite this early experimentation with the new product, most salmon canners did not immediately adopt machine-made cans. As with the soldering machine, the principal cause of this hesitation was a reluctance to antagonize the Chinese cannery workers. The Chinese objected to ready-made cans because they enabled canners to eliminate the solderers, a significant portion of the work force, and deprive the remainder of the cannery gang of several weeks of light duty while the cans were being fabricated. Packers who purchased ready-made cans in the mid-1880s often found it difficult to secure all the workers they required. The Chinese frequently refused to work at these canneries,

[15]*Pacific Fisherman* 25 (August 1927): 19; *American Machinist* 6 (July 14, 1883): 1-2.
[16]*Pacific Fisherman Annual* 10 (February 1912): 36; *Pacific Fisherman* 25 (August 1927): 18; Joseph A. Craig and Robert L. Hacker, "The History and Development of the Fisheries of the Columbia River," in U.S. Department of the Interior, *Bulletin of the Bureau of Fisheries No. 32*, 49 (Washington, D.C., 1940): 155.

preferring to sign on with firms that hand-fabricated cans and consequently offered longer terms of employment.[17]

Ready-made cans were first widely used in Alaska, where canning began on a commercial basis in the mid-1880s. Alaskan canners discovered that using ready-made cans reduced the time the crews had to spend at the remote cannery sites where they had to be fed and sheltered. In the minds, and on the books, of the canners these savings outweighed any benefits gained by placating the Chinese. As early as 1890 Alaskan canners shipped millions of ready-made cans north, despite the objections of the Chinese and despite sacrificing the valuable cargo space that the cases of empty cans occupied on the crowded cannery transports.[18]

In the mid-1890s, Pacific Coast machine shops introduced their own can-making machinery, more rugged and faster-operating versions of eastern machines (fig. 4). These improved machines made it possible for salmon canners to fabricate cans mechanically at their own plants, which enabled canners to offer their Chinese workers continuing em-

Fig. 4.—The Astoria Iron Works produced this can-bodymaker. (*Pacific Fisherman* 1 [September 1903]: 21.)

[17]Harry K. Ralston, "The 1900 Strike of the Fraser River Sockeye Fishermen" (master's thesis, University of British Columbia, 1965), p. 6.

[18]A. B. Alexander, "Report of A. B. Alexander, Fishery Expert," in Z. L. Tanner, "Report upon Investigations of the U.S. Fish Commission Steamer *Albatross* from July 1, 1889 to June 30, 1891," in U.S. Commission of Fish and Fisheries, *Report of the Commissioner of Fisheries: 1889–1891* (Washington, D.C., 1893), p. 286.

ployment, assuring the goodwill of the labor contractors and an adequate supply of workers, and eliminated the need to take up precious space on the cannery transports with cases of empty cans. It also gave cannery superintendents greater flexibility with which to respond to unforeseen variations in the size of the runs.[19]

By 1900, most Alaskan canneries used machine-made cans either fabricated at the cannery or purchased ready-made. Yet canners in British Columbia and the United States continued to rely on hand-made cans. These canners did not need to support their crews at the canneries for as long as the Alaskan packers because they were closer to the population centers of the Pacific Coast. A factor in British Columbia's continuing commitment to handmade cans was Canada's continuing admittance of Chinese workers.[20]

* * *

Not every innovation that followed the retort onto the canning line was aimed to replace highly paid Chinese, as were the soldering machine and can-making machinery. In 1883 a Columbia River fisherman named Mathias Jensen perfected the machine that eventually eliminated most hand filling, which was unskilled labor. Jensen's machine used a plunger to force pieces of fish through a chamber and into a waiting can. A knife sliced off the mass of fish when the can was full. Early models (fig. 5) filled about fifty cans per minute, but by 1900 improved versions could fill seventy cans per minute.[21]

As with previous innovations, canners did not immediately adopt Jensen's filler. Canners operating on the Columbia River, the most important salmon stream on the Pacific Coast in the 1880s, refused to use the new machine after English customers complained about the mangled appearance of machine-packed salmon. Columbia River canners marketed most of their pack in England, so, rather than irritate their best customers, they rejected Jensen's machine and continued to hand fill their cans.[22]

Although canners in other regions were not as wedded to the English market as those on the Columbia, adoption of the filling machine

[19]*Pacific Fisherman* 25 (August 1927): 19; *Pacific Fisherman Statistical Number* 25 (1927): 116.

[20]Ralston (n. 17 above), p. 6; Stacey (n. 8 above), p. 14.

[21]*Pacific Fisherman Statistical Number* 25 (1927): 116; Jefferson F. Moser, "Alaska Salmon Investigations in 1900–1901," in U.S. Commission of Fish and Fisheries, *Bulletin of the U.S. Fish Commission: 1901,* 21 (Washington, D.C., 1902): 225; M. L. Dodge, "The Mechanical Features of Salmon Canning," *Mechanical Engineering* 47 (August 1925): 612.

[22]Henry Doyle, "Rise and Decline of the Pacific Salmon Fisheries," 2 vols., ca. 1957, 1:82, Henry Doyle Papers, University of British Columbia Library, Vancouver.

FIG. 5.—Mathias Jensen's first filling machine. (*Pacific Fisherman Statistical Number* 25 [1927]: 116.)

proceeded slowly until 1895. In that year the Alaska Packers Association (APA) purchased the patent rights to Jensen's filler and began installing the machine in its Alaskan canneries.[23] The APA produced about 70 percent of the Alaskan salmon pack in the late 1890s, and, indeed, was the world's largest producer of canned salmon. Most of this output consisted of red salmon, a different species than that canned on the Columbia and one not highly regarded by the English market. The association marketed this salmon in the urban centers of the eastern United States, a new, developing market where few consumers were familiar with canned Pacific salmon or had preconceptions about its proper appearance in the can. The APA's size enabled it to flood the new eastern markets with machine-packed salmon, which was accepted virtually without consumer resistance. The host of new filling machines that appeared on the market following expiration of

[23]John N. Cobb, "Pacific Salmon Fisheries," 3d ed., Appendix 1 to U.S. Department of Commerce, *Report of the Commissioner of Fisheries: 1921*, Bureau of Fisheries Doc. 902 (Washington, D.C., 1922), p. 29; U.S. Circuit Court, Western Division of Washington, Alaska Packers Association v. J. M. L. Letson and F. W. Burpee (1901), File 911, Carton 74535, Record Group 21, U.S. Federal Records Center, Seattle; Alaska Packers Association v. Letson et al., 130 F. 129 (1904).

the APA's monopoly rights to the Jensen filler in 1901 testifies to the association's success in introducing machine-packed salmon to American consumers. Canners in all regions, except the Columbia River and British Columbia, rushed to install the new machines.[24]

The filler's popularity stemmed not only from the canners' need to compete with the APA in the marketplace but also from the desire to replace human workers with machines. In the United States the Chinese labor pool continued to shrink, forcing contractors to substitute other ethnic workers, whom the canners viewed as unsatisfactory, for the Chinese. After the turn of the 20th century, only the Columbia River, where the English market dictated the actions of canners, and British Columbia, where canners could still obtain all the Chinese workers they required, failed to adopt filling machines. The history of the filling machine illustrates the variety of factors that could influence mechanization of the canning lines. Even if a new machine proved practical, regional considerations that at first might seem totally unrelated to questions of technology could impede or prevent its adoption in some locales.

* * *

The canned-salmon industry's first wave of technological innovation came to a close about 1900. By that date virtually every operation within the cannery that manipulated tin cans had been at least partially mechanized. The wave broke on the problem of developing a mechanical means for butchering and cleaning salmon. A second period of innovative activity began about 1905, following the solution of this complex technical problem.

The first innovative wave contributed to large increases in cannery productivity. Prior to the use of machinery, a cannery gang of 130–150 workers could produce 240 cases of salmon in a day. By 1883, with the widespread adoption of retorts and an increasing use of soldering machines and other innovations, the same number of workers could produce 1,000 cases per day. Productivity continued to rise as more machinery appeared on the canning lines. In 1900 the industry's most heavily mechanized plants, those run by the Alaska Packers Association, packed 2,400 cases per day. These canneries employed more workers, but most of the work force consisted of unskilled machine tenders, so payrolls remained relatively stable.[25]

[24]*Cathlamet* (Washington) *Gazette*, February 7, 1902; Alaska Packers Association, "History: 1891–1940," 8 vols., Alaska Packers Association Papers, Alaska State Historical Library, Juneau, 1: passim; Cobb (n. 5 above), p. 572.

[25]Stacey (n. 8 above), p. 26; Moser (n. 21 above), p. 235; Alaska Packers Association, "History" (n. 24 above), 1:43, 50–54.

The only canning operation not partially mechanized by 1900 was butchering. Skilled Chinese workers continued to clean virtually every salmon put into cans on the Pacific Coast. Despite the skill of these workers, who could clean up to six fish per minute, butchering constituted the industry's single greatest obstacle to increased productivity. The butchers controlled the productivity of the entire plant, since all subsequent operations on the canning line required cleaned salmon. By 1900, with the mechanization of the rest of the line, the butchers could not supply enough salmon to permit the line to operate at full speed. Some canners started their butchering gangs earlier than the rest of the line in the hope that the fish cleaned during this period would enable the cannery to run at full speed throughout the day.[26] But persisting production bottlenecks caused the introduction of newer, faster-operating machinery elsewhere on the line to grind to a halt. If the butchers could not supply the salmon needed to run an existing machine at full speed, little incentive existed for the adoption of an even more efficient device. The logical solution—hiring additional butchers to boost production—proved impossible. Skilled Chinese butchers were now in short supply in the United States, and those still working earned twice as much as unskilled cannery laborers. For these reasons canners resolved to eliminate this production bottleneck by mechanizing the butchering operation.[27]

The physical variations among individual salmon made development of a butchering machine very difficult. Canners required a machine that peformed all the tasks of the hand butchers—removal of the head, tail, and fins, as well as opening and cleaning the body cavity. The difficulties involved in accomplishing all these tasks are apparent in the half-dozen different butchering machines that operated on canning lines between 1901 and 1904, all of which failed to perform at least one of the operations performed by the hand butchers.[28]

The 1904 season marked the commercial introduction of the machine that eventually mechanized the butchering operation in most salmon canneries. Edmund A. Smith, a corpulent former mining-camp cook, developed his butchering machine during 1902 and 1903.[29] A large vertical carrier wheel, with the salmon attached along the rim, carried the fish past a series of knives and brushes that removed the fins

[26]*Pacific Fisherman Statistical Number* 25 (1927): 116.

[27]*Seattle Times*, August 22, 1905. In 1903 an Alaskan cannery sent 100 Chinese workers north. The average age of these men was forty-five and 20 percent were estimated to be at least seventy years old. *Seattle Post-Intelligencer*, April 9, 1904.

[28]For early butchering machines, see O'Bannon, "Technological Change" (n. 6 above), pp. 195–96.

[29]*Pacific Fisherman Annual* 4 (January 1906): 47; *Pacific Fisherman* 7 (July 1909): 19.

and split and cleaned the body cavity. Workers removed the heads and tails from the salmon by running them through band saws prior to placing them on the carrier wheel. The trials of Smith's first machine, conducted in a Seattle cannery during 1903, proved very successful. Operated by three unskilled workers, the device cleaned forty salmon per minute, the equivalent of an eighteen-man Chinese butchering gang.[30] Smith Cannery Machines Co. immediately dubbed its product the "Iron Chink," a name by which it is still known today. (See fig. 6.)

Six canners leased Smith butchering machines for the 1904 season. Smith prominently featured the testimonials of these canners, one of whom claimed in his advertising that the device enabled him to pack up to 1,500 cases per day without Chinese butchers.[31] Smith first sold his

Fig. 6.—Advertisement for a 1904-model Smith Fish Cleaner, the "Iron Chink." (*Pacific Fisherman Annual* 3 [January 1905]: 95.)

[30]*Pacific Fisherman Statistical Number* 25 (1927): 112; *Pacific Fisherman* 1 (September 1903): 12; ibid., 2 (August 1904): 5; ibid., 7 (June 1909): 12.
[31]*Pacific Fisherman* 2 (December 1904): 16.

machines, for about $2,600 each, in 1905.[32] Testimonials solicited at the close of that season focused on its labor-saving qualities. One canner exulted that he had "made my last contract, I hope, with Chinese butchers," while another belligerently declared, "hereafter I want no Chinese butchers in the plant. . . ."[33]

Smith's machine rapidly and efficiently performed all of the tasks of the hand butchers and in such a superior manner to the other machines on the market that it quickly drove its competition from the field. By 1910 few, if any, salmon canneries used a butchering machine other than Smith's.[34] Yet not all canners embraced the butchering machine, and, again, regional conditions determined its reception. Columbia River operators could not use Smith's machine because it could not handle the large chinook salmon that constituted the major-ity of their pack. Canners in this region had no choice but to continue to employ hand butchers. In 1917, however, Smith's firm introduced a new model capable of processing chinooks.[35]

More than any other single innovation, Smith's butchering machine revolutionized the canned-salmon industry. It eliminated the last im-portant production bottleneck on the canning lines and permitted the virtual total mechanization of the canning process. The new machine did not merely eliminate a production bottleneck, it shattered it. Just one could keep two full lines of cannery machinery amply supplied with salmon. This enabled canners to double the capacity of their plants by simply installing a new line of machinery. Smith's machine also unleashed a second wave of technological innovation, lasting from roughly 1905 to 1914, characterized by the refinement, improvement, and replacement of many of the canning machines introduced during the first wave.

The most important innovation to follow the butchering machine onto the canning lines, the sanitary can, epitomizes this process of refinement and replacement. Machines known as double seamers crimped the ends onto cans without using solder, eliminating the need for soldering machines and greatly reducing the risk to consumers of lead contamination (fig. 7). Although sanitary cans were a major refine-ment that simplified production on the line and facilitated increased output, they were not a wholly new innovation. Double seaming had originated in Europe, but the European technology proved far too slow for use in American canneries. Despite a few experiments with the

[32]*Pacific Fisherman Statistical Number* 25 (1927): 112.

[33]*Pacific Fisherman Annual* 4 (January 1906): 45–46.

[34]Smith Cannery Machines Company v. Seattle-Astoria Iron Works et al., 261 F. 85 (1919).

[35]*Pacific Fisherman* 15 (January 1917): 35.

FIG. 7.—A battery of double seamers (*Pacific Fisherman* 10 [November 1912]: 27)

new system, American salmon canners did not begin to explore its potentials seriously until after the development of high-speed can-bodymaking machines about 1906,[36] though Pacific Coast fruit and vegetable canners used sanitary cans by then. The slowness of the double seamers, which closed only ten cans per minute, precluded introduction of the new system into the heavily mechanized, high-speed salmon canneries. Only after the 1906 development of a double seamer that closed thirty cans per minute did salmon packers express any interest in the new technology.[37]

The American Can Company, the nation's largest producer of tin cans, controlled the patent rights to the improved double seamer.[38] American Can attempted to secure a market for its ready-made sanitary cans by requiring the leasees of double seamers to purchase all of their cans ready-made. This gambit failed because few salmon canners proved willing to abandon their own can-making machinery and revert to the wasteful practice of shipping cases of empty cans to the canneries.[39] Prior to the start of the 1912 season American Can dropped its leasing restrictions and agreed to provide canners with both sanitary can-bodymaking machines and double seamers. Now

[36]James W. McKie, *Tin Cans and Tin Plate: A Study in Competition in Two Related Markets* (Cambridge, 1959), p. 190; Judge (n. 2 above), p. 94; May (n. 2 above), p. 92; Dodge (n. 21 above), p. 613; *Pacific Fisherman* 9 (October 1911): 11.

[37]*Pacific Fisherman* 4 (February 1906): 20; ibid. (July 1906): 21.

[38]*Pacific Fisherman Yearbook*, January 1916, p. 75.

[39]McKie (n. 36 above), pp. 91, 182.

that canners could manufacture sanitary cans themselves the new system quickly became commonplace in salmon canneries. In 1911 sanitary cans accounted for only 25 percent of the industry's pack. Two years later, after elimination of the leasing restrictions, the new-style can made up 65 percent of the output.[40] By 1917, American Can Co. ads implied that sanitary cans had vanquished "old-style soldered cans" (fig. 8).

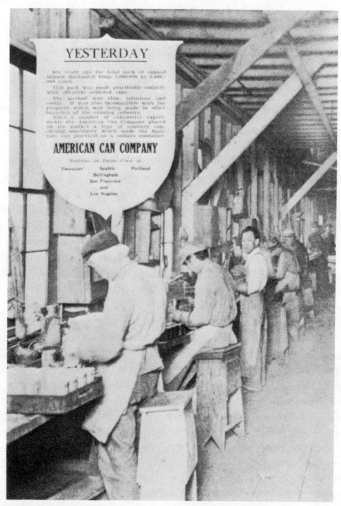

FIG. 8.—American Can Co. ran this advertisement on behalf of its can-making machines in the *Pacific Fisherman Yearbook*, January 1917, p. 83.

[40]*Pacific Fisherman Yearbook*, January 1912, p. 33; ibid., January 1915, p. 54; *Pacific Fisherman* 13 (May 1915): 15.

The double-seaming process refined and improved an existing technology. Its incorporation into the canning line permitted faster and more efficient operations by eliminating several steps in the canning process and reducing the time needed to perform the remaining steps. But the second wave of innovation consisted of more than just the introduction of a new-style can. Machines attached to the fillers replaced the early hand jigs used to add salt to the product. Filling machines equipped with turrets operated on several cans simultaneously. Weighing machines prevented the waste of salmon that resulted from overfilled cans and assured that canners complied with the Pure Food and Drug Act of 1906. Can washers replaced workers armed with wet rags, while lacquering and labeling machines prepared the final product for delivery to market. Several of these innovations existed in rudimentary form prior to 1905, but the opportunities and imperatives for innovation that stemmed from the development of the butchering machine led to their perfection, refinement, and widespread adoption in the decade afterward.

By 1914 the salmon canneries of the Pacific Coast operated as fully mechanized fish-processing factories. Further refinement of the canning process occurred during the next decade, but the essential ingredients of the mechanized cannery existed throughout most of the industry by then. The productivity of the average cannery increased by about 50 percent during the industry's second period of innovation. By 1914 canneries routinely packed 30,000 cases of salmon per year, compared to an average of about 20,000 cases in 1900 at the close of the first wave of innovation.[41]

* * *

The general pattern of technological innovation described here for the canned-salmon industry is just that, a general pattern. It serves as an ordering device with which the history of the industry may be explored, but it does not accurately describe the course of mechanization at all times and in all locations. Labor, market, and environmental conditions all influenced the course of innovation in specific locales.

It is a mistake to view the mechanization of the industry as a powerful independent force moving inexorably toward a foreseeable goal. The process of mechanization could be easily derailed or shunted aside by seemingly extraneous forces: the peculiar prejudices of canners in favor of Chinese workers, the preconceptions of English consumers as

[41]Statistics based on data in Cobb (n. 5 above).

to the proper appearance of salmon in a can, or the physical properties of the fish themselves. It is simplistic and wrongheaded to speak of a monolithic industry that operated in as many local environments as the canned-salmon industry. For historical analysis, the course of mechanization within the Pacific Coast canned-salmon industry demonstrates the importance of the microcosm.

"Touch Someone": The Telephone Industry Discovers Sociability

CLAUDE S. FISCHER

The familiar refrain, "Reach out, reach out and touch someone," has been part of American Telephone and Telegraph's (AT&T's) campaign urging use of the telephone for personal conversations. Yet, the telephone industry did not always promote such sociability; for decades it was more likely to discourage it. The industry's "discovery" of sociability illustrates how structural and cultural constraints interact with public demand to shape the diffusion of a technology. While historians have corrected simplistic notions of "autonomous technology" in showing how technologies are produced, we know much less about how consumers use technologies. We too often

CLAUDE S. FISCHER is professor of sociology at the University of California, Berkeley. Some material presented in this article was initially delivered to the Social Science History Association, Washington, D.C., October 1983. The research was supported by the National Endowment for the Humanities (grant RO-20612), the National Science Foundation (grant SES83-09301), the Russell Sage Foundation, and the Committee on Research, University of California, Berkeley. Further work was conducted as a Fellow at the Center for Advanced Study in the Behavioral Sciences, Stanford, California, with financial support from the Andrew W. Mellon Foundation. Archival research was facilitated by the generous assistance of people in the telephone industry: at AT&T, Robert Lewis, Robert Garnet, and Mildred Ettlinger; at the San Francisco Pioneer Telephone Museum, Don Thrall, Ken Rolin, and Norm Hawker; at the Museum of Independent Telephony, Peggy Chronister; at Pacific Bell, Robert Deward; at Bell Canada Historical, Stephanie Sykes and Nina Bederian-Gardner; at Illinois Bell, Rita Lapka; John A. Fleckner at the National Museum of American History also provided assistance. Thanks to those interviewed for the project: Tom Winburn, Stan Damkroger, George Hawk Hurst, C. Duncan Hutton, Fred Johnson, Charles Morrish, and Frank Pamphilon. Several research assistants contributed to the work: Melanie Archer, John Chan (who conducted the interviews), Steve Derné, Keith Dierkx, Molly Haggard, Barbara Loomis, and Mary Waters. And several readers provided useful comments on prior versions, including Victoria Bonnell, Paul Burstein, Glenn Carroll, Bernard Finn, Robert Garnet, Roland Marchand, Michael Schudson, John Staudenmaier, S.J., Ann Swidler, Joel Tarr, Langdon Winner, and auditors of presentations. None of these colleagues, of course, is responsible for remaining errors.

This essay originally appeared in *Technology and Culture*, vol. 29, no. 1, January 1988.

87

88   *Claude S. Fischer*

take those uses (especially of consumer products) for granted, as if
they were straightforwardly derived from the nature of the technology or dictated by its creators.[1]

In the case of the telephone, the initial uses suggested by its promoters were determined by—in addition to technical and economic
considerations—its cultural heritage: specifically, practical uses in
common with the telegraph. Subscribers nevertheless persisted in
using the telephone for "trivial gossip." In the 1920s, the telephone
industry shifted from resisting to endorsing such sociability, responding, at least partly, to consumers' insistent and innovative uses of
the technology for personal conversation. After summarizing telephone history to 1940, this article will describe the changes in the
uses that telephone promoters advertised and the changes in their attitudes toward sociability; it will then explore explanations for these
changes.[2]

[1] See C. S. Fischer, "Studying Technology and Social Life," pp. 284–301 in *High Technology, Space, and Society: Emerging Trends*, ed. M. Castells (Beverly Hills, Calif.,
1985). For a recent example of a study looking at consumers and sales, see M. Rose,
"Urban Environments and Technological Innovation: Energy Choices in Denver and
Kansas City, 1900–1940," *Technology and Culture* 25 (July 1984): 503–39.

[2] The primary sources used here include telephone and advertising industry journals; internal telephone company reports, correspondence, collections of advertisements, and other documents, primarily from AT&T and Pacific Telephone (PT&T);
privately published memoirs and corporate histories; government censuses, investigations, and research studies; and several interviews, conducted by John Chan, with retired telephone company employees who had worked in marketing. The archives
used most are the AT&T Historical Archives, New York (abbreviated hereafter as
AT&T ARCH), and the Pioneer Telephone Museum, San Francisco (SF PION MU),
with some material from the Museum of Independent Telephony, Abilene (MU
IND TEL); Bell Canada Historical, Montreal (BELL CAN HIST); Illinois Bell Information Center, Chicago (ILL BELL INFO); and the N. W. Ayer Collection of Advertisements and the Warshaw Collection of Business Americana, National Museum of
American History, Smithsonian Institution, Washington, D.C. A bibliography on the
social history of the telephone is unusually short, especially in comparison with those
on later technologies such as the automobile and television. There are industrial and
corporate histories, but the consumer side is largely untouched. For some basic
sources, see J. W. Stehman, *The Financial History of the American Telephone and Telegraph Company* (Boston, 1925); A. N. Holcombe, *Public Ownership of Telephones on the
Continent of Europe* (Cambridge, Mass., 1911); H. B. MacMeal, *The Story of Independent
Telephony* (Chicago: Independent Pioneer Telephone Association, 1934); J. L. Walsh,
Connecticut Pioneers in Telephony (New Haven, Conn.: Morris F. Tyler Chapter of the Telephone Pioneers of America, 1950); J. Brooks, *Telephone: The First Hundred Years*
(New York, 1976); A. Hibbard, *Hello-Goodbye: My Story of Telephone Pioneering* (Chi-
cago, 1941); Robert Collins, *A Voice from Afar: The History of Telecommunications in Can-
ada* (Toronto, 1977); R. L. Mahon, "The Telephone in Chicago," ILL BELL INFO,
MS, ca. 1955; J. C. Rippey, *Goodbye, Central; Hello, World: A Centennial History of North-*

A Brief History of the Telephone

Within about two years of A. G. Bell's patent award in 1876, there were roughly 10,000 Bell telephones in the United States and fierce patent disputes over them, battles from which the Bell Company (later to be AT&T) emerged a victorious monopoly. Its local franchisees' subscriber lists grew rapidly and the number of telephones tripled between 1880 and 1884. Growth slowed during the next several years, but the number of instruments totaled 266,000 by 1893.[3] (See table 1.)

As long-distance communication, telephony quickly threatened telegraphy. Indeed, in settling its early patent battle with Western Union, Bell gave financial concessions to Western Union as compensation for loss of business. As local communication, telephony quickly overwhelmed nascent efforts to establish signaling exchange systems (except for stock tickers).

During Bell's monopoly, before 1894, telephone service consisted basically of an individual line for which a customer paid an annual flat fee allowing unlimited calls within the exchange area. Fees varied widely, particularly by size of exchange. Bell rates dropped in the mid-1890s, perhaps in anticipation of forthcoming competition. In 1895, Bell's average residential rate was $4.66 a month (13 percent of an average worker's monthly wages). Rates remained high, especially in the larger cities (the 1894 Manhattan rate for a two-party line was $10.41 a month).[4]

On expiration of the original patents in 1893–94, thousands of new telephone vendors, ranging from commercial operations to

---

western Bell (Omaha, Nebr.: Northwestern Bell, 1975); G. W. Brock, *The Telecommunications Industry: The Dynamics of Market Structure* (Cambridge, Mass, 1981); I. de S. Pool, *Forecasting the Telephone* (Norwood, N.J., 1983); R. W. Garnet, *The Telephone Enterprise: The Evolution of the Bell System's Horizontal Structure, 1876–1909* (Baltimore, 1985); R. A. Atwood, "Telephony and Its Cultural Meanings in Southeastern Iowa, 1900–1917" (Ph.D. diss., University of Iowa, 1984); Lana Fay Rakow, "Gender, Communication, and the Technology: A Case Study of Women and the Telephone" (Ph.D. diss., University of Illinois at Urbana-Champaign, 1987); and I. de S. Pool, ed., *The Social Impact of the Telephone* (Cambridge, Mass., 1977). (Note that AT&T, Bell, and similar corporate names refer, of course, to these companies—or their direct ancestors—up to the U.S. industry reorganization of January 1, 1984.)

[3]Statistics from AT&T, *Events in Telecommunications History* (New York: AT&T, 1979), p. 6; U.S. Bureau of the Census (BOC), *Historical Statistics of the United States*, Bicentennial Ed., pt. 2 (Washington, D.C., 1975), pp. 783–84.

[4]Rates are reported in scattered places. For these figures, see BOC, *Telephones and Telegraphs 1902*, Special Reports, Department of Commerce and Labor (Washington, D.C., 1906), p. 53; and *1909 Annual Report of AT&T* (New York, 1910), p. 28. Wage data are from *Historical Statistics* (n. 3 above), tables D735–38.

TABLE 1
TELEPHONE DEVELOPMENT, 1880–1940

	Number of Tele- phones	Tele- phones per 1,000 People	Per- centage in Bell System	Percentage Inde- pendent, Connected to Bell	Per- centage Residen- tial, Connected to Bell
1880	54,000	1	100	0	...
1885	156,000	3	100	0	...
1890	228,000	4	100	0	...
1895	340,000	5	91	0	...
1900	1,356,000	18	62	1	...
1905	4,127,000	49	55	6	...
1910	7,635,000	82	52	26	...
1915	10,524,000	104	57	30	...
1920	13,273,000	123	66	29	68
1925	16,875,000	145	75	24	67
1930	20,103,000	163	80	20	65
1935	17,424,000	136	82	18	63
1940	21,928,000	165	84	16	65
1980	180,000,000	790	81	19	74

SOURCES.—U.S. Bureau of the Census, *Historical Statistics of the United States*, Bicentennial Ed., pt. 2 (Washington, D.C., 1975), pp. 783–84; and U.S. Bureau of the Census, *Statistical Abstract of the United States 1982–83* (Washington, D.C., 1984), p. 557.

small cooperative systems, sprang up. Although they typically served areas that Bell had ignored, occasional head-to-head competition drove costs down and spurred rapid diffusion: almost a nine-fold increase in telephones per capita between 1893 and 1902, as compared to less than a twofold increase in the prior nine years.[5]

Bell responded fiercely to the competition, engaging in price wars, political confrontations, and other aggressive tactics. It also tried to reach less affluent customers with cheaper party lines, coin-box telephones, and "measured service" (charging by the call). Still, Bell lost at least half the market by 1907. Then, a new management under Theodore N. Vail, the most influential figure in telephone history, changed strategies. Instead of reckless, preemptive expansion and price competition, AT&T bought out competitors where it could and ceded territories where it was losing. With tighter fiscal con-

[5]BOC, *Telephones, 1902* (n. 4 above); Federal Communications Commission (FCC), *Proposed Report: Telephone Investigation* (Washington, D.C., 1938), p. 147. AT&T has always officially challenged this interpretation; see, e.g., *1909 Annual Report of AT&T*, pp. 26–28.

trol, and facing capital uncertainties as well, AT&T's rate of expansion declined.[6] Meanwhile, the "independents" could not expand much beyond their small-town bases, partly because they were unable to build their own long-distance lines and were cut off from Bell-controlled New York City. Many were not competitive because they were poorly financed and provided poor service. Others accepted or even solicited buyouts from AT&T or its allies. By 1912, the Bell System had regained an additional 6 percent of the market.

During this competitive era, the industry offered residential customers a variety of economical party-line plans. Bell's average residential rate in 1909 was just under two dollars a month (about 4 percent of average wages).[7] How much territory the local exchange covered and what services were provided—for example, nighttime operators—varied greatly, but costs dropped and subscriber lists grew considerably. These basic rates changed little until World War II (although long-distance charges dropped).

In the face of impending federal antitrust moves, AT&T agreed in late 1913 to formalize its budding accommodation with the independents. Over several years, local telephone service was divided into regulated geographic monopolies. The modern U.S. telephone system—predominantly Bell local service and exclusively Bell long-distance service—was essentially fixed from the early 1920s to 1984.

The astronomical growth in the number of telephones during the pre-Vail era (a compound annual rate of 23 percent per capita from 1893 to 1907) became simply healthy growth (4 percent between 1907 and 1929). The system was consolidated and technically improved, and, by 1929, 42 percent of all households had telephones. That figure shrank during the Depression to 31 percent in 1933 but rebounded to 37 percent of all households in 1940.

Sales Strategies

The telephone industry believed, as President Vail testified in 1909, that the "public had to be educated . . . to the necessity and ad-

---

[6]See, e.g., *Annual Report of AT&T*, 1907–10; and FCC, *Proposed Report* (n. 5 above), pp. 153–154. On making deals with competitors, see, e.g., Rippey (n. 2 above), pp. 143ff.

[7]*1909 Annual Report of AT&T*, p. 28. Charges for minimal, urban, four-party lines ranged from $3.00 a month in New York (about 6 percent of the average manufacturing employee's monthly wages) to $1.50 in Los Angeles (about 3 percent of wages) and much less in small places with mutual systems; see BOC, *Telephones and Telegraphs and Municipal Electric Fire-Alarm and Police-Patrol Signaling Systems, 1912* (Washington, D.C., 1915); and *Historical Statistics* (n. 3 above), table D740.

vantage of the telephone."[8] And Bell saluted itself on its success in an advertisement entitled "Blazing the Way": Bell "had to invent the business uses of the telephone and convince people that they were uses. . . . [Bell] built up the telephone habit in cities like New York and Chicago. . . . It has from the start created the need of the telephone and then supplied it."[9]

"Educating the public" typically meant advertising, face-to-face solicitations, and public relations. In the early years, these efforts included informational campaigns, such as publicizing the existence of the telephone, showing people how to use it, and encouraging courteous conversation on the line.[10] Once the threat of nationalization became serious, "institutional" advertising and publicity encouraged voters to feel warmly toward the industry.[11]

As to getting paying customers, the first question vendors had to ask was, Of what use is this machine? The answer was not self-evident.

For roughly the first twenty-five years, sales campaigns largely employed flyers, simple informational notices in newspapers, "news" stories supplied to friendly editors (many of whom received free service or were partners in telephony), public demonstrations, and personal solicitations of businessmen. As to uses, salesmen typically

[8]Testimony on December 9, 1909, in State of New York, *Report of the Committee of the Senate and Assembly Appointed to Investigate Telephone and Telegraph Companies* (Albany, 1910), p. 398.

[9]Ayer Collection of AT&T Advertisements, Collection of Business Americana, National Museum of American History, Smithsonian Institution.

[10]See, e.g., *Pacific Telephone Magazine* (PT&T employee magazine, hereafter PAC TEL MAG), 1907–40, passim; 1914 advertisements in SF PION MU folder labeled "Advertising"; MU IND TEL "Scrapbook" of Southern Indiana Telephone Company clippings; advertisements in directories of the day; "Educating the Public to the Proper Use of the Telephone," *Telephony* 64 (June 21, 1913): 32–33; "Swearing over the Telephone," *Telephony* 9 (1905): 418; and "Advertising and Publicity—1906 –1910," box 1317, AT&T ARCH.

[11]On AT&T's institutional advertising, see R. Marchand, "Creating the Corporate Soul: The Origins of Corporate Image Advertising in America" (paper presented to the Organization of American Historians, 1980), and N. L. Griese, "AT&T: 1908 Origins of the Nation's Oldest Continuous Institutional Advertising Campaign," *Journal of Advertising* 6 (Summer 1977): 18–24. FCC, *Proposed Report* (n. 5 above), has a chapter on "Public Relations"; see also N. R. Danielian, *AT&T: The Story of Industrial Conquest* (New York, 1939), chap. 13. For a defense of AT&T public relations, see A. W. Page, *The Bell Telephone System* (New York, 1941). Among the publicity efforts along these lines were "free" stories, subsidies of the press, and courting of reporters and politicians (documented in AT&T ARCH). In one comical case, AT&T frantically and apparently unsuccessfully tried in 1920 to pressure Hal Roach to cut out from a Harold Lloyd film he was producing a burlesque scene of central exchange hysteria (see folder "Correspondence—E. S. Wilson, V.P., AT&T," SF PION MU).

stressed those that extended applications of telegraph signaling. For example, an 1878 circular in New Haven—where the first exchange was set up—stated that "your wife may order your dinner, a hack, your family physician, etc., all by Telephone without leaving the house or trusting servants or messengers to do it." (It got almost no response.)[12] In these uses, the telephone directly competed with— and decisively defeated—attempts to create telegraph exchanges that enabled subscribers to signal for services and also efforts to employ printing telegraphs as a sort of "electronic mail" system.[13]

In this era and for some years later, the telephone marketers sought new uses to add to these telegraphic applications. They offered special services over the telephone, such as weather reports, concerts, sports results, and train arrivals. For decades, vendors cast about for novel applications: broadcasting news, sports, and music, night watchman call-in services, and the like. Industry magazines eagerly printed stories about the telephone being used to sell products, alert firefighters about forest blazes, lullaby a baby to sleep, and get out voters on election day. And yet, industry men often attributed weak demand to not having taught the customer "what to do with his telephone."[14]

In the first two decades of the 20th century, telephone advertising became more professionally "modern."[15] AT&T employed a Bos-

[12]Walsh (n. 2 above), p. 47.

[13]S. Schmidt, "The Telephone Comes to Pittsburgh" (master's thesis, University of Pittsburgh, 1948); Pool, *Forecasting* (n. 2 above), p. 30; D. Goodman, "Early Electrical Communications and the City: Applications of the Telegraph in Nineteenth-Century Urban America" (unpub. paper, Department of Social Sciences, Carnegie-Mellon University, n.d., courtesy of Joel Tarr); and "Telephone History of Dundee, Ontario," City File, BELL CAN HIST.

[14]On special services and broadcasting, see Walsh (n. 2 above), p. 206; S. H. Aronson, "Bell's Electrical Toy: What's the Use? The Sociology of Early Telephone Usage," pp. 15–39, and I. de S. Pool et al., "Foresight and Hindsight: The Case of the Telephone," pp. 127–58, both in Pool, ed., *Social Impact* (n. 2 above); "Broadening the Possible Market," *Printers' Ink* 74 (March 9, 1911): 20; G. O. Steel, "Advertising the Telephone," *Printers' Ink* 51 (April 12, 1905): 14–17; and F. P. Valentine, "Some Phases of the Commercial Job," *Bell Telephone Quarterly* 5 (January 1926): 34–43. For illustrations of uses, see, e.g., PAC TEL MAG (October 1907), p. 6, (January 1910), p. 9, (December 1912), p. 23, and (October 1920), p. 44; and the independent magazine, *Telephony*. E.g., the index to vol. 71 (1916) of *Telephony* lists the following under "Telephone, novel uses of": "degree conferred by telephone, dispatching tugs in harbor service, gauging water by telephone, telephoning in an aeroplane." On complaints about not having taught the public, see the quotation from H. B. Young, ca. 1929, pp. 91, 100 in "Publicity Conferences—Bell System— 1921–34," box 1310, AT&T ARCH, but similar comments appear in earlier years, as well as positive claims, such as Vail's in 1909.

[15]The following discussion draws largely from examination of advertisement collections at the archives listed in n. 2. Space does not permit more than a few examples

ton agency to dispense "free publicity" and later brought its chief, J. D. Ellsworth, into the company. It began national advertising campaigns and supplied local Bell companies with copy for their regional presses. Some of the advertising was implicitly competitive (e.g., stressing that Bell had long-distance service), and much of it was institutional, directed toward shaping a favorable public opinion about the Bell System. Advertisements for selling service employed drawings, slogans, and texts designed to make the uses of the telephone—not just the technology—attractive. (The amount and kind of advertising fluctuated, especially in the Bell System, in response to competition, available supplies, and political concerns.)[16]

From roughly 1900 to World War I, Bell's publicity agency advertised uses of the telephone by planting newspaper "stories" on telephones in farm life, in the church, in hotels, and the like.[17] The national advertisements, beginning around 1910, addressed mostly businessmen. They stressed that the telephone was impressive to customers and saved time, both at work and at home, and often noted the telephone's convenience for planning and for keeping in touch with the office during vacations.

A second major theme was household management. A 1910 series, for example, presented detailed suggestions: Subscribers could telephone dressmakers, florists, theaters, inns, rental agents, coal dealers, schools, and the like. Other uses were suggested, too, such as conveying messages of moderate urgency (a businessman calling home to say that he will be late, calling a plumber), and conveying invitations (to an impromptu party, for a fourth at bridge).

Sociability themes ("visiting" kin by telephone, calling home from a business trip, and keeping "In Touch with Friends and Relatives")

---

of hundreds of advertisements in the sources. See esp. at AT&T ARCH, files labeled "Advertising and Publicity"; at SF PION MU, folders labeled "Advertising" and "Publicity Bureau"; at BELL CAN HIST, "Scrapbooks"; at ILL BELL INFO, "AT&T Advertising" and microfilm 384B, "Adver."; and at the Ayer Collection (n. 9 above), the AT&T series.

[16]For explicit discussions, see Mahon (n. 2 above), e.g., pp. 79, 89; Publicity Vice-President A. W. Page's comments in "Bell System General Commercial Conference, 1930," microfilm 368B, ILL BELL INFO; and comments by Commercial Engineer K. S. McHugh in "Bell System General Commercial Conference on Sales Matters, 1931," microfilm 368B, ILL BELL INFO. On the origins of in-house advertising, see N. L. Griese, "1908 Origins" (n. 11 above).

[17]See correspondence in "Advertising and Publicity—Bell System—1906–1910, Folder 1," box 1317, AT&T ARCH. Some reports claimed that thousands of stories were placed in hundreds of publications. Apparently no national advertising campaigns were conducted prior to these years; Bell marketing strategy seemed largely confined to price and service competition. See N. C. Kingsbury, "Results from the American Telephone's National Campaign," *Printers' Ink* (June 29, 1916): 182–84.

appeared, but they were relatively rare and almost always suggested sending a message such as an invitation or news of safe arrival rather than having a conversation. A few advertisements also pointed out the modernity of the telephone ("It's up to the times!"). But the major uses suggested in early telephone advertising were for business and household management; sociability was rarely advised.[18]

With the decline of competition and the increase in regulation during the 1910s, Bell stressed public relations even more and pressed local companies to follow suit. AT&T increasingly left advertising basic services and uses to its subsidiaries, although much of the copy still originated in New York, and the volume of such advertising declined. Material from Pacific Telephone and Telegraph (PT&T), apparently a major advertiser among the Bell companies, indicates the substance of "use" advertising during that era.[19]

PT&T advertisements for 1914 and 1915 include, aside from informational notices and general paeans to the telephone, a few suggestions for businessmen (e.g., "You fishermen who feel these warm days of Spring luring you to your favorite stream. . . . You can adjust affairs before leaving, ascertain the condition of streams, secure accommodations, and always be in touch with business and home"). Several advertisements mention the home or women, such as those suggesting that extension telephones add to safety and those encouraging shopping by telephone. Just one advertisement in this set explicitly suggests an amiable conversation: A grandmotherly woman is speaking on the telephone, a country vista visible through the window behind her, and says: "My! How sweet and clear my daughter's voice sounds! She seems to be right here with me!" The text reads: "Let us suggest a long distance visit home today." But this sort of advertisement was unusual.

During and immediately after World War I, there was no occasion to promote telephone use, since the industry struggled to meet demand pent up by wartime diversions. Much publicity tried to ease customer irritation at delays.

Only in the mid-1920s did AT&T and the Bell companies refo-

---

[18]In addition to the advertising collections, see A. P. Reynolds, "Selling a Telephone" (to a businessman), *Telephony* 12 (1906): 280–81; id., "The Telephone in Retail Business," *Printers' Ink* 61 (November 27, 1907): 3–8; and "Bell Encourages Shopping by Telephone," ibid., vol. 70 (January 19, 1910).

[19]Letter from AT&T Vice-President Reagan to PT&T President H. D. Pillsbury, March 4, 1929, in "Advertising," SF PION MU; W. J. Phillips, "The How, What, When and Why of Telephone Advertising," talk given July 7, 1926, in ibid.; and "Advertising Conference—Bell System—1916," box 1310, AT&T ARCH, p. 44.

cus their attention, for the first time in years, to sales efforts.[20] The system was a major advertiser, and Bell leaders actively discussed advertising during the 1920s. Copy focused on high-profit services, such as long distance and extension sets; modern "psychology," so to speak, influenced advertising themes; and Bell leaders became more sensitive to the competition from other consumer goods. Sociability suggestions increased, largely in the context of long-distance marketing.

In the United States, long-distance advertisements still overwhelmingly targeted business uses, but "visiting" with kin now appeared as a frequent suggestion. Bell Canada, for some reason, stressed family ties much more. Typical of the next two decades of Bell Canada's long-distance advertisements are these, both from 1921: "Why night calls are popular. How good it would sound to hear mother's voice tonight, he thought—for there were times when he was lonely—mighty lonely in the big city"; and "it's a weekly affair now, those fond intimate talks. Distance rolls away and for a few minutes every Thursday night the familiar voices tell the little family gossip that both are so eager to hear." Sales pointers to employees during this era often suggested providing customers with lists of their out-of-town contacts' telephone numbers.

In the 1920s, the advertising industry developed "atmosphere" techniques, focusing less on the product and more on its consequences for the consumer.[21] A similar shift may have begun in Bell's advertising, as well: "The Southwestern Bell Telephone Company has decided [in 1923] that it is selling something more vital than distance, speed or accuracy. . . . [T]he telephone . . . almost brings [people] face to face. It is the next best thing to personal contact. So the fundamental purpose of the current advertising is to sell the company's subscribers their voices at their true worth—to help them realize that 'Your Voice is You.'. . . to make subscribers think of the telephone whenever they think of distant friends or relatives. . . . "[22] This attitude was apparently only a harbinger, because during most of the 1920s the sociability theme was largely re-

[20]See n. 16 above.

[21]D. Pope, *The Making of Modern Advertising* (New York, 1983); S. Fox, *The Mirror Makers: A History of American Advertising and Its Creators* (New York, 1984); M. Schudson, *Advertising: The Uneasy Persuasion* (New York, 1985), pp. 60ff; R. Marchand, *Advertising the American Dream: Making Way for Modernity, 1920–1940* (Berkeley, Calif., 1985); and R. Pollay, "The Subsiding Sizzle: A Descriptive History of Print Advertising, 1900–1980," *Journal of Marketing* 49 (Summer 1985): 24–37.

[22]W. B. Edwards, "Tearing Down Old Copy Gods," *Printers' Ink* 123 (April 26, 1923): 65–66.

stricted to long distance and did not appear in many basic service advertisements.

Bell System salesmen spent the 1920s largely selling ancillary services, such as extension telephones, upgrading from party lines, and long distance, to current subscribers, rather than finding new customers. Basic residential rates averaged two to three dollars a month (about 2 percent of average manufacturing wages), not much different from a decade earlier, and Bell leaders did not consider seeking new subscribers to be sufficiently profitable to pursue seriously.[23] The limited new subscriber advertising continued the largely practical themes of earlier years. PT&T contended that residential telephones, especially extensions, were useful for emergencies, for social convenience (don't miss a call about an invitation, call your wife to set an extra place for dinner), and for avoiding the embarrassment of borrowing a telephone, as well as for its familiar business uses. A 1928 Bell Canada sales manual stressed household practicality first and social invitations second as tactics for selling basic service.[24]

Then, in the late 1920s, Bell System leaders—prodded perhaps by the embarrassment that, for the first time, more American families owned automobiles, gas service, and electrical appliances than subscribed to telephones—pressed a more aggressive strategy. They built up a full-fledged sales force. And they sought to market the telephone as a "comfort and convenience"—that is, as more than a practical device—drawing somewhat on the psychological, sensualist themes in automobile advertising. They focused not only on upgrading the service of current subscribers but also on reaching those car owners and electricity users who lacked telephones. And the *social* character of the telephone was to be a key ingredient in the new sales strategies.[25]

Before "comfort and convenience" could go far, however, the Depression drew the industry's attention to basic service once again. Subscribers were disconnecting. Bell companies mounted campaigns to

[23]On rates, see W. F. Gray, "Typical Schedules for Rates of Exchange Service," and related discussion, in "Bell System General Commercial Engineers' Conference, 1924," microfilm 364B, ILL BELL INFO.

[24]Bell Telephone Company of Canada, "Selling Service on the Job," ca. 1928, cat. 12223, BELL CAN HIST.

[25]Comments, esp. by AT&T vice-presidents Page and Gherardi, during "General Commercial Conference, 1928," and "Bell System General Commercial Conference, 1930," both microfilm 368B, ILL BELL INFO, expressed a view that telephones should be part of consumers' "life-styles," not simply their practical instruments. One hears many echoes of "comfort and convenience" at lower Bell levels during this period.

save residential connections by mobilizing *all* employees to sell or save telephone hookups on their own time (a program that had started before the Crash), expanding sales forces, advertising to current subscribers, and mounting door-to-door "save" and "nonuser" campaigns in some communities.[26] The "pitches" PT&T suggested to its employees included convenience (e.g., saving a trip to market), avoiding the humiliation of borrowing a neighbor's telephone, and simply being "modern." Salesmen actually seemed to rely more on pointing out the emergency uses of the telephone—an appeal especially telling to parents of young children—and suggesting that job offers might come via the telephone. Having a telephone so as to be available to friends and relatives was a lesser sales point. By now, a half-century since A. G. Bell's invention, salespeople did not have to sell telephone service itself but had to convince potential customers that they needed a telephone in their own homes.[27]

During the Depression, long-distance advertising continued, employing both business themes and the themes of family and friendship. But basic service advertising, addressed to both nonusers and would-be disconnectors, became much more common than it had been for twenty years.

The first line of argument in print ads for basic service was practicality—emergency uses, in particular—but suggestions for sociable conversations were more prominent than they had been before. A 1932 advertisement shows four people sitting around a woman who is speaking on the telephone. "Do Come Over!" the text reads, "Friends who are linked by telephone have good times." A 1934 Bell Canada advertisement features a couple who have just resubscribed and who testify, "We got out of touch with all of our friends and missed the good times we have now." A 1935 advertisement asks, "Have you ever watched a person telephoning to a friend? Have you noticed how readily the lips part into smiles . . . ?" And 1939 copy states, "Some one thinks of some one, reaches for the telephone, and all is well." A 1937 AT&T advertisement reminds us that "the telephone is vital in emergencies, but that is not the whole of its service. . . . Friendship's path often follows the trail of the telephone wire." These family-and-friend mo-

[26]See A. Fancher, "Every Employee Is a Salesman for American Telephone and Telegraph," *Sales Management* 28 (February 26, 1931): 45–51, 472; "Bell Conferences," 1928 and 1930 (n. 25 above), esp. L. J. Billingsley, "Presention of Disconnections," in 1930 conference; *Pacemaker*, a sales magazine for PT&T, ca. 1928–31, SF PION MU; and *Telephony*, passim, 1931–36.

[27]PT&T *Pacemaker*; interviews by John Chan with retired industry executives in northern California; see also J. E. Harrel, "Residential Exchange Sales in New England Southern Area," in "Bell Conference, 1931" (n. 16 above), pp. 67ff.

tifs, more frequent and frank in the 1930s, forecast the jingles of today, such as " . . . a friendly voice, like chicken soup/is good for your health/Reach out, reach out and touch someone."[28]

This brief chronology draws largely from prepared copy in industry archives, not from actual printed advertisements. A systematic survey, however, of two newspapers in northern California confirms the impression of increasing sociability themes. Aside from one 1911 advertisement referring to farm wives' isolation, the first sociability message in the *Antioch Ledger* appeared in 1929, addressed to parents: "No girl wants to be a wallflower." It was followed in the 1930s with notices for basic service such as "Give your friends straight access to your home," and "Call the folks now!" In 1911, advertisements in the *Marin* (County) *Journal* stressed the convenience of the telephone for automotive tourists. Sociability became prominent in both basic and long-distance advertisements in the late 1920s and the 1930s with suggestions that people "broaden the circle of friendly contact" (1927), "Voice visit with friends in nearby cities" (1930), and call grandmother (1935), and with the line, "I got my telephone for convenience. I never thought it would be such fun!" (1940).[29]

The emergence of sociability also appears in guides to telephone salesmen. A 1904 instruction booklet for sales representatives presents many selling points, but only one paragraph addresses residential service. That paragraph describes ways that the telephone saves time and labor, makes the household run smoothly, and rescues users in emergencies, but the only barely social use it notes is that the telephone "invites one's friends, asks them to stay away, asks them to hurry and enables them to invite in return." Conversation— telephone "visiting"—per se is not mentioned.

A 1931 memorandum to sales representatives, entitled "Your Tele-

---

[28]There is some variation among the advertising collections I examined. Illinois Bell's basic service advertisements used during the Depression are, for the most part, similar to basic service ads used a generation earlier. The Pacific Bell and Bell Canada advertisements feature sociable conversations much more. On the other hand, the Bell Canada ads are distinctive in that sociability is almost exclusively a family matter. Friendship, featured in U.S. ads all along, emerges clearly in the Canadian ads only in the 1930s. The 1932 ad cited in the text appears in the August 17 issue of the *Antioch* (Calif.) *Ledger*. The "chicken soup" jingle, sung by Roger Miller, was a Bell System ad in 1981. On the "Touch Someone" campaigns, see M. J. Arlen, *Thirty Seconds* (New York, 1980). See also "New Pitch to Spur Phone Use," *New York Times*, October 23, 1985, p. 44.

[29]These particular newspapers were examined as part of a larger study on the social history of the telephone that will include case studies of three northern California communities from 1890 to 1940.

phone," is, on the other hand, full of tips on selling residential service and encouraging its use. Its first and longest subsection begins: *"Fosters friendships.* Your telephone will keep your personal friendships alive and active. Real friendships are too rare and valuable to be broken when you or your friends move out of town. Correspondence will help for a time, but friendships do not flourish for long on letters alone. When you can't visit in person, telephone periodically. Telephone calls will keep up the whole intimacy remarkably well. There is no need for newly-made friends to drop out of your life when they return to distant homes." A 1935 manual puts practicality and emergency uses first as sales arguments but explicitly discusses the telephone's "social importance," such as saving users from being "left high and dry by friends who can't reach [them] conveniently."[30]

This account, so far, covers the advertising of the Bell System. There is less known and perhaps less to know about the independent companies' advertising. Independents' appeals seem much like those of the Bell System, stressing business, emergencies, and practicality, except perhaps for showing an earlier sensitivity to sociability among their rural clientele.[31]

In sum, the variety of sales materials portray a similar shift. From the beginning to roughly the mid-1920s, the industry sold service as a practical business and household tool, with only occasional mention of social uses and those largely consisting of brief messages. Later sales arguments, for both long-distance and basic service, featured social uses prominently, including the suggestion that the telephone be used for converations ("voice visiting") among

---

[30]Central Union Telephone Company Contracts Department, *Instructions and Information for Solicitors,* 1904, ILL BELL INFO. Note that Central Union had been, at least through 1903, one of Bell's most aggressive solicitors of business. Illinois Bell Commercial Department, *Sales Manual 1931,* microfilm, ILL BELL INFO. Ohio Bell Telephone Company, "How You Can Sell Telephones," 1935, file "Salesmanship," BELL CAN HIST.

[31]Until 1894, independent companies did not exist. For years afterward, they largely tried to meet unfilled demand in the small cities and towns Bell had underserved. In other places, they advertised competitively against Bell. Nevertheless, advertising men often exhorted the independents to use "salesmanship in print" to encourage basic service and extensive use. See, e.g., J. A. Schoell, "Advertising and Other Thoughts of the Small Town Man," *Telephony* 70 (June 10, 1916): 40–41; R. D. Mock, "Fundamental Principles of the Telephone Business: Part V, Telephone Advertising," series in ibid., vol. 71 (July 22–November 21, 1916); D. Hughes, "Right Now Is the Time to Sell Service," ibid., 104 (June 10, 1933): 14–15; and L. M. Berry, "Helpful Hints for Selling Service," ibid., 108 (February 2, 1935): 7–10. See also Kellogg Company, "A New Business Campaign for ———" (Chicago: Kellogg, 1929), MU IND TEL.

friends and family. While it would be helpful to confirm this impressionistic account with firm statistics, for various reasons it is difficult to draw an accurate sample of advertising copy and salesmen's pitches for over sixty years. (For one, we have no easily defined "universe" of advertisements. Are the appropriate units specific printed ads, or ad campaigns? How are duplicates to be handled? Or ads in neighboring towns? Do they include planted stories, inserts in telephone bills, billboards, and the like? Should locally generated ads be included? And what of nationally prepared ads not used by the locals? For another, we have no clear "population" of ads. The available collections are fragmentary, often preselected for various reasons.) An effort in that direction appears, however, in table 2, in which the numbers of "social" advertisements show a clear increase, both absolutely and relatively.

TABLE 2
COUNTS OF DOMINANT ADVERTISING THEMES BY PERIOD

Sources and Types of Advertisements	Prewar		1919–29		1930–40	
Antioch (Calif.) *Ledger*:						
Social, sociability	1	(1)	1	(1)	6	(4)
Business, businessmen	6	(5)	1	(1)	2	(1)
Household, convenience, etc.	5	(5)	3	(3)	4	(3)
Public relations, other	0	(0)	4	(3)	1	(1)
Total	12	(11)	9	(8)	13	(9)
Approximate ratio of social to others	1:11	(1:10)	1:8	(1:7)	1:1	(1:1)
Marin (Calif.) *Journal*:						
Social, sociability	1	(1)	5	(2)	43	(20)
Business, businessmen	2	(2)	8	(2)	10	(3)
Household, convenience, etc.	12	(12)	3	(3)	20	(20)
Public relations, other	0	(0)	19	(13)	25	(16)
Total	15	(15)	35	(20)	98	(59)
Approximate ratio of social to others	1:14	(1:14)	1:6	(1:9)	1:1	(1:2)
Bell Canada:						
Social, sociability	5	(2)	25	(1)	59*	(9)
Business, businessmen	20*	(20)	15	(2)	24*	(4)
Household, convenience, etc.	28	(28)	3	(3)	23*	(6)
Public relations, other	30*	(30)	25	(40)	2	(2)
Total	83*	(80)	68	(46)	108*	(21)
Approximate ratio of social to others	1:16	(1:39)	1:2	(1:45)	1:1	(1:1)

TABLE 2 *(continued)*

Sources and Types of Advertisements	Prewar		1919–29	1930–40
Pacific Telephone, 1914–15:				
Social, sociability	2	(1)	...	...
Business, businessmen	7	(6)	...	...
Household, convenience, etc.	18	(16)	...	...
Public relations, other	16	(9)	...	...
Total	43	(32)	...	...
Approximate ratio of social to others	1:21	(1:31)	...	...
Assorted Bell ads, 1906–10:				
Social, sociability	4	(4)	...	...
Business, businessmen	13	(12)	...	...
Household, convenience, etc.	11	(11)	...	...
Public relations, other	9	(9)	...	...
Total	37	(36)	...	...
Approximate ratio of social to others	1:8	(1:8)	...	...

Sources.—Advertisements in the *Antioch Ledger* were sampled from 1906 to 1940 by Barbara Loomis; those in the *Marin Journal* were sampled from 1900 to 1940 by John Chan. The Bell Canada collection appears in scrapbooks at Bell Canada Historical; the Pacific collection is in the San Francisco Pioneer Telephone Museum. The AT&T advertisements are from AT&T ARCH, box 1317. Other, spotty collections were used for the study but not counted here because they were not as systematic. All coding was done by the author.

Note.—Counts in parentheses exclude explicitly long-distance advertisements. Usually each ad had one dominant theme. When more than one seemed equal in weight, the ad was counted in both categories. "Social, sociability" refers to the use of the telephone for personal contact, including season's greetings, invitations, and conversation between friends and family. (Note that the inclusion of brief messages in this category makes the analysis a conservative test of the argument that there was a shift toward sociability themes.) "Business, businessmen" refers to the explicit use of the telephone for business purposes or general appeals to businessmen—e.g., that the telephone will make one a more forceful entrepreneur. "Household, convenience, etc." includes the use of the telephone for household management, personal convenience (e.g., don't get wet, order play tickets), and for emergencies, such as illness or burglary. "Public relations, other" includes general institutional advertising, informational notices (such as how to use the telephone), and other miscellaneous. Perhaps the most conservative index is the ratio of non-long-distance social ads to non-long-distance household ads. (Business ads move to speciality magazines over the years; public information ads fluctuate with political events; and long-distance ads may be "inherently" social.) In the *Antioch Ledger*, this ratio changes from 1:5 to 4:3; in the *Marin Journal*, from 1:12 to 1:1; and in Bell Canada's ads, from 1:14 to 1.5:1. Even these ratios understate the shift, for several reasons. One, I was much more alert to social than to other ads and was more thorough with early social ads than any other category. Two, the household category is increased in the later years by numerous ads for extension telephones. Three, the nature of the social ads counted here changes. The earlier ones overwhelmingly suggest using the telephone for greetings and invitations, not conversation. With rare exception, only the later ones discuss friendliness and "warm human relationships" and suggest chats.

*Estimated.

Industry Attitudes toward Sociability

This change in advertising themes apparently reflected a change in the actual beliefs industry men held about the telephone. Alexander Graham Bell himself forecast social chitchats using his invention. He predicted that eventually Mrs. Smith would spend an hour on the telephone with Mrs. Brown "very enjoyably . . . cutting up Mrs. Robinson."[32] But for decades few of his successors saw it that way.

Instead, the early telephone vendors often battled their residential customers over social conversations, labeling such calls "frivolous" and "unnecessary." For example, an 1881 announcement complained, "The fact that subscribers have been free to use the wires as they pleased without incurring additional expense [i.e., flat rates] has led to the transmission of large numbers of communications of the most trivial character."[33] In 1909, a local telephone manager in Seattle listened in on a sample of conversations coming through a residential exchange and determined that 20 percent of the calls were orders to stores and other businesses, 20 percent were from subscribers' homes to their own businesses, 15 percent were social invitations, and 30 percent were "purely idle gossip"—a rate that he claimed was matched in other cities. The manager's concern was to reduce this last, "unnecessary use." One tactic for doing so, in addition to "education" campaigns on proper use of the telephone, was to place time limits on calls (in his survey the average call had lasted over seven minutes). Time limits were often an explicit effort to stop people who insisted on chatting when there was "business" to be conducted.[34]

[32]Quoted in Aronson, "Electrical Toy" (n. 14 above).

[33]Proposed announcement by National Capitol Telephone Company, in letter to Bell headquarters, January 20, 1881, box 1213, AT&T ARCH. In a similar vein, the president of Bell Canada confessed, ca. 1890, to being unable to stop "trivial conversations"; see Collins, *A Voice* (n. 2 above), p. 124. The French authorities were also exasperated by nonserious uses; see C. Bertho, *Télégraphes et téléphones* (Paris, 1980), pp. 244–45.

[34]C. H. Judson, "Unprofitable Traffic—What Shall Be Done with It?" *Telephony* 18 (December 11, 1909): 644–47, and PAC TEL MAG 3 (January, 1910): 7. He also writes, "the telephone is going beyond its original design, and it is a positive fact that a large percentage of telephones in use today on a flat rental basis are used more in entertainment, diversion, social intercourse and accommodation to others, than in actual cases of business or household necessity" (p. 645). MacMeal, *Independent* (n. 2 above), p. 240, reports on a successful campaign in 1922 to discourage gossipers through letters and advertisements. Typically, calls were—at least officially—limited to five minutes in many places, although it is unclear how well limits were enforced.

An exceptional few in the industry, believing in a more "populist" telephony, did, however, try to encourage such uses. E. J. Hall, Yale-educated and originally manager of his family's firebrick business, initiated the first "measured service" in Buffalo in 1880 and later became an AT&T vice-president. A pleader for lower rates, Hall also defended "trivial" calls, arguing that they added to the total use-value of the system. But the evident isolation of men like Hall underlines the dominant antisociability view of the pre–World War I era.[35]

Official AT&T opinions came closer to Hall's in the later 1920s when executives announced that, whereas the industry had previously thought of telephone service as a practical necessity, they now realized that it was more: it was a "convenience, comfort, luxury"; its value included its "trivial" social uses. In 1928, Publicity Vice-President A. W. Page, who had entered AT&T from the publishing industry the year before, was most explicit when he criticized earlier views: "There had also been the point of view [in the Bell System and among the public] about not using the telephone for frivolous conversation. This is about as commercial as if the automobile people should advertise. 'Please do not take out this car unless you are going on a serious errand. . . .' We are faced, I think, with a state of public consciousness that the telephone is a necessity and not to be trifled with, certainly in the home." Bell sales officials were told to sell telephone service as a "comfort and convenience," including as a conversational tool.[36]

Although this change in opinion is most visible for the Bell System, similar trends can be seen in the pages of the journal of the independent companies, *Telephony*, especially in regard to rural customers. Indeed, early conflict about telephone sociability was most acute in rural areas. During the monopoly era, Bell companies largely neglected rural demand. The depth and breadth of

[35]Hall's philosophy is evident in the correspondence over measured service before 1900, box 1127, AT&T ARCH. Decades later, he pushed it in a letter to E. M. Burgess, Colorado Telephone Company, March 30, 1905, box 1309, AT&T ARCH, even arguing that operators should stop turning away calls made by children and should instead encourage such "trivial uses." The biographical information comes from an obituary in AT&T ARCH. Another, more extreme populist was John L. Sabin, of PT&T and the Chicago Telephone Co.; see Mahon (n. 2 above), pp. 29ff.

[36]A. W. Page, "Public Relations and Sales," "General Commercial Conference, 1928," p. 5, microfilm 368B, ILL BELL INFO. See also comments by Vice-President Gherardi and others in same conference and related ones of the period. On Page and the changes he instituted, see G. J. Griswold, "How AT&T Public Relations Policies Developed," *Public Relations Quarterly* 12 (Fall 1967): 7–16; and Marchand, *Advertising* (n. 21 above), pp. 117–20.

that demand became evident in the first two decades of this century, when proportionally more farm than urban households obtained telephones, the former largely from small commercial or cooperative local companies. Sociability both spurred telephone subscription and irritated the largely non-Bell vendors.

The 1907 Census of Telephones argued that in areas of isolated farmhouses "a sense of community life is impossible without this ready means of communication. . . . The sense of loneliness and insecurity felt by farmers' wives under former conditions disappears, and an approach is made toward the solidarity of a small country town." Other official investigations bore similar witness.[37] Rural telephone men also dwelt on sociability. One independent company official stated: "When we started the farmers thought they could get along without telephones. . . . Now you couldn't take them out. The women wouldn't let you even if the men would. Socially, they have been a godsend. The women of the county keep in touch with each other, and with their social duties, which are largely in the nature of church work."[38]

Although the episodic sales campaigns to farmers stressed the practical advantages of the telephone, such as receiving market prices, weather reports, and emergency aid, the industry addressed the social theme more often to them than to the general public. A PT&T series in 1911, for example, focused on the telephone in emergencies, staying informed, and saving money. But one additional advertisement said it was: "A Blessing to the Farmer's Wife. . . . It relieves the monotony of life. She CANNOT be lonesome with the Bell Service. . . ."[39] For all that, telephone professionals who dealt with farm-

---

[37]BOC, *Special Reports: Telephones: 1907* (Washington, D.C., 1910), pp. 77–78; see also U.S. Congress, Senate, Country Life Commission, 60th Cong., 2d sess., 1909, S. Doc. 705; and F. E. Ward, *The Farm Woman's Problems*, USDA Circular 148 (Washington, D.C., 1920). See also C. S. Fischer, "The Revolution in Rural Telephony," *Journal of Social History* (in press).

[38]Quoted in R. F. Kemp, "Telephones in Country Homes," *Telephony* 9 (June 1905): 433. A 1909 article claims that "[t]he principle use of farm line telephones has been their social use. . . . The telephones are more often and for longer times held for neighborly conversations than for any other purpose." It goes on to stress that subscribers valued conversation with anyone on the line; see G. R. Johnston, "Some Aspects of Rural Telephony," *Telephony* 17 (May 8, 1909): 542. See also R. L. Tomblen, "Recent Changes in Agriculture as Revealed by the Census," *Bell Telephone Quarterly* 9 (October 1932): 334–50; and J. West (C. Withers), *Plainville, U.S.A.* (New York, 1945), p. 10.

[39]The PT&T series appeared in the *Antioch* (Calif.) *Ledger* in 1911. For some examples and discussions of sales strategies to farmers, see Western Electric, "How to Build Rural Lines," n.d., "Rural Telephone Service, 1944–46," box 1310, AT&T ARCH; Stromberg-Carlson Telephone Manufacturing Company, *Telephone Facts for*

ers often fought the use of the line for nonbusiness conversations, at least in the early years. The pages of *Telephony* overflow with complaints about farmers on many grounds, not the least that they tied up the lines for chats.

More explicit appreciation of the value of telephone sociability to farmers emerged later. A 1931 account of Bell's rural advertising activities stressed business uses, but noted that "only within recent years [has] emphasis been given to [the telephone's] usefulness in everyday activities . . . the commonplaces of rural life." A 1932 article in the *Bell Telephone Quarterly* notes that "telephone usage for social purposes in rural areas is fundamentally important." Ironically, in 1938, an independent telephone man claimed that the social theme *had been* but was *no longer* an effective sales point because the automobile and other technologies had already reduced farmers' isolation![40]

As some passages suggest, the issue of sociability was also tied up with gender. When telephone vendors before World War I addressed women's needs for the telephone, they usually meant household management, security, and emergencies. There is evidence, however, that urban, as well as rural, women found the telephone to be useful for sociability.[41] When industry men criticized chatting

Farmers (Rochester, N.Y., 1903), Warshaw Collection, Smithsonian Institution; "Facts regarding the Rural Telephone," *Telephony* 9 (April 1905): 303. In *Printers' Ink*, "The Western Electric," 65 (December 23, 1908): 3–7; F. X. Cleary, "Selling to the Rural District," 70 (February 23, 1910): 11–12; "Western Electric Getting Farmers to Install Phones," 76 (July 27, 1911): 20–25; and H. C. Slemin, "Papers to Meet 'Trust' Competition," 78 (January 18, 1912): 28.

[40]R. T. Barrett, "Selling Telephones to Farmers by Talking about Tomatoes," *Printers' Ink* (November 5, 1931): 49–50; Tomblen (n. 38 above); and J. D. Holland, "Telephone Service Essential to Progressive Farm Home," *Telephony* 114 (February 19, 1938): 17–20. See also C. S. Fischer, "Technology's Retreat: The Decline of Rural Telephones, 1920–1940," *Social Science History* (in press).

[41]A 1925 survey of women's attitudes toward home appliances by the General Federation of Women's Clubs showed that respondents preferred automobiles and telephones above indoor plumbing; see M. Sherman, "What Women Want in Their Homes," *Woman's Home Companion* 52 (November 1925): 28, 97–98. A census survey of 500,000 homes in the mid-1920s reportedly found that the telephone was considered a primary household appliance because it, with the automobile and radio, "offer[s] the homemaker the escape from monotony which drove many of her predecessors insane"; reported in *Voice Telephone Magazine*, in-house organ of United Communications, December 1925, p. 3, MU IND TEL. One of our interviewees who conducted door-to-door telephone sales in the 1930s said that women were attracted to the service first in order to talk to kin and friends, second for appointments and shopping, and third for emergencies, while, for men, employment and business reasons ranked first. See also Rakow, "Gender" (n. 2 above), and C. S. Fischer, "Women and the Telephone, 1890–1940," paper presented to the American Sociological Association, 1987.

on the telephone, they almost always referred to the speaker as "she." Later, in the 1930s, the explicit appeals to sociability also emphasized women; the figures in such advertisements, for example, were overwhelmingly women.

In rough parallel with the shift in manifest advertising appeals toward sociability, there was a shift in industry attitudes from irritation with to approval of sociable conversations as part of the telephone's "comfort, convenience, and luxury."

Economic Explanations

Why were the telephone companies late and reluctant to suggest sociable conversations as a use? There are several, not mutually exclusive, possible answers. The clearest is that there was no profit in sociability at first but profit in it later.

Telephone companies, especially Bell, argued that residential service had been a marginal or losing proposition, as measured by the revenues and expenses accounted to each instrument, and that business service had subsidized local residential service. Whether this argument is valid remains a matter of debate. Nevertheless, the belief that residential customers were unprofitable was common, especially among line workers, and no doubt discouraged intensive sales efforts to householders.[42] At times, Bell lacked the capital to construct lines needed to meet residential demand. These constraints seemed to motivate occasional orders from New York not to advertise basic service or to do so only to people near existing and unsaturated lines.[43] And, at times, there was a technical incompatibility

[42]See, e.g., J. W. Sichter, "Separations Procedures in the Telephone Industry," paper P-77-2, Harvard University Program on Information Resources (Cambridge, Mass., 1977); *Public Utilities Digest*, 1930s–1940s, passim; "Will Your Phone Rates Double?" *Consumer Reports* (March 1984): 154–56. Chan's industry interviewees believed this cross subsidy to be true, as, apparently, did AT&T's commercial engineers; see various "Conferences" cited above, AT&T ARCH and ILL BELL INFO.

[43]E.g., commercial engineer C. P. Morrill wrote in 1914 that "we are not actively seeking new subscribers except in a few places where active competition makes this necessary. Active selling is impossible due to rapid growth on the Pacific Coast." He encouraged sales of party lines in congested areas, individual lines in place of party lines elsewhere, extensions, more calling, directory advertisements, etc., rather than expanding basic service into new territories; see PAC TEL MAG 7 (1914): 13–16. And, in 1924, the Bell System's commercial managers decided to avoid canvassing in areas that would require plant expansion and to stress instead long-distance calls and services, especially for large business users; see correspondence from B. Gherardi, vice-president, AT&T, to G. E. McFarland president, PT&T, July 14, 1924, and November 26, 1924, folder "282—Conferences," SF PION MU, and exchage with McFarland, May 10 and May 20, 1924, folder "Correspondence—B. Gherardi," SF PION MU.

between the quality of service Bell had accustomed its business subscribers to expect and the quality residential customers were willing
to pay for. Given these considerations, Bell preferred to focus on
the business class, who paid higher rates, bought additional equipment, and made long-distance calls.[44]

Still, when they did address residential customers, why did telephone vendors not employ the sociability theme until the 1920s, relying for so long only on practical uses? Perhaps social calls were an
untouched and elastic market of consumer demand. Having sold
the service to those who might respond to practical appeals—and perhaps by World War I everyone knew those practical uses—vendors
might have thought that further expansion depended on selling
"new" social uses of the telephone.[45] Similarly, vendors may have
thought they had already enrolled all the subscribers they
could—42 percent of American households in 1930—and shifted attention to encouraging use, especially of toll lines. We have seen
how sales efforts for intercity calls invoked friends and family. But
this explanation does not suffice. It leaves as a puzzle why the sociability themes continued in the Depression when the industry focused
again on simply ensuring subscribers and also why the industry's internal attitudes shifted as well.

Perhaps the answer is in the rate structures. Initially, telephone
companies charged a flat rate for unlimited local use of the service.
In such a system, extra calls and lengthy calls cost users nothing
but are unprofitable to providers because they take operator time
and, by occupying lines, antagonize other would-be callers. Some industry men explicitly blamed "trivial" calls on flat rates.[46] Discouraging "visiting" on the telephone then made sense.

Although flat-rate charges continued in many telephone exchanges, especially smaller ones, throughout the period, Bell and others instituted "measured service" in full or in part—charging
additionally per call—in most large places during the era of competition. In St. Louis in 1898, for example, a four-party telephone cost
forty-five dollars a year for 600 calls a year, plus eight cents a call
in excess.[47] This system allowed companies to reduce basic subscrip-

[44]The story of the Chicago exchange under John L. Sabin illustrates the point.
See R. Garnet, "The Central Union Telephone Company," box 1080, AT&T ARCH.

[45]This point was suggested by John Chan from the interviews.

[46]See n. 33, 34. This is also the logic of a recent New York Telephone Co. campaign to encourage social calls: The advertising will not run in upstate New York
"since the upstaters tend to have flat rates and there would be no profit in having
them make unnecessary calls" (see "New Pitch," n. 28 above).

[47]Letter to AT&T President Hudson, December 27, 1898, box 1284, AT&T
ARCH. On measured service in general, see "Measured Service Rates," boxes 1127,

tion fees and thus attract customers who wanted the service only for occasional use.

Company officials had conflicting motives for pressing measured service. Some saw it simply as economically rational, charging according to use. Others saw it as a means of reducing "trivial" calls and the borrowing of telephones by nonsubscribers. A few others, such as E. J. Hall, saw it as a vehicle for bringing in masses of small users.

The industry might have welcomed social conversations, if it could charge enough to make up for uncompleted calls and for the frustrated subscribers busy lines produced. In principle, under measured service, it could. (As it could with long distance, where each minute was charged.) Although mechanical time metering was apparently not available for most or all of this period, rough time charges for local calls existed in principle, since "messages" were typically defined as five minutes long or any fraction thereof. Thus, "visiting" for twenty minutes should have cost callers four "messages." In such systems, the companies would have earned income from sociability and might have encouraged it.[48]

However, changes from flat rates to measured rates do *not* seem to explain the shift toward sociability around the 1920s. Determining the extent that measured service was actually used for urban residential customers is difficult because rate schedules varied widely from town to town even within the same states. But the timing does not fit. The big exchanges with measured residential rates had them early on. For example, in 1904, 96 percent of Denver's residential subscribers were on at least a partial measured system, and, in 1905, 90 percent of those in Brooklyn, New York, were as well. (Yet, Los Angeles residential customers continued to have flat

---

1213, 1287, 1309, AT&T ARCH; F. H. Bethell, "The Message Rate," repr. 1913, AT&T ARCH; H. B. Stroud, "Measured Telephone Service," *Telephony* 6 (September 1903): 153–56, and (October 1903): 236–38; and J. E. Kingsbury, *The Telephone and Telephone Exchanges* (London, 1915), pp. 469–80.

[48]Theodore Vail claimed in 1909 that mechanical time metering was impossible (in testimony to a New York State commission, see n. 8 above, p. 470). See also Judson (n. 34 above), p. 647. In 1928, an operating engineer suggested overtime charges on five-minute calls and stated that equipment for monitoring overtime was now available; see L. B. Wilson, "Report on Commercial Operations, 1927," in "General Commercial Conference, 1928," p. 28, microfilm 368B, ILL BELL INFO. On the five-minute limit, see "Measured Service," box 1127, AT&T ARCH, passim; and Bell Canada, *The First Century of Service* (Montreal, 1980), p. 4. There is no confirmation on how strict operators in fact were in charging overtime. The Bell System, at least, was never known for its laxness in such matters.

rates.)[49] There is little sign that these rate systems altered significantly in the next twenty-five years while sociability themes emerged.

Conversely, flat rates persisted in small exchanges beyond the 1930s. Moreover, sociability themes appeared more often in rural sales campaigns than in urban ones, despite the fact the rural areas remained on flat-rate schedules.

Although concern that long social calls occupied lines and operators—with financial losses to the companies—no doubt contributed to the industry's resistance to sociability, it is not a sufficient explanation of those attitudes or, especially, of the timing of their change.

Technical Explanations

Industry spokesmen early in the era would probably have claimed that technical considerations limited "visiting" by telephone. Extended conversations monopolized party lines. That is why companies, often claiming customer pressure, encouraged, set—or sought legal permission to set—time limits on calls. Yet, this would not explain the shift toward explicit sociability, because as late as 1930, 40–50 percent of Bell's main telephones in almost all major cities were still on party lines, a proportion not much changed from 1915.[50]

A related problem was the tying up of toll lines among exchanges, especially those among villages and small towns. Rural cooperatives complained that the commercial companies provided them with only single lines between towns. The companies resisted setting up more, claiming they were underpaid for that service. This

[49]Denver: letter from E. J. Hall to E. W. Burgess, 1905, box 1309, AT&T ARCH; Brooklyn: BOC, *Telephones, 1902* (n. 4 above); Los Angeles: "Telephone on the Pacific Coast, 1878–1923," box 1045, AT&T ARCH.

[50]On company claims, see, e.g., "Limiting Party Line Conversations," *Telephony* 66 (May 2, 1914): 21; and MacMeal (n. 2 above), p. 224. On party-line data, compare the statistics in the letter from J. P. Davis to A. Cochrane, April 2, 1901, box 1312, AT&T ARCH, to those in B. Gherardi and F. B. Jewett, "Telephone Communications System of the United States," *Bell System Technical Journal* 1 (January 1930): 1–100. The former show, e.g., that, in 1901, in the five cities with the most subscribers, an average of 31 percent of telephones were on party lines. For those five cities in 1929, the percentage was 36. Smaller exchanges tended to have even higher proportions. See also "Supplemental Telephone Statistics, PT&T," "Correspondence—Du Bois," SF PION MU. The case of Bell Canada also fails to support a party-line explanation. Virtually all telephones in Montreal and Toronto were on individual lines until 1920.

single-line connection would create an incentive to suppress social conversations, at least in rural areas. But this does not explain the shift toward sociability either. The bottleneck was resolved much later than the sales shift when it became possible to have several calls on a single line.[51]

The development of long distance might also explain increased sociability selling. Over the period covered here, the technology improved rapidly, AT&T's long-distance charges dropped, and its costs dropped even more. The major motive for residential subscribers to use long distance was to greet kin or friends. Additionally, overtime was well monitored and charged. Again, while probably contributing to the overall frequency of the sociability theme, long-distance development seems insufficient to explain the change. Toll calls as a proportion of all calls increased from 2.5 percent in 1900 to 3.2 percent in 1920 and 4.1 percent in 1930, then dropped to 3.3 percent in 1940. They did not reach even 5 percent of all calls until the 1960s.[52] More important, the shift toward sociability appears in campaigns to sell basic service and to encourage local use, as well as in long-distance ads. (See table 2.)

Cultural Explanations

While both economic and technical considerations no doubt framed the industry's attitude toward sociability, neither seems sufficient to explain the historical change. Part of the explanation probably lies in the cultural "mind-set" of the telephone men.

In many ways, the telephone industry descended directly from the telegraph industry. The instruments are functionally very similar; technical developments sometimes applied to both. The people who developed, built, and marketed telephone systems were predominantly telegraph men. Theodore Vail himself came from a family involved in telegraphy and started his career as a telegrapher. (In contrast, E. J. Hall and A. W. Page, among the supporters of "triviality," had no connections to telegraphy. J. L. Sabin, a man of the

---

[51]"Carrier currents" allowed multiple conversations on the same line. The first one was developed in 1918, but for many years they were limited to use on long-distance trunk lines, not local toll lines. See, e.g., R. Coe, "Some Distinguishing Characteristics of the Telephone Business," *Bell Telephone Quarterly* 6 (January 1927): 47–51, esp. pp. 49–50; and R. C. Boyd, J. D. Howard, Jr., and L. Pederson, "A New Carrier System for Rural Service," *Bell System Technical Journal* 26 (March 1957): 349–90. The first long-distance carrier line was established in Canada in 1928, after the long-distance sociability theme had emerged; see Bell Canada, *First Century*, no. 46, p. 28.

[52]BOC, *Historical Statistics* (n. 3 above), p. 783.

same bent, did have roots in telegraphy.) Many telephone companies had started as telegraph operations. Indeed, in 1880, Western
Union almost displaced Bell as the telephone company. And the organization of Western Union served in some ways as a model for Bell.
Telephone use often directly substituted for telegraph use. Even
the language used to talk about the telephone revealed its ancestry.
For example, an early advertisement claimed that the telephone system was the "cheapest telegraph service ever." Telephone calls were
long referred to as "messages." American telegraphy, finally, was
rarely used even for brief social messages.[53]

No wonder, then, that the uses proposed first and for decades to
follow largely replicated those of a printing telegraph: business
communiqués, orders, alarms, and calls for services. In this context,
industry men reasonably considered telephone "visiting" to be an
abuse or trivialization of the service. Internal documents suggest
that most telephone leaders typically saw the technology as a business instrument and a convenience for the middle class, claimed
that people had to be sold vigorously on these marginal advantages,
and believed that people had no "natural" need for the telephone—
indeed, that most (the rural and working class) would never need
it. Customers would have to be "educated" to it.[54] AT&T Vice-

[53]On the telegraph background of early telephone leaders, see, e.g., A. B. Paine, *Theodore N. Vail* (New York, 1929); Rippey (n. 2 above); and W. Patten, *Pioneering the Telephone in Canada* (Montreal: Telephone Pioneers, 1926). Interestingly, this was true of
Bell and the major operations. But the leaders of small-town companies were typically businessmen and farmers; see, e.g., *On the Line* (Madison: Wisconsin State Telephone Association, 1985). On Western Union and Bell, see G. D. Smith, *The Anatomy
of a Business Strategy: Bell, Western Electric, and the Origins of the American Telephone Industry* (Baltimore, 1985). The "cheapest telegraph" appears in a Buffalo flier of November 13, 1880, box 1127, AT&T ARCH. On the infrequent use of the telegraph for
social messages, see R. B. DuBoff, "Business Demand and Development of the Telegraph in the United States, 1844–1860," *Business History Review* 54 (Winter 1980):
459–79.

[54]In the very earliest days, Vail had expected that the highest level of development would be one telephone per 100 people; by 1880, development had reached
four per 100 in some places; see Garnet (n. 2 above), p. 133, n. 3. It reached one
per 100 Americans before 1900 (see table 1). In 1905, a Bell estimate assumed that
twenty telephones per 100 Americans was the saturation point and even that "may appear beyond reason"; see "Estimated Telephone Development, 1905–1920," letter
from S. H. Mildram, AT&T, to W. S. Allen, AT&T, May 22, 1905, box 1364, AT&T
ARCH. The saturation date was forecast for 1920. This estimate was optimistic in its
projected *rate* of diffusion—twenty per 100 was reached only in 1945—but very pessi-
mistic in its projected *level* of diffusion. That level was doubled by 1960 and tripled
by 1980. One reads in Bell documents of the late 1920s of concern that the automobile and other new technologies were far outstripping telephone diffusion. Yet, even
then, there seemed to be no assumption that the telephone would reach the near uni-
versality in American homes of, say, electricity or the radio.

President Page was reacting precisely against this telegraphy perspective in his 1928 defense of "frivolous" conversation. At the same conference, he also decried the psychological effect of telephone advertisements that explicitly compared the instrument to the telegraph.[55]

Industry leaders long ignored or repressed telephone sociability—for the most part, I suggest, because such conversations did not fit their understandings of what the technology was supposed to be for. Only after decades of customer insistence on making such calls—and perhaps prodded by the popularity of competing technologies, such as the automobile and radio—did the industry come to adopt sociability as a means of exploiting the technology.

This argument posits a generation-long lag, a mismatch, between how subscribers used the telephone and how industry men thought it would be used. A variant of the argument (posed by several auditors of this article) suggests that there was no mismatch, that the industry's attitudes and advertising accurately reflected public practice. Sales strategies changed toward sociability around the mid-1920s because, in fact, people began using the telephone that way more. This increase in telephone visiting occurred for perhaps one or more reasons—a drop in real costs, an increase in the number of subscribers available to call, clearer voice transmission, more comfortable instruments (from wall sets to the "French" handsets), measured rates, increased privacy with the coming of automatic dial switching, and so on—and the industry's marketing followed usage.

To address this argument fully would require detailed evidence on the use of the telephone over time, which we do not have. Recollections by some elderly people suggest that they visited by telephone less often and more quickly in the "old days," but they cannot specify exact rates or in what era practices changed.[56] On the other hand, anecdotes, comments by contemporaries, and fragments of numerical data (e.g., the 1909 Seattle "study") suggest that residential users regularly visited by telephone before the mid-1920s, whatever the etiquette was supposed to be, and that such calls at least equaled calls regarding household management. Yet, telephone advertising in the period overwhelmingly stressed practical use and ignored or suppressed sociability use.

Changes in customers' practices may have helped spur a change

[55] Page 53 in L. B. Wilson (chair), "Promoting Greater Toll Service," "General Commercial Conference, 1928," microfilm 368B, ILL BELL INFO.

[56] This comment is based on the oral histories reported by Rakow (n. 2 above) and by several interviews conducted in San Rafael, Calif., by John Chan for this project. See also Fischer, "Women" (n. 41).

in advertising—although there is no direct evidence of this in the industry archives—but some sort of mismatch existed for a long time between actual use and marketing. Its source appears to be, in large measure, cultural.

This explanation gains additional plausibility from the parallel case of the automobile, about which space permits only brief mention. The early producers of automobiles were commonly former bicycle manufacturers who learned their production techniques and marketing strategies (e.g., the dealership system, annual models) during the bicycle craze of the 1890s. As the bicycle was then, so was the automobile initially a plaything of the wealthy. The early sales campaigns touted the automobile as a leisure device for touring, joyriding, and racing. One advertising man wondered as late as 1906 whether "the automobile is to prove a fad like the bicycle or a lasting factor in the industry of the country."[57]

That the automobile had practical uses dawned on the industry quickly. Especially after the success of the Ford Model T, advertisements began stressing themes such as utility and sociability—in particular, that families could be strengthened by touring together. Publicists and independent observers alike praised the automobile's role in breaking isolation and increasing community life.[58] As with the telephone, automobile vendors largely followed a market-

[57] Among the basic sources on the history of the automobile drawn from are: J. B. Rae, *The American Automobile: A Brief History* (Chicago, 1965); id., *The Road and Car in American Life* (Cambridge, Mass., 1971); J. J. Flink, *America Adopts the Automobile, 1895–1910* (Cambridge, Mass., 1970); id., *The Car Culture* (Cambridge, Mass., 1976); and J.-P. Bardou, J.-J. Chanaron, P. Fridenson, and J. M. Laux, *The Automobile Revolution*, trans. J. M. Laux (Chapel Hill, N.C., 1982). The advertising man was J. H. Newmark, "Have Automobiles Been Wrongly Advertised?" *Printers' Ink* 86 (February 5, 1914): 70–72. See also id., "The Line of Progress in Automobile Advertising," ibid., 105 (December 26, 1918): 97–102.

[58] G. L. Sullivan, "Forces That Are Reshaping a Big Market," *Printers' Ink* 92 (July 29, 1915): 26–28. Newmark (n. 57 above, p. 97) wrote in 1918 that it "has taken a quarter century for manufacturers to discover that they are making a utility." A 1930s study suggested that 80 percent of household automobile expenditures was for "family living"; see D. Monroe et al., *Family Income and Expenditures. Five Regions*, Part 2. *Family Expenditures*, Consumer Purchases Study, Farm Series, Bureau of Home Economics, Misc. Pub. 465 (Washington, D.C., 1941), pp. 34–36. Recall the 1925 survey of women's attitudes toward appliances (n. 41 above). The author of the report, Federation President Mary Sherman, concluded that "Before toilets are installed or washbasins put into homes, automobiles are purchased and telephones are connected . . . [b]ecause the housewife for generations has sought escape from the monotony rather than the drudgery of her lot" (p. 98). See also *Country Life* and Ward (n. 37 above); E. de S. Brunner and J. H. Kolb, *Rural Social Trends* (New York, 1933); and F. R. Allen, "The Automobile," pp. 107–32 in F. R. Allen et al., *Technology and Social Change* (New York, 1957).

ing strategy based on the experience of their "parent" technology; they stressed a limited and familiar set of uses; and they had to be awakened, it seems, to wider and more popular uses. The automobile producers learned faster.

No doubt other social changes also contributed to what I have called the discovery of sociability, and other explanations can be offered. An important one concerns shifts in advertising. Advertising tactics, as noted earlier, moved toward "softer" themes, with greater emphasis on emotional appeals and on pleasurable rather than practical uses of the product. They also focused increasingly on women as primary consumers, and women were later associated with telephone sociability.[59] AT&T executives may have been late to adopt these new tactics, in part because their advertising agency, N. W. Ayer, was particularly conservative. But in this analysis, telephone advertising eventually followed general advertising, perhaps in part because AT&T executives attributed the success of the automobile and other technologies to this form of marketing.[60]

Still, there is circumstantial and direct evidence to suggest that the key change was the loosening, under the influence of public practices with the telephone, of the telegraph tradition's hold on the telephone industry.

Conclusion

Today, most residential calls are made to friends and family, often for sociable conversations. That may well have been true two or three generations ago, too.[61] Today, the telephone industry encourages such calls; seventy-five years ago it did not. Telephone salesmen then claimed the residential telephone was good for emergencies; that function is now taken for granted. Telephone salesmen then claimed the telephone was good for marketing; that function

[59]Recall that, early on, women were associated in telephone advertising with emergencies, security, and shopping.

[60]On changes in advertising, see sources cited in n. 21 above. The comment on N. W. Ayer's conservatism comes from Roland Marchand (personal communication).

[61]It is difficult to establish for what purpose people actually use the telephone. A few studies suggest that most calls by far are made for social reasons, to friends and family. (This does not mean, however, that people subscribe to telephone service for such purposes.) See Field Research Corporation, *Residence Customer Usage and Demographic Characteristics Study: Summary*, conducted for Pacific Bell, 1985 (courtesy R. Somer, Pacific Bell); B. D. Singer, *Social Functions of the Telephone* (Palo Alto, Calif.: R&E Associates, 1981), esp. p. 20; M. Mayer, "The Telephone and the Uses of Time," in Pool, *Social Impact* (n. 2 above), pp. 225–45; and A. H. Wurtzel and C. Turner, "Latent Functions of the Telephone," ibid., pp. 246–61.

persists ("Let your fingers do the walking. . . . ") but never seemed to be too important to residential subscribers.[62] The sociability function seems so obviously important today, and yet was ignored or resisted by the industry for almost the first half of its history.

The story of how and why the telephone industry discovered sociability provides a few lessons for understanding the nature of technological diffusion. It suggests that promoters of a technology do not necessarily know or determine its final uses; that they seek problems or "needs" for which their technology is the answer (cf. the home computer business); but that consumers may ultimately determine those uses for the promoters. And the story suggests that, in promoting a technology, vendors are constrained not only by its technical and economic attributes but also by an interpretation of its uses shaped by its and their own histories, a cultural constraint that can be enduring and powerful.

---

[62]A 1934 survey found that up to 50 percent of women respondents with telephones were "favorable" to shopping by telephone. Presumably, fewer actually did so; see J. M. Shaw, "Buying by Telephone at Department Stores," *Bell Telephone Quarterly* 13 (July 1934): 267–88. This is true despite major emphases on telephone shopping in industry advertising. See also Fischer, "Women" (n. 41 above).

More "Small Things Forgotten": Domestic Electrical Plugs and Receptacles, 1881–1931

FRED E. H. SCHROEDER

"The household," wrote A. E. Kennelly in 1890, "is in itself the condensed history of a nation's past, the centre of its present, and the cradle of its future."[1] Such a microcosm would certainly seem to deserve detailed study. And, when properly read, household artifacts ought therefore to disclose more than another page in the history of decorative arts and furnishings, for there is also a technology that underlies the ornamentation of domestic life. Domestic technology has certainly not been neglected by historians, yet a close look at one family of artifacts reveals something important about the nation's past, a legacy that continues to be central today.[2]

Fred E. H. Schroeder is professor of humanities at the University of Minnesota, Duluth. His publications include historical studies of rural school buildings, feminine hygiene supplies, and, in *Outlaw Aesthetics* (Bowling Green, Ohio, 1977), mass-produced decorative art and entertainments. The author acknowledges the help of Julian D. Tebo, secretary of the Electric History Association; Michael Lane, director of Glensheen Mansion Museum; Al Kuhfeld, curator at the Bakken Library of Electricity in Life; Bill Peavler of the Oklahoma Historical Society; Bruce Maston, historian of the GE Realty Plot Historic District; Merwin Brandon and Richard Lloyd, chairmen of the National Electrical Code; Lenore Swoiskin, archivist of Sears Roebuck; John Bowditch, curator of machinery at the Edison Institute; Bernard Carlson of Michigan Technological University; Erskine Stanberry; and the able staff members of the Patent and Trademark Office, the General Electric Main Library, the Northeast Minnesota Historical Center, the University of Minnesota Engineering Library, the Minnesota Historical Society, the Minneapolis Public Library, the University of Minnesota, Duluth, Library, and the Duluth Public Library.

[1]A. E. Kennelly, "Electricity in the Household," *Scribners*, January 1890, p. 115.

[2]Sigfried Giedion's *Mechanization Takes Command: A Contribution to Anonymous History* (Oxford, 1948) is the pioneer in studies of domestic technology. During the past decade the subject has been addressed several times in *Technology and Culture*, for example by Ruth Schwartz Cowan, "The 'Industrial Revolution' in the Home: Household Technology and Social Change in the 20th Century" (January 1976, pp. 1–23); Joann Vanek, "Household Technology and Social Status: Rising Living Standards and Status and Residence Differences in Housework" (July 1978, pp. 361–75); and Charles A. Thrall,

This essay originally appeared in *Technology and Culture*, vol. 27, no. 3, July 1986.

118   *Fred E. H. Schroeder*

The commonplace act of plugging an electrical appliance into a wall outlet can be regarded as an act that connects directly into an industrial system—even though in the normal activities of a day, people are no more likely to feel aware that the receptacle connects to a dynamo than they are to think of Canadian forests when turning a newspaper page. How the plug and receptacle developed to make this connection an everyday thing is the topic of this essay.

Flexible cords, attachment plugs, and receptacles utilizing lighting circuits were conceived of almost simultaneously with the installation of Edison's first central-station system in 1882. By 1890, many of the necessary manufactured components were available in the United States, England, and Germany, and most were exhibited at the 1893 World's Columbian Exposition in Chicago. Yet the industry did not engage in active promotion of domestic appliances until the 20th century and did not promote them vigorously until after 1915, when rival schemes were finally resolved into a standardized system of convenience outlets and interchangeable appliances.[3]

The electrical appliance plug is something that Thomas Edison did not invent. It was a curious oversight, because Edison anticipated almost everything that might relate to the incandescent light bulb and its applications. The *Official Gazette* of the U.S. Patent Office for December 27, 1881, contains an astonishing five pages of inventions ranging from "a slip or filament . . . made of bamboo or similar fiber" to a vacuum pump for exhausting the air from a glass bulb, to an insulated conducting tube, a dynamo, a current regulator, a meter, a chandelier, processes for manufacture of these various components, and, in Patent no. 251,551, the entire "System of Electric Lighting" for houses. In that system, the appliance plug is conspicuously absent.[4]

"The Conservative Use of Modern Household Technology" (April 1982, pp. 175–94). An important recent addition to the literature is Ruth Cowan's *More Work for Mother: The Ironies of Household Technology from the Open Hearth to the Microwave* (New York, 1983). At the same time, domestic historic preservation has encouraged professional preservation architecture and such journals as *The Old House Journal* (Brooklyn, 1973–) and *Technology and Conservation* (Boston, 1976–), as well as the microfiche publication of the Winterthur Museum collection of decorative-arts trade catalogs (New York, 1984).

[3]National statistics on electrical household appliances and supplies were not available until 1899, when an output value of manufactures of $1.9 million was reported; this doubled over the next four years. The largest percentage increase (42 percent) in a single year was from 1915 to 1916. *Historical Statistics of the United States: Colonial Times to 1970, Bicentennial Edition* (Washington, D.C., 1975), p. 700.

[4]References to patents by number will not be footnoted. Brief descriptions with a single view can be found in the *Official Gazette*, whereas full copies are available in official patent repositories.

Within two years Edison was selling electric lighting to Wall Street, with 8,000 bulbs illuminated by power from one central station, and by 1890 Edison central electric stations were providing light throughout the world.[5] But there was no convenient way of tapping into the system for other purposes.

The idea of applying the new household lighting circuits to other uses was immediately seized on by many inventors, and the term "appliance" as referring to electrical devices that can operate off household current became common.[6] Kennelly's 1890 article on "Electricity in the Household"—the first intended for general readership—is illustrated with a photo of a sewing machine run by electricity along with a diagram for wiring a house for an electric thermostat, for fire-alarm, burglar-alarm, clock, and "annunciator" systems, and for an electric fan, phonograph, and stove.[7] "Nor is it to be supposed," says Kennelly, "that any of the applications above alluded to are visionary, for all are in actual use." This was true enough, though all appliances were novelties in the household.[8] Three important points should be mentioned about Kennelly's article: first, in 1890 both the technology and the inventive mind were ready for home appliances, and home wiring was not unheard of.[9] Second, Kennelly regarded household electricity

[5]Thomas Parke Hughes, "Thomas Alva Edison and the Rise of Electricity," in *Technology in America,* ed. Carroll W. Pursell, Jr. (Cambridge, Mass., 1981), pp. 123–25. The industrial backdrop for this essay can be found in Harold Passer, *The Electrical Manufacturers 1875–1900* (Cambridge, Mass., 1953), and Thomas P. Hughes, *Networks of Power: Electrification in Western Society, 1880–1930* (Baltimore, 1983).

[6]"The general idea of the plug and socket is such an obvious one it must have been thought of independently by many different people and no individual 'inventor' can ever be named" (John Mellanby, *The History of Electric Wiring* [London, 1957], p. 165). The term "electric appliances" first appears in a U.S. patent in 1887 (no. 362,108); the generic "appliance" as apparatus dates back to the 16th century (*Oxford English Dictionary*).

[7]Kennelly (n. 1 above), pp. 102–15.

[8]Aside from fans, the first small-motor applications were for sewing machines, which were seen at the Paris Exhibition in 1881; in the United States the C & C Electric Motor Company, formed in 1886 by Charles Curtis, Francis Bacon Crocker, and Schuyler Skaats Wheeler, began to manufacture low-voltage sewing-machine motors, introducing in 1887 a 110-volt model to take advantage of lighting circuits. (Malcolm MacLaren, *The Rise of the Electrical Industry during the Nineteenth Century* [Princeton, N.J., 1943], pp. 91–93.) Nicola Tesla's first small-electric-motor application was to a fan in 1889; in the same year patents for a large ceiling fan were granted to Philip Diehl of Elizabeth, New Jersey (nos. 414,757 and 414,758). (Giedion [n. 2 above; Norton Library edition, 1969], pp. 558–60.) Most of the phonograph exhibits at the 1893 Columbian Exposition "were run by electric motors," including some run "by the direct incandescent light circuit." (J. P. Barrett, *Electricity at the Columbian Exposition* [Chicago, 1894], p. 154; cf. Hughes, *Networks of Power,* pp. 82–83.)

[9]On the number of American generating plants and lamps prior to 1891 see Passer (n. 5 above), p. 121, and Paul W. Keating, *Lamps for a Brighter America* (New York, 1954),

as applicable to illumination, heat, and small motors. But the third point is something of a negative, because all the appliances that he describes were wired in permanently. Otherwise, his foresight, as well as his futuristic enthusiasm, was a decade ahead of its time.[10]

With the new century came a sense of being on the edge of a revolution in housekeeping, but George E. Walsh, writing in *The Independent* in 1901, still couched his statements in future tense: "With an invisible power that can be converted at will into light, heat and power, the tendency will be to invent all sorts of implements for reducing the inconveniences of living. For instance, the sewing machine will have an electric attachment that can be employed at any moment to run the machine as long or as short as needed. Many an overheated housewife must have viewed with envy the electric fans that cool the air on hot days in restaurants, and it would not be long before appropriate fans would be placed in every household for private use." The deterrent, Walsh says, is cost. Stoves, ovens, chafing dishes, and teakettles were all available, yet too expensive in energy costs. "It only needs the cheapening of electrical power to introduce them in nine-tenths of the homes in this broad land."[11] Undoubtedly, electricity rates were a deterrent factor (as is the case today for electric heating in some areas), but it appears that the real technological roadblock was the requirement for permanent wiring. If only there were some way of tapping into the lighting circuit in a flexible manner, appliances might become more attractive to consumers.

A few such schemes had been patented in the 1880s. Sigmund Bergmann, a former Edison employee and later a partner in the manufacture of accessories, patented on April 10, 1883, a "Connection

---

p. 39. MacLaren points out that most uses were in businesses, not residences (p. 92). For occasional use battery operation of small appliances, especially fans, continued throughout the period. The earliest census report on domestic electrification in 1907 reported that 8% of U.S. dwellings had electric service; this doubled by 1912. Rural-urban differences were not reported, but it is reasonable to assume that nearly all such dwellings were in cities. (*Historical Statistics of the United States,* p. 827.)

[10]The *Nineteenth-Century Readers Guide* has only Kennelly's article under the subject heading of "Electric apparatus and appliances, Domestic." There is another article on heating houses electrically. From 1900 on there is a heading "Electricity in the home [or household]," which has two entries from 1900–4, eleven from 1905–9, twenty-one from 1910–14, and three in the 1907–15 supplement. It is curious that although electric saucepans, broilers, boilers, flatirons, curling irons, cigar lighters, phonographs, and more from the United States, England, and Germany were exhibited at the Columbian Exposition, none received mention in any popular magazines, newspapers, or fair guidebooks. See Barrett (n. 8 above), pp. 400–8.

[11]George E. Walsh, "Electricity in the Household," *Independent,* March 7, 1901, pp. 556–69.

for Electric-Light Fixtures" (no. 275,749) that not only utilized a screw plug to connect into Edison-type sockets but suggests that this was already a common practice. One historian states that the first "normal" type of plug and socket in England was introduced by T. T. Smith, also in 1883, and he finds two-pin designs as early as 1885.[12] One such arrangement appeared in a General Electric catalog in 1889.

In 1887, Charles G. Perkins of Hartford, Connecticut, patented a "Connector for Electrical Appliances" (no. 362,108), and in the early 1890s we have patents for a "flexible electric connector" (no. 421,802) and an "electrical [ceiling] fixture" (no. 459,704) "to make connections . . . to translating devices, such as electric lights, electric motors and kindred apparatus." And a "*plug* and *receptacle* for electrical purposes" (italics added) was patented in 1894 (no. 530,066), incidentally introducing the nomenclature.

Some of this apparatus went into production, presumably for special applications, but certainly none caught on for domestic uses.[13] During the 1890s, however, several inventions did render household current available for convenience appliances. Two of these, a flush wall receptacle and a box-shaped ceramic plug (the "Chapman Plug"), led the way to a score of different models for walls and baseboards (which will be discussed more fully below). But the most common approach was to utilize the existing Edison light sockets with their familiar spiral screw base. Legend has it that Edison got this idea while screwing the cap on a

---

[12]Mellanby (n. 6 above), p. 165. "Non-normal" antecedents include one for series application by Lord Kelvin in 1881 and single-prong plugs for telegraph and telephone switchboards. L. E. Heaton's 1878 patent for "Tip for Flexible Electric Conducting Cords" (no. 199,827) anticipates the versatility of applications "for use on telegraphic switch cords and also on flexible cords for therapeutic apparatus." M. D. Fagen, ed., *A History of Engineering and Science in the Bell System: The Early Years (1875–1925)* (Whippany, N.J.: Bell Telephone Laboratories, 1975), p. 514, shows an illustration with the original 1882 plug and jack "designed to make multiple connections."

[13]An 1890 patent, no. 421,802, assigned to John F. Wollensak of Chicago has two prongs and closely resembles "Wood's Attachment Plug and Receptacle" in the *Illustrated Catalogue of Electric Light and Power Supplies* of the Electric Supply Company, Chicago (March 1892), p. 198. In the same catalog a whole group may derive from Perkins's invention. The 1891 ceiling fixture (no. 459,704) is no direct antecedent of modern plugs, but, in purpose, like the subsequent "rosette" of 1892 (no. 484,077), it is an attempt to render a ceiling outlet into a convertible unit. Cf. no. 434,509, spring-mounted "Ceiling block connector," and no. 444,807, "Combined electric motor and lamp-socket." ("Branch block" and "cut-out block" are alternate terms.) One special attachment plug in the collections of the National Museum of American History was designed to connect a bouquet of flowers filled with tiny Edison lamps and intended for presentation to the Crown Princess of Germany by the chief engineer of the German Edison Company at an exhibition, August 28, 1883. The plug shorted out, and the bare wires were successfully connected to main leads.

122   *Fred E. H. Schroeder*

kerosene can.[14] It had the advantage of firmly seating the bulb without having to snap, pull, or otherwise jar the lamp and its delicate filament. There were rival lamps before 1900, each with its own base, but, of the dozen or so major types, Edison's lamp base had 70 percent of the market.[15] For all practical purposes, it was the standard.

Yet, regardless of such early attachment devices as Bergmann's, and regardless of the actual availability of light-socket plugs in manufacturers' catalogs by 1892, there are no published indications of any real market or of any domestic usage until the turn of the century. For twenty-five years after that, scores of lamp-socket connectors were invented, designed, and manufactured, primarily by three companies that are still active leaders in wiring equipment: Harvey Hubbell of Bridgeport, Reuben Benjamin of Chicago, and General Electric of Schenectady. All utilized the Edison light socket. Nevertheless, popular knowledge of the lamp-socket connections lagged behind. Not until 1904 did *Scientific American* publish an article on "Electricity in the Household," showing photographs of people using lamp-socket connectors for an electric sewing machine, a chafing dish (chafing-dish cookery was a fad at the time), a "hot-water bag" (i.e., a heating pad), and a curling-iron heater such as was "to be found on the dressing tables of many fashionable hotel bedrooms." This article stated that "aside from the electrical devices illustrated herewith, there are many others which are coming into practical use. Electric griddles, cake irons, toasters, cereal boilers, and coffee urns are but a few of the many devices now finding their way into homes equipped with electricity." It is an "electrical age," the author asserted with more anticipation than accuracy, adding that "no new house is considered complete unless it be fitted with electric lighting circuits, whether the owner intends to use electricity or gas as an illuminant."[16]

Harking back to the year 1904, S. M. Kennedy, general agent for the Southern California Edison Company, recounted in 1915 his experiences selling appliances "for a period of eleven years, almost from the date of their earliest commercial practicability." His statistics include appliances sold by retailers as well as those marketed door-to-door by his own sales staff. In 1904, there were 500 appliances in Southern California; in 1906, 12,500; in 1910, 44,635 (79 percent of them

[14]Robert Conot, *A Streak of Luck* (New York, 1979), p. 187. The first patent is no. 251,549, December 27, 1881.

[15]John W. Howell and Henry Schroeder, *The History of the Incandescent Lamp* (Schenectady, N.Y., 1927), pp. 182–92.

[16]"Electricity in the Household," *Scientific American*, March 19, 1904, p. 232; cf. n. 9 above on the relative rarity of electrified homes.

electric flatirons); and in 1914, 141,705.[17] All of these plugged into light sockets, a practice that will be recognized as a mitigated convenience. One might plug in an iron at the cost of being left in the dark. Screwing in the plug necessarily twists the cord. And, if an iron is accidentally dropped, the cord will have to separate from either the plug or the appliance and a short circuit or shock is likely.

As one might imagine, solutions to these problems were actively sought. Some houses already had multisocket lighting fixtures and chandeliers, so one could be used for an appliance and the others for lights. Adapters were soon on the market, making it possible to screw a double-socket "cluster" into a single light outlet. (These are still available at any hardware store.) On the matter of twisting the cord (a problem that Bergmann had anticipated in 1883), two solutions were devised. The one that seems to have dominated the market from about 1911 to as late as 1925 was the Benjamin plug. Reuben Benjamin had been working on electrical inventions from at least 1901, his first marketable invention apparently being a "wireless cluster" adapter of the type mentioned above, manufactured in his basement by high school boys working after school. The $2,400 investment grossed sales of $10,000 in the first year. Around 1909 Benjamin developed a plug that allowed the light-socket connector to rotate while the cord remained stationary. The specific date is indeterminate, partly because of the time lag between patent application and the patent (an invention can of course be marketed while a patent is pending), partly because Benjamin Electric bought rights to similar inventions, and partly because Benjamin was constantly refining his inventions.[18] Possibly most significant is the fact that the Bergmann patent would have expired around 1911.

In the meantime, Harvey Hubbell was following another path. He invented as early as 1904 a separable attachment plug (fig. 1). The inner portion screwed into the Edison-type lamp socket while the outer portion plugged into the inner portion by means of pins or blades. The inner screw-plug portion is of a type still available today, whereas the outer portion, which became known as the *plug cap,* is the device from

[17]S. M. Kennedy, "Selling Lamp-Socket Appliances," *Electrical World,* May 29, 1915, pp. 1412–14.

[18]Reuben Benjamin's life is touched on in the biography of his partner Walter David Steele in the *National Cyclopedia of America Biography.* The early relevant patents are nos. 670,376 and 693,864. Patents 861,238 (July 23, 1907) and 1,005,119 (August 3, 1911), both invented by William Tregoning of Cleveland, clearly influenced Benjamin. The latter patent is dated on a Benjamin plug in the author's collection, along with Benjamin's 1,103,250 and 1,103,251 (July 14, 1914). All three inventions had been filed in 1909, but Tregoning's patent was awarded three years earlier.

which evolved our modern two-prong plug. The advantages of the separable plug are clear. Not only would an accidental pull on the cord merely separate the two elements rather than damaging the cord, the socket, or the appliance, but a homemaker could also leave the inner part installed while using the plug-cap end of the appliance cord to insert into other outlets similarly supplied with the threaded inner part, thereby making it possible to move a lamp, fan, or iron from room to room as needed. When Hubbell patented the separable plug, two plug-cap designs were granted patents on the same day. One, filed for in 1903, had pins, whereas the other, filed in 1904, had blades "in tandem"—that is, on the same axis rather than parallel to one another. A small point, but, as we shall see, this affected the design of receptacles for several decades.[19]

Both these solutions to the problem of conveniently tapping into the household current were posited on the availability of light-socketed receptacles, and for that reason they were readily adaptable to houses that had been wired from the 1880s on. But this remained only a partial convenience because, for obvious reasons, light outlets were located either high on walls or, most commonly, in the center of the

FIG. 1.—The "separable plug" was invented in 1904, with many later improvements like this 1912 "push-in" two-blade "cap" designed for greater ease in using light-socket outlets. Specialized appliance receptacles that would directly accept the "push-in cap" were a later development. As late as 1930, electrical appliances were ordinarily sold with light-socket attachment plugs, usually of this separable variety, which gave the option of discarding the old-fashioned portion. (*Electrical World* 60 [August 17, 1912]: 371.)

[19]On Harvey Hubbell, see *National Cyclopedia of American Biography*, 22:153. Hubbell started manufacturing electrical parts in 1888. Patent nos. 774,250 and 774,251 (November 8, 1904) appear to be his first separable plugs, and no. 923,179 (June 1, 1909) the first with parallel blades. Cf. note 13 above for antecedents to pronged domestic appliance plugs.

ceiling. Thus the use of portable appliances necessitated awkward reaching, often requiring a chair or stepladder to plug in an appliance. The first patent specifically naming an extension-cord plug as such was granted in 1901 (no. 670,376, "for connecting the wires of an incandescent lamp to a stationary fixture"), but, although an extension cord could render the appliance plug more accessible, the entire system could and did lead to an almost carnival festooning of cords in the home (fig. 2). The aesthetic solution was to develop a system of permanently installed receptacles at convenient heights and, insofar as possible, to mask or disguise these and their cords.

The actual date of the introduction of wall receptacles for portable appliances is elusive. A concealed floor plate with a two-prong plug was patented as early as 1890 (no. 421,802), and there are English wall

FIG. 2.—This 1906 photo shows the inelegance of the rudimentary system for connecting appliances to light sockets but also suggests the potential usefulness of the arrangement. (*Electrical World* 47 [February 3, 1906]: 249.)

126   *Fred E. H. Schroeder*

sockets dated ca. 1893.[20] In 1895 Frederick A. Chapman of Philadelphia patented a "cut-out block" and "box" for both wall and ceiling applications for light or for power (no. 539,725), with added potential for flush installation, "thus prevent[ing] an unsightly appearance." The Chapman plug does not resemble any modern apparatus and clearly bypasses all the Edison-Bergmann patents. Rather than having prongs or blades, it is rectangular, made of porcelain with broad copper contact strips on the sides. The receptacle is also made of porcelain. When the plug is inserted, brass doors are closed over the cord and the receptacle is concealed with only the cord to be seen coming out of the flush brass wall plate. The design definitely was effective, and a number of manufacturers made interchangeable elements and refinements. The Glensheen Mansion historic home in Duluth, Minnesota (built 1906–8), has these receptacles and plugs in many rooms, and they are still in use.[21] (See fig. 3.) But finding these is

FIG. 3.—This obsolete porcelain plug and receptacle has been in continuous use since 1908. The brass doors close over the recess, leaving only a lamp cord as evidence of the utilitarian current tap. The first baseboard receptacles were installed in an experimental Schenectady home in 1906; the installation illustrated here was a luxury item used only for semipermanent floor, table, and mantel lamps. (Courtesy of Glensheen Mansion Museum.)

[20]Mellanby (n. 6 above), p. 167.
[21]No. 659,547, receptacle (1900), assigned to Bryant Electric Company; no. 668,213, plug (1901); no. 707,516, receptacle (1902); also, Western Electric Company's *General Catalogue of Electrical Supplies* (Chicago, 1901) has several pages (pp. 250–54) of Chapman plugs, receptacles, and wall lamps designed to plug into the Chapman-Bryant receptacle. The Glensheen Mansion Museum's curator, Michael Lane, has located Chelten replacement receptacles for the Chapman system.

like finding living dinosaurs in a lost world. They are members of a line that did not evolve.

Recall, however, that Edison had not anticipated wall receptacles in his original system, and he seems not to have wavered from a predilection for fixed lighting outlets with the incidental use of Bergmann's attachment plug. The result was that the industry became awash with competing wall-receptacle designs. Until well into the 1920s some receptacles had an Edison screw socket into which one might plug a Benjamin plug, a nonrotating plug, or a Hubbell-type separable plug for which the plug cap might have pins, blades in tandem, or parallel blades. And there were others. By 1915 matters had come to such a pass that the National Electric Light Association (NELA) called a meeting in New York to try to establish some degree of uniformity. *Electrical World* accompanied a story on this meeting with a photograph of seventeen different types of wall receptacles, several of which were marketed by the same manufacturer.[22] (See fig. 4.)

The differing designs were not merely whimsical, however; some reflected differing amperage, voltage, polarity, and AC or DC current needs, much as today's different systems prevent plugging a 240-volt clothes dryer into a low-voltage outlet, discourage the use of ungrounded tools, or prevent reversing the polarity of electronic equipment. Nonetheless, the rivalry and confusion in 1915 were regarded as excessive by the industry, and, most important, salesmen knew that potential customers were growing suspicious of receptacle installations, not to mention their irritation with systems that would not accept whatever plug was provided with a new appliance. Consumer advertising sometimes tells more about this than technical literature, as, for example, in a 1910 *Colliers* advertisement by the Automatic Vacuum Cleaner Company, which states that "You Don't Need Electricity for Thorough Vacuum Cleaning."[23] There is evidence here for both sales resistance and a transition period in domestic labor-saving devices.

In the Glensheen Mansion not all rooms have wall receptacles, and so the archaeology of the house can tell something of the conception of household electricity at this time. The vacuum-cleaning system is permanently installed with a suction motor in the basement and intake tubes throughout the building. The permanently installed lighting

[22]"Standardization of Plugs and Receptacles," *Electrical World*, February 27, 1915, pp. 567–68.

[23]*Colliers*, October 29, 1910, p. 9. Advertisements for electric vacuum cleaners were commonplace in both *Colliers* and *Ladies Home Journal*. See the 1922 Montgomery Ward Catalog (Golden Jubilee Reprint, 1972), pp. 542–43, for such descriptions as "it takes any make standard attachment plug caps."

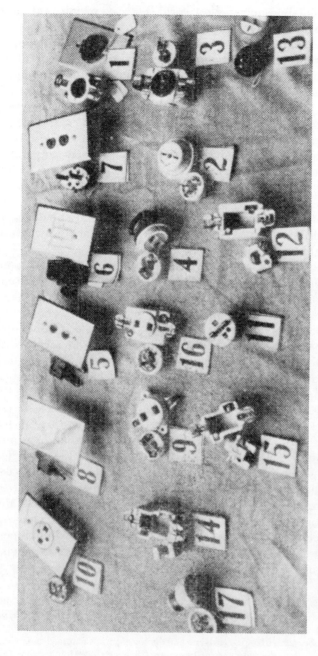

FIG. 4.—The public's acceptance of electrical appliances prompted rival manufacturers to develop exclusive and noncompatible plug-and-receptacle systems. In less than a decade the confusion was causing sales resistance, and in 1915 the National Electric Light Association supplied this photograph as evidence of the need for standardization, which was achieved in 1917. (*Electrical World* 65 [February 27, 1915]: 567.)

fixtures are so abundant and well located that most rooms do not need additional lights even today, and the few installations of modern outlets tend to be extension cords tapped into the wires of a wall-mounted lighting fixture. Their locations suggest use only for bedside clocks and radios and, in the library, for a radio and a television set. The original receptacles were limited in purpose to floor and table lamps. For that matter, none of the plug-connected lamps is really portable; Chapman plugs do not grip easily, and even these movable lamps are aesthetically designed for each room's specific decor. The advantage of portability, therefore, seems to have been limited to the slight "fine-tuning" of position that a cord allows for reading or needlework at a desk or in a sitting-room chair.

Servants' rooms do not have receptacles; nor do work areas. The reason for the former is obviously class related, but the reason for the latter is a reflection of the very early state of the art. Light-socket appliances were becoming significant by the time this house was designed, but a house—indeed an estate—amply staffed by servants hardly required labor-saving devices. In addition there is evidence that the year in which Glensheen's construction was planned may be the very year that baseboard receptacles were first introduced.

In 1905, H. W. Hillman designed "the house without a chimney," an all-electric home in Schenectady, New York. The name is somewhat of a misnomer: Hillman was obliged to install a coal furnace, although he also had electric heat in all the rooms and there was no kitchen chimney, since he had an electric "cooking and baking outfit." Reminiscing twenty years later in *Electrical World*, Hillman said that "it was a new idea to specify outlets in baseboards and sidewalls so that electric household utensils might be freely used without removing lights from their sockets."[24]

This demonstration home was highly publicized and almost immediately became internationally famous. A full-page Sunday feature in the New York *Herald* was copied by local papers in the United States and in London, Paris, and Berlin and was followed quickly by articles in *Good Housekeeping, Cassier's Magazine,* and *American Homes and Gardens,* this last being reprinted in the *Scientific American Supplement.* Boasting such electrical delights as a corn popper and a massage vibrator, the floor plan shows wall outlets in several rooms and three portable lamps. The chafing dish and coffee percolator are located on a side table in

[24]"Electricity in the Home," *Electrical World,* July 31, 1926, pp. 221–23. The Hillman house is now part of the GE Realty Plot Historic District; see Bruce Maston, *An Enclave of Elegance* (Schenectady, N.Y., 1983), pp. 204–8. See also GE's Bulletin no. 4921, *Electric Heating and Cooking Appliances* (1912).

130   *Fred E. H. Schroeder*

the dining room, which "has a backboard fitted with the necessary switches." Such tables, according to *Scientific American*, were "considered standard articles in a department store in Schenectady."[25]

But a lot of electricity would pass through America's wires before the innovations of an engineer in Schenectady and a millionaire in Duluth became commonplace. We can attempt to trace the evolution from novelty to mainstream in a number of ways. A 1913 rural home near Chelsea, Oklahoma (still in mint condition), was built from mail-order materials from Sears Roebuck; although electric power was at first unavailable, the house was supplied and constructed with complete lighting circuits and fixtures but no wall receptacles. The owner recalls plugging in the iron, toaster, washing machine, and refrigerator via extensions from ceiling fixtures until "the early thirties" when baseboard outlets were added.[26]

As late as 1915, the wholesale hardware catalog of the Marshall-Wells company in Duluth, serving hundreds of retailers from Minnesota to the Pacific coast of the United States and Canada, listed no wall receptacles, extension cords, or plug-cap adapters, although among its 3,800 pages it has Hotpoint Domestic Irons and El Bako, El Boilo, El Comfo, El Stovo, and El Glostovo—all from Hotpoint and all equipped with Edison-type light-socket plugs.[27] Marshall-Wells has over twenty pages of electrical ceiling and wall fixtures, as well as several pages of "Wakefield Interchangeable Fixtures . . . For Electric, Gas and Combination Lights," switch boxes, wire, and both gas and combination gas-and-electrical boxes (the gas pipe doubling as conduit for wire) but no wall receptacles.[28] The year of this catalog, 1915, is a handy milestone, for it will be recalled that this was the same year that NELA was pressing for standardization of wall receptacles and plugs, and it was

[25]Harold Stannard, "Electricity in the Home," *Scientific American Supplement* no. 1587, June 2, 1906. See also photographs in Maston; on p. 207 there is an electrical oven of the same design as that illustrated in Columbian Exposition publications a dozen years earlier (Giedion [n. 2 above], p. 544; Barrett [n. 8 above], p. 403).

[26]Communication to author from Erskine Stanberry, July 1983.

[27]See pp. 365, 366, 366A, 366B, 366½, 366¾, 419, 454 (discontinued items were sometimes removed, and pages with fractions were inserted). Most pages are dated, hence a 1915 catalog will have several years of items.

[28]"The gas/electric combination fixtures so frequently reproduced today as appropriate for Victorian lighting schemes had a surprisingly short period of production and popularity . . . [but] even in purely electric lights between 1890–1910, the average electric fixture derived most of its elements from gas lighting functions and esthetics. Until the 1910s electric fixtures continued to be made of gas pipes and tubes, often of brass" (Melissa L. Cook and Maximilian L. Ferro, "Electric Lighting and Wiring in Historic American Buildings," *Technology and Conservation*, Spring 1983, p. 32).

the year that S. M. Kennedy looked back on the first eleven years of saturating Southern California with lamp-socket appliances.

By 1915, appliances were becoming an American way of life, yet houses wired for the convenient use of appliances were still in an evolutionary stage. Ten years later double outlets that would accommodate modern plugs without a lamp-socket adapter were standardized; nevertheless, George Adler, an electrical engineer, could still open a *Good Housekeeping* article on "Bringing Your Wiring Up to Date" by asking: "When you want to use your electric toaster in the morning, do you have to unscrew a lamp from some lighting fixture to secure an outlet convenient to the table? When you wish to use the vacuum cleaner in your bedroom, do you have to connect to a wall fixture and have the cord dangling across the dresser or table?"[29] These simple questions provide a social historian with pictures of a reality that is otherwise forgotten or suppressed: forgotten, because the lamp-socket appliance has disappeared completely and is now a half-century and more back in time; suppressed, because neither catalogs nor magazine photographs of home interiors illustrate the disorderly inconvenience of appliance usage from 1904 to 1930. Advertisements in *Ladies Home Journal* between 1911 and 1917 do show housewives plugging appliances into light sockets (fig. 5), but after 1917 the attachment process is no longer depicted.[30] Such views would neither sell appliances nor show homes as owners and appliance manufacturers wanted them to be envisioned. An article published in 1924 in *House and Garden* underscores the domestic situation: "Because folk make inconvenience outlets out of their convenience outlets and plugs, and because builders need a little 'talking up' to in order to attain right electric comfort, this very short story about a lengthy subject is written. . . . It is computed that you use the vacuum cleaner 135 hours a year—or about 500 times a year. If your convenience outlet (or receptacle) is at knee or waist high, think of your release from stretching to chandelier heights!"[31]

Both the *Good Housekeeping* and *House and Garden* articles aimed to persuade homeowners to rewire using the new convenience outlets designed to accommodate plug blades whether tandem or parallel. Such "duplex flush receptacles" had been introduced into the market

---

[29]George W. Alder, "Bring Your Wiring Up to Date," *Good Housekeeping*, August 1925, pp. 88–89.

[30]Maston (n. 24 above), p. 206, has a photograph of the residence occupied by H. W. Hillman before the "all-electric house" showing a table lamp attached to a chandelier.

[31]"Plugs and Convenient Outlets," *House and Garden*, July 1924, p. 124.

nine years earlier (again, in 1915) by Hubbell.[32] (See fig. 6.) As far as plugs are concerned, the *House and Garden* article is unequivocal, describing the Hubbell-style design of separable plug as "the plug to get." Thus, between the separable plug and the T-receptacle, the electrical industry finally set the stage for standardization, which occurred quietly in 1917 when six manufacturers agreed on that receptacle.[33] In 1926 the NELA Wiring Committee issued a report stating that "within a few years the plugs for attaching the ordinary appliances to the sockets, and the receptacles or convenience outlets for attaching the ordinary appliance to the circuit otherwise than through the socket, have been standardized in the sense that the plugs and receptacles of practically all manufacturers are interchangeable."[34]

FIG. 5.—This washer/wringer is shown rather hazardously plugged into a light socket. (*Ladies Home Journal,* November 1917, p. 122.)

[32]*Electrical World,* February 13, 1915, p. 435.
[33]Ibid., March 3, 1917, p. 440. Wartime priorities very likely encouraged manufacturers to eliminate redundancies.
[34]R. S. Hale, "Report on Plugs and Receptacles," *National Electric Light Association Bulletin,* April 1926, pp. 247–48.

It is also noteworthy that the wiring code had recently been liberalized to "permit a circuit with several receptacles for 10 ampere devices."[35] Previously, the code required a separate circuit for every individual device in excess of 660 watts. The NELA Wiring Committee noted that "the screw plugs with tandem slots and the cap with tandem blades are still being manufactured to a limited and diminishing extent. The screw plug with tandem slot should disappear, but there will continue to be a use for the cap with tandem blade." This use, the committee proposed, would be for higher-wattage appliances, not because it would prevent improper use of these but as a reminder to the consumer that there is danger in overloading the circuit.[36]

By 1930 the transition was nearly complete. Although the 1927 Sears Roebuck catalog illustrated all appliances with lamp-socket plugs (the specific model is not clear), the 1928 Marshall-Wells catalog shows some appliances with a Benjamin plug and some with a separable plug,

FIG. 6.—Among the many competing plug-and-receptacle systems in 1915, this familiar-looking newcomer was to become the standard. The duplex feature was an innovation. T-slots permitted the use of the now obsolete tandem-bladed plug as well as our common (American) parallel blades. (*Electrical World* 65 [February 13, 1915]: 435.)

[35]Hillman appears to have been the first to wire a house for two circuits, one for lights and one for heat appliances. The voltage of the second circuit is not recorded. Maston (n. 24 above), p. 205.

[36]Hale (n. 34 above).

whereas others (not clearly shown) appear to have only bladed plugs. The 1930 Sears Roebuck catalog is the first to show a similar mixture. With its fall 1931 catalogs, Sears Roebuck adds irons to the list of bladed-plug appliances, thus ending the era.[37]

In the years since there have been changes, but not at the expense of the convenient flexibility of standardized access to the centrally produced current (in the United States, at least; internationally the situation is not so flexible). Although the basic design is the parallel-bladed plug, since 1962 standard receptacles have had a third hole for grounding.[38] The variety and number of appliances used in a home has undoubtedly increased—electric toothbrushes, knives, televisions, air conditioners, computers, patio rotisseries, for example; yet not only are the basic appliances the same as in the 1927 Sears Roebuck catalog—lamps, vacuums, irons, grills, hot plates, toasters, percolaters, mixers, hair dryers, heating pads, fans, space heaters, washing machines, corn poppers, ranges, radios, sewing machines, bandsaws, and toy trains—but many of these appliances had been anticipated by inventors as early as 1890. If there has been any significant change, it probably is in the growing number of appliances that function independently of household circuits. The battery, which antedated dynamos and circuitry systems and was employed in the earliest motorized appliances such as tabletop fans, has been greatly improved, and, along with the high efficiency of printed circuitry and semiconductors, it has freed dozens of appliances—such as drills, radios, lawn trimmers, tape recorders, and calculators—from cords and receptacles.

One practical use for this history of a commonplace technology is in the researching, reconstructing, and interpreting of historic homes of the 20th century. Now we have a timetable of important developments such as the commercial introduction of lamp-socket appliances in 1904, the appearance of the standardized T-receptacle in 1917, and the disappearance of lamp-socket appliances in 1931. It is clear that our households are indeed archaeological sites, containing not only our present and our plans for the future but a condensation of the past. Rarely do we encounter such a perfectly undisturbed technological midden as Glensheen Mansion. Far more often a house embodies the residue of change. To pursue the archaeological analogy, houses that

[37] 1928 Marshall-Wells catalog, pp. 1206, 1207, 1209, 1303, 1323; 1932 catalog, pp. 1207, 1210, 1323. The 1932 Marshall-Wells catalog has a few hot plates with the old plug, but these appear to be old cuts. Sears Roebuck references from 1930 and 1931 were supplied by Sears Roebuck Archives, Chicago.

[38] Communication to author from Richard Lloyd, former chairman of National Electrical Code, March 1983.

were constructed or first wired ca. 1880 to ca. 1918 have strata of various stages in the evolution of domestic electrification. The strata do not appear only in the surface manifestations of wiring; other aspects of the system have their own archaeologies as well—wire, cable, conduit, fusing, entrance panels being almost "underground," whereas chandeliers, lamps, and other appliances are "up front," sharing in the histories of decorative arts and industrial design.[39]

"Small things forgotten" is a phrase that historical archaeologist James Deetz extracted from colonial probate records for the title of his book on the archaeology of everyday things such as eating utensils.[40] Lamp-socket appliance plugs are small things that have been all but forgotten by electricians, electrical engineers, and hardware merchants, yet neither being forgotten nor smallness is indicative of insignificance. These plugs represent a necessary technological step in the conversion of our nation's households from hand labor and inconvenient fuels to automation and boundless flexibility in interior arrangements, while patterns of luxury and necessity reversed completely during that first quarter of the century. Today, candlelight dinners prepared on an alcohol-heated chafing dish are for luxurious entertaining, whereas a generous supply of convenience outlets in every room is a necessity few persons would willingly forgo.

[39]Cook and Ferro (n. 28 above), passim.
[40]James Deetz, *In Small Things Forgotten: The Archaeology of Early American Life* (Garden City, N.Y., 1977).

The Garbage Disposer, the Public Health, and the Good Life

SUELLEN HOY

By the 1960s the garbage disposer, a mundane household appliance introduced to Americans in the years immediately following World War II, had become recognized as a public health benefit as well as an appropriate accoutrement of the Good Life.[1] After years of debate the disposer had finally won the approval of sanitary engineers, public health officers, and municipal officials for its ability to improve community sanitation practices. And in an affluent society whose material progress became the envy of the world, the "grinder," as it was initially called, also captured the attention of middle-class women and their families, who found that it relieved them of the unpleasant task of handling and storing putrescible food wastes. In essence this "hunk of better living" touched a responsive chord in a generation of Americans who, having survived years of depression grayness and wartime scarcity, resumed their search for a healthier environment and a "greater ease of living" through goods and amenities that offered more cleanliness, convenience, and comfort.[2]

SUELLEN HOY is adjunct associate professor, Department of History, University of Notre Dame. She is coeditor of *History of Public Works in the United States, 1776–1976* (Chicago, 1976) and *Public Works History in the United States: A Guide to the Literature* (Nashville, 1982). The author acknowledges the help of Robert D. Bugher, American Public Works Association; Edward J. Cleary, formerly of *Engineering News-Record;* William S. Foster, formerly of *American City;* Martin V. Melosi, University of Houston; Walter Nugent, University of Notre Dame; William S. Price, Jr., North Carolina Division of Archives and History; Carmine Prioli, North Carolina State University; Joel A. Tarr, Carnegie-Mellon University; and Kenneth S. Watson, *Industrial Wastes.*

[1] The appliance is often called a "disposal" or "disposall," but this is not generically accurate since it appropriates a particular (General Electric) brand name, much as "fridge" (from Frigidaire) entered the language as a substitute for the generic "refrigerator." Professionals in the fields of sanitary engineering and waste management would prefer "kitchen disposer" or "food-waste disposer." At the risk of making both engineers and historians unhappy, I shall compromise and call the appliance the "grinder," "garbage disposer," or simply "disposer."

[2] References to "hunk of better living" and "greater ease of living" can be found in "Is

This essay originally appeared in *Technology and Culture*, vol. 26, no. 4, October 1985.

The adoption of the disposer can be examined in several ways: as a partial solution (though not without initial resistance) to a major public health problem; as a symbol of middle-class consumerism; as a labor-saving device attractive to women who were either working outside their homes or helping create the baby boom; or even as a profit maker for appliance dealers and plumbing contractors (and perhaps even city officials, though direct proof is lacking). The following pages will touch on all of these forces contributing to the garbage disposer's popularity. However, some must be treated briefly, either because evidence for them is slender, or because they are more suitably discussed in a separate essay. The major focus here is on how the disposer reflected postwar environmental concerns, a heightened consumer culture, and changes in the lives of American women.

Very probably, the shifting role of women in the home, beginning in the 1920s and accelerating in the years following World War II, contributed to the acceptance of the disposer. More women, especially married women, were working outside the home.[3] Their employment figured strongly in the substantial improvement after 1939 in median family income.[4] Consumer debt for durable goods became more acceptable and widespread.[5] And a suburban "life-style," manifest in the new single-family houses of Park Forest and Levittown, became first a target of emulation and then reality for millions of people.[6]

The acceptance of the garbage disposer took place contemporaneously with these pervasive social changes. That much is clear. The causal connections, however, are not. Did the disposer, in combination

America Getting Ready to Junk It?" *Domestic Engineering* 202 (July 1963): 59, and in "The House for Modern Living," *Architectural Forum* 62 (April 1935): 275. For an excellent discussion of Americans' search for a "better quality of life" in the post–World War II period, see Samuel P. Hays, "From Conservation to Environmental Politics in the United States since World War II," *Environmental Review* 6 (Fall 1982): 19–24.

[3]U.S. Department of Commerce, Bureau of the Census, *Historical Statistics of the United States: Colonial Times to 1970* (Washington, D.C., 1975), p. 133 (series D 49 and D 51).

[4]Ibid., p. 303 (series G 356), gives median family income as $1,319 in 1939, $3,042 in 1947, and $10,169 in 1970 (current dollars).

[5]Ibid., p. 1009 (series X553 and X554).

[6]For discussions of the postwar economy and consumer culture, see Walter T. K. Nugent, *Modern America* (Boston, 1973), pp. 312–14, 330–36; William E. Leuchtenburg, *A Troubled Feast: American Society since 1945* (rev. ed., Boston, 1979), pp. 31–69; Carl N. Degler, *At Odds: Women and the Family in America from the Revolution to the Present* (New York, 1980), pp. 418–35; John Kenneth Galbraith, *The Affluent Society* (Boston, 1958), pp. 200–202; Richard Wightman Fox and T. J. Jackson Lears, eds., *The Culture of Consumption: Critical Essays in American History, 1880–1980* (New York, 1983), pp. ix–xvii; Herbert J. Gans, *The Levittowners: Ways of Life and Politics in a New Suburban Community* (New York, 1967), pp. 34, 38–39; and Richard Polenberg, *One Nation Divisible: Class, Race, and Ethnicity in the United States since 1938* (New York, 1980), pp. 128–33.

with other laborsaving devices, reduce the time it took women to clean kitchens to such an extent that it provided them with unoccupied hours with which to earn money outside the home? Possibly; perhaps even probably. Or did women already working outside the home adopt the disposer eagerly because it reduced their total hours of labor both inside and outside the home? In other words, as Ruth Schwartz Cowan has asked, was the disposer a "pusher" or "puller" of women into the work force?[7] There is also the possibility that the disposer helped husbands and children more than wives and mothers, if it is true that "taking out the garbage" was indeed a chore reserved for males and the young.[8] In the absence of demographic profiles on the families that actually bought disposers (working wife or not; married couples, single people, or one-parent households; income level before and after installation of the disposer), these connections remain obscure.

We remain on firm ground, however, in recalling the availability of small, versatile electric motors and low-cost electric power that caused consumer use of electricity to nearly triple in the 1950s and made possible the adoption of a wide array of laborsaving devices by homeowners. When electricity was first introduced into the household in the late 19th century, it was used largely for purposes of illumination. With the advent of a practical small electric motor, electricity gradually transformed household operations by mechanizing appliances. With few exceptions, consumption of electricity continued to increase throughout the 20th century. While the years of greatest national growth on a year-by-year basis were between 1938 and 1959, growth rates were particularly high in 1944 and 1954.[9]

* * *

[7]Cowan gives the best answer to this question in her recent monograph. In explaining the effect of modern household appliances on married women's participation in the work force, she points out that "the washing machine, the dishwasher, and the frozen meal have not been *causes* of married women's participation in the workforce, but they have been *catalysts* of this participation." When housewives decided for whatever reasons that they needed to work full time, they subsequently discovered that "with the help of a dishwasher, a washing machine, and an occasional frozen dinner, they could undertake that employment without endangering their family's living standards." Ruth Schwartz Cowan, *More Work for Mother: The Ironies of Household Technology from the Open Hearth to the Microwave* (New York, 1983), pp. 208–9.

[8]In an investigation of the relationship between modern household equipment and family division of labor, Charles A. Thrall demonstrates that "in families which had a garbage disposal, husbands and young children were significantly less involved in taking care of the garbage. . . ." Thrall, "The Conservative Use of Modern Household Technology," *Technology and Culture* 23 (April 1982): 175–94 (quotation found on page 191).

[9]On electricity consumption, see Bonnie Maas Morrison, "Household Energy Consumption, 1900–1980" in George H. Daniels and Mark H. Rose, eds., *Energy and*

Although it was the modern "all-electric" kitchen of postwar America that welcomed the garbage disposer, the disposer's origins can be traced to the shredders, comminutors, and grinders installed to reduce large solids to fine pulp at grinding stations near municipal sewers or sewage plants in the 1920s and 1930s. The "Disposall," as developed and manufactured for household use by General Electric beginning in 1935, was a modified version of these earlier devices. In 1923 at Lebanon, Pennsylvania, C. R. Fox and W. S. Davis made the first attempt to grind garbage and discharge it into the sewers, to be disposed of at a sewage plant. Other municipal experiments followed in 1929 by Morris M. Cohn and General Electric's Engineering Department in Schenectady, New York; in 1933 by C. E. Keefer in Baltimore; in 1934 by Frank J. McDevitt in St. Louis; and in 1935 by C. K. Calvert in Indianapolis. In each instance, the investigators reported favorably on the ability of sewage-treatment processes to handle the additional load of garbage solids.[10]

No single individual is more responsible for encouraging the disposer's development for home use and for convincing public works officials and public health officers of its merits than Morris M. Cohn, who held a variety of important posts in Schenectady from 1921 to 1952 and served as editor of *Wastes Engineering* for at least fifteen years.[11] Born in Schenectady in 1898, Cohn earned bachelor's and master's degrees in civil engineering at Union College, and in 1952 his alma mater awarded him an honorary doctorate. His first position with

---

Transport: Historical Perspectives on Policy Issues (Beverly Hills, Calif., 1980), pp. 201–34. See also A. E. Kennelly, "Electricity in the Household," *Scribner's Magazine* 7 (January 1890): 102–15; and Nathan Rosenberg, "Technological Interdependence in the American Economy," *Technology and Culture* 20 (January 1979): 47–50. For tables showing increased use of various home comforts over time, consult Stanley Lebergott, *The American Economy: Income, Wealth, and Want* (Princeton, N.J., 1976). And for a discussion of how the home was connected to the surrounding community through a network of power and service lines, see chap. 7, "The Heart of the Home," in David P. Handlin, *The American Home: Architecture and Society, 1815–1915* (Boston, 1979), pp. 452–89.

[10] Mark B. Owen, "Grinding as a Process in Garbage Disposal," *Public Works Engineers' Yearbook* (1936): 118–33; Morris M. Cohn, "Recent Developments in Dual Disposal," *Sewage & Industrial Wastes* 23 (January 1951): 54–55; J. H. Powers, "The Disposall . . . Now in Military Service on Land and Also at Sea," *General Electric Review* 46 (March 1943): 175–77; William S. Foster, retired engineering editor of *American City*, to Suellen Hoy, January 25, 1983.

[11] During the 1930s, this journal was known as *Municipal Sanitation*, in the 1940s as *Sewage Works Engineering and Municipal Sanitation*, in the 1950s as *Sewage and Industrial Wastes Engineering*, and finally, in the 1960s, as *Wastes Engineering*. Cohn's obituary in the *New York Times*, December 10, 1975, incorrectly reported that Cohn had been editor of three magazines; actually he had been editor of a magazine that changed names three times during his tenure.

Schenectady in 1921 was as a sanitary chemist with the Bureau of Sewage. Four years later he became superintendent of the bureau, then sanitary engineer in the Department of Public Service, director of environmental sanitation in the Department of Health, and finally city manager in 1952. Until his death in 1975, he remained actively involved in state and regional engineering and health organizations as well as national groups such as the American Society of Civil Engineers, American Public Works Association, National Society of Professional Engineers, and American Public Health Association. Besides his efforts on behalf of the disposer, Cohn is most remembered by his colleagues for three books, *Sewers for Growing America* (1966), *The Pollution Fighters: A History of Environmental Engineering in New York State* (1973), and *By the Magic of Chemistry: Pipe Lines for Progress* (1975).

Although few descriptions exist of the exchanges that took place between engineers in General Electric's Schenectady laboratory and Cohn, there is little doubt that they occurred regularly.[12] Cohn describes the first visit around 1929 or 1930 of "two research men with inquiring minds, spurred on by a president of a great electrical firm who saw no reason why electricity could not replace the garbage can, just as the vacuum sweeper had replaced the broom. . . ." They came, according to Cohn, "to see what sewage looked like" and to find out whether garbage could be "put down the sewer." Well aware of the 1923 experiments conducted in Lebanon, Pennsylvania, Cohn explained that "garbage could go down the sewer if it were converted into sewage by maceration." By 1933 General Electric had created a unit "ready for test"; two years later the company began manufacturing and selling its "Disposall."[13]

Few specifics are known of the research and development undertaken in Schenectady and elsewhere between the first visit recorded by Cohn and the beginning of commercial sales in 1935. What is known is that early in the 1930s General Electric President Gerard Swope initiated an "intra-company competition" for the best disposal unit design. The Fort Wayne and Schenectady Works laboratories both submitted designs. The Fort Wayne group, which had cooperated with the com-

---

[12]Former associates and professional colleagues vividly recall Cohn's involvement with General Electric engineers during the early 1930s. Foster to Hoy, January 25 and March 28, 1983; Edward J. Cleary, former editor of *Engineering News-Record*, to Suellen Hoy, March 5, 1983; conversation between Robert D. Bugher, executive director of the American Public Works Association, and Suellen Hoy, March 24, 1983. On copies of resumés found in the files at the headquarters of the American Public Works Association in Chicago and of the American Society of Civil Engineers in New York, Cohn listed his service as consultant to General Electric from 1933 to 1939.

[13]Cohn, "Recent Developments in Dual Disposal" (n. 10 above), pp. 54–55.

pany's Plumbing and Testing Laboratory in Chicago, won the competition and gave special credit to engineer J. H. Powers.[14] During the same period, Cohn not only instructed some of his employees to investigate the kinds and condition of garbage found in the city's sewage but also began an experiment in his own home. For months he ground varying amounts and types of food wastes in a meat grinder, disposed of it in the toilet drain, tracked its movement through the plumbing and sewer systems, and reported his findings to his colleagues at General Electric and in other cities. In the October and November 1934 issues of *Municipal Sanitation*, he published the first of many articles that would explain the benefits of what he and others were calling "dual disposal."[15]

Throughout the 1930s and 1940s, Cohn contended that it was not merely "wishful thinking" to devise a process to eliminate "the foul garbage can from the American scene," for sanitary engineering had already "wiped out the blot of the nauseating backhouse."[16] He demonstrated again and again the similarities in character and composition of sewage and shredded garbage and argued that, because they are so much alike, "suitably designed sewers" could perform "two vital sanitary disposal functions at one and the same time."[17] He also believed that in most instances "the cost of handling sewage and garbage as one waste, through one sewer system and in one plant," would be cheaper than "handling the two wastes separately."[18] And Cohn was convinced beyond a single doubt that if Americans—particularly housewives—

[14]George Wise, historian for General Electric Company, to Suellen Hoy, February 2, 1983.

[15]Cohn, "Recent Developments in Dual Disposal" (n. 10 above), p. 55; and Morris M. Cohn, "Like Sweeping Back the Waves . . . It Cannot Be Done," *Wastes Engineering* 32 (November 1961): editorial page. In another article Cohn explained in detail how he placed "all waste food from his home into the sanitary sewer, with the permission of the City." He reported that, after months of use and a thorough examination, "the house drain was free from deposition" as was "the sewer at the first manhole below the lateral." Cohn, "The Combined Collection and Disposal of Sewage and Food Wastes," *Sewage Works Journal* 7 (January 1935): 49.

[16]Morris M. Cohn, "Eliminating Waste Food Electrically—a Fact, Not a Fad," *Plumbing and Heating Journal* 119 (September 1948): 46.

[17]Morris M. Cohn, *Sewers for Growing America* (Valley Forge, Pa., 1966), p. 54.

[18]Cohn, "Eliminating Waste Food Electrically" (n. 16 above), p. 50. For an important discussion of costs related to the earlier adoption of the water-carriage system of wastewater removal, see Joel A. Tarr and Francis C. McMichael, "The Evolution of Wastewater Technology and the Development of State Regulation: A Retrospective Analysis," in Joel A. Tarr, ed., *Retrospective Technology Assessment—1976* (San Francisco, 1977), pp. 179–83. See also Joel A. Tarr, James McCurley III, Francis C. McMichael, and Terry Yosie, "Water and Wastes: A Retrospective Assessment of Wastewater Technology in the United States, 1800–1932," *Technology and Culture* 25 (April 1984): 226–63.

were freed from the garbage can "the health, comfort, convenience, and the nicety of the art of living" would be advanced.[19]

But not everyone in public works and public health circles agreed with Cohn. In fact, in many quarters, the thought of mixing sewage and garbage and disposing of them simultaneously was considered "preposterous." Then, when it was successfully demonstrated that sewage and food wastes were "one and the same" and that dual disposal was "a reasonable, feasible process," doubters frequently argued that the practice was undesirable because "sewers would be clogged and the sewage plant processes upset."[20] There also arose a fear that the widespread use of the disposer would overload existing facilities.[21]

Cohn's most critical and articulate opponents were several public health professionals employed by New Jersey—Harry P. Croft, chief, and Robert R. Shaw, principal engineer of the Bureau of Engineering and Sanitation in the New Jersey Department of Health; and Willem Rudolfs, chief of the Department of Water and Sewage at the New Jersey Agricultural Experiment Station and professor of sanitary engineering at Rutgers University. While they did not deny that well-designed and -constructed public sewers were capable of conveying ground garbage, they said that in New Jersey more than 75 percent of the municipal sewage treatment plants were already inadequate and that this inadequacy would be "intensified greatly by the addition of ground garbage to the sewers."[22] They openly questioned what they called the "faulty" published data on the volume and strength characteristics of ground garbage and pointed out that it would require at least a 100 percent increase in sludge-digestion capacity and a 30 percent increase in oxidation-unit capacity at treatment plants if the use of disposers became widespread.[23] And, since ground garbage settles quickly, they stated that it could result in larger deposits of putrescible matter in plant grit chambers. They argued finally that

[19]Cohn, "Eliminating Waste Food Electrically" (n. 16 above), p. 46. For a fine description of late-19th-century "townsite consciousness" which included "freedom from organic wastes, stagnant water, ground moisture, and human congestion," see Jon A. Peterson, "The Impact of Sanitary Reform upon American Urban Planning, 1840–1890," *Journal of Social History* 13 (Fall 1979): 91–94.

[20]Morris M. Cohn, "Kitchen Waste Grinders—in the Specification Stage . . . an Editorial," *Sewage Works Engineering and Municipal Sanitation* 20 (January 1949): editorial page.

[21]"Dual Disposal of Garbage and Sewage Poses Problems for Treatment Plants," *Engineering News-Record* 136 (March 28, 1946): 12.

[22]Harry P. Croft and Robert S. Shaw, "The Disposal of Ground Garbage in Sewerage Systems," *Public Health News* 29 (July 1948): 221–23 (quotation found on page 221); idem, "Kitchen Garbage Disposal Means Sewage-Plant Expansion," *American City* 63 (November 1948): 110–11.

[23]"Dual Disposal of Garbage and Sewage" (n. 21 above), p. 12.

home garbage grinders represented "a creeping menace to stream pollution" and "an additional investment of public funds in plant expansion" at a time "when satisfactory means of collecting garbage with other refuse already exist."[24]

Regarding treatment-plant capacity, Cohn contended that dual disposal meant total sewage flow would increase "about 1 to 2 gallons per capita per day" or 1 to 2 percent, hence "any treatment works having sufficient 'cushion' capacity" could handle this nominal increase in plant loading. He also observed that, if a treatment plant were already inadequate, it should be enlarged to meet current and future demands.[25] While regarding the points made by the New Jersey public health officials as well taken, an *American City* editorial agreed with Cohn: although disposers had been installed in varying numbers in various communities for over a decade, there was not "a single sewage-treatment plant anywhere" that could "trace any appreciable amount of its load to kitchen grinders." If responsible authorities in New Jersey admitted that 75 percent of their sewage-treatment facilities were overloaded, the state had "a stream sanitation problem needing immediate attention." The editorial then suggested that the problem would be solved by requiring "construction of treatment facilities adequate for present needs, not banning a useful household device" whose effect on sewage treatment would be "negligible for years to come."[26]

During the early years of World War II, when the debate over dual disposal reached full strength, production of the home grinder came to a complete halt. In response, however, to requests from the nation's armed forces (particularly the navy) for a larger unit, General Electric began producing a commercial "Disposall" and in the process refined the home version. The basic unit consisted of a control element, cylindrical waste-receiving chamber, grinding or rotating plate at the base, strainer, pump, and motor. During the war years, General Electric added a unique device called the "water flow interlock." Installed in the cold-water pipe to the sink's faucet, the device was electrically connected in series with the control switch and responded only to the flow of water. The interlock prevented operation until the faucet had been turned on and there was a sufficient supply of cold water to flush waste particles through the plumbing drain line. By adding this mechanism

[24]Croft and Shaw, "Kitchen Garbage Disposal" (n. 22 above), pp. 110–11.
[25]Cohn also reported that "the suspended solids in the mixed flow would be approximately doubled" and "the B.O.D. [biochemical oxygen demand] . . . increased from 15 to 30 per cent." See "Dual Disposal of Garbage and Sewage" (n. 21 above), p. 12; "Dual Disposal of Garbage and Sewage," *Water & Sewage Works* 93 (April 1946): 157–58.
[26]"Kitchen Grinders—a 'Creeping Menace,'" *American City* 63 (November 1948): 11.

to the basic unit, General Electric responded directly to critics who were arguing that the grease found in ground garbage would clog sewers. Cold water solidified the grease, and the Disposall's high-speed grinding and aeration action homogenized the particles into buoyant, noncongealing forms that prevented clogging.[27]

Although wartime exigencies had temporarily stopped the sale of home disposal units, at the war's end General Electric had ready a simpler product that was more efficient and less noisy. When redesigning the Disposall, company engineers had not only added the water-flow interlock but had also eliminated sixty-one parts, reducing the total number from 198 to 137. The disposer's weight and height of approximately 75 pounds and 20 inches were also reduced by 10 pounds and 4 inches, respectively. Yet, despite smaller dimensions, waste storage was increased by 11 cubic inches, the vibration and noise diminished through the use of neoprene resilient gaskets, and the shredding made more effective by means of improved impellers.[28]

* * *

The availability of a better appliance and an improved economy at the conclusion of World War II thrust to center stage the debate over the future of the kitchen garbage disposer. In a March 1947 editorial in *Sewage Works Engineering*, Cohn reported that numerous United States cities were seriously considering "the economic and engineering desirability of disposing of all community garbage via the sanitary sewer system." He stated that it would be only "a matter of time" until some community undertook "a program of completely eliminating garbage collections and substituting disposal of ground wastes" into their sewers. If municipalities remained uninvolved, "the home grinding process" would "develop slowly"; but, if a community made "home grinding a city-sponsored project," the conversion from surface to underground collection and disposal would occur "within a few years." Cohn, of course, hoped for the latter.[29]

[27]Powers (n. 10 above), pp. 175–77; R. N. Clark and Arthur Heifetz, "The Army Tries Garbage Disposal by Grinding," *Public Works* 74 (March 1943): 21, 38; Foster to Hoy, March 28, 1983; Morris M. Cohn, "Effect of Food Wastes on Sewers and Sewage Treatment," *Sewage Works Journal* 18 (May 1946): 479–80.

[28]"Thorough Redesign Job Eliminates 61 Parts," *Product Engineering* 12 (November 1941): 580–81. Later, with the introduction of plastics, total weights of garbage disposal units often ranged "from 23 to 42 lbs" and they were anywhere "from 10¾ to 15⅝ inches long." See "Garbage Disposal Unit," *Modern Plastics* 38 (May 1961): 171; and Herbert O. Johansen, "The Controversial Garbage Disposer," *Popular Science* 174 (June 1959): 147.

[29]Morris M. Cohn, "Untouched by Human Hands," *Sewage Works Engineering and Municipal Sanitation* 18 (March 1947): editorial page.

In response, an *American Journal of Public Health* editorial raised two questions: "What will the process accomplish for the public health?" and "What will it cost?" Taking up the second question first, the editorial said that the cost of the kitchen disposal unit was high but that "its capital cost and maintenance must be balanced against the cost of collection of garbage and its transportation to a point of final disposal." Responding to the most important question—the grinder's effect on public health—the American Public Health Association's journal stated for the first time that "from the standpoint of the sanitarian" there were "great advantages" to dual disposal "even if the cost is the same or slightly greater." In conclusion, the editorial predicted that the garbage can would "ultimately follow the privy along the same road" and become "an anachronism" in urban communities.[30]

Following the APHA's acknowledgment of the disposer's numerous health benefits, city officials and public works administrators across the country who had long been troubled by costly yet inadequate refuse collection and disposal practices began to consider seriously how the disposer might improve their operations and the well-being of the communities they served. For decades municipal officials had been acutely aware of the threat of garbage to the public health. While residents of America's earliest towns regarded the accumulation of garbage as a nuisance or an annoyance and late-19th-century urbanites saw it as a health hazard, turn-of-the-century municipal engineers and sanitarians recognized it as part of a much larger environmental concern as well. For this reason, they monitored community sanitation practices, compiled statistical data, developed procedures for street cleaning and refuse collection and disposal, designed sewer and drainage systems, and promoted sound sanitary practices and epidemic-control programs.[31]

But even after years of professional investigation and experimentation, refuse collection and disposal remained difficult and costly municipal problems. The efficiency of methods depended largely on the volume of wastes a city had to remove. And, by world standards, the United States produced exceptionally large quantities of wastes as diverse as they were plentiful.[32] In the throwaway society of postwar

[30]"The Kitchen Garbage Grinder (Editorial)," *American Journal of Public Health* 37 (May 1947): 574.
[31]For a brief historical discussion of the subject, consult the chapter on "Solid Wastes" in Ellis L. Armstrong, Michael C. Robinson, and Suellen M. Hoy, eds., *History of Public Works in the United States, 1776–1976* (Chicago, 1976), pp. 431–56; for a fuller treatment, see Martin V. Melosi, *Garbage in the Cities: Refuse, Reform, and the Environment, 1880–1980* (College Station, Tex., 1981).
[32]Between 1888 and 1913, the annual per capita weight of mixed refuse for fourteen

America, during which time the packaging industry flourished, in addition to organic wastes—garbage, manure, human excrement, and dead animals—there were paper, plastics, cans, ashes, street sweepings, and yard trimmings.[33] Some wastes were especially troublesome, particularly in densely populated areas, because they decompose rapidly. Left unattended in the kitchen, outside the back door, or in the alley, garbage is not only unsightly and the source of offensive odors but is also a breeding ground for flies and an attraction to rats. It is not surprising, then, that public health and public works officials regularly examined new ways of collecting and disposing of garbage. If they had neglected to do so, they would have failed to address a major environmental challenge resulting from the twin forces of urbanization and industrialization.

According to a survey of state departments of health conducted by *American City* in 1948, most health departments seemed to agree with the position taken by the American Public Health Association a year earlier. Twenty-nine of forty-eight state health departments responded, only seven expressing a fear that garbage grinders represented "a dangerous factor in the maintenance of adequate sewage facilities." The remainder were not apprehensive. They generally believed that the grinder's use was neither sufficiently widespread nor soon about "to warrant concern," that an ordinance banning it would be "impractical and probably more expensive to enforce than the cost of the added sewage facilities," that the grinder was "a step forward in public sanitation, since it helps solve fly and rat problems," that any city able to afford grinders on a large scale "certainly should be able to afford adequate sewage treatment," and that those cities with sewer service charges should adjust them "to compensate for the added solids load."[34]

During the annual meeting of the American Public Works Association in October 1948, Mark B. Owen, a former president of the association and an expert in the field of sewage treatment and disposal, stated

---

American cities was reported as 860 pounds, sometimes even higher. Comparisons with several European cities disclosed that eight English cities generated 450 pounds per capita and that seventy-seven German cities produced 319 pounds per capita. See Rudolph Hering and Samuel A. Greeley, *Collection and Disposal of Municipal Refuse* (New York, 1921), p. 70.

[33]In 1920 Americans individually produced an average of 2.8 pounds of solid wastes daily; in 1975 they produced about 6 pounds. With increased packaging in the postwar era, the ratio of paper in municipal solid wastes rose almost 50 percent. See Armstrong, Robinson, and Hoy (n. 31 above), p. 431.

[34]"What Other State Departments of Health Think about Kitchen Grinders," *American City* 63 (November 1948): 111.

unequivocally that "garbage grinding in the home is with us to stay."[35] During the 1930s, while commissioner of public works and engineering in Dearborn, Michigan, Owen had conducted a series of experiments in an attempt to solve that community's sewage disposal problems. He eventually designed an innovative treatment plant where sewage was chemically and mechanically processed into a solid and then incinerated to a clean ash.[36] As early as 1936 Owen had predicted that the home disposal unit would some day "be available at a price easily within the reach and purse of the average homeowner" and "be almost as commonly used as electric refrigerators."[37] By the late 1940s he was as convinced as Cohn that it was simply a matter of time.

Cost, more than any other factor, prevented widespread adoption of the disposer during the immediate postwar years. Prior to World War II, when General Electric was the sole manufacturer, it was estimated that there were 175,000 units in use in American kitchens; by the end of 1948, when there were seventeen companies producing the appliance, approximately 200,000 units were being installed annually. The price of individual units varied from $75 to $135, and the installation cost ranged from $20 to $150 in an old home and was about $10 in a new home.[38] For a municipality that permitted the disposal of ground garbage through the sewers, the costs depended on local conditions and practices and thus varied from place to place. In an important summary article on the effect of ground garbage on sewerage systems in the February 1948 issue of *American City*, engineering editor William S. Foster pointed out that municipal refuse collection costs could be reduced by altering the customary practice of collecting garbage two or three times each week and initiating a single pickup.[39]

*   *   *

[35]Mark B. Owen, "Refuse Disposal—Old and New," *Proceedings of the 1948 Public Works Congress* (1948): 23.
[36]Anne Spray, "People in Public Works: Mark Owen," *APWA Reporter* 45 (September 1978): 4–5.
[37]Owen, "Grinding as a Process" (n. 10 above), p. 129.
[38]On the number of companies manufacturing grinders by 1949, see Mark B. Owen, "The Future of Home Garbage Grinders," *Water & Sewage Works* 96 (May 1949): 189. For data on costs of individual units and installation fees, see "What Garbage Grinding Costs the Individual Householder," *American City* 63 (June 1948): 146.
[39]William S. Foster, "Ground Garbage: What Is Its Effect on the Sewerage System," *American City* 63 (February 1948): 87. In a question-and-answer format, Foster "review[ed] the record to answer questions most frequently raised in this development in municipal sanitation" (ibid., pp. 85–87). The cost of collecting solid wastes is largely determined by the amount of equipment and labor required, which in turn is influenced by the frequency of the collection. Although the garbage disposer did not significantly reduce the amount of garbage/rubbish to be collected, its widespread use made it possible

In February 1950 the residents of Jasper, Indiana, population 6,800, voted to require the installation of home garbage disposers. On February 15 the local (county) newspaper announced this decision (a first for an American community) in a banner headline that read: "Garbage Man Gets Walking Papers in Jasper." An outbreak of cholera among garbage-fed hogs in the vicinity of Jasper in 1947, followed two years later by a polio epidemic, encouraged such drastic action. But the forceful leadership of a young and energetic mayor as well as a precedent-setting decision by the Indiana legislature in March 1949 were also responsible for ousting the garbage man and his unsavory can.[40]

Jasper is located approximately 120 miles southwest of Indianapolis, on the Patoka River, which flows westward and discharges into the Wabash River. In 1950, the town had approximately 1,200 homes, of which 90 percent were connected to municipal sewers. Because Jasper's sewage disposal practices were contributing to the pollution of the Patoka River, the Indiana Stream Pollution Control Board had issued preliminary and final abatement orders in August and December 1945. The city then hired the Indianapolis engineering firm of Couch and Kulin, Inc., to study Jasper's sewage treatment needs. The preliminary report proposed a million-gallon-per-day activated sludge plant, with the necessary intercepting sewers; it also recommended additional trunk, relief, and lateral sewers to reduce overloading in the existing system. In September 1948 the Stream Pollution Control Board and the Indiana State Board of Health approved the overall plan and specifications. However, while the project was under consideration, the hog cholera had broken out and Jasper was subsequently unable to find contractors to handle its garbage at a reasonable cost. Confronted with this critical problem, Mayor Herbert E. Thyen began investigating alternative disposal methods—individual home grinders, central grinding station, and sanitary landfill.[41]

Following Thyen's advice, the city council asked the engineering firm of Couch and Kulin, already in its employ, to prepare cost data for

---

to store other types of waste for longer periods without creating health problems. This fact permitted reduced frequency and costs of collection.

[40]"Garbage Man Gets Walking Papers in Jasper," *Daily Herald*, February 15, 1950; "Grind Your Own Refuse," *Newsweek*, February 27, 1950, p. 66; "Electricity Ousts Garbage Man and Unsavory Garbage Can," *Water & Sewage Works* 97 (April 1950): 52; Sylvia Wright, "No More Garbage in This Town," *McCall's*, August 1950, p. 86; "Indiana Legislation on Garbage Grinders," *American City* 64 (July 1949): 17.

[41]L. I. Couch and H. J. Kulin, "Municipal Garbage Disposal by Household Grinders at Jasper, Indiana," *Sewage and Industrial Wastes* 22 (September 1950): 1138–46; L. I. Couch, "A Kitchen Grinder in Every Home," *American City* 65 (May 1950): 112–14.

each of the proposed methods. The final estimates on total annual cost included the original investment and interest as well as depreciation, maintenance, and operation; they figured as follows: $11,805, home grinders (66¢ per family per month); $11,742, central grinding station (65¢ per family per month); and $10,930, sanitary landfill (61¢ per family per month). Even though the household grinder would be slightly more expensive, the city administration expressed a preference for it, stating that the grinder would not only eliminate the garbage can but would also remove garbage trucks from Jasper's streets and narrow alleys and would improve the community's appearance and health.[42]

When the city administration announced that it favored the home disposal unit, plans for a new sewage treatment plant had already been approved, but no construction had begun. The mayor directed the engineers to adjust the plans as necessary to ensure that the new plant would be able to treat ground garbage from all of Jasper's homes. Accordingly, the engineers added one aeration unit, two sludge-digestion tanks, and 12,000 square feet of sludge-drying beds to the plant's original design. The Stream Pollution Control Board and the State Board of Health approved the revised plans on March 10, 1949, and construction began two months later.[43]

During the period in which the plans for the sewage treatment plant were being redrawn, the mayor and city council undertook a vigorous campaign to win public acceptance of the proposed method of garbage disposal. They first secured the backing of the leaders of the largest civic organizations; and then, as a united front, they wrote newspaper articles, spoke before community groups of all kinds, conducted public demonstrations of disposers, and went from door to door promoting the idea. The mayor also enlisted the support of his fellow townsmen, state senator Leo Stemle and state representative Frank Seng, in his effort to secure authority from the state legislature to issue revenue bonds to meet the costs of purchasing and installing grinders in residences throughout the town.[44]

On March 7, 1949, the Indiana State Legislature passed a bill which gave every city and town with an adequate sewage treatment plant "power to acquire, install, equip, own, operate and maintain . . . a garbage disposal system consisting of garbage grinders to be installed in private residences, business places or any other building within or

---

[42]Ibid. Complete cost estimates appear in a chart in Couch and Kulin (n. 41 above), p. 1139.

[43]Couch and Kulin, pp. 1138–46.

[44]Ibid.

without the city or town, with the consent of the owners. . . ."[45] Under
the provisions of the act, a municipality could issue revenue bonds to
pay the costs of purchase, installation, and upkeep in all houses or
other buildings whose owners desired such service; set just and equitable charges or rates to be paid by the equipment's users; and discon-
tinue garbage collection and disposal by other methods. The *American
Journal of Public Health* hailed this action as "a courageous and imaginative step . . . to advance scientific sanitation."[46] At the conclusion of an
editorial entitled "Home Grinders Become a Public Utility" in *Sewage
Works Engineering*, Cohn declared that Indiana and Jasper deserved
"the applause of the sanitary engineering profession for . . . approving
a new health and comfort achievement and setting up sound fiscal
practices for making this dual disposal process a self-liquidating
utility."[47]

Following passage of the state legislation, the city set the bidding date
for December 6, 1949, and asked the consulting engineering firm of
Couch and Kulin to prepare the specifications and proposal forms.
The base proposal called for a price on an installed unit with a water-
flow interlock device. In drafting the specifications, the engineers
attempted to give some indication of the difficulties that might be
encountered in installing disposers. They conducted a survey of potential users (about 1,400) and learned that approximately 60 percent of
the total number of sinks had drain openings of less than 3½ inches,
which meant they would have to be enlarged. Couch and Kulin also
discovered that about 80 percent of the sinks were porcelain-enamel
cast iron, 10 percent porcelain-enamel steel, 6 percent vitreous china,
and 4 percent stainless steel. This information was especially important
since the specifications held the contractor liable for any damage done
to the sinks in the process of enlarging the drains. Another condition of
the specifications required that all bidders be prepared to present a
complete demonstration of their appliances.[48]

Eighteen prospective bidders requested specifications and proposal
packets when the material was released thirty days before the bidding

[45]*Laws of the State of Indiana: Passed at the Eighty-sixth Regular Session of the General
Assembly, Begun on the Sixth Day of January, A.D. 1949* (Indianapolis, 1949), p. 221.

[46]"Garbage Grinders—a Public Utility (Editorial)," *American Journal of Public Health* 39
(September 1949): 1180.

[47]Morris M. Cohn, "Home Grinders Become a Public Utility," *Sewage Works Engineering
and Municipal Sanitation* 20 (May 1949): editorial page.

[48]B. A. Poole and G. K. Erganian, "Public Health Benefits from the Disposal of
Garbage in Sewers," *American Journal of Public Health* 41 (September 1951): 1108; Couch,
"A Kitchen Grinder in Every Home" (n. 41 above), p. 114; and Couch and Kulin,
"Municipal Garbage Disposal" (n. 41 above), pp. 42–43.

date. In the end, the city received bids from only six manufacturers and awarded a contract to the General Electric Company, which agreed to scale down its price from $125 (retail and installed) to $75. The city then set August 1, 1950, as the date when the electric "Disposall" would take over the work previously performed by a private scavenger under contract with the city.[49]

Although the city council did not require Jasper residents to purchase grinders, it not only discontinued public garbage collection as of August 1 but also prohibited the storage of garbage in outside cans. A few points were designated within the city where garbage could be disposed of, but the city ordinance made it illegal for any person to make a business of collecting or transporting garbage without first obtaining a permit. And a permit of this kind could be secured only after the collection vehicle and proposed method of disposal were approved by the local health officer.[50] Thus, Jasper assumed almost complete responsibility for the collection and disposal of the town's garbage.

Once Jasper's citizens learned of the agreement with General Electric, they decided against issuing revenue bonds to finance the project. To guarantee its successful completion, the mayor asked that at least half of the city's homeowners file applications with the Board of Public Works and Safety signifying their intention to install disposers. They were also requested to make a deposit on the cost of the unit and to pay the remainder prior to installation. The city placed the money collected in this fashion into a trust fund from which it paid GE for its work as it progressed. For those householders unable to pay the required $75, local banks made short-term, low-interest loans. In this way, Jasper incurred no financial obligations.[51]

Four plumbing and two electrical teams installed the new Disposall units. Gordon H. Roney, commercial engineer for GE and developer of an effective sink-boring tool, supervised the project. He reported that the plumbers and electricians found their major problem to be numerous instances of amateur or defective wiring. Thus, the discov-

---

[49]Couch and Kulin, "Municipal Garbage Disposal" (n. 41 above), pp. 42–43. General Electric agreed to furnish grinders at a unit price of $36.69 each and to furnish and install units at a cost of $74.17 per grinder, including the interlock device.

[50]B. A. Poole and George Erganian, "Recent Developments in Dual Disposal—Discussion," *Sewage and Industrial Wastes* 23 (March 1951): 278; Poole and Erganian, "Public Health Benefits" (n. 48 above), pp. 1107–8; "Garbage Collections Cease; Home Grinders to Be Installed," *Public Works* 81 (March 1950): 73. The collection of other garbage, largely rubbish and trash, continued on a once-a-week basis.

[51]Couch and Kulin, "Municipal Garbage Disposal" (n. 41 above), pp. 40–41; Poole and Erganian, "Public Health Benefits" (n. 48 above), p. 1108.

ery of many electrical fire hazards proved an unanticipated benefit. By the end of October 1950, nearly 800 grinders had been installed in Jasper.[52]

After part of this project had been completed, the United States Public Health Service and the Indiana State Board of Health decided to undertake a study of "the effects of these installations on the environmental sanitation" of Jasper.[53] In their investigation, covering the period from March 1950 to October 1951, they found that the grinders caused "no noticeable per capita increase in residential water consumption" and that ground garbage created "no deleterious effect on the sewers."[54] Although the raw sewage was stronger in suspended solids and in biochemical oxygen demand, it posed no problem to the recently constructed treatment plant.[55] On the subject of flies and rodents, the study indicated that "the lower average number of flies per grill count" in Jasper, when compared with the nearby control town of Huntingburg, was the result of the former's improved garbage-handling practices.[56] But the study also showed that the open dump owned by the city—where it deposited rubbish and where garbage was deposited by homeowners and merchants who did not own disposers—was the cause of a major problem with flies and rodents. The city, for its part, acknowledged the problem and indicated that, once all householders had ample opportunity to install grinders, it would rigidly enforce the local ordinance.[57]

Professional engineers directly involved in Jasper's experiment did not recommend it as "the solution to garbage disposal problems for all communities."[58] Instead they urged careful study of each situation and

[52]Poole and Erganian, p. 1109. By October 1951 over 900 household grinders were in use, "serving 75% of the community's population." See "Jasper, Ind., Measures Its Garbage-Grinder Sanitation Progress," *American City* 68 (February 1953): 108.

[53]U.S. Public Health Service, *Effects of Community-Wide Installation of Household Garbage-Grinders on Environmental Sanitation* (Washington, D.C., 1952), p. v. The authors of this booklet, no. 224 in the Public Health Service Publication Series, were George K. Erganian and Walter G. Belter, sanitary engineers on the staff of the Indiana State Board of Health, and Ralph C. Graber, senior sanitary engineer of the United States Public Health Service.

[54]Ibid., p. 34.

[55]Ibid., pp. 34–35.

[56]Ibid., p. 36.

[57]Ibid. See also Poole and Erganian, "Public Health Benefits" (n. 48 above), p. 1110.

[58]Frank D. Wraight (chief, Sewage Disposal Section, Indiana State Board of Health), "Community-Wide Installation of Household Garbage Grinders a Success at Jasper, Indiana." Paper presented at a "Local Government Conference on Refuse Disposal Methods," University of Pittsburgh, April 22–23, 1954 (from "Garbage Grinders" file in headquarters of American Public Works Association, Chicago).

stressed Jasper's unique conditions. L. I. Couch, president of the consulting engineering firm employed by the city from the project's beginning, emphasized Jasper's public ownership of all utilities as well as its diversified and stable economy. While many residents were engaged in farming, most others worked in one of the city's eighteen manufacturing firms (of wood products), the majority of which were owned by Jasper residents. Couch and others also pointed out that over 92 percent of the homes in the middle-class community were owned by their occupants. And, since a private scavenger had been employed by the city prior to the cholera outbreak, it had made no previous investment in garbage-collection equipment. Not unlike the cautious position taken by these engineers, the American Public Health Association advised that the experiment "should be watched with keen interest by health authorities in other states."[59]

*   *   *

Given the widespread publicity of Jasper's mass installation of "food-waste disposers,"[60] public officials in other cities and states could not help but take notice—some even took action. Early in 1951 a committee of the Federation of Civic Associations in Dearborn, Michigan, a community of 95,000, invited several of Jasper's public officials to visit and explain the considerations that led to their unusual experiment. Following their presentation and additional study, the committee recommended enactment of an ordinance calling for the installation of disposal units in all new homes and food-handling establishments. Such an ordinance was passed in September 1951, and by 1954 over 5,000 units were in use. Henry A. Hoxie, Dearborn's public works director, reported that this development had resulted in weekly savings of $1,500. For that reason and because the sewage treatment plant had so little difficulty handling the additional load, he urged the enactment of a second ordinance which would set "a time limit in

[59]Couch, "A Kitchen Grinder in Every Home" (n. 41 above), p. 113; U.S. Public Health Service (n. 53 above), p. 1; Frank D. Wraight, "Garbage Grinder Experiences, Jasper, Indiana," *Sewage and Industrial Wastes* 28 (January 1955): 44, 48; n. 46 above.

[60]Between 1945 and 1950, "grinders" became more widely known as "food waste disposers." Foster and Kenneth S. Watson (former manager of General Electric's Water Management Lab in Louisville, Kentucky, and later of General Electric's Research and Development Center in Schenectady, N.Y.) explained that with this more "palatable name" the product was easier to sell. It was regularly pointed out in advertisements that food wastes disposed of in an electric grinding unit did not even become garbage! Foster to Hoy, January 25, 1983; Kenneth S. Watson to Suellen Hoy (telephone conversation), April 14, 1983. See also "The Case for Food Waste Disposers!" *Domestic Engineering* 176 (November 1950): 102.

various districts for the universal installation of garbage disposal units."[61]

Dearborn was not the only community to follow Jasper's lead. In 1951, for example, the city councils of two other small Midwestern communities demonstrated their preference for the disposal of garbage through grinding. In South Euclid, Ohio, the city council passed an ordinance similar to that enacted in Dearborn; it required the installation of disposers in all new residences. The city council in Herrin, Illinois, encouraged the use of disposers by becoming, in effect, the local distributor for General Electric. The company sold units ($60 each) directly to the city; local electricans and plumbers installed them ($39.50 each); and banks offered time-payment plans which operated through the city's water department (down payment of $9.95, $4.18 monthly).[62]

Although developments in South Euclid, Herrin, and elsewhere were newsworthy, they were insignificant compared either with Jasper's initial experiment or with a subsequent campaign in Detroit.[63] In 1955, Detroit's Mayor Albert E. Cobo launched a crusade to make that city—which had a population of 2 million—"garbage free." Cobo's first step was to create a "Detroit Committee for a Garbage-Free City," headed by the public works director and made up of civic leaders, disposer manufacturers, and plumbers. Although he advocated using disposal units, Cobo insisted that the committee's primary purpose was not to sell appliances but to promote a sanitation philosophy that would signify a new "quality of life" for the community. Proud that Detroit was "the first city of its size to undertake such a program," he also expressed pleasure in government and industry's support of the project.[64]

Whatever the mayor's purposes may actually have been, after a five-month study of Detroit's garbage-disposal practices the committee urged the placement of "a food waste disposer in virtually every home

[61]Harry A. Hoxie, "Kitchen Garbage Grinders Mean a Cleaner City," *American City* 69 (May 1954): 150–51.

[62]"Two Cities Take Action to Encourage Use of Grinders," *American City* 66 (May 1951): 99.

[63]For brief reports on similar experiments in several other cities, namely, Boulder and Aurora, Colo., Quincy, Mass., and Sherwood Hills, Wis., see "In Order to Be 'Garbage-Free,'" *American City* 75 (May 1960): 232; Herbert S. Roth, "Sixth Year with Garbage Grinders," *American City* 75 (April 1960): 162; "Garbage Outlawed in Aurora, Colo.," *Wastes Engineering* 25 (June 1954): 281; K. S. Watson and Curtis Clark, "What Ground Garbage Does to a Sewerage System," *American City* 76 (July 1961): 110. Los Angeles County was one of the earliest and largest areas to encourage use of the disposer. For a discussion of this county's experience, see A. M. Rawn, "Some Effects of Home Garbage Grinding upon Domestic Sewage," *American City* 66 (March 1951): 110–11.

[64]Albert E. Cobo, "Detroit to Be Garbage Free," *American City* 70 (October 1955): 118.

and restaurant." The committee argued forcefully that if the city were to install about 250,000 disposers they would not only rid Detroit of filthy alleys and cluttered streets but would also reduce by $1.7 million the $3.5 million spent annually on garbage collection. To achieve this goal, it sponsored radio announcements explaining the disposer's benefits, prepared television spots comparing "backbreaking old-fashioned garbage hauling with the easy, modern method," printed and distributed window posters that read "Let's Get Rid of Garbage," conducted evening sales meetings for plumbing contractors, and mailed pamphlets and brochures to potential buyers.[65] After reviewing these activities in an April 1956 editorial in *Wastes Engineering*, Morris M. Cohn applauded Detroit's "large-scale application of the grass roots demonstration of 'outlawing' garbage at Jasper, Indiana." He also observed, undoubtedly with a great deal of satisfaction, that Detroit's campaign was "the culmination of predictions made . . . twenty-two years ago, in answer to skeptics who labeled the idea of . . . the disposal of dual wastes . . . as 'dangerous,' 'ill-advised,' 'ridiculous,' and 'idle-dreaming.'"[66]

To have seen to the purchase and installation of 250,000 food waste disposers, ranging in cost from $90 to $145, in a city where there were large disparities in income and a relatively small number of individually owned, single-family dwellings would have been a remarkable feat. Even in his enthusiasm for Detroit's undertaking, Cohn had remarked that whether or not the city succeeded in achieving its goal did "not alter the importance of this sanitation development." What was significant, he contended, was that one of the largest and fastest-growing American communities had given itself "the task of becoming a 'garbage-free' city" and had made the sewage works "an important factor in the plan."[67] Thus it probably did not surprise him or others when the campaign came to an "abrupt halt" in August 1956, eighteen months after it had begun.[68] Estimates indicated that by then 50,000 homes had installed units. Glenn L. Richards, commissioner of public works, who was asked why Detroit's mayoral committee had ceased promotion of the garbage disposer, responded that the committee believed the process and product had been "thoroughly sold to the public." Moreover, the city had passed an ordinance requiring the

[65] "The Detroit Plan for a Garbage Free City," *Domestic Engineering* 186 (August 1955): 102–6.

[66] Morris M. Cohn, "And Now Detroit—Garbage-Free City!" *Wastes Engineering* 27 (April 1956): editorial page.

[67] Ibid.

[68] "Last Leaflet Marks End of City Garbage Grinder Push," *Engineering News-Record* 157 (August 30, 1956): 28.

installation of disposers in new homes. Although Richards denied that the program had ended because of complaints filed with the Better Business Bureau, the bureau reported that a large number of home-owners had become irritated with the high-handed techniques of disposer dealers—some had posed as city employees, while others had threatened passage of a new ordinance that would require universal use of an expensive model.[69]

Certainly disposer dealers and plumbing contractors, often one and the same, knew full well the opportunity afforded them by "the 'baby' in the household appliance family."[70] *Domestic Engineering* had stated its case in a two-part series beginning in November 1950. It told its readers, largely plumbing and heating contractors, that "the big boom in automatic food waste disposer sales" was on—that "individual homeowners, apartment house operators, restaurant managers, project builders and entire communities" had demonstrated "a show of enthusiasm seldom displayed for any labor-saving product."[71] In fact, the consumer had been "ahead of the dealer in accepting this new product" and had "until recently . . . to shop for a disposer rather than be sold one."[72] Projecting sales of a half-million units in 1950, *Domestic Engineering* explained succinctly the profitability of disposers: "they are simple to install, trouble-free in operation, and a high profit item when sold in quantity."[73]

Disposer dealers recognized that builders of housing developments and middle-class women were the key to the "98 percent unsold market." They also believed that with a "readily accepted product" they had only to "acquaint prospective customers with its many advantages."[74] Developers proved the easier group to reach because by selling "in quantity" dealers could offer them substantially lower prices. In Lakewood Park, a housing development 12 miles from Los Angeles where 7,200 homes were constructed and equipped with disposal units in 1950 and 1951, Given Manufacturing Company charged low installation and service costs in return for the large order of its Waste King Pulverator. According to the builders of Lakewood

[69]Ibid.

[70]"The Case for . . . Food Waste Disposers! (Part II)," *Domestic Engineering* 176 (December 1950): 106.

[71]"The Case for . . . Food Waste Disposers! (Part I)," *Domestic Engineering* 176 (November 1950): 102.

[72]"The Case for . . . Food Waste Disposers! (Part II Continued)," *Domestic Engineering* 177 (January 1951): 216.

[73]N. 71 above, p. 220.

[74]N. 70 above, p. 109; "Meet Mrs. America: She's the Key to Your Market Break-Through in Disposers," *Domestic Engineering* 202 (July 1963): 64–69; "Attract the Feminine Trade," *Domestic Engineering* 183 (February 1954): 159.

158   *Suellen Hoy*

Park, however, there were additional reasons for equipping these homes with disposers. From a survey they conducted among prospective homeowners, federal and state housing authorities, and local banking and credit institutions, they learned not only that the disposer was quickly becoming "a necessary rather than luxury item" but also that "the addition of a garbage grinder would increase the value of the house." They also consulted health and engineering professionals in Los Angeles and found out from them that the automatic disposal unit was the "most logical and sanitary method of eliminating garbage."[75]

*   *   *

Since disposer dealers and plumbing contractors had had little practice in selling their product to women, the latter presented a greater challenge than did the developers. Following World War II, with a large number of married women in the labor force and with the widespread shortage in household help, the American home underwent a final transformation and became a center of consumption rather than one of production. And women, who were themselves partly responsible for the expanding middle class in this postwar period, became major purchasers of consumer products and services. While it was apparent that many of the durable goods that had been invented to reduce the burden of household tasks frequently created new demands and heavier responsibilities, women continued to look for timesaving devices that would make their homes more comfortable, healthful, and efficient.[76] Most women, even the most affluent, were

[75]"No Garbage . . . ," *American City* 66 (September 1951): 104.

[76]On how laborsaving devices have raised the standards of household care, see especially Janet L. Wolff, *What Makes Women Buy: A Guide to Understanding and Influencing the New Woman of Today* (New York, 1958); Ruth Schwartz Cowan, "A Case Study of Technological and Social Change: The Washing Machine and the Working Wife," in Mary S. Hartman and Lois Banner, eds., *Clio's Consciousness Raised: New Perspectives on the History of Women* (New York, 1974), pp. 245–53; Ruth Schwartz Cowan, "The 'Industrial Revolution' in the Home: Household Technology and Social Change in the 20th Century," *Technology and Culture* 17 (January 1976): 1–23; Thrall (n. 8 above), pp. 175–94; and Christine E. Bose, Philip L. Bereano, and Mary Malloy, "Household Technology and the Social Construction of Housework," *Technology and Culture* 25 (January 1984): 53–82. See also David M. Katzman, *Seven Days a Week: Women and Domestic Service in Industrializing America* (New York, 1978); Starley M. Hunter, "Homemakers Name Their Home Problems," *Journal of Home Economics* 53 (June 1961): 425–27; Elizabeth Sweeney Herbert, "When the Homemaker Goes to Work," *Journal of Home Economics* 44 (April 1952): 257–59; Irene L. Muntz, "How Modern Equipment Is Changing Homemaking Practices," *Journal of Home Economics* 45 (January 1953): 20–22; and Louisa M. Comstock, "How To Get Your Household Help Back," *Better Homes & Gardens* 24 (April 1946): 27, 134–36.

The Garbage Disposer   159

doing their own housework; the processes of housework, in the post-war years, had become homogenized.[77]

Although the garbage disposer was never listed among the "glamour products" for "the modern living kitchen," it became a popular item, indeed a "must" for the "complete kitchen."[78] In October 1958 the United Industry Committee for Housing and the National Association of Home Builders sponsored a Women's Conference on Housing in Washington, D.C. During the conference, eighty-two women indicated how they would spend an imaginary $2,500 on home improvements. From a list of nineteen items with their prices ($90 for a disposer), a majority selected the half bath (forty-one votes) as their first need and the fireplace (twenty-five votes) as second. The food-waste disposer took third place with nineteen votes. Some of the items receiving ten votes or less were dishwasher (ten), dryer (six), central air conditioning (five), and den or extra bedroom (two). There were no votes for the two-car garage.[79] In 1949, in a "How's Your Home?" contest sponsored by the Home Improvement Council, the disposer again ranked third—after "more cabinets" and "clothes washer"—when 80,000 women listed their kitchen needs.[80]

Once it became apparent that the garbage disposer had "sales appeal," dealers employed a variety of techniques used successfully in selling other household products to make "Mrs. America" aware of the appliance's positive features.[81] Encouraged by their trade journal to "hire a hall" or "use your own store" for mass demonstrations, dealers and contractors found this form of promotion especially successful. It enabled them to present their case to "a large number of prospects," obtain an "inexhaustible list of leads," receive "free publicity in local newspapers," and increase their "prestige as a progressive mer-chandiser."[82] Dealers sometimes cooperated with disposer manu-

---

[77]Cowan, *More Work for Mother* (n. 7 above), pp. 196–97.

[78]"Where Are Your Customers?" *Domestic Engineering* 184 (October 1954): 140; "She'll Buy This Dream!" *Domestic Engineering* 181 (February 1953): 106–7. The "complete kitchen" was sometimes referred to as the "packaged kitchen" or the "unit kichen." See, e.g., Helen E. McCullough, "The Kitchen of Tomorrow," *Journal of Home Economics* 37 (January 1945): 8–10.

[79]"Mrs. Smith (82 of 'Em) Goes to Washington," *Domestic Engineering* 192 (November 1958): 110–12.

[80]"80,000 Tell What They Want in Home Improvements . . . ," *Domestic Engineering* 193 (May 1959): 123.

[81]"Products with Sales Appeal," *Domestic Engineering* 180 (July 1952): 86.

[82]"Teach 'Em First . . . Sell 'Em Later," *Domestic Engineering* 178 (November 1951): 148. Similar techniques were used to sell gas and electric ranges. See Jane Busch, "Cooking Competition: Technology on the Domestic Market in the 1930s," *Technology and Culture* 24 (April 1983): 222–45.

facturers in staging programs at home shows or displays in store windows, and they used direct-mail campaigns to inform former customers how they could "refit" their kitchens at reasonable costs.[83]

Middle-class housewives in particular responded to these promotional efforts. In 1958, disposer sales topped $50 million, for some half-million new units, and in 1959 figures showed that more than 4 million homes had garbage disposers.[84] By 1961 at least fourteen companies manufactured models ranging in price from $60 to $130 including installation. The cost of the latter varied from $20 to $50 and depended on whether there had been a unit before and whether the house was old or new.[85]

When asked why they bought a disposer, women responded consistently that with it "there was no more garbage."[86] And once they eliminated garbage they also did away with "insects and rodents," "trips to the back alley in rain and snow," "nauseous odors," "clutter in the sink," "nasty scrubbing and relining of garbage pails," and "arguments about 'whose turn it is to take out the garbage.'" Repeating again and again that the disposer was "indispensable" and that they "wouldn't trade it in for anything," few women complained about the appliance's performance. Some disliked the grinding noise, but most said that since it lasted such a short time it was only a minor annoyance.[87]

By the 1960s the garbage disposer had found a niche. Marketed as a convenient household appliance that was not only "simple, safe, and

[83]"Cooperation Is the Keynote of Two Successful Sale Promotions in Our Industry Last Month," *Domestic Engineering* 179 (May 1952): 89; "Display Pays Off," *Domestic Engineering* 179 (February 1952): 83; "Attract the Feminine Trade" (n. 74 above), p. 159; "Don't You Love Me Any More, Mr. Plumbing & Heating Contractor," *Domestic Engineering* 179 (April 1952): 102–3; "They Use the Shock Sell and Soft Sell to Move 250 Disposers a Year," *Domestic Engineering* 202 (July 1963): 70–71.

[84]Johansen, "The Controversial Garbage Disposer" (n. 28 above), p. 148; "Food-Waste Disposers," *Consumer Reports* 24 (August 1959): 418. By comparison, approximately 100,000 units were sold in 1947. And in 1968, according to a national survey of community solid-wastes practices conducted by the American Public Works Association, there were "63.5 home grinders installed per 1,000 population on a countrywide basis." In urban areas the figure was "61.0 per 1,000"; and in nonurban (largely suburban) areas, where there was more new housing as well as newer sewer lines and sewage treatment facilities, it was higher—"76.0 per 1,000." See Institute for Solid Wastes of the American Public Works Association, *Municipal Refuse Disposal* (Chicago, 1970), p. 244.

[85]"Food Waste Disposers," *Consumer Bulletin* 44 (March 1961): 6–10; and "What You Want to Know about Garbage Disposers," *American Home* 64 (August 1961): 79–80.

[86]Ellen Staunton, "I Take It All Back," *House Beautiful* 87 (December 1945): 100, 178.

[87]Frances Meyer, "What a Waste Disposer Can Mean to You," *Better Homes & Gardens* 27 (August 1949): 93–95, 117; "Meet Mrs. America" (n. 74 above), pp. 65–68; Edith Ramsay and Hubbard H. Cobb, "Disposers and Incinerators," *American Home* 52 (September 1954): 83–84, 92.

sanitary" to operate but also quiet and efficient, the disposer removed the burden of handling and storing putrescible food wastes.[88] And in those cities where the appliance was banned because of overtaxed sewerage systems and/or undersized sewage treatment plants, women were being urged to join together to modify "antiquated codes and laws" so they would have "the right to use a garbage disposer."[89] Ordinances prohibiting disposers frequently dated from the years immediately following World War II when city officials, particularly those in the densely populated Northeast, feared the consequences of subjecting their community sewers to an increased load.

According to a questionnaire sent to all state health departments and to 1,271 cities with populations of 10,000 or more by the editors of *Public Works* in 1960, 23 of the 527 cities that replied had such ordinances—disposers were forbidden in parts of Philadelphia and throughout Boston and New York City.[90] F. H. Zurmuhlen, New York City's commissioner of public works, cited the prevalence of flat gradients as one reason for banning the discharge of ground garbage into the sewerage system. He also acknowledged that "during periods of intense rainfall" 90 percent of the sanitary flow of the city's sewers (which were combined with storm drains) sometimes escaped to the harbor and beaches. Emphasizing the $500 million being spent on intercepting sewers and treatment plants in the city's pollution control program, he contended that, if the home garbage disposers were allowed, "a heavy additional capital expense" for "aeration tanks and other units" would be required to handle "a probable increase of 50 percent in capacity." That, Zurmuhlen insisted, New York City could not afford.[91]

In contrast to the relatively few cities with proscriptions, other cities not only allowed the installation of disposers but required it in all new residences. For example, by 1960 a food-waste disposer had to be installed in every new home built in Denver, Detroit, and Columbus, and in many cities in California (35 percent of all Los Angeles homes had disposers in 1959). This was also widely required in Indiana, Michigan, and Ohio.[92] Yet for the greater part of the nation, the

---

[88]Republic Heater Corporation's new "Pulverizer Disposal" was said to be so quiet that "she can hear the radio playing low" and so efficient that it "takes garbage as fast as she can feed it." *Domestic Engineering* 181 (January 1953): ad. on p. 166.

[89]John Mack Carter, "Will There Be Garbage Cans on the Moon?" *American Home* 64 (August 1961): 4.

[90]"A Study of the Use of Home Food Waste Disposers," *Public Works* 91 (November 1960): 82.

[91]Ibid., p. 85.

[92]"Food-Waste Disposers" (n. 84 above), p. 419. In some cities, disposal units were

individual consumer could make a choice. While many chose to purchase disposers or homes equipped with them, others did not. Those
who did not usually lived in older homes, especially in ones served by
septic tanks, and found the price of the unit plus the cost of installation
too high.[93]

The garbage disposer had not become a standard home appliance by
the 1960s, but it did reach a level of consumption and popularity that
few would have imagined prior to the 1950s. Part of its appeal related
to its tangible health and environmental benefits. At most, the disposer
practically eliminated the garbage can and the unpleasantries and
difficulties associated with it from many households and communities.
At least, it offered individuals and municipalities an alternative in
confronting the long-standing problems related to the handling and
storage of putrescible food wastes.

But the other part of the disposer's attractiveness can be understood
only if this ordinary piece of technology is seen as a product favored by
an expanding middle-class and suburbanized society of Americans

---

permitted in homes but not in commercial establishments and institutions. Like the home
units, commercial ones have proved an excellent solution to food-waste disposal problems, especially where large quantitites of garbage are produced. In hotels, restaurants,
hospitals, etc., garbage is produced not only in large quantities but also in relatively short
periods; and storage facilities are often inadequate and frequently located in the areas
where food is prepared. Commercial grinders differ from home ones in that the former
put large amounts of suspended solids into the sewer system. Commercial units have,
therefore, been banned where the water supply is limited, where sewers are inadequate
or faulty, and/or where the sewage treatment plant cannot handle the additional (and
often very large) quantities of ground garbage. For a full discussion of the disposer in
commercial establishments, see Institute for Solid Wastes (APWA), *Municipal Refuse
Disposal* (n. 84 above), pp. 253–59. According to a list (dated February 22, 1971) of "U.S.
Cities Requiring Garbage Grinders in New Residential Construction" found in "Garbage
Grinders" file in the headquarters of the American Public Works Association, there were
fifty-eight cities in twelve states that had such a requirement. California and Michigan led
the list with nineteen and sixteen cities, respectively.

[93] In 1970, according to the American Public Works Association, "average annual costs
to a householder for a $150 garbage grinder with a 20-year life expectancy installed
when the house is built, if the costs are included in the mortgage, are about $10.30 for
purchase and installation at 5 per cent interest, $10 for repairs, $1 for water and
electricity, and 75 cents for sewage treatment, for a total of about $22 a year." Estimates
are 50 percent more for the same installation in an old house. See Institute for Solid
Wastes (APWA), *Municipal Refuse Disposal* (n. 84 above), p. 252. See also "Food-Waste
Disposers" (n. 84 above), p. 419. For discussions of the use of the disposer with a septic
tank, see "The Food Waste Disposer and the Septic Tank: Can They Live in Peace?"
Domestic Engineering 202 (July 1963): 61–63, 153; and Public Health Service, *Manual of
Septic-Tank Practice* (Washington, D.C., 1960). They conclude that a home served by a
septic tank can safely use a disposer if the tank has not already shown itself inadequate
and if the owner is willing to clean out the tank more regularly.

eager not only to make their homes and communities cleaner and healthier but also to make their own lives easier, simpler, and safer. Once the disposer's sanitary advantages became apparent, it won the approval of women, many of whom were married, employed outside their homes, and responsible for most household purchases. Since these women worked in large part to acquire goods and conveniences for themselves and their families, it is not surprising that the garbage disposer captured their attention and received their endorsement. And in adapting the disposer to the modern home, appliance dealers, plumbing contractors, and home builders were not unaware of the heightened consumer interests of postwar Americans. Thus these businessmen too quickly found a way to profit from this "hunk of better living."

Government and Technology in the Great Depression

CARROLL W. PURSELL

Even before the onslaught of the Great Depression of 1929, misgivings about the role of technology in Western culture were gaining wide currency. Aggressive insistence upon the inevitability and superiority of machine civilization were countered by denunciations of a new Dark Age of dehumanized enslavement for the soul. With the coming of the depression and its signal characteristic of unemployment in the midst of seeming overproduction, this philosophical and literary debate took on new significance for the shaping of public policy. Throughout the New Deal years, the question of the machine was constantly before the government.

Officials in Washington, however, were torn by that same ambivalence which had marked much of the concern of the 1920s: on the one hand, there was a general agreement that technology (whether out of control or merely under the control of the wrong forces) had made and was continuing to produce great changes in American society, not all of them for the best. On the other hand, there was an agreement that some of these changes *were* for the best, there was a hope that these good changes outweighed the bad, and the additional hope that some invisible hand would *continue* to keep the balance favorable. Actual government policy tended to studies of the bad effects of technology, encouragement of the presumed good effects, and some measure of relief for the more obvious victims of the Technological Age.

The motto so evident at the 1933 Chicago world's fair, "Science Finds—Industry Applies—Man Conforms," was evidence of not simply "A Century of Progress" but also of an aggressive, confident thrust of a machine civilization.[1] The duPont Company's promise of "Better Things for Better Living through Chemistry" was only a huckster's

CARROLL W. PURSELL is Adeline Barry Davee Distinguished Professor of History, and director of the Program in the History of Technology and Science, at Case Western Reserve University. He is currently president (1990–92) of the Society for the History of Technology.

[1]See Lowell Tozer, "American Attitude toward Machine Technology, 1893–1933" (Ph.D. diss., University of Minnesota, 1953).

This essay originally appeared in *Technology and Culture,* vol. 20, no. 1, January 1979.

phrasing of that larger hope expressed by the exposition's head of the division of basic sciences: "It is not unlikely," he assured the readers of the *Scientific Monthly,* "that, before the end of this century, science will play a role quite as dominating as that of the church during the thirteenth century."[2] The claim was as baldly assertive as that expressed a generation before by the scientist-inventor, Leo Baekeland: "I dare say," he had boasted, "that the last hundred years under the influence of the modern engineer and the scientist have done more for the betterment of the race than all the art, all the civilizing efforts, all the so-called classical literature, of past ages, for which some people want us to have such an exaggerated reverence."[3]

A contemporary expression of this mood which found a wide audience could also be found in the writings of the Technocracy movement. During the winter of 1932–33 the Energy Survey of the United States, begun in April 1932 in rooms provided by Columbia University's Department of Industrial Engineering, catapulted the opinions and pronouncements of the group's leader, Howard Scott, into instant prominence.[4] In an article entitled "A Rendezvous with Destiny," Scott proclaimed his message that "an economy of abundance on the North American continent is only possible when political government has been abolished." God, Scott assured the nation, "in His kindness is on the side of the greatest technology. . . . This generation of Americans has the technology, the men, the materials, and the machinery" for the accomplishment of "a new civilization."[5]

The fear that Howard Scott and the Chicago world's fair were correct in their predictions was also widespread. The soft underbelly of technological progress was exposed in such popular offerings as Charlie Chaplin's 1936 film *Modern Times.* In this film, although the little tramp is found as often in a prison or a restaurant kitchen as a factory, the image of his struggle against the insane rationality of industrial rhythms emerges as *the* memorable statement against technology in the entire depression decade.

The works of other artists of the period show perhaps a greater ambivalence toward the machine. The prolific Stuart Chase, in his 1929 book *Men and Machines,* admitted both his dependence upon

---

[2]Quoted in ibid., pp. 217–18.

[3]Quoted in Melvin Kranzberg and Carroll W. Pursell, Jr., *Technology in Western Civilization* (New York, 1967), 2:695.

[4]Two histories of Technocracy are Henry Elsner, Jr., *The Technocrats: Prophets of Automation* (Syracuse, N.Y., 1967), and William E. Akin, *Technocracy and the American Dream: The Technocrat Movement, 1900–1941* (Berkeley, 1977).

[5]Howard Scott, "A Rendezvous with Destiny," reprinted from *Technocracy* in the *American Engineer* 6 (October 1936): 8–10, 24.

machines and his realization that they might, in fact, come to control his life. Looking ahead he saw three choices: "We can drift with the tide as at present. We can officially adopt some simple formula like 'government by business,' or 'state socialism,' and thus attempt to run a dreadnaught with a donkey engine. Or we can face the full implications of the machine, relying on no formulas because none adequate have been created, with nothing to guide us but our naked intelligence and a will to conquer. . . . From our brains," he concluded, "have sprung a billion horses, now running amuk. Where are the riders with their whirling ropes; where the light-hearted youths to mount, be thrown, and rise to mount again?" Significantly, his book was illustrated by W. T. Murch in the fashionable and streamlined art deco style of the period. Two years later, when he wrote of the "machineless men" in his book *Mexico: A Study of Two Americas*, it was illustrated by the sensuous and organic drawings of Diego Rivera.[6]

Artists and journalists were joined by scholars in questioning the influence of the machine on contemporary society. Harry Jerome, studying *Mechanization in Industry* for the National Bureau of Economic Research in 1934, would venture only the cautious belief that, while mechanization was important, it tended to proceed without dramatic changes of pace and that, while it did "result in a substantial period of unemployment for the men displaced and frequently necessitated their taking employment at a lower wage," he did "not find convincing the evidence or theoretical arguments sometimes advanced to demonstrate an inherent tendency for mechanization to create an ever larger permanent body of unemployed."[7] Despite an introduction which noted that critics had seen mechanization as either "a Frankenstein monster, threatening the very life of its creator," or "a dawning millennium of ease and plenty in a world of push-buttons and buzzers," Jerome lamely admitted after 415 pages that "the preceding discussion of the effects of mechanization does not even touch upon many of the ways in which the increasing use of machines alters for better or worse the social and cultural life of the modern world."[8] *Fortune* magazine was more blunt, but equally indecisive. Noting that after the new immigration laws of the early 1920s "the hunkies thinned out of the employment offices, [but] engineers came into the plants," the journal went on to state the problem: "From the purely productive point of view, a part of the human race is already obsolete and a further part is obsolescent. But from the consuming point of

[6]Stuart Chase, *Men and Machines* (New York, 1929), pp. 347–48, and *Mexico: A Study of Two Americas* (New York, 1931).
[7]Harry Jerome, *Mechanization in Industry* (New York, 1934), p. 387.
[8]Ibid., pp. xxii, 416.

view, no human being is obsolete: on the contrary, an ever-increasing human consumption is not only desirable but necessary. These are the hard and pointed horns of the dilemma of our time."[9]

On at least one rare occasion the question was raised by the very men who were helping create the problem. In 1936, John D. Rust and his brother Mack made successful field tests of their new cotton-picking machine. "It will," they claimed, "do the work of 50 to 100 men. Thrown on the market in the manner of past inventions, it would mean, in the sharecropped country, that 75% of the labor population would be thrown out of employment. We are not willing that this should happen. How can we prevent it?" The Rust brothers tried several ways of avoiding this disaster, including giving market control of the machine to the Southern Tenant Farmers Union, but at last called upon "federal and state aid in working out a program for painlessly absorbing the picker into the South's economy."[10] The potential disruption of the machine, and the Rust brothers' concern, was widely publicized with major articles in such journals as *Harper's Magazine* and the *American Mercury*, the last article being reprinted in *Reader's Digest.*[11]

On several occasions the acolytes and unbelievers met head on. In 1928 the historian Charles A. Beard edited a volume of essays entitled *Whither Mankind: A Panorama of Modern Civilization.* The book included statements by Bertrand Russell on science, Sidney and Beatrice Webb on labor, Lewis Mumford on the arts, John Dewey on philosophy, among others. Noting that "the machine civilization" was open to attack on three grounds—aesthetic, religious, and humanistic—Beard denied that these values were inevitably sacrificed to technology. Indeed, he maintained, "these ancient forces will become powerful in the modern age just in the proportion that men and women accept the inevitability of science and the machine, understand the nature of the civilization in which they must work, and turn their faces resolutely to the future."[12]

The question of the humanists, "Whither mankind?" was answered vigorously two years later by a group of engineers who titled their book *Toward Civilization.* In this volume Beard brought together essays by Robert Millikan on science, Elmer Sperry on invention, Lillian Gilbreth on work and leisure, Michael Pupin on idealism, and

[9]"Obsolete Men," *Fortune* 6 (December 1932): 27, 94.

[10]Quoted in *Time* (March 23, 1936), p. 60.

[11]John Rust, "The Origin and Development of the Cotton Picker," *West Tennessee Historical Society Papers*, no. 7 (1953), p. 49.

[12]Chalres A. Beard, ed. *Whither Mankind? A Panorama of Modern Civilization* (New York, 1928), p. 24.

others. Beard was pleased to discover that these people, "having solved the problem of production, have brought the abolition of undeserved poverty and misery within the range of the practicable for the first time in human history." Even better was the fact that "those who have wrought this miracle are now deeply concerned about the next stage—a wider distribution of wealth and a nobler use of riches and leisure."[13] Again the message was the inevitability of technology—and the responsibility of the humanities to help mankind adjust to it.

Another forum for the argument over technology was provided by the idea of a moratorium on research which agitated the popular press sporadically for a decade after its first suggestion in 1927. In that year the bishop of Ripon, addressing a sermon to the annual meeting of the British Association for the Advancement of Science, suggested, as he said, "at the risk of being lynched by some of my hearers, that the sum of human happiness, outside of scientific circles, would not necessarily be reduced if for, say ten years, every physical and chemical laboratory were closed and the patient and resourceful energy displayed in them transferred to recovering the lost art of getting together and finding a formula for making the ends meet in the scale of human life."[14] The idea that our scientific and technical prowess had somehow outstripped our moral and social ability to control them (and therefore that the former should be restrained until the latter are strengthened) found an echo even in the second inaugural address of Franklin D. Roosevelt. Without government aid, he declared, "we had been unable to create those moral controls over the services of science which are necessary to make science a useful servant instead of a ruthless master of mankind."[15] Later that same year the president wrote to Karl T. Compton, President of the Massachusetts Institute of Technology, that the whole subject of engineering responsibility must be opened up to also "consider social processes and problems, and modes of more perfect adjustment to environment, and must cooperate in designing accommodating mechanisms to absorb the shocks of the impact of science."[16]

To a remarkable degree, the New Deal administrations of Franklin D. Roosevelt did address themselves to the "social processes and problems" which made up both cause and effect of technological change in

[13]Charles A. Beard, ed., *Toward Civilization* (London, 1930), p. 304.

[14]Quoted in Carroll Pursell, " 'A Savage Struck by Lightning': The Idea of a Research Moratorium, 1927–37," *Lex et Scientia* 10 (October–December 1974): 146.

[15]Quoted in ibid., p. 158.

[16]Quoted in Carroll W. Pursell, Jr., *Readings in Technology and American Life* (New York, 1969), p. 358.

America. The New Deal shared the ambivalence of those who hoped to minimize the bad and maximize the good effects of technology. Given the realities of power in America, it was perhaps inevitable that while the good was actively promoted by a score of federal programs and encouragements the bad were more often merely subjected to the harmless scrutiny of academic investigation.

The earliest major report was that of President Hoover's Research Committee on Social Trends, published in 1933. Taking an upbeat approach, the committee went on record that it did "not believe in a moratorium upon research in physical science and invention, such as has sometimes been proposed. On the contrary, it holds that social invention has to be stimulated to keep pace with mechanical invention." In his chapter on "The Influence of Invention and Discovery," W. F. Ogburn declared that "science and technology are the most dynamic elements of our material culture," and, to help prove it, he listed no less than 150 of what he called the "effects of the radio telegraph and telephone and of radio broadcasting."[17] In chapter after chapter, on such subjects as population, the arts, women, labor, and the law, Hoover's committee documented the broad impact of technology, and always with the same message—the need to adapt to change.

In June of 1937 the government issued another major report even more sharply focused on technology. Through its subcommittee on technology, chaired by Ogburn, the National Resources Committee reported on *Technological Trends and National Policy,* including, as the title had it, the social implications of new inventions. The document was, in the words of Harold Ickes, "the first major attempt to show the kinds of new inventions which may affect living and working conditions in America in the next 10 to 25 years. It indicates some of the problems which the adoption and use of these inventions will inevitably bring in their train. It emphasizes the importance of national efforts to bring about prompt adjustment to these changing situations, with the least possible social suffering and loss, and sketches some of the lines of national policy directed to this end."[18]

It was Ogburn's belief that since it took perhaps a quarter of a

[17]President Hoover's Research Committee on Social Trends, *Recent Social Trends,* Report of the President's Research Committee on Social Trends (New York, 1933), 1:xv, 122, 153–56.

[18]National Resources Committee, *Technological Trends and National Policy, including the Social Implications of New Inventions* (Washington, D.C., June 1937), p. iii. Also see Arlene Inouye and Charles Süsskind, " 'Technological Trends and National Policy,' 1937: The First Modern Technology Assessment," *Technology and Culture* 18 (October 1977): 593–621.

century for basic science to be embodied in technological application, and even longer for social effects to become obvious, the shape of events ten to twenty-five years in the future could be discovered from current research. His attempt to circulate the National Academy of Sciences for insights and predictions, however, turned up a welter of very specific suggestions and defensive disclaimers. Karl T. Compton of M.I.T. warned that it "is far more important to support the progress of science generally rather than to try to pick out certain fields of anticipated practical value." Columbia University's Harold Urey replied that it seemed to him that "if the National Government wishes to do something to aid in the development of technologies, that it would do well to supply the National Research Council or the National Academy of Sciences with a fund of money to be administered for this purpose. . . ."

William D. Coolidge of General Electric denied that either "adequate organization" or "governmental intervention of any kind will effectively speed those researches or mitigate the severities, if any, of the resulting economic and social problems," and warned specifically that "imagination would . . . transcend the bounds of reasonable possibility if it forecast the supersession of existing sources of energy by the industrial utilization of the energy within the atom." Frank B. Jewett of Bell Laboratories expressed the opinion that "the restraints almost certain to be imposed by governmental participation and guidance would more than offset the advantages." E. B. Wilson of Harvard's School of Public Health, pointing out that "Ogburn has been 'hipped' on the devastation that the mechanical cotton picker would bring to the South," noted that even so ardent a New Dealer as Secretary of Agriculture Henry A. Wallace was known to "sneer at the proposition pointing out the very obvious difficulties of a mechanical cotton picker which would be satisfactory—difficulties which Ogburn with his ignorance of the problems of machinery doesn't see."[19]

The claims of the published report were modest indeed. While insisting that "invention is a great disturber and it is fair to say that the greatest general cause of change in our modern civilization is invention," the committee also admitted that "there is as yet no science capable of predicting the social effects of inventions. . . ." As an early effort at technology assessment the report may have been modest, but it did not escape criticism. The columnist Mark Sullivan, adopting a

[19]William F. Ogburn to Frank R. Lillie, April 2, 1936; Karl T. Compton to Frank R. Lillie, April 8, 1936; Harold C. Urey to F. Lillie, April 9, 1936; William D. Coolidge to Frank R. Lillie, April 13, 1936; Frank B. Jewett to F. R. Lillie, April 14, 1936; E. B. Wilson to Frank R. Lillie, March 14, 1936, all in files of Government Relations and Science Advisory Committee, National Academy of Sciences, Washington, D.C.

folksy commonsensical approach, informed his readers that "professors down in Washington have thought up a new one. They are going to regulate inventions." Comparing this with the Agricultural Adjustment Act's effort to cut back on farm production, Sullivan warned that "we are fairly confident that no Chester County jury would send a man to jail for planting potatoes when Secretary Wallace said he mustn't. Neither will our juries send us to jail for adopting a new invention, or sticking to an old way, whichever we prefer, the professors to the contrary notwithstanding."[20]

Two Department of Agriculture films also addressed the effects of technology on the land. In *The Plow That Broke the Plains,* in 1936, Pare Lorentz documented in dramatic images the devastation that resulted when an inappropriate technology is forced upon the land. On the Great Plains, under the spur of wartime prices and speculative greed, a powerful machine technology destroyed the natural cover and prepared the way for a dust bowl. The film ends with a stream of Okies making their way to California and an empty bird's nest in a dead tree. The following year, in 1937, Lorentz produced *The River,* a film relating a story of equal devastation—of a landscape cut over and mined out by cotton culture. This time the result was not too little water but too much—the repeated and tragic flooding of the Mississippi drainage basin. Unlike his last film, however, this one had a somewhat artificial upbeat ending: the Tennessee Valley Authority would put the land back together. The means was a massive job of civil, agricultural, and social engineering, and the end was to be control of both social and natural destructive forces.[21]

The USDA also provided the obligatory "serious, factual book, but a cheering one withal, because every page discloses or implies the great inventiveness of Americans, new opportunities and progress, new plans and hopes for conquering problems." Entitled *Technology on the Farm* and issued during the summer of 1940, the report first described changes in machines, animals, plants, land use, and processes, then tried to assess their effects. "It would be useless for us to try to curb this march of technology," the author warned, "for we know that it gives jobs, as well as takes them away. Our task, rather, is to study ways to equalize the advantages brought by technology and to help plan a more stable economy." Again, as in past studies, the task of technology assessment was undertaken with great humility: "It is impossible to forecast the nature of inventions, whims, fashions, and movements that will affect agriculture," they warned, "but it is possi-

[20]*Washington Star* (August 10, 1937).
[21]Both of these films are available from the National Audiovisual Center in Washington, D.C.

ble to forecast that there will be inventions, whims, fashions, and movements." The study accepted the growth of a mechanized and integrated agribusiness as inevitable (although it was certainly as much a result of deliberate policy as immutable natural forces) and concentrated on "the basic problem . . . to provide employment and security to the displaced and underprivileged persons most adversely affected by technology."[22]

A final, almost anticlimactic, study was released in 1941 with the final report of the Temporary National Economic Committee (TNEC). Established by the Congress in 1938 to look into the problems of "monopoly and the concentration of economic power in and financial control over production and distribution of goods and services," the TNEC was conceived in depression but born in war. Because Dr. New Deal had been sent away and Dr. Win-the-War called in instead, the committee found that "it is quite conceivable that the democracies might attain a military victory over the aggressors only to find themselves under the domination of economic authority far more concentrated and influential than that which existed prior to the war."[23]

After taking 1,753 pages of testimony and exhibits specifically on the subject of "Technology and Concentration of Economic Power" and the publication of two monographs, one covering patents and the other technology in our economy, the tone of the final report hardly reflected its radical possibilities. It was agreed by all that the patent system was being "shamefully abused," and the committee spoke of the need to "pass on the technological gains" made. Aside from patents, technological unemployment was most carefully looked at. A long description of historic opinion on the question was given, and the problems of loss of jobs and skill were admitted, but in the end the classic benefits were claimed. The committee insisted that "a free competitive system offers the best opportunity for the widest participation in such gains achieved through a reduction in prices of goods, in the stimulation of new industries and extension of existing ones, fuller employment, reduction of working hours, increase in consumers' purchasing power, and a more equitable distribution of the value added by manufacture." In the end the committee merely suggested a number of rather obvious devices, such as dismissal wage contracts and job retraining programs, which "may be incorporated

[22]U.S. Department of Agriculture, *Technology on the Farm* (Washington, D.C., August 1940), pp. vi, v, xi.
[23]U.S. Congress, Senate, Temporary National Economic Committee, *Investigation of Concentration of Economic Power, Final Report and Recommendations*, 77th Cong., 1st sess., March 31, 1941, pp. 691–93.

into law and industrial practice in order to soften the impact of technological advance in highly mechanized society."[24]

While the putative ill effects of technology were being carefully studied, those effects which were perceived as benefits were enthusiastically promoted by the New Deal. As one historian has written, "To conservationist planners and 'technological liberals' like Morris L. Cooke the first ten years of the Roosevelt administration offered much genuine opportunity and also much that was mere semblance."[25] One apparently possible innovation of the period that failed to be carried out was a large new program of federal subsidy for both basic and applied research. Late in 1933 a plan put forward by Karl T. Compton, head of the Science Advisory Board, and Alfred D. Flinn, director of the Engineering Foundation, called for the government to invest $16 million over a period of some years in scientific and technical research that would be self-liquidating in the sense that industrial savings would more than pay for the costs. This "Recovery Program for Science Progress," as it was called, was a clear attempt to win governmental support for those arguments in favor of industrial research and the ability of new technology to fructify the stagnant economy.[26] Other plans to subsidize research in federal bureaus and state land-grant engineering stations or through grants in colleges and universities, while sometimes formally embodied in congressional legislation, almost always failed to become law.[27] It was a deeply held belief that if such research could turn up just one device such as the radio or automobile the resulting new industry would solve the problems of depression. Looking ahead to the fate of the unemployed in the next winter rather than the next generation, the administration did not give much support to these measures.

Where the needs of technology and the unemployed did intersect, the New Deal could move quickly. Already the Hoover administration had, in 1928, approved the construction of a dam in Boulder Canyon,

[24]Ibid., pp. 22, 91. The two monographs were no. 22, *Technology in Our Economy* (Washington, D.C., 1941), and no. 31, *Patents and Free Enterprise* (Washington, D.C., 1941); see also *Investigation of Concentration of Economic Power*, Hearings before the Temporary National Economic Committee, Part 30, *Technology and Concentration of Economic Power* (Washington, D.C., 1940).

[25]Jean Christie, "The Mississippi Valley Committee: Conservation and Planning in the Early New Deal," *Historian* 32 (May 1970): 469.

[26]Carroll W. Pursell, Jr., "The Anatomy of a Failure: The Science Advisory Board, 1933–1935," *Proceedings of the American Philosophical Society* 109 (December 1965): 342–51.

[27]See, for example, Carroll W. Pursell, Jr., "A Preface to Government Support of Research and Development: Research Legislation and the National Bureau of Standards, 1935–41," *Technology and Culture* 9 (April 1968): 145–64.

Nevada. Bids for the work were opened in 1931 and in June 1933 the first concrete was poured. That same year work was begun on Grand Coulee Dam, and just four years later Congress appropriated money to begin construction of the Colorado–Big Thompson Project.[28] Perhaps no government work of the 1930s better expressed the technological faith that bold engineering could control the forces of nature for the benefit of humankind than did these dramatic and graceful monuments.

In terms of both social and civil engineering, the authorization in 1933 of the long-debated Tennessee Valley Authority cast this same faith in more controversial terms. The rampaging Tennessee River, the Power Trust, and the social rot of southern agricultural life were all to be brought under control by the TVA. In terms of what some scholars have called "The Mythos of the Electronic Revolution," the supporters of the TVA attributed "intrinsically benign and progressive properties to electricity and its applications. [They also displayed] . . . a faith that electricity will exorcise social disorder and environmental disruption, eliminate political conflict and personal alienation, and restore ecological balance and a communion of man with nature."[29]

Both the mythos and the economics of electricity dictated that people must be convinced to use as much power as possible. Both the good life and the economies of scale made it necessary for the government to undertake an intensive campaign to get people to buy and use more electric appliances. An Electric Home and Farm Authority was set up which granted "low-interest loans for appliance purchases and worked with manufacturers to get low-cost appliances onto the market."[30] The whole TVA, but especially its electrification program, was a giant advertisement for the good which technology could do if only people had it available and learned to use it fully.

The benefits of electrification were spread even wider by a second New Deal agency, the Rural Electrification Administration (REA) set up in 1935 with Morris L. Cooke, the Progressive engineer, as director. In that year only 10 percent of American farms were served by electricity from central power stations. Because private power companies refused to do so, the REA began to bring power to the remain-

---

[28]U.S. Department of the Interior, *The Story of Hoover Dam* (Washington, D.C., 1961), *The Story of the Columbia Basin Project* (Washington, D.C., 1964), and *The Story of the Colorado–Big Thompson Project* (Washington, D.C., 1962).

[29]James W. Carey and John J. Quirk, "The Mythos of the Electronic Revolution" *American Scholar* 39 (Spring 1970): 222.

[30]Thomas K. McCraw, *TVA and the Power Fight, 1933–1939* (Philadelphia, 1971), p. 62.

ing 90 percent. Once again the fear was expressed that the farmers would not use enough electricity to make the project worthwhile. A broad-scale campaign was launched, including demonstration workers, pamphlets, 4-H projects for children, meetings, and a demonstration farm equipment tour, called the REA Circus, which featured a tent seating 1,000 and "a dozen equipment sideshows, furnished by manufacturers." Farm wives led their husbands in electrifying, buying first irons and radios, then washing machines, vacuum cleaners, and other appliances. The REA officials were pleased to discover that, in the face of this campaign, farmers actually used more kilowatt-hours than did city dwellers.[31] A film released by the government in 1940, entitled *Power and the Land,* made the theme explicit and even set it to music. Technology, specifically electricity (the cleanest, most ecological, cheapest, most flexible and democratic of modern technologies) has the potential of carrying the American dream to all the nation's citizens. The happiness and well-being of its citizens being the grand object of government, the American government would promote the spread of technology to all its people.

The motto of the 1933 Century of Progress fair in Chicago, that "Science Finds—Industry Applies—Man Conforms," stood revealed by the end of the decade as a fair summary statement of a relationship agreed upon by most humanists, technologists, and government officials in America. There appeared to be a growing consensus that the federal government should use its power to assist in the stimulation of basic research, the support of something like industrial applied research, and, most important, in shaping social expectations and institutions in such a way that most citizens could comfortably conform to the new technologies and that those who unfortunately could not might be taken care of by some form of special welfare.

Like most humanists and technologists, government policymakers tended to analyze the impact of technology on society in terms of some form of cost/benefit analysis. The strength of this approach was its flexibility—by studying the costs and subsidizing the benefits, the New Deal brought actual improvement to many people and threatened the economic position of few powerful vested interests. The weakness of this type of approach was not that it was wrong (technology does, after all, share with all the rest of this imperfect world the characteristic of being partly bad, partly good) but that it could not provide any analysis that might lead to sound public policy. At base this strategy was informed by a reasonable desire to maximize

[31]*Rural Lines—USA: The Story of the Rural Electrification Administration's First Twenty-five Years, 1935–1960, REA.* Miscellaneous Publication no. 811 (Washington, D.C., January 1960), p. 26.

the good and minimize the bad effects of that technological change which was such a signal characteristic of the 1920s and 1930s. Unfortunately, it turned out that not only were good and bad closely mixed in real life, but, even worse, one person's good was another person's bad. For an administration that sought no radical reconstruction of American institutions and that eschewed any serious attempt at national planning, it was perhaps inevitable that it should avoid— and indeed intensify—the problems of technology in society.

"Very Risky Business": A Power Reactor for New York City

GEORGE T. MAZUZAN

Public concern about the safety of nuclear power continues unabated in the United States. The industry as well as its federal regulators are scrutinized and criticized regularly. One needs only to sample the voluminous literature published to date to see that much of it is harsh and often rings with emotion rather than scholarly detachment.[1] Enough time has now passed and enough records are currently open, however, to permit us to glance backward a few years and look with detail at one of the earliest and significant safety controversies that faced the fledgling nuclear industry.[2] The case involved an attempt by the Consolidated Edison Company of New York (Con Edison) to construct a power reactor in the middle of New York City. It under-

---

Formerly a historian at the U.S. Nuclear Regulatory Commission, GEORGE T. MAZUZAN became the National Science Foundation Historian in 1986. He is the coauthor, with J. Samuel Walker, of *Controlling the Atom: The Beginnings of Nuclear Regulation, 1946–1962* (Berkeley, 1984).

[1]The most noted stridently antinuclear works include the following: Gerard H. Clarfield and William M. Wiecek, *Nuclear America: Military and Civilian Nuclear Power in the United States, 1940–1980* (New York, 1984); Richard Curtis, *The Perils of the Peaceful Atom: The Myth of Safe Nuclear Power Plants* (New York, 1969); Daniel Ford, *The Cult of the Atom: The Secret Papers of the Atomic Energy Commission* (New York, 1982); John G. Fuller, *We Almost Lost Detroit* (New York, 1975); Richard S. Lewis, *The Nuclear-Power Rebellion: Citizens vs. the Atomic Industrial Establishment* (New York, 1972); and H. Peter Metzger, *The Atomic Establishment* (New York, 1972). More balanced accounts include Irvin C. Bupp and Jean-Claude Devian, *Light Water: How the Nuclear Dream Dissolved* (New York, 1978); Mark Hertsgaard, *Nuclear Inc.: The Men and Money behind Nuclear Energy* (New York, 1983); and Peter Pringle and James Spigelman, *The Nuclear Barons* (New York, 1981).

[2]The voluminous records of the United States Atomic Energy Commission, the Congressional Joint Committee on Atomic Energy, newspaper accounts, and the periodical literature form the primary sources for this article. Other archival collections that are open for research, such as the papers of Chet Holifield at the University of Southern California, Clinton P. Anderson at the Library of Congress, and the White House records at the John F. Kennedy Library, have been searched but contain no important items about this event. Additional records that would be used if access could be gained include the archives of Westinghouse and Con Edison. Eventually, too, the papers of Glenn Seaborg will be open to researchers, but they are unavailable at this time.

This essay originally appeared in *Technology and Culture*, vol. 27, no. 2, April 1986.

scored the issue of federal regulation of an acceptable level of risk for not only the people of New York but as a precedent for urban populations elsewhere. Equally important, the attempt prompted the first organized grass-roots protest over the siting and safety of a power reactor and induced an active role in the matter by the New York City Council. In retrospect, the unfolding technological drama stands out as a historical milestone in both the development and the regulation of nuclear power in the United States.

When commercial nuclear power appeared to be competitive with other energy sources in the early 1960s, the utilities that invested in nuclear units were generally large corporations located near or in urban centers. Con Edison, the Philadelphia Electric Company, the Commonwealth Edison Company of Chicago, the Detroit Edison Company, the Pacific Gas and Electric Company in San Francisco, the Southern California Edison Company in Los Angeles, and the San Diego Gas and Electric Company were among the leading companies wanting to add nuclear power to their mix of energy sources.[3] While these metropolitan utilities represented different geographic areas of the United States, each one advocated locating nuclear plants close to its customer load centers. In the early period of commercial nuclear power development, Con Edison was a pioneer. Between the time it brought its original Indian Point nuclear plant into operation in July 1962 and when it applied for a construction permit for a second Indian Point unit in December 1965, the utility sought approval for another reactor. The location of that reactor was an important issue not only for Con Edison but also for other metropolitan utilities throughout the nation because it was so closely tied in with the competitive economics of nuclear energy. The projected capital cost of any central power station had to include the cost of transmitting the electricity from its source to its customers. Con Edison wanted to locate its station as close as possible to the population center it served. In this instance—with its site in the Ravenswood neighborhood of Queens—the utility pushed for what came to be truly called metropolitan siting.[4]

The U.S. Atomic Energy Commission (AEC) was the federal agency totally responsible for approving sites, licensing reactors, and setting safety guidelines and standards for power reactor technology under its statutory mandate of protecting the public health and safety. Development of official siting criteria had evolved into both an important and a controversial question at the agency in the late 1950s and early 1960s.

[3]U.S. Department of Energy, Technical Information Center, *Nuclear Reactors Built, Being Built, or Planned in the United States* (DOE/TID-8200-R47, August 1983).

[4]*Nucleonics Week*, December 13, 1962, pp. 1–2; *Electrical World*, December 17, 1962, p. 46, March 25, 1963, p. 69.

The guide the AEC finally adopted in 1962 was the product of experience with its own reactors, case-by-case evaluation of several early commercial reactor applications, demands for guidance from industry and the congressional Joint Committee on Atomic Energy, and collective knowledge about various elements of nuclear technology.[5]

Before private enterprise was allowed to own nuclear plants, the earliest government-owned research and testing reactors had been constructed in the late 1940s at sites far from population centers. Although those reactors had very low power ratings, remote siting was an important safety criterion because of the experimental nature of the technology. By 1950, however, the AEC approved designs for newer reactors at sites closer to populated areas. This trend was exemplified by two early government-sponsored reactors, one at the Argonne National Laboratory near Chicago and the other at General Electric's West Milton, New York, site, some 25–30 miles from the tri-city area of Schenectady, Troy, and Albany. To compensate for the additional risks of placing reactors close to populated regions, designers relied on "engineered safety features," devices designed to mitigate the consequences of any assumed accidents. Architects designed the West Milton reactor, for example, with a large steel containment structure, and builders enclosed the Argonne reactor in a gastight concrete building. The containment structure was also a major design element of the government-owned demonstration power reactor at Shippingport, Pennsylvania, that in 1957 supplied the first American commercial power by nuclear energy through the generating facilities of the Duquesne Light Company. Except for a few experimental reactors constructed at remote sites, and some gas-cooled reactors, all power reactors constructed in the United States after 1957 included provisions for containment buildings, which allowed them to be sited closer to population centers. But the AEC was unable to devise satisfactory standards delineating the specific relationship between distance from population centers on the one hand and containment or additional engineered safety features on the other. Consequently, it continued to make individual judgments for each proposed reactor and site on a case-by-case basis.[6]

---

[5]George T. Mazuzan and J. Samuel Walker, *Controlling the Atom: The Beginnings of Nuclear Regulation 1946–1962* (Berkeley, Calif., 1984), pp. 214–45.

[6]AEC Report WASH-3 (rev.), "Summary Report of the Reactor Safeguard Committee," March 31, 1950, AEC/NRC; Charles R. Russell, *Reactor Safeguards* (New York, 1962), pp. 98–101; T. J. Thompson and C. Rogers McCullough, "The Concepts of Reactor Containment," in *The Technology of Nuclear Reactor Safety*, ed. T. J. Thompson and J. G. Beckerley, 2 vols. (Cambridge, Mass., 1964, 1973), 2:111; Richard G. Hewlett and Francis Duncan, *A History of the United States Atomic Energy Commission*, vol. 2, *Atomic Shield, 1947–1952* (University Park, Pa., 1969), pp. 202, 204, 423–24.

The AEC began developing site guidelines in the late 1950s. Compromise between the agency's initial stress on isolation of reactors and industry's preference for engineered safety features (instead of remote sites) took several years of work and finally resulted in publication of the 1962 reactor site criteria. Advice from industry representatives and from members of the AEC's prestigious Advisory Committee on Reactor Safeguards (Safeguards Committee) greatly influenced the regulators' conclusions. The document balanced distance factors against a list of engineered design features. Important components included the extent to which generally accepted engineering standards were applied to the reactor design, the presence of unique or unusual features of the site of the reactor having a significant bearing on the probability or consequences of an accident, the special safety features designed for the facility, and the physical barriers that had to be breached before a release of radioactive material to the environment would occur.[7]

Early drafts of the siting document contained a sample calculation for determining acceptable distances from population areas. Industry groups objected strongly to its inclusion because they thought the sample made the guide seem unduly rigid. The final draft of the siting criteria deleted the calculation in the body but referred to it as a separately published AEC "Technical Information Document" (commonly cited by its agency designation, TID-14844). The document, "Calculation of Distance Factors for Power and Test Reactor Sites," showed the computations used to arrive at an acceptable distance and provided supplementary explanatory information.[8]

The key words in the 1962 site criteria, however, were written in the prefatory "statement of consideration" which specified that applicants were "free—and indeed encouraged—to demonstrate to the Commission the applicability and significance of considerations other than those set forth in the guides." The staff analysis of the final document also concluded that it was "intended as an interim measure until the state of the art allows more definitive standards to be developed."[9] The criteria, then, reflected the realities imposed by a developing industry and the rapidly changing nature of the technology. The AEC regulators were confident that the guides provided an ample margin of safety while at the same time allowing the industry to build commercial power

---

[7]Mazuzan and Walker, *Controlling the Atom*, pp. 214–21; AEC-R 2/32 (June 8, 1961); AEC-R 2/39 (February 23, 1962), AEC/NRC. When the AEC was disbanded in 1975, its regulatory records were retained by the United States Regulatory Commission (NRC). AEC records are cited as AEC/NRC. AEC records consist of docket files, minutes of meetings, position papers, drafts, reports, correspondence, press releases, and other background material on a given subject, cited by paper number and location.

[8]AEC-R 2/39, AEC/NRC.

[9]Ibid.; *Federal Register*, June 1, 1962.

reactors as close to populated areas, where the greatest demand for electricity existed, as possible.

While accepting the industry position for the site criteria, the AEC regulatory staff in practice continued a cautious, conservative approach toward actually substituting engineered safety features for remote siting. In an important November 1962 report to President John F. Kennedy on the status of nuclear power, the AEC recognized that remote siting raised the cost of electricity from reactors. Safety considerations, however, were behind the agency's statement that, until utilities gained operating experience and engineered safeguards were proved, "prudence dictates that large reactor installations be fairly far removed from population centers." This annoyed the industry greatly.[10] Subsequently, throughout the 1960s, several metropolitan utilities attempted to show the AEC regulators that sites in densely populated areas were safe for power reactors because of the incorporation of new engineered safety features.

Even before the new site guidelines went into effect, Con Edison, along with Westinghouse, its nuclear reactor vendor, proposed a commercial power reactor at a location that did not meet any of the distance factors in the site criteria. Instead, the planned site would have to be judged strictly on the basis of its designs for engineered safeguards. On December 10, 1962, Con Edison applied to the AEC for a construction permit to build a 1,000-electrical-megawatt facility at its Ravenswood site, in Queens, in the heart of New York City. The proposed generating station would be between the East River and Vernon Boulevard, a long stone's throw from Welfare Island in the East River. Slightly over ½ mile to the south stood the Queensboro Bridge connecting Queens with Manhattan. Central Park was approximately 1½ miles west of the site, and the United Nations complex rose at the same distance southwest of the site. The 1,000 electrical megawatts would be derived from the combination of a Westinghouse pressurized water reactor rated at 750 electrical megawatts and from two oil-fired superheaters. When announced, the Ravenswood plant was the largest power reactor planned in the world. Only two other large plants in the United States, both in the preliminary stages, approached Ravenswood in size. Southern California Edison and the San Diego Gas and Electric Company planned a 436-electrical-megawatt reactor for a Camp Pendleton, Cali-

---

[10]AEC, "Civilian Nuclear Power—a Report to the President," 1962, in U.S. Congress, Joint Committee on Atomic Energy (JCAE), committee print, *Nuclear Power Economics— 1962 through 1967*, 90th Cong., 2d sess., 1968, p. 154; JCAE, *Hearings on the Development, Growth, and State of the Atomic Energy Industry*, 88th Cong., 1st sess., 1963, pp. 788–89; *Nucleonics Week*, April 1963, p. 4.

fornia, site (operating today as the San Onofre Nuclear Generating Station, Unit 1), and the Connecticut Yankee Atomic Company was proceeding with a facility at Haddam Neck that would generate 500 electrical megawatts. Among the several operating reactors in the nation, Con Edison's Indian Point plant rated at 275 electrical megawatts and Commonwealth Edison's Dresden station near Chicago at 202 electrical megawatts were the largest.[11]

Con Edison's application for the Ravenswood site was based mainly on economic considerations. In planning for the facility, the company had determined that a 1,000-megawatt nuclear plant, by making use of economy of size, would be competitive with a fossil-fueled facility at the outset and more economical than a conventional plant over its lifetime. Transmission costs were particularly vital in the selection of the site. While these were expensive anywhere, Con Edison incurred much-higher-than-usual expense in New York City. The company figured transmission costs in the urban area at $3 million per mile because many lines had to go underground. If the proposed plant were constructed at Indian Point, for example, Con Edison officials estimated that transmission costs would be $75–$100 million more than they would be at Ravenswood.[12]

The problems of air pollution and availability of fuel also weighed heavily in favor of a nuclear plant at the Ravenswood site. Air pollution from the existing oil-fired plant at Ravenswood would be aggravated if another fossil-fueled plant was constructed there. A nuclear facility would ease that problem. Con Edison's other major concern about constructing a coal-fired plant at the site was the possible interruption of coal. Labor strikes in the mines and by carriers had caused critical difficulties in the past, and storage of large supplies of coal on site was not a good alternative because of cost and space requirements. Utility

[11]Notice of Application for Construction Permit, December 10, 1962, "Ravenswood Preliminary Hazards Report," vol. 1, p. 1-1, "Ravenswood Site Data," pp. 1-1–2, AEC Docket no. 50-204, AEC/NRC; Edward J. Bauser to John T. Conway, December 10, 1962, Harold L. Price to Conway, December 11, 1962 (Ravenswood), Joint Committee on Atomic Energy (JCAE) Papers, RG 128 (Records of the Joint Committees of Congress), National Archives; *Christian Science Monitor*, December 12, 1962, p. 2; *Nucleonics Week*, December 13, 1962, p. 2; *Electrical World*, December 17, 1962, p. 46; *Nuclear News*, January 1963, p. 27.

[12]Bauser to Conway, December 10, 1962, JCAE Papers; U.S. Congress, JCAE *Hearings on the Development, Growth, and State of the Atomic Energy Industry*, 88th Cong., 1st sess., 1963, pp. 621–22, 626–28; minutes of Consolidated Edison (Ravenswood) Subcommittee of Advisory Committee on Reactors Safeguards (ACRS), September 11, 1963, ACRS File, AEC/NRC; *Electrical World*, March 25, 1963, p. 69. Indian Point is 24 miles direct-line distance from downtown New York City. Transmission-line distance, however, is 38 miles, of which approximately 13 miles is underground.

officials saw the nuclear option at Ravenswood as a welcome lifting of those burdens.[13]

Con Edison's 1962 proposal gave credence to the AEC's recent milestone report to the president, an analysis which argued that commercial light-water reactors were on the threshold of being competitive with conventional plants. But the Ravenswood site posed a delicate problem for the agency's regulatory staff. It had to judge the potential hazards of allowing construction of a nuclear plant in the heart of the nation's largest city knowing very well the precedent such a reactor would set for future site applications. To guide them, the federal regulators turned first to their recently published reactor site criteria.[14]

To aid in evaluating the site, the criteria required Con Edison to make projections about certain factors: the dangerous fission product release from the nuclear core of the reactor based on a major hypothesized credible accident, the expected demonstrable leak rate from the containment structure, and the meteorological conditions pertinent to the site. On the basis of its assumptions and predictions, the utility could then calculate the isolation distances spelled out in the site criteria: the "exclusion zone," "low population zone," and "population center distance." The criteria defined the exclusion area as the vicinity surrounding a reactor in which the licensee had the authority to determine all activities. Normally, residence within the exclusion area was prohibited. The criteria determined that the exclusion area be of such size that an individual located at any point on its boundary for two hours following the postulated fission product release in the event of an accident would not receive radiation exposure to the whole body in excess of 25 rem, or a radiation dose to the thyroid from iodine exposure in excess of 300 rem.

The low population zone provided an area immediately surrounding the exclusion area which contained a density and total number of residents who, in the event of a serious accident, could be given appropriate protective measures (e.g., evacuation). The criteria did not specify a permissible population density or a total population for the zone because the situation may vary from case to case. Instead, they determined that the zone should be an area in size so that an individual who was exposed to the radioactive cloud resulting from the postulated release of fission products and who was located on the zone's outer boundary during the entire period of the cloud's passage would not receive radiation exposure to the whole body in excess of 25 rem or to the thyroid in excess of 300 rem from iodine exposure.

[13]U.S. Congress, JCAE, *Hearings on Development*, 1963, pp. 622–23.

[14]AEC, "Civilian Nuclear Power—a Report to the President," pp. 124–25; *Code of Federal Regulations (CFR)*, 10 pt. 100—Reactor Site Criteria, 1962.

The criteria defined the third element, the population center distance, as the span from the reactor to the nearest boundary of a built-up area "containing more than about 25,000 residents." They determined that this should be at least one-and-one-third times the distance from the reactor to the outer boundary of the low population zone. The guidelines further pointed out that, where large cities were close by, a greater distance might be necessary. The criteria suggested that TID-14844, the procedural method and sample calculation for a hypothetical reactor, be used as a beginning point for evaluation of any proposed site. The calculated distances could then be adjusted upward or downward, depending on the physical characteristics of a site and the specific features of a reactor, such as the leak rate of the containment or engineered safety features.[15]

Population statistics obviously precluded application of the calculated low population zone and population center distance for the Ravenswood reactor. Application of the sample calculation in TID-14844 to a hypothetical reactor with the equivalent power rating of the proposed Con Edison unit produced an exclusion distance of 1 mile, a low population zone distance of 16.5 miles, and a population center distance of 21.5 miles. Ravenswood's actual proposed exclusion area was 675 by 550 feet. Within a 5-mile radius, a daytime population of five million people lived and worked. At night the number dropped to three million. Within a ½ mile, Con Edison estimated the population to be 28,000 people during the day and 18,800 at night. Engineered safeguards, then, would have to compensate for the lack of remoteness from the large population. So it fell to the AEC regulatory staff and the Safeguards Committee to evaluate Con Edison's reactor design and determine its suitability for the Ravenswood site.[16]

As one of the pioneering power companies in the nuclear field, Con Edison appeared to be the type of utility that could make the Ravenswood facility a reality. The company's experience with the Indian Point reactor, its application for Ravenswood stated, had been "invaluable in aiding our determination to bring the benefits of atomic power to our customers at the earliest possible time." Harland C. Forbes, who in 1957 became chairman of the board, was, like his predecessor Hudson R. Searing, an aggressive engineer who believed that nuclear energy would be an important part of Con Edison's mixture of fuel sources.

[15]*CFR*, 10 pt. 100—Reactor Site Criteria, 1962; AEC, Technical Information Document (TID)-14844, "Calculation of Distance Factors for Power and Test Reactor Sites," March 23, 1963.
[16]Robert Lowenstein to Duncan C. Clark, n.d., Industrial Research and Application—6 (Reg. Consolidated Edison—Ravenswood Site), AEC/NRC; TID-14844; minutes of Consolidated Edison (Ravenswood) Subcommittee of ACRS, ACRS File, AEC/NRC.

Forbes and his senior staff felt absolutely no apprehension about the safety of the proposed facility. Shortly after the Ravenswood announcement, the chairman told a reporter that operating Indian Point had given the company confidence that a nuclear plant could be built at Ravenswood "or in Times Square for that matter" without hazard to employees or the community. Questioned a few months later before the Joint Committee on Atomic Energy about his faith in the safety design of the plant, Forbes retorted, "If we didn't have [confidence] we would never have proposed it in the first place." He believed that the future of nuclear power as a source of electrical energy in large cities was at stake in the Ravenswood case. Forbes later suggested that Ravenswood raised a key question that the AEC found in making decisions about siting: "Either these plants are safe to build or they're not," he said, "whether it would be 500 people affected or 5,000,000."[17]

Con Edison's plans for Ravenswood soon sparked vociferous opposition from local citizens. The utility's announcement of the Ravenswood application in December 1962 came at a time when all the city's newspapers were shut down by a strike. This might have delayed organization of opposition for a short time, but by January 1963 a group of residents neighboring the Ravenswood site was seeking more information about the company's plans. The Astoria–Long Island City Community Council, consisting of nearly all the civic and religious organizations in Queens, arranged a public information meeting that representatives of Con Edison, the AEC, the governor of New York, the mayor of the city, and the president of the borough of Queens would attend.[18]

Sleet and snow in New York on the night of February 19 did not prevent a crowd of some 250–300 people from filling the auditorium at St. Rita's Roman Catholic Church in Queens. The three-hour session quickly became as stormy as the weather outside. Politely at first, the audience listened to Con Edison spokesmen give details about the proposed plant, including the safety devices designed to ensure that the reactor posed virtually no danger to public health. The AEC Division of Reactor Licensing and Regulation director Robert Lowen-

[17]Philip L. Cantelon, "Engineers and Alchemists: Electricity from Nuclear Energy," draft of unpublished manuscript in progress, pp. 10–11, 32–34; Application for Construction Permit, December 10, 1962, AEC Docket no. 50-204, AEC/NRC; *Christian Science Monitor*, December 12, 1962, p. 2; U.S. Congress, JCAE, *Hearings on Development*, 1963, p. 624; *New York Times*, May 10, 1963, p. 18.

[18]*Electrical World*, December 24, 1962, p. 22; Morton Kulick to Atomic Energy Commission, December 14, 1962, James Angiola to Atomic Energy Commission, January 21, 30, 1963, Folder no. 1 (December 7, 1962–May 20, 1963), AEC Docket no. 50-204, AEC/NRC.

stein stressed that he could not discuss the merits of Con Edison's application but assured the crowd that the agency would evaluate it carefully. He asserted that neither the AEC staff nor the Safeguards Committee had yet reached any conclusions on the proposal.[19]

The mood of the meeting changed dramatically after Robert C. Beardsley, an associate professor of biology at Manhattan College, challenged the optimistic assessment of the plant's risks presented by Con Edison. He gave his scientific opinion that there was no safe dose of atomic radiation and that there was ample reason to suspect that even the smallest amounts had ill effects on the human body. Beardsley was followed by Queens borough president Mario J. Cariello, who minced no words in opposing the Ravenswood application: "I was opposed to this project, I am opposed, and I will continue in that stand until convinced otherwise." The audience roundly applauded him. The subsequent question-and-answer period demonstrated strong criticism toward the utility and particularly toward the Ravenswood project. The chairman of the Astoria–Long Island City Community Council, who had called the meeting, later accurately reported that "although there was a difference of opinion between the speakers of the evening as to the dangerous effects of atomic radiation, the audience showed no such disagreement, and unanimously applauded all opposition to the building of such a plant in our community."[20]

The concern of the Ravenswood community about the safety implications of its proposed new nuclear neighbor marked the first organized movement against a commercial nuclear power plant in the United States. In the background, however, there had been, since the early 1950s, a growing anxiety nationwide about the expanding nuclear weapons race between the United States and the Soviet Union. Debates over nuclear fallout from weapons tests grabbed headlines as both nations conducted several series of atmospheric tests that ended only with the signing of the limited test ban treaty in October of 1963. The local opposition to Ravenswood, while not directly affected by the larger fallout controversy, has to be considered in the context of that national concern that had made the public particularly anxious generally about radiation hazards and nuclear explosions.[21]

[19]Duncan Clark to Harold L. Price, February 21, 1963 in AEC-R 102 (March 4, 1963), AEC/NRC; *Nucleonics Week*, February 28, 1963, p. 6.

[20]J. B. Graham to John T. Conway, February 20, 1963 (Ravenswood), JCAE Papers; *Nucleonics Week*, February 28, 1963, p. 6; James V. Angiola to Jacob K. Javits, March 18, 1963, Mario J. Cariello to AEC, April 15, 1963, Price to Javits, May 2, 1963, Folder no. 1 (December 7, 1962–May 20, 1963), AEC Docket no. 50-204, AEC/NRC.

[21]For the debate, see: Robert A. Divine, *Blowing on the Wind: The Nuclear Test Ban Debate, 1954–1960* (New York, 1978), and Mazuzan and Walker, *Controlling the Atom*, pp. 32–58, 246–72.

Grass-roots feelings against the Ravenswood facility continued to grow. A trickle of correspondence to the AEC early in 1963 increased in the spring and summer. Most letters came from New York City residents. Nineteen messages requested more information, three indicated approval of Con Edison's plans, and fifty-nine opposed the plant. The bulk of the correspondence in opposition expressed the opinion that nuclear plants had no place in a metropolitan area, although very few were opposed generally to nuclear power.[22]

Meanwhile, ad hoc committees and established groups in the local area rallied against the Ravenswood reactor. The February 19 meeting spawned the creation of the hundred-member Committee against Nuclear Power Plants in New York City, headed by Irving Katz, a biochemist who lived in Ravenswood. By late spring, another ad hoc group, the Committee for a Safe New York, was urging citizens to write to their congressmen claiming that the dividends of Con Edison stockholders "should not be raised at the expense of the safety of millions of New Yorkers." A political organization, the Queens County New Frontier Regular Democratic Club, adopted a resolution opposing the Con Edison application. In addition, it sponsored another community-wide information meeting on April 25 in Forest Hills. Although not as volatile as the crowd that attended the February meeting, the large gathering still displayed unequivocal opposition to the plant. All this turmoil prompted an inquiry into the Con Edison project by the New York City Council. The Democratic majority leader, Eric J. Treulich, set up the hearing through introduction on May 4 of a bill prohibiting industrial reactors in the city. In early June, the bill gained the support of the New York State Americans for Democratic Action.[23]

The February meeting also caused members of the local scientific community to lend their expertise to the growing debate. The Scientists' Committee for Radiation Information, an independent, nonpartisan group, had been active since 1958 in educating the public on matters associated with nuclear energy applications. The Ravenswood proposal now prompted the committee to start a new project, headed

[22]The letters are in Folders no. 1–3 (December 7, 1962——), AEC Docket no. 50-204, AEC/NRC.

[23]Richard P. Hunt, "Atomic Question for the City," *New York Times Magazine*, October 6, 1963, p. 46; Duncan Clark to Harold L. Price, May 6, 1963, in AEC-R 102/1 (May 10, 1963), AEC/NRC; Committee for a Safe New York statement: "Hiroshima—New York," n.d.; Queens County New Frontier Regular Democratic Club, Inc., program April 25, 1963 (Ravenswood), JCAE Papers; New Frontier Regular Democratic Club, "Resolution," n.d.; Robert K. Otterbourg to Joseph C. Clarke, March 15, 1963, Folder no. 1 (December 7, 1962–May 20, 1963), AEC Docket no. 50-204, AEC/NRC; *New York Times*, May 10, 1963, p. 1, May 15, 1963, p. 30, June 12, 1963, p. 42; *Nuclear News*, June 1963, p. 23; *Nucleonics Week*, May 2, 1963, p. 1.

by physiologist and anesthesiologist Stanley Deutsch, aimed at publishing a report "soon enough to be useful to the people of New York City as they strive to crystallize their thinking on the siting proposal for the first large urban power reactor." The scientists' group hoped "to render an accounting of hazards and safeguards, of advantages and drawbacks, as objectively, concretely, and lucidly as science can do for a general audience." Although its final report was overtaken by events and apparently was never published, the committee mimeographed a preliminary report that the Ravenswood reactor opposition used for scientific credibility.[24]

Con Edison chairman Forbes was questioned about the expanding local opposition to Ravenswood when he testified before the congressional Joint Committee on Atomic Energy on April 3, 1963. Forbes disparaged the protests by commenting that there had been little public interest either in favor or opposition. He told the committee that "there have been a few community meetings at which one or two people have raised some question about the genetic effects of radiation and so forth, some of which is rather silly. I think some of that has to be expected." While admitting that public opposition "could develop," he thought it unlikely. "It seems to me that the public in general has reached the point where it has accepted nuclear plants as a matter of course as they would any other plants," Forbes declared.[25]

The opposition that Forbes deprecated gained some national publicity the following day when David E. Lilienthal, the first chairman of the AEC (1946–50), testified before the Joint Committee. He had been asked to appear to elaborate on and explain a lecture he had given at Princeton University in February 1963. At that time, he had criticized the 1962 AEC report to the president for overstating the need for nuclear power and for understating the fact that, even if it was cost competitive, it differed significantly from other forms of energy because of the hazards associated with it. In his testimony before the Joint Committee, Lilienthal remarked that if he lived in Queens, he would consider operation of a reactor at Ravenswood "very risky business." Recalling that isolation of reactors had been the policy during his tenure as AEC chairman, Lilienthal questioned whether enough safety features had been developed in the interim period to justify metropoli-

[24]Scientists' Committee for Radiation Information, proposal for a "Conference for Scientific Information on Nuclear Age Problems," November 17, 1962, Stanley Deutsch to James Terrill, May 9, 1963, with enclosure, Sidney J. Socolar to Terrill, September 18, 1963, with enclosure, File 22, U.S. Public Health Service Records, Division of Radiological Health, U.S. Public Health Service, Rockville, Maryland. The preliminary report is excerpted in Sheldon Novick, *The Careless Atom* (Boston, 1968), p. 59.

[25]U.S. Congress, JCAE, *Hearings on Development*, 1963, p. 624.

tan siting. He declared that he "would not dream of living in the Borough of Queens if there were a large atomic power plant in that region." Lilienthal's statements elicited sharp rejoinders from several members of the Joint Committee. Senator John O. Pastore accused him of being "unfair" and "making these statements rather loosely," and Congressman Chet Holifield suggested that he was influenced by oil interests. But Lilienthal's comments, coming from a person of stature, gave opponents of Ravenswood an unexpected windfall of prominence and credibility.[26]

The increasing discord over Ravenswood became a political issue when Democratic majority leader Treulich introduced his bill banning industrial reactors in New York City. As a representative from Queens, Treulich stated that he would reserve judgment on the wisdom of his legislation until after hearings were held. But he emphasized that an inquiry into the matter was needed, and he hoped that the introduction of his bill would ensure that the questions surrounding Ravenswood were thoroughly aired.[27]

The City Council hearing on the Treulich bill, held on June 14, 1963, was the growing controversy's longest and loudest gathering to date. Demonstrators marched and distributed literature in the plaza outside City Hall. Inside the council chamber, a packed crowd of 350 people listened as fifty-nine witnesses spoke on the bill during the seven-and-one-half-hour session. The speakers, including scientists, engineers, lawyers, and concerned citizens, represented the utility, the AEC, civic groups, and parents' organizations. Earl L. Griffita, senior vice-president of Con Edison, outlined the utility's proposal for Ravenswood, backed by four company scientists and engineers. The AEC's Robert Lowenstein outlined the regulatory process the Con Edison application would have to pass before the agency granted a permit. He also read a statement from AEC chairman Glenn T. Seaborg that raised a serious question about the legality of the proposed city legislation. Seaborg suggested that the Atomic Energy Act gave the U.S. government exclusive regulatory authority on such questions as the Ravenswood site. State senator Seymour R. Thayler of Queens made one of the strongest protests against the plant. He told the city legislators that four out of five Queens residents opposed the plant, and that, in spite of all the safety precautions the engineers could build

---

[26]Ibid., pp. 704–44; David E. Lilienthal, *The Journals of David E. Lilienthal: The Harvest Years, 1959–1963* (New York, 1971), pp. 460–63; *New York Times*, April 5, 1963, p. 11; *Nucleonics Week*, April 11, 1963, p. 5.

[27]*New York Times*, May 9, 1963, p. 1, May 15, 1963, p. 30.

into the reactor, "the mind of man has not yet invented an accident-proof piece of mechanical equipment."[28]

Although the hearing was inconclusive, the presentations by Con Edison and the AEC greatly disturbed a careful observer and strong proponent of nuclear power. In a rare editorial, the trade sheet *Nucleonics Week* depicted the New York hearing as a missed opportunity for the industry. Noting that more and more attention would be focused on siting nuclear plants in urban centers, the weekly newsletter argued that many people were asking intelligent questions that could not be "brushed under the carpet."[29]

What was needed at the hearing, the editorial suggested, was an authoritative presentation for laymen on the "ABCs" of nuclear power. It criticized the AEC for sending a lawyer (Lowenstein) instead of a technical expert to testify. Lowenstein had to "duck vital technical questions" and therefore reinforced doubt in the minds of some of the listeners. But in the editor's opinion, Con Edison's representatives were even less satisfactory. The editor criticized the utility's cavalier assumption that it did not have to "go all out on educating the City Council and the public." Instead, Con Edison spokesmen failed "to give immediate and full answers to some good questions." The editorial concluded that "the net tone of the hearing was negative to nuclear power" and warned that "if the public does not accept nuclear power, there will be no nuclear power."[30]

The *New York Times* echoed *Nucleonics Week*'s opinion. In an August 6 editorial, the newspaper complained that Con Edison had not presented a "compelling reason why the construction of a nuclear reactor inside the city limits" was necessary. "What is still lacking," the editorial concluded, "is a clear statement of why there is no other place to put the plant than [in] the heart of the metropolitan area."[31]

The issue continued to generate controversy and gain headlines during the fall of 1963. Lilienthal's earlier questioning of the benefits of nuclear power had irritated many nuclear proponents. Seaborg, for one, waited for the right occasion to rebut the former AEC chairman. In early November, he used an invitation to address Sigma Delta Chi, a national fraternity of journalists, to join the debate. He later said he

[28]Statement at June 14, 1963, Public Hearing by Mary Hays Weik (Ravenswood), JCAE Papers; *New York Times*, June 15, 1963, p. 1; Glenn Seaborg to Paul R. Screvene, June 11, 1963, AEC Press Release no. F-120, AEC/NRC; *Nucleonics Week*, June 20, 1963, p. 2; *Nuclear News*, July 1963, pp. 25–26; *Electrical World*, July 1, 1963, p. 60.
[29]*Nucleonics Week*, June 20, 1963, p. 1.
[30]Ibid., pp. 1–2.
[31]*New York Times*, August 26, 1963, p. 26.

spoke out because it was "timely and necessary ... that the public understand the stringent safety standards which these nuclear power reactors must meet before construction and operation are authorized." Without mentioning Lilienthal by name, Seaborg's speech to the journalists included a point-by-point refutation of both Lilienthal's Joint Committee testimony and his charges in earlier lectures. While dealing with several issues, Seaborg stressed reactor siting. He explained why utilities wanted to locate facilities in metropolitan areas and pointed out that any application had to pass AEC regulatory review, which had been "ultra conservative with respect to safety." Seaborg declared, in contrast to Lilienthal, that he would "not fear having my family residence within the vicinity of a modern nuclear power plant built and operated under our regulations and controls."[32]

Seaborg's widely reported talk set the stage for further bitter discussion within the industry. At the annual joint meeting of the American Nuclear Society and the Atomic Industrial Forum, Lilienthal reiterated his criticism of the nuclear establishment. He again questioned whether enough was known about the hazards to the public to permit nuclear plants in congested areas. Furthermore, he charged that Seaborg's recent comments at the Sigma Delta Chi convention had in effect prejudged the Ravenswood application. Lilienthal's speech stirred a sharp reaction. Shortly afterward, the press was invited to meet with a group of men to dispute the former chairman's views. AEC commissioner James Ramey; Emerson Jones, consultant to the managers of the Consumers Power District of Nebraska; Robert E. Ginna, chairman of the Rochester Gas and Electric Corporation; and Joseph Howland of the University of Rochester formed the group. They maintained that Lilienthal's remarks were "entirely uncalled for," and they vigorously defended the safety record of the nuclear industry. Later that day, Lilienthal wrote privately in his journal that he thought the "truth squad" tactic was a "stupid, reckless stunt." He predicted that the AEC would hear more misgivings about its role in protecting the public from the hazards of nuclear power plants. "Just booing me, or having Senators bark at me," Lilienthal wrote, "won't make the real issue go away."[33]

In the midst of this year-long public debate over the siting of the Ravenswood facility, the AEC regulatory staff and the Safeguards

---

[32]Seaborg, Remarks to the National Convention—Sigma Delta Chi, November 7, 1963, AEC Speech File, S-33-63, AEC/NRC; *Nucleonics Week*, November 14, 1963, p. 6.

[33]*New York Times*, November 8, 1963, p. 16; November 20, 1963, p. 61; *Nucleonics Week*, November 14, 1963, p. 1; November 10, 1963, p. 1; *Nuclear News*, December 1963, pp. 17-18; *Wall Street Journal*, November 20, 1963, p. 32; Lilienthal, *Harvest Years* (n. 26 above), pp. 521–22.

Committee (established by statute as an independent advisory body to the AEC) quietly worked on their evaluation of the Con Edison application. Following its usual procedures, the staff reviewed the preliminary hazards summary report on the reactor submitted with its application by the utility. It also met informally on several occasions with Con Edison representatives. The Safeguards Committee, likewise following its standard format, established a Ravenswood subcommittee that proceeded independently to evaluate the hazards report.[34]

Because of the dense population around the site, the proposed reactor's acceptance would have to be based solely on engineered design features. Without distance to rely on as a safety factor, the AEC's regulators were forced to consider the reactor design and project ways in which the engineered safeguards might fail to perform satisfactorily. This procedure would determine whether the reactor could be erected at the proposed site. It made the Ravenswood application the most difficult one they had faced to that time.

The most important engineered safety feature incorporated into the plant design was the so-called double containment. According to the Con Edison preliminary hazards report, the containment would withstand any leakage to the outside environment of radioactive water, air, steam, and fission products even in the "worst conceivable accident" (instantaneous escape of the radioactive primary cooling system from the piping into the containment with a subsequent 100 percent of the nuclear core melted). Con Edison reported confidently that the containment would be so rigorous that it would meet not only the standards set for the AEC site criteria but also the agency's more rigid standards for protection against radiation. The structure was a reinforced concrete "igloo," approximately 150 feet in diameter, 167 feet in height, and 7 feet thick, that rested on a solid concrete pad. The outer shell consisted of 5½ feet of reinforced concrete. This provided the bulk of the shielding from radiation inside the reactor. On the inside of the outer concrete shell was a welded steel vessel or membrane, fabricated from quarter-inch carbon steel plate. Within that shell, the designers placed another quarter-inch welded steel membrane that was separated from the outer one by a distance of 2 feet. The space between the two membranes would be filled with low-density, pervious concrete. Called the "negative pressure zone," it would be maintained at a level below atmospheric pressure by means of

[34]Lowenstein to Consolidated Edison Company, August 9, 1963, Folder no. 2 (May 21–November 13, 1963), Division of Reactor Licensing and Regulation Report no. 1 on Ravenswood to Advisory Committee on Reactor Safeguards, September 25, 1963, AEC Docket no. 50-204; minutes of Reactor Safeguards Subcommittee (Ravenswood) of ACRS, April 10, 1963, ACRS File, AEC/NRC.

a pump-back system (another engineered safety feature) that would force air from this area into the interior of the containment. Thus any radioactivity that leaked into this space could be discharged back into the inner vessel. The designers also included in the containment plans a spray system to reduce any pressure that may build up within the containment structure in the event of an accident.[35]

The pressurized water reactor that Westinghouse designed for Ravenswood consisted of a primary coolant system that transferred heat from the fission process in the reactor core by means of ordinary water through piping loops to five parallel steam generators. The primary system was maintained under pressure to prevent the formation of steam (thus the pressurized water reactor got its name). The steam needed to turn the turbines was raised instead in a secondary system that allowed the heat to transfer from the primary system to the secondary fluid through the walls of tubes in the steam generators. The nonradioactive steam that formed in the steam generators was transported through piping out of the containment building to the turbine-generator. Within the primary system, the pressure vessel, which housed the core of the reactor where the high-density uranium fuel fissioned, acted as another safety barrier. Finally, within the core itself, metal cladding around the fuel served as an additional safety feature. Westinghouse also designed two independent emergency safety injection systems, which would supply borated water to maintain fluid coverage of the nuclear core in the event of a major loss-of-coolant accident (the preliminary hazards report postulated that the loss-of-coolant accident, defined as the complete severance of the largest pipe connected in the primary coolant system, was the "maximum credible accident" that could happen to the reactor).[36]

Because Con Edison's preliminary safety evaluation report emphasized that the integrity of the double containment structure would not be breached, it considered that this safety feature alone would more than offset the need for the distance factors in the site criteria. Therefore, the AEC regulators decided to evaluate the design of the containment first. By concentrating their effort on that system, they thought that they could determine whether the Ravenswood site would be suitable. In other words, the regulatory staff maintained that until the design features of containment proved to be sound, it would be premature to analyze the remainder of the proposed plant.[37]

[35]Preliminary Hazards Report, chap. 2, p. 2-1, chap. 4, p. 4-1, AEC Docket no. 50-204, AEC/NRC; *Nucleonics Week*, December 20, 1962, p. 3.

[36]Preliminary Hazards Report, chap. 1, pp. 1-4–1-5, chap. 3, pp. 2-1–2-2, 3-1–3-4, 4-3–4-4, chap. 4, pp. 3-5–3-7.

[37]Ibid., chap. 3, pp. 1-1–1-8; Division of Reactor Licensing and Regulation Report no. 1 on Ravenswood to ACRS, September 25, 1963, AEC Docket no. 50-204, AEC/NRC.

The AEC regulatory staff needed more technical information before reaching a decision. After several meetings with Con Edison officials, the staff formally requested additional data on August 9, 1963. Most of the questions the AEC asked related to technical items, such as how adequate the containment design was, how to measure radioactive leakage rates in the containment, how penetrations through the containment could be monitored, and how filter systems could remove radioactivity from the containment.[38]

While waiting for Con Edison's reply, the regulators continued their analysis of the available data. They also conferred with the Ravenswood subcommittee of the Safeguards Committee and with members of the Con Edison staff. Although it made no formal decisions as a result of the meetings, the AEC staff subtly suggested both to the Safeguards Committee and to Con Edison that the Ravenswood site probably would prove to be unacceptable. For example, in September, Edson Case, assistant director in the Division of Reactor Licensing and Regulation, reported to the subcommittee on a recent computer study that incorporated the available information on the Ravenswood reactor. The study calculated the potential hazards to the public in the event of an accident in which fission products were released. It analyzed such factors as containment spray rates, leakage hole size in the containment, safety injection system efficiency, and pump-back system rates. The computer program assumed a history of maintained power level for the reactor (in order to determine the fission product buildup) and projected a significant loss of primary coolant as a result of the accident. Case told the subcommittee that while the study could not be used to show that the Con Edison application was acceptable, it might show that reliance on designed safety features alone at Ravenswood would be unacceptable.

In a report to the subcommittee later that month, the regulatory staff questioned Con Edison's main assumption that, in the event of either a maximum credible accident or a worst conceivable accident, there would be no net escape of fission products from the containment. The staff cautioned that "we have not accepted the premise that the net outleakage in the event of such accidents would be absolutely zero." It further observed that, as more emphasis was placed on engineered safety features and less on isolation, the evaluation of hazards would become more complex.[39]

[38]Lowenstein to Con Edison, August 9, 1963, Division of Reactor Licensing and Regulation Report no. 1 on Ravenswood to ACRS, September 25, 1963, AEC Docket no. 50-204, AEC/NRC.

[39]Minutes of Reactor Safeguards Subcommittee (Ravenswood) of ACRS, September 11, 1963, ACRS File; Division of Reactor Licensing and Regulation Report no. 1 on Ravenswood to ACRS, September 25, 1963, AEC Docket no. 50-204, AEC/NRC.

In October 1963, licensing director Lowenstein reported further results of the computer study to the Safeguards Committee. Initial runs of the program showed that, if all the engineered safety features operated as planned, the facility as currently designed still could not meet minimum radiation exposure requirements established in the site criteria. Lowenstein confided his belief that the regulatory staff would reject the application on the basis that the proposal entailed "too much of an advancement in reactor technology for this location." A month later, the staff sent a draft report to the Safeguards Committee that summarized Lowenstein's earlier conclusion. It stated that the proposal was unacceptable because it was "based upon the uncertainties involved in determining the adequacy of the engineered safeguards in the event of a fission product release accident in light of the definite expectation of significant leakage [from the containment]. The problem of demonstrating a guaranteed essentially zero release of fission products in the event of such an accident . . . appears overwhelming." Other engineering schemes might exist, the report said, but they "would have to be evaluated on their own merits."[40]

The AEC regulators, in other words, privately agreed with the public opposition to Ravenswood on the general supposition that this humanly engineered nuclear power technology was fallible. They did not have confidence that, at this stage of development, the technology could reasonably assure the safety features of its machine in an urban setting. Like David Lilienthal, the regulators deemed Ravenswood very risky.

The staff conveyed its conclusion on Ravenswood to Con Edison, although not officially. In November, the utility formally responded to the agency's August 9 request for supplemental information. In addition to submitting the analyses requested, Con Edison acknowledged that, as a result of its several meetings with the regulators, various aspects of the design had to be clarified and amplified. It believed that particular attention had to be given to "detailed studies of additional engineered safeguards not utilized to date in existing plants," and it planned to file a formal amendment to the preliminary hazards report about April 15, 1964. The company also hinted that it had not made a final decision on the Ravenswood plant and that it would weigh both economic and safety factors as it progressed through its planning stages.[41]

[40]Minutes of 50th ACRS meeting, October 10–11, 1963, ACRS File; Staff Conclusion on Ravenswood, November 12, 1963, cited in "Preapplication Meeting for Proposed Boston Edison Plant, 26 January 1966," AEC Docket no. 50-293, AEC/NRC.
[41]F. F. Brower to R. L. Lowenstein, November 14, 1963, AEC Docket no. 50-204, AEC/NRC; *Nuclear News*, January 1964, p. 23.

While the regulatory staff's reaction to the Ravenswood application was negative, the Safeguards Committee initially seemed ambivalent as it undertook its independent review. Members of the subcommittee assigned to the project approached Con Edison's application with an open mind, agreeing that the committee review should be based on a thorough evaluation for the engineered safeguards rather than make an "arbitrary determination that the plant is located unnecessarily close to a large center of population." After initial study, however, some members began to question whether adequate safety features could be built into the facility. In its first meeting with the utility representatives, the subcommittee chairman, Franklin Gifford, director of the Atmospheric Turbulence and Diffusion Laboratory at Oak Ridge, commented that the "lousy" site required undue emphasis on designed safety elements. Committee member William Ergen, a physicist at the Oak Ridge National Laboratory, suggested that Con Edison consider more remote sites. At another subcommittee meeting in October, committee members remarked among themselves that "many paths exist by which the double containment scheme might be by-passed" and that even a "very small release [of fission products] may be intolerable at this site." Ergen later advised Con Edison officials that he thought it "unrealistic to design and operate a plant with assurance that the required very low leak rates will be met in the event of an accident." In executive session at its monthly meeting in November, one committee member observed that if Ravenswood was to be rejected "because of the elementary state of the reactor art," Con Edison should be informed soon to avoid waste of time and money. Another member considered the utility ill-advised in submitting the proposal, but noted that it probably would not be difficult to withdraw, "particularly in view of the opposition to nuclear power . . . in recent Lilienthal articles."[42]

The precise effect on Con Edison officials of the reservations expressed informally by the regulatory staff and the Safeguards Committee cannot be absolutely determined. Circumstantially it seems clear that they played a decisive role in Con Edison's decision, announced on January 3, 1964, to withdraw the application. Con Edison chairman Forbes officially told Glenn Seaborg that the action was based on the utility's opportunity to purchase a large block of hydroelectric power from Canada on an "economically advantageous basis." Forbes stressed that his company still looked to nuclear energy to "supply the additional thermal power needs for our system in the years ahead" and

[42]Minutes of Reactor Safeguards Subcommittee (Ravenswood) of AEC, April 10, September 11, October 21, 1963, minutes of 50th and 51st ACRS meetings, October 10–11, November 7–8, 1963, ACRS File, AEC/NRC.

that withdrawal of the application did not devalue the "role which nuclear energy will play in our service area."[43]

Earlier in 1963, Con Edison had begun negotiations with the British Newfoundland Corporation for the purchase of Canadian electricity. The *New York Times* reported in January 1964 that the estimated cost of the Canadian power delivered to the edge of Con Edison's service area in Westchester County varied from 5 to 6 mills per kilowatt hour. This compared favorably to Con Edison's projection that electricity from Ravenswood would run 6½ to 7 mills per kilowatt hour. The *Times* report did not take into account, however, the high cost of new transmission lines from the edge of the utility's service area into the heart of New York City. At the April 1963 Joint Committee hearing, Forbes had emphasized that particular expense as the main economic attraction for constructing the Ravenswood facility. Con Edison officials who met with the Safeguards Committee had underscored the same consideration. Those earlier statements were not forgotten by Safeguards Committee members. In a brief discussion of the Ravenswood abandonment at a January 1964 meeting, one member spotted something of a red herring in observing that Con Edison's reason for withdrawal was "in variance with [its earlier] argument for the need of short transmission lines and hence lower costs in the New York area." Moreover, utility spokesmen early in 1963 had said that regardless of the comparative economic aspects of the Canadian scheme, the company intended to stick with the Ravenswood project at least through the stage of getting an AEC decision on the license.[44]

Con Edison's withdrawal of the Ravenswood proposal in the face of opposition from the AEC regulatory staff left the question of metropolitan siting unresolved. The first time the full Safeguards Committee had discussed the application in October 1963, one member had voiced some doubt that Con Edison's stated reasons for pursuing the Ravenswood site were its primary concerns. He conjectured that the proposal "may be more of an attempt to see if approval for city locations could be obtained." Other public voices suggested similar rationales. *Electrical World* had editorially praised Con Edison in September for its effort to gain approval for a city reactor "at the present level of knowledge and with the present degree of public confidence in nuclear technology." *Nuclear News* noted that a decision on Ravenswood "would settle the [metropolitan] siting problem forever." Now the jettisoning of the

[43]Forbes to Seaborg, January 3, 1964, AEC Docket no. 50-204, AEC/NRC.

[44]*New York Times*, May 10, 1963, p. 1; January 8, 1964, p. 47; *Nucleonics Week*, January 9, 1964, p. 1; U.S. Congress, JCAE, *Hearings on Development*, April 3, 1963, pp. 626–27; minutes of Reactor Safeguards Subcommittee (Ravenswood) of ACRS, September 11, 1963, minutes of 50th ACRS meeting, October 10–11, 1963, minutes of 52d ACRS meeting, January 9–10, 1964, ACRS File, AEC/NRC.

Ravenswood proposal left open the possibility of metropolitan siting in the future not only for Con Edison but for other utilities as well. Had Con Edison pursued the application to a formal decision and been rejected by the AEC regulatory staff (as it appears it would have been), it would have settled the issue by effectively ending the chances of locating plants in populous areas. By strategically retreating on Ravenswood, Con Edison postponed a final decision on metropolitan siting until a later time.[45]

Although not recognized then, the anti-Ravenswood demonstrations from the local citizenry appeared as a harbinger of the antinuclear movement that developed in the later 1960s. Earlier, a few nuclear waste disposal incidents in different parts of the nation had produced some short-lived local protests. But those actions were never connected with safety issues of nuclear power reactors. Prior to the Ravenswood case, no power reactor had been challenged by the local population on the basis of safety. Local groups had opposed a reactor proposed for a site at Bodega Bay on the California coastline, but that protest was an environmental one over the possible destruction of the natural beauty of the area rather than over any safety issues related to the reactor. In the only formal legal intervention prior to 1962 involving a commercial power reactor—the Power Reactor Development Company episode—the labor unions that intervened continued throughout the case as strong supporters of nuclear power.[46]

The significance of the Ravenswood episode is twofold. First, it

[45]Minutes of 50th ACRS meeting, October 10–11, 1963, ACRS File, AEC/NRC; *Electrical World*, September 16, 1963, p. 19; *Nuclear News*, December 1963, p. 30. Several utilities subsequently submitted reactor applications for metropolitan sites. In 1965, Boston Edison applied to site a reactor in Weymouth approximately 9 miles from downtown Boston; in 1966, the Public Service Electric and Gas Company in New Jersey submitted an application for a reactor to be located at Burlington, N.J., between Philadelphia and Trenton; the following year, several southern California utilities applied for a construction permit to build two reactors at Bolsa Island, just south of Los Angeles; and in 1969, Public Service Electric and Gas in New Jersey asked for site review of Newbold Island, again located in the densely populated Philadelphia–Trenton corridor. None of these applications met the AEC's site criteria for population densities, and the regulators considered the proposals very risky. The AEC informally suggested alternative, more remote sites in three of the cases, and, just as in the Ravenswood case, all the applications were withdrawn before formal decisions were made. By the early 1970s, the pressure from utilities to gain AEC approval for urban nuclear sites had waned. D. F. Brunch, *Metropolitan Siting—a Historical Perspective*, NUREG-0478 (Washington, D.C., 1978); George T. Mazuzan, "The AEC and Metropolitan Siting," draft of unpublished manuscript in progress.

[46]Richard J. Lewis, *The Nuclear-Power Rebellion: Citizens vs. the Industrial Establishment* (New York, 1972); Steven Ebbin and Raphael Kasper, *Citizen Groups and the Nuclear Power Controversy: Uses of Scientific and Technological Information* (Cambridge, Mass., 1974); Joseph Shatten, "The No-Nuke Wind Ensemble," *The American Spectator*, March 1980, pp. 7–12; Mazuzan and Walker, *Controlling the Atom*, pp. 122–82, 354–64.

marked the beginning of local protests against nuclear power reactor facilities in the United States. Although it is difficult to judge the precise effect of the public protests, they brought unwanted publicity to Con Edison and the nuclear industry just as protests would do in the 1970s and 1980s. Second and equally important, Ravenswood underscored the difficult but strong position taken by the AEC regulators against the industry's advocacy of urban siting. The regulators wanted a better-developed technology and more operating experience with reactors before allowing such a large risk to the population of New York City. Minimizing risk from this dangerous technology was an important part of the AEC's statutory mandate to protect the public health and safety. The regulators' stand against the Ravenswood reactor places them in a notable position for which they seldom gain credit.

Nuclear Power and the Environment: The Atomic Energy Commission and Thermal Pollution, 1965–1971

J. SAMUEL WALKER

During the latter half of the 1960s, the decline of environmental quality in the United States took on growing urgency as a public policy issue. A series of controversies over the effects of substances such as DDT, mercury, and phosphates, ecological disasters such as a huge oil spill off the coast of California and the death of Lake Erie from industrial pollution, and easily visible evidence of foul air and dirty water fueled public alarm about the deterioration of the environment. At the same time that the environmental crisis commanded increasing attention, questions about the availability of electrical power triggered deepening concern. Since the early 1940s, the use of electricity in the United States had expanded by an average of 7 percent per year, which meant that it roughly doubled every decade. Utility and government planners found no indications that the pace of growth was likely to slow in the near future. A report prepared by the White House Office of Science and Technology in 1968 predicted that the nation would need about 250 "mammoth-sized" new power plants by 1990. Power blackouts and brownouts became increasingly common-place in the late 1960s, graphically illustrating the discomfort and inconvenience that a shortage of electricity could cause.[1]

J. SAMUEL WALKER is historian of the U.S. Nuclear Regulatory Commission. He is the coauthor, with George T. Mazuzan, of *Controlling the Atom: The Beginnings of Nuclear Regulation, 1946–1962* (Berkeley, 1984).

[1]*Considerations Affecting Steam Power Plant Site Selection* (Washington, D.C.: Executive Office of the President, Office of Science and Technology, 1968); *Nucleonics Week*, December 12, 1968, pp. 4–5; Jeremy Main, "A Peak Load of Trouble for the Utilities," *Fortune* 80 (November 1969): 116–19 ff.; "Why Utilities Can't Meet Demand," *Business Week*, November 29, 1969, pp. 48–62; "Conservation Forces Thwart Utilities' Hunt for Power Plant Sites," *Wall Street Journal*, March 23, 1970, p. 1; "Danger of More Power 'Blackouts,' " *U.S. News and World Report*, April 20, 1970, pp. 48–50. For the best overviews of environmental issues, see Samuel P. Hays, *Beauty, Health, and Permanence: Environmental Politics in the United States, 1955–1985.* (New York, 1987); Martin V. Melosi, *Coping with Abundance: Energy and Environment in Industrial America* (Philadelphia, 1985); Martin V. Melosi, "Lyndon Johnson and Environmental Policy," in Robert A. Divine,

204 J. Samuel Walker

The growing public and political concern with environmental quality and the continually increasing demand for electricity put utilities in a quandary. Electrical generating stations were major polluters; fossil fuel plants, which provided over 85 percent of the nation's electricity in the 1960s, spewed millions of tons of noxious chemicals into the atmosphere annually. Coal, by far the most commonly used fuel, placed a much greater burden on the environment than other fossil fuels. The sulfur dioxide and nitrogen oxides that coal plants released were important ingredients in air pollution, and the carbon dioxide they emitted raised the possibility of harmful climatic changes over a long period of time. The difficulties caused by burning coal, and to a lesser extent oil and natural gas, defied easy solutions. The concurrent demands for sufficient electricity and clean air created, in the words of the Conservation Foundation, "a most vexing dilemma: How do we protect the environment from further destruction and, at the same time, have the electricity we want at the flick of a switch?" An article in *Fortune* magazine depicted the problem in even starker terms: "Americans do not seem willing to let the utilities continue devouring ever increasing quantities of water, air, and land. And yet clearly they also are not willing to contemplate doing without all the electricity they want. These two wishes are incompatible. That is the dilemma faced by the utilities."[2]

After the mid-1960s, utilities increasingly viewed nuclear power as the answer to that dilemma. While conforming with their plans to achieve "economies of scale" by building larger plants, it promised the means to produce sufficient electricity without fouling the air. Envi-

ed., *The Johnson Years*, vol. 2: *Vietnam, the Environment, and Science* (Lawrence, Kans., 1987); Edward W. Lawless, *Technology and Social Shock* (New Brunswick, N.J., 1977); Rihard H. K. Vietor, *Environmental Politics and the Coal Coalition* (College Station, Tex. 1980); and Roderick Nash, *Wilderness and the American Mind*, 3d ed. (New Haven, Conn., 1982).

[2]*Considerations Affecting Steam Power Plant Site Selection* (n. 1 above), chap. 4; James G. Terrill, Jr., E. D. Harward, and I. Paul Leggett, Jr., "Environmental Aspects of Nuclear and Conventional Powerplants," *Journal of Industrial Medicine and Surgery* 36 (July 1967): 412–19, reprinted in Joint Committee on Atomic Energy (JCAE), *Selected Materials on Environmental Effects of Producing Electric Power*, 91st Cong., 1st sess., 1969, pp. 121–33; *Nucleonics Week*, November 11, 1965, p. 2; *Restoring the Quality of Our Environment: Report of the Environmental Pollution Panel* (Washington, D.C.: President's Science Advisory Committee, 1965); Main, "A Peak Load of Trouble" (n. 1 above), p. 205; National Rural Electric Cooperative Association, *The Electric Power Crisis: Its Impact on Workers and Consumers*, 1971, copy in Box 35 (Reaction of Utilities, JCAE, etc.), Office Files of James T. Ramey, Atomic Energy Commission Records, Department of Energy, Germantown, Md. (hereafter cited as AEC/DOE); Conservation Foundation, *CF Letter*, March 1970, copy in Box 181 (Pollution), Office Files of Glenn T. Seaborg, AEC/DOE.

ronmental concerns were a major spur to the rapid growth of nuclear power, and industry voices emphasized the environmental benefits of nuclear generation. In a rare editorial, entitled "Let the Public Choose the Air It Breathes," the trade publication *Nucleonics Week* concluded in 1965 that, in comparison with coal, "the one issue on which nuclear power can make an invincible case is the air pollution issue." In a memorandum to senior staff members, public information officials of Atomics International, a leading nuclear vendor, itemized environmental assets of nuclear power. Describing it as "safe, clean, quiet, and odorless," they observed that atomic plants "do not release harmful amounts of pollutants to the atmosphere . . . [or] to water" and that they "assure continued supply of low cost power and conserve our natural resources." Like Atomics International, other nuclear vendors stressed the cleanliness of atomic power; it was an important selling point in their effort to expand their markets.[3]

As the buyers of generating facilities, many utilities found the case for the environmental advantages of nuclear power to be compelling. Sherman R. Knapp, chairman of the board of Connecticut Light and Power, told an American Nuclear Society meeting in February 1965: "Atomic power is bound to be increasingly attractive to communities as concern over air pollution intensifies." Other utility executives echoed the same sentiments and took actions that proved the accuracy of Knapp's prediction. Northern States Power of Minneapolis, for example, decided in 1967 to build a 550-megawatt nuclear unit because of environmental considerations, even though the estimated costs were higher than for a comparable fossil fuel plant. Richard D. Furber, vice-president of the utility, explained that Northern States had just suffered through a lengthy controversy over the construction of a coal plant and added: "Many times during the three-year controversy the opposition indicated they would lay off if we would convert this plant to a nuclear plant."[4]

This was not an isolated case in which environmentalists expressed support for nuclear power, though they clearly were less enthusiastic

[3]*Nucleonics Week*, February 25, 1965, p. 1; J. H. Wright, "Nuclear Power and the Environment," *Atomic Power Digest*, published by Westinghouse Nuclear Energy Systems, 1969, copy in Box 53 (Westinghouse Electric Co.), Seaborg Office Files, AEC/DOE; JCAE, *Environmental Effects of Producing Electric Power*, 91st Cong., 2d sess., 1970, pp. 1512–26; "Suit on Pollution to Seek A.E.C. Aid," *New York Times*, September 29, 1970, p. 25; AI-Public Information to AI Supervision, January 18, 1971, Box 194 (Anti-Nuclear Organizations), Craig Hosmer Papers, University of Southern California, Los Angeles; Richard F. Hirsh, "Conserving Kilowatts: The Electric Power Industry in Transition," *Materials and Society* 7 (1983): 295–305.

[4]"News about Industry," *Nuclear Industry* 12 (March 1965): 7–11, and "Northern States Power Puts the Accent on Environment," ibid. 14 (November 1967): 32–33.

about the technology than were industry representatives. While acknowledging the advantages of nuclear power in combating air pollution, some environmentalists cautioned that radioactive effluents could also pose a serious problem. Malcolm L. Peterson, a spokesman for the Greater St. Louis Committee for Nuclear Information, declared in 1965: "Because nuclear power plants do not pollute the air with smoke, nor produce any of the ingredients of photochemical smog, they are regarded as 'clean,' but it should not be forgotten that radioactivity, though invisible, is also a contaminant." Another prominent environmental organization, the Sierra Club, was ambivalent in its position on nuclear power. It protested plans to build a power reactor at Bodega Head on the California coast in the early 1960s, but as a policy matter it neither endorsed nor opposed the construction of nuclear plants. The attitudes of environmental groups were perhaps best summarized in the equivocal assessment of Thomas E. Dustin, president of the Izaak Walton League of America, in 1967: "I think most conservationists may welcome the oncoming of nuclear plants, though we are sure they have their own parameters of difficulty."[5]

The attitudes of the general public about the environmental effects of nuclear power were seldom evaluated. One poll published in early 1966 suggested that many members of the public lacked strong views or informed opinions about the subject. The survey, conducted with residents of Buchanan, New York (site of the Indian Point nuclear plant), Philadelphia, and Atlanta, asked, among other questions, "How 'clean' are nuclear plants in operation?" In each location, from 40 to 50 percent of the respondents had no answer. Those who did respond, however, overwhelmingly expressed a favorable outlook on the cleanliness of nuclear power.[6]

Officials of the U.S. Atomic Energy Commission (AEC) actively promoted the idea that nuclear power provided the answer to both the environmental crisis and the energy crisis. Under its statutory mandate, the AEC was responsible both for encouraging the use of atomic energy for peaceful purposes and for regulating its safety, and

[5]"Conservation Policy Guide: Abstract of Directors' Actions, 1946–1968" (Minutes), rev. ed., July 1968, Sierra Club Records, William E. Colby Memorial Library, Sierra Club, San Francisco; Thomas E. Dustin to Glenn T. Seaborg, February 17, 1967, Box 7717 (MH&S-11, Industrial Hygiene), and Thomas L. Kimball to Seaborg, November 6, 1970, Box 181 (Pollution), Seaborg Office Files, AEC/DOE; Malcolm L. Peterson, "Environmental Contamination from Nuclear Reactors," *Scientist and Citizen* 8 (November 1965): 1–11; Norman Cousins, "Breakfast with Dr. Teller," *Saturday Review*, March 19, 1966, pp. 26, 54.

[6]"Are Nuclear Plants Winning Acceptance?" *Electrical World,* January 24, 1966, pp. 115–17; "Nuclear Power and the Community: Familiarity Breeds Confidence," *Nuclear News* 9 (May 1966): 15–16.

it saw the energy/environment dilemma as an opportunity to enhance the attractiveness of nuclear power. Chairman Glenn T. Seaborg told the National Conference on Air Pollution in 1966 that, in light of expanding demand for electricity and deteriorating air quality, "we can be grateful that, historically speaking, nuclear energy arrived on the scene when it did." Although he acknowledged that nuclear power had some adverse impact on the environment, he insisted that its effects were much less harmful than those of fossil fuels. In comparison with coal, he once declared, "there can be no doubt that nuclear power comes out looking like Mr. Clean." Other AEC officials expressed the same views on numerous occasions.[7]

Other than radiation protection, the focus of its regulatory functions, the AEC did not view environmental issues as a central part of its responsibilities. Although the AEC expressed concern about environmental matters in general, it insisted that its statutory mandate for regulating its licensees did not extend beyond radiation hazards. The agency conducted numerous research projects around its own installations to seek information about the consequences of nuclear weapons tests, underground explosions, and reactor wastes for the natural environment and animal life. In nearly every case, the projects focused on the effects of radiation; the major exception was a series of studies done on heated water in the Columbia River from the plutonium reactors on the Hanford reservation.[8]

The AEC cooperated on an informal basis with other government agencies in assessing the environmental aspects of reactor licensing and operation, particularly the U.S. Public Health Service, a part of the Department of Health, Education, and Welfare, and the Fish and Wildlife Service (FWS), a part of the Department of the Interior. Relations between the AEC and other agencies were usually cordial

[7]U.S. Atomic Energy Commission (USAEC), *Nuclear Power and the Environment* (one of a series of booklets on "Understanding the Atom"), 1969, Atomic Energy Commission Records, Nuclear Regulatory Commission, Rockville, Md. (hereafter cited as AEC/NRC); Glenn T. Seaborg speeches, December 13, 1966, Box 7717 (MH&S-11, Industrial Hygiene, vol. 1), May 5, 1969, Box 25 (Pollution of the Environment), and April 20, 1970, Box 35 (Regulatory—General), Nixon Library Materials, Seaborg Office Diary, August 7, 1968, James T. Ramey speech, August 13, 1970, Box 35 (H. Peter Metzger), Ramey Office Files, AEC/DOE; "Atom and Environment," *Washington Evening Star*, June 16, 1969, p. A-10.

[8]John G. Palfrey to Donald F. Hornig, September 5, 1964, Box 168 (Office of Science and Technology), Seaborg Office Files, Glenn T. Seaborg to Edward Wenk, Jr., January 19, 1966, Box 1362 (MH&S-3-3, Contamination and Decontamination), AEC/DOE; John R. Totter speech, December 3, 1969, Box 194 (Environment—General), Hosmer Papers; USAEC, *Atoms, Nature, and Man* (one of a series on "Understanding the Atom"), 1966, and USAEC, *Nuclear Power and the Environment*, AEC/NRC.

and mutually respectful, but on occasion the arrangements led to disputes. One of those disagreements occurred when the FWS questioned the AEC's denial of regulatory authority over nonradiological environmental matters. The FWS, under an interagency understanding, reviewed power reactor applications submitted to the AEC to evaluate the effects of the proposed plant on the animal and marine environment. The FWS began to suggest in the mid-1960s that the AEC should take nonradiological environmental effects into account in licensing cases, especially the consequences of discharging large quantities of heated water for aquatic life. The AEC responded that it lacked authority to set requirements for any nonradiological effect that a nuclear plant might have on the environment.[9]

What began as a dispute between the AEC and the FWS soon flared into a major public debate over "thermal pollution." As it developed, the controversy not only embroiled the AEC in a conflict with Interior but also antagonized some prominent members of Congress, generated unfavorable publicity, and raised questions about the extent to which nuclear power was environmentally superior to fossil fuels. As a result of the thermal pollution issue, nuclear power, rather than being seen as an answer to environmental degradation from electrical production, appeared to a growing number of observers to be a part of the problem.

Thermal pollution resulted from cooling the steam that drove the turbines to produce electricity in a fossil fuel or nuclear plant. The steam was condensed by the circulation of large amounts of water, and in the process the cooling water was heated, usually by 10–20 degrees Fahrenheit, before being returned to the body of water from which it came. This problem was not unique to nuclear power plants; fossil fuel plants also discharged waste heat from their condensers. It was more acute in nuclear plants, however, for two reasons. Fossil fuel plants, unlike nuclear ones, dispelled some of their heat into the atmosphere through smokestacks. More important, fossil plants used steam heat more efficiently than nuclear ones, meaning that nuclear plants generated 40–50 percent more waste heat than did comparably sized fossil fuel plants. The cooling water that nuclear power stations

[9]U.S. Senate, Subcommittee on Air and Water Pollution, *Hearings on Clean Air,* 88th Cong., 2d sess. 1964, pp. 1069–97, and *Hearings on Thermal Pollution—1968,* 90th Cong., 2d sess., 1968, pp. 1248–62; Lester R. Rogers to Harold L. Price and others, June 13, 1963, Glenn T. Seaborg to Stewart L. Udall, March 27, 1964, John F. Newell to the Files, June 9, 1964, Troy Connor to the Separated Legal Files, July 9, 1964, Connor to Harold L. Price, May 25, 1965, Harold L. Price to Lewis A. Sigler, July 6, 1965, Price to Commissioner Ramey, February 2, 1968, L-4-1 (Memo of Understanding, AEC–Dept. of Interior and Fish and Wildlife), AEC/NRC.

released was not radioactive; it circulated in a separate loop from the water used to cool the reactor core.[10]

The problem of thermal pollution was not new in the mid-1960s, but it created more anxiety at that time because of the growing number of power plants being constructed, the greater size of those plants, and the increasing inclination of utilities to order nuclear units. Those trends combined to amplify concern about the effects of waste heat on the environment. Although the precise impact of thermal pollution was uncertain, there appeared to be ample cause to be disturbed about its implications. Some scientists suggested that waste heat deposited in lakes and rivers from steam power plants posed a grave threat both to fish and to other forms of aquatic life.[11]

The effects of thermal discharges on fish were worrisome because many species were highly sensitive to changes in temperature. A rise in water temperature could alter their reproductive cycles, respiratory rates, metabolism, and other vital functions. A drastic or a sudden shift in temperature could be lethal. Between 1962 and 1967, the Federal Water Pollution Control Administration found at least ten cases in which fish were killed by waste heat from fossil fuel power stations. The most serious incident occurred in the Sandusky River in Ohio, where over 300,000 fish died in January 1967; the others were much less severe. It was more common for fish to be killed indirectly by heat discharges. In the Hudson River around the Indian Point nuclear power station, for example, tens of thousands of bass died in 1963 after being attracted during cold weather to the warm currents coming from the plant. As nearly as experts could determine, the fish got caught in the water intake system of the plant and died from exhaustion or from contact with pumps or other equipment. Large fish kills attracted a great deal of attention, but the more subtle threats to the marine environment were at least as troubling. As one writer argued: "In the long run temperature levels that adversely affect the

[10]Federal Power Commission, *Problems in Disposal of Waste Heat from Steam-Electric Plants*, 1969, Box 7763 (MH&S-11, Bulky Package), AEC/DOE; USAEC, *Thermal Effects and U.S. Nuclear Power Stations*, WASH-1169, 1971, MH&S-3-1 (Thermal Effects, Nov. 1970–), AEC/NRC; Ralph E. Lapp, "Power and Hot Water," *New Republic*, February 6, 1971, pp. 20–23.

[11]Federal Power Commission, *Problems in Disposal of Waste Heat* (n. 10 above), pp. 1–2, 17–22; Roger Don Shull, "Thermal Discharges to Aquatic Environments," June 9, 1965, attachment to Clifford K. Beck to James T. Ramey, November 6, 1967, Legal-4-1 (Federal Water Pollution Agency), AEC/NRC; CW [Charles Weaver] memorandum, April 27, 1967, File 23-1-10 (Vermont Yankee Nuclear Power Plant Material, 1967), George D. Aiken Papers, University of Vermont, Burlington; John R. Clark, "Thermal Pollution and Aquatic Life," *Scientific American* 220 (March 1969): 19–26; Wolfgang Langewiesche, "Can Our Rivers Stand the Heat?" *Reader's Digest* 96 (April 1970): 76–80.

animals' metabolism, feeding, growth, reproduction and other vital functions may be as harmful to the fish population as outright heat death."[12]

The concern about thermal pollution extended not only to its hazards for fish but also to other potential consequences. It could disrupt the ecological balance by killing certain kinds of plant life while causing other kinds to flourish. Water warmed by thermal discharges, for example, contained relatively greater quantities of blue-green algae than of other species, and an excess of blue-green algae made water look, taste, and smell unpleasant. Rising temperatures also reduced the capacity of water to retain dissolved oxygen, which was needed to chemically convert waste matter into innocuous forms. As the amount of oxygen in the water diminished, the amount of undesirable wastes and pollutants increased.[13]

The nature and severity of the environmental damage attributable to waste heat depended on variables that differed widely from place to place, including the size and efficiency of the power plant, the type and adaptability of the fish and plant life in the affected body of water, the rate and volume of water flow, and the natural thermal characteristics of the water. While many questions about thermal pollution remained unanswered, the prospect that scores of new power plants, over half of them nuclear, would be built within two decades generated substantial alarm about its long-term effects. An article on the subject in *Scientist and Citizen*, the publication of the Committee for Environmental Information (the successor to the Committee for Nuclear Information), declared in 1968: "We cannot continue to expand our production of electric power with present generating methods without causing a major ecological crisis." Television newsman Edwin Newman informed his viewers of an even drearier prognosis. "The gloomiest forecast we know of about the future of our water resources is that by the end of the decade our

[12]Federal Power Commission, *Problems in Disposal of Waste Heat* (n. 10 above), pp. 18–21; Clark, "Thermal Pollution and Aquatic Life" (n. 10 above), pp. 19–22; JCAE, *Hearings on Participation by Small Electrical Utilities in Nuclear Power*, 90th Cong., 2d sess., 1968, pp. 89–92; "Con Ed Abolishes Fish 'Death Trap,' " *New York Times*, July 1, 1966, p. 37; Robert H. Boyle, "A Stink of Dead Stripers," *Sports Illustrated*, April 26, 1965, pp. 81–84; Allan R. Talbot, *Power along the Hudson: The Storm King Case and the Birth of Environmentalism* (New York, 1972), pp. 112–14.

[13]William M. Holden, "Hot Water: Menace and Resource," *Science News* 94 (August 17, 1968): 164–66; John Cairns, Jr., "We're in Hot Water," *Scientist and Citizen* 10 (October 1968): 187–98; Frank Graham, Jr., "Tempest in a Nuclear Teapot," *Audubon* 72 (March 1970): 13–19; Federal Power Commission, *Problems in Disposal of Waste Heat* (n. 10 above), pp. 21–22; USAEC, *Thermal Effects and U.S. Nuclear Power Stations* (n. 10 above), pp. 18–23.

rivers may have reached the boiling point," he reported in 1970. "Three decades more and they may evaporate." Newman added: "This vision of an ultimate cataclysm is based on the assumption that we will continue to discharge heat into our rivers at the rate at which we're doing it now." Most warnings about thermal pollution were far less apocalyptic than the one that Newman cited, but anxiety about the dangers of waste heat from power plants was widespread among both experts and laymen.[14]

Some observers, however, found less cause for concern. Although they acknowledged that thermal pollution was a problem, they also argued that its threat to the environment had been exaggerated. Scientists who took this point of view noted that laboratory experiments demonstrating serious effects of waste heat sometimes conflicted with actual field experience. They also showed that, contrary to the impression that newspaper and magazine articles often gave, only a small percentage of fish kills were caused by heated water from power plants. In addition, some scientists argued that heated water from generating stations could be beneficial. While certain kinds of fish were adversely affected, others throve in warmer water. The Pacific Gas and Electric Company, citing studies by the California Department of Fish and Game, asserted in 1970: "Fishermen rarely criticize utility companies for the warmer temperature of water near power plants. That's where the fishing is likely to be best." Heated water offered other potential advantages. Glenn Seaborg, for example, suggested that waste heat could be put to work irrigating fields to extend the growing season and reduce frost damage. In this regard, he and others maintained that the proper term for waste heat was not "thermal pollution" but "thermal enrichment."[15]

Yet even those who were most sanguine about the implications of waste heat recognized that its harmful effects could not be ignored. The disagreement of opinion arose over the severity of the problem, not the existence of one. In order to find out more about the

[14]Cairns, "We're in Hot Water" (n. 13 above), p. 187; Clark, "Thermal Pollution and Aquatic Life" (n. 10 above), p. 19; "Operators of Nuclear Plants Fear Heat Pollution," *Philadelphia Inquirer,* September 30, 1970, p. 1; "The Problem of Thermal Pollution," NBC television broadcast, May 24, 1970, Box 37 (Environmental Effects, including Thermal), Nixon Library Materials, AEC/DOE.

[15]Holden, "Hot Water: Menace and Resource" (n. 13 above), pp. 164–65; "Problems Associated with U.S. Thermal Effects Standards Examined," *Nuclear Industry* 17 (August 1970): 32–36; Atomic Industrial Forum, *Info: Thermal Effects,* February 20, 1970, copy in Box 18 (AIF Meeting, Thermal Considerations), Ramey Office Files, AEC/DOE; John A. Harris to the Commission, April 8, 1970, MH&S-3-1 (Thermal Effects), AEC/NRC: Glenn T. Seaborg and William R. Corliss, *Man and Atom: Building a New World through Nuclear Technology* (New York, 1971), pp. 81–83, 117–20.

consequences of thermal pollution and ways to control it, several government agencies and a number of utilities sponsored research programs. But most utilities could not wait for research to produce conclusive results about waste heat; they needed to build plants immediately to meet anticipated demand for electricity. Public concern about thermal pollution and newly established state water quality standards made it imperative for many of them to act promptly to curb thermal discharges.[16]

Technical solutions were available to deal with the problem of waste heat, but they required extra expenses in the construction and operation of steam-electric plants. Gradually, and often reluctantly, a growing number of utilities decided to pay the costs of mitigating the effects of thermal pollution. To do so, they built systems to replace their traditional, and preferred, practice of "once-through cooling," in which water was drawn into the plant, used to cool steam in the condenser, and then directly returned to its source. Utilities generally elected to use alternatives to once-through cooling because the volume and flow of the water available for cooling were insufficient, environmental groups raised vocal protests, and/or limits set by state agencies required them to reduce the temperature of waste heat discharges. The federal Water Quality Act of 1965 encouraged states to establish water quality standards for interstate streams and coastal waterways, and many states moved promptly to control water temperatures. The increasing concern about environmental quality, the imposition of state standards, the growing number and size of power stations, and the paucity of good sites for plants accelerated the trend away from once-through cooling, although utilities still employed it where they could.[17]

Utilities could choose from several options to reduce the effects of waste heat. The cheapest and easiest approach was to limit the environmental impact of heated water without building a separate system. This could be done, for example, by pumping more water through the condenser, which raised its temperature less, or by providing a long channel to discharge the heated water into different

[16]"The Effects and Control of Heated Water Discharges: A Report to the Federal Council for Science and Technology by the Committee on Water Resources Research," November 1970, copy in Box 169 (Office of Science and Technology), Seaborg Office Files, and "Thermal Effects Studies by Nuclear Power Plant Licensees and Applicants," 1969, Box 5625 (Environmental Pollution), OGM Files, AEC/DOE.

[17]R. E. Hollingsworth to Joseph D. Tydings, January 23, 1970, MH&S-3-1 (Thermal Effects), SECY-812 (December 28, 1970), AEC/NRC; Milton Shaw to Commissioner Larson, February 20, 1970, Box 7751 (ID&R-6, Hazards, vol. 2), AEC/DOE; Nucleonics Week, May 4, 1967, pp. 1–2.

sections of the source body of water. In many cases, however, a more elaborate system was essential. The available alternatives offered the means to resolve or greatly alleviate the problem of waste heat but also exacted significant costs. One method was to dig a cooling pond, where contact with air would cool the heated water on the surface. The primary disadvantage of a cooling pond was that it required a sizable area of land. A large plant would need a pond of several hundred acres (the rule of thumb was 2 acres for every megawatt), and, except in rural regions, the cost of that much land was prohibitive.[18]

Utilities generally found it more economical to build cooling towers. Several different designs were available, but the most commonly used were natural draft or mechanical draft towers. Either type of tower dumped waste heat into the atmosphere as warm vapor or warmed air. A natural draft tower could rise as high as a 30-story building. It worked like a chimney, drawing air warmed by contact with heated water upward and out the top of the tower. This process cooled the water, some of which evaporated; the rest either was recirculated in the condenser or returned to its source. The principal drawback to a natural draft tower was its cost, estimated in 1967 to be four thousand to ten thousand dollars per megawatt. Mechanical draft towers used fans to circulate air and cool the water from the condenser. They were less expensive to build than natural draft towers because they did not need to be nearly as high, but they were more expensive to operate. In addition to their costs, cooling towers posed other problems. They reduced the generating capacity of the plant by a small, but not negligible, amount. The water that cooling towers added to the atmosphere raised concern that they would cause localized fog and icing conditions, although there was little evidence that this was a common occurrence. Finally, natural draft towers were aesthetically objectionable to those who disliked the way they dominated the skyline for miles around.[19]

[18]Steve Elonka, "Cooling Towers: A Special Report," *Power*, March 1963, copy in Box 16 (Reactors—General), Office Files of Wilfrid E. Johnson, and P. N. Ross, "Presentation to President's Water Pollution Control Advisory Board," December 6, 1968, Box 3 (Water Pollution-Muskie Bill), Ramey Office Files, AEC/DOE; *Considerations Affecting Steam Power Plant Site Selection* (n. 1 above), chap. 4.

[19]Elonka, "Cooling Towers"; Ross, "Presentation to . . . Advisory Board"; Frank H. Rainwater, "Thermal Waste Treatment and Control," June 29, 1970, Box 18 (AIF Meeting, Thermal Considerations), Ramey Office Files; Glenn T. Seaborg to Sally Morrison, February 3, 1970, Box 7763 (MH&S-11, Environmental Studies, vol. 5), AEC/DOE; *Nucleonics Week*, May 4, 1967, pp. 1–2; "Outlook for Cooling Towers," *Nuclear Industry* 14 (October 1967): 8–14; "Wealth of New Data on Nuclear Plant Cooling Methods, Costs," ibid. 17 (July 1970): 7–15; "Utilities Burn over Cooling

The problem of cooling waste heat discharges was not peculiar to nuclear plants, but it was particularly troublesome in them. A utility that considered building a nuclear unit in the late 1960s inevitably confronted the issue of thermal pollution. In 1967, only a handful of power companies planned to use cooling towers, but, by early 1970, over half of the eighty-five plants on order or under construction were designed with cooling systems. Most of those without cooling apparatus were located on oceans, bays, or the Great Lakes, where the threat of waste heat seemed less acute. Although the trend was clear, it did not emerge without major controversies over the effects of thermal pollution and the role of the AEC in regulating them.[20]

Control over thermal pollution was, in the phrase of a writer for the trade journal *Nuclear Industry,* "a jurisdictional 'no man's land.' " The Department of the Interior, including both the Federal Water Pollution Control Administration and the Fish and Wildlife Service, took particular interest in the problem, but its statutory power extended only to advising other federal agencies and state governments on the protection of aquatic life. Enforcement of water standards remained a function of the states, but their regulations were not always adequate or uniform. Some members of Congress and officials of the FWS suggested that the AEC should assume greater responsibility over thermal discharges from nuclear plants, but it denied that it had the statutory authority to do so.[21]

The AEC's refusal to regulate thermal effects stirred private expressions of concern and, later, unusually blunt protests from the FWS. The differing views of the two agencies emerged clearly, and publicly, in a disagreement over an application for a construction permit for the Millstone Nuclear Power Station in Waterford, Connecticut. In November 1965, the AEC, as a part of its customary procedures, sent a copy of the Millstone application to the FWS for comment. The FWS, in turn, forwarded the document to one of its subdivisions, the Radiobiological Laboratory of the Bureau of Com-

Towers," *Business Week,* April 3, 1971, pp. 52–54; *Considerations Affecting Steam Power Plant Site Selection* (n. 1 above), chap. 5.

[20]Shaw to Larson, February 20, 1970, AEC/DOE; Hollingsworth to Tydings, January 23, 1970, SECY-812, H. L. Price to the Commission, July 27, 1971, Job 9, Box 19 (Legal-11 REG Litigation), AEC/NRC; "Outlook for Cooling Towers" (n. 19 above), pp. 8–12.

[21]Troy Conner to Harold L. Price, May 25, 1965, L-4-1 (Memo of Understanding, AEC–Department of Interior and Fish and Wildlife), AEC/NRC; "A Jurisdictional 'No Man's Land,' " *Nuclear Industry* 15 (March 1968): 3–5; Ellen Thro, "The Controversy over Thermal Effects," *Nuclear News* 11 (December 1968): 49–53.

mercial Fisheries. Theodore R. Rice, director of the laboratory, prepared an evaluation of the possible effects of the proposed plant on fish in the vicinity. He concluded that the reactor could be operated without radiological injury to fish. Rice appended a section cautioning that thermal discharges from the plant might have adverse consequences, but he accepted the AEC's view that its jurisdiction was "limited to matters pertaining to radiological safety."[22]

To that point, the comments of the FWS had followed well-established patterns. Clarence F. Pautzke, head of the FWS, made a major departure from routine procedures, however, when he sent Rice's report to the AEC in March 1966. Pautzke announced that, even though his agency had in the past submitted comments similar to Rice's, it had changed its position because of growing federal concern for environmental quality. "We wish to make clear that Dr. Rice's statements . . . concerning the jurisdiction and responsibility of the Atomic Energy Commission in regard to thermal pollution," he declared, "does [sic] not represent the policy of the Fish and Wildlife Service." Pautzke asserted that the AEC's regulatory authority covered thermal pollution and suggested that it ask the Department of Justice to review the question. If Justice supported the AEC, he thought that "legislation to provide this necessary authority should be sought by the Commission."[23]

Pautzke's letter caught the AEC by surprise. Harold L. Price, the AEC's director of regulation, complained that the FWS had not only sent it to several state agencies but also had "openly and publicly challenge[d] the position of the Commission with respect to authority over thermal effects." The Joint Committee on Atomic Energy, the AEC's congressional oversight committee, was equally startled by the implied effrontery and concerned about the possible effect of Pautzke's arguments. It had recently heard similar criticism from John D. Dingell, chairman of the House Subcommittee on Fisheries and Wildlife Conservation, who suggested that the AEC was evading the provisions and the intentions of the Fish and Wildlife Coordination Act. "The effect of this has been," he charged, "that they have

[22]"Preliminary Evaluation of Possible Effects on Fish and Shellfish of the Proposed Millstone Nuclear Reactor," December 15, 1965, Box 587 (Reactors: Millstone Point), Papers of the Joint Committee on Atomic Energy, Record Group 128 (Records of the Joint Committees of Congress), National Archives, Washington, D.C. (hereafter cited as JCAE Papers). This document is printed in U.S. Congress, House, Committee on Merchant Marine and Fisheries, Subcommittee on Fisheries and Wildlife Conservation, *Hearings on Miscellaneous Fisheries Legislation*, 89th Cong., 2d sess., 1966, pp. 191–94.

[23]Clarence F. Pautzke to Harold L. Price, March 23, 1966, Box 587 (Reactors: Millstone Point), JCAE Papers. See also Subcommittee on Fisheries and Wildlife Conservation, *Hearings on Miscellaneous Fisheries Legislation* (n. 22 above), pp. 191–92.

proceeded without due care for either the enhancement or the preservation of fish and wildlife values." In response to a request from Joint Committee Chairman Chet Holifield and for its own information, the AEC reviewed its legal stance on regulating against thermal pollution and applying the Fish and Wildlife Coordination Act to its activities.[24]

Howard K. Shapar, who, as assistant general counsel for licensing and regulation, was the AEC staff's authority on the legal aspects of regulatory issues, reaffirmed the agency's position in a lengthy analysis. He argued that the Atomic Energy Act of 1954 and its subsequent amendments restricted the AEC's regulatory power to hazards peculiar to nuclear facilities and that, therefore, its statutory mandate extended only to radiological health and safety.

Shapar further contended that the Fish and Wildlife Coordination Act, which Congress had passed in 1934 and strengthened in 1958, did not apply to AEC licensees. The act required federal agencies to consult with the FWS "with a view to the conservation of wildlife resources" if they undertook or licensed activities in which water would be "impounded, diverted, . . . controlled or modified." Shapar submitted that nuclear plants simply circulated and returned water to its source "essentially unchanged." They did not impound, divert, control, or modify it in the way that dredging, irrigation, or flood control projects did. Shapar acknowledged that a nuclear facility would raise the temperature of the water it used, but he did not view that as sufficient grounds to require AEC compliance with the Fish and Wildlife Coordination Act. Moreover, the act did not expand the regulatory authority of the AEC or any other federal agency. Consequently, even if the AEC were to agree that the law was binding, it would apply "only with respect to the radiological effects of licensed activities."[25]

Shapar's brief demonstrated that the AEC could make a strong legal case for not regulating thermal pollution. But the problem

---

[24]Harold L. Price to the Commission, March 28, 1966, L-4-1 (Memo of Understanding, AEC–Department of Interior and Fish and Wildlife), AEC/NRC; Chet Holifield to Glenn T. Seaborg, March 21, 1966, Box 202 (Regulatory Matters—General Files), Seaborg Office Files, AEC/DOE; John D. Dingell to Chet Holifield, March 17, 1966, John T. Conway to All Committee Members, April 2, 1966, Box 512 (Pollution: Thermal Pollution), JCAE Papers; John D. Dingell to Clinton P. Anderson, March 18, 1966, Box 845 (Joint Committee on Atomic Energy—General 1966), Clinton P. Anderson Papers, Library of Congress, Washington, D.C.

[25]Howard K. Shapar to the Files, April 18, 1966, Box 512 (Pollution: Thermal Pollution), JCAE Papers; Joseph F. Hennessey to the Commission, April 21, 1966, L-4-1 (Memo of Understanding, AEC–Department of Interior and Fish and Wildlife), AEC/NRC.

remained, and the AEC offered no alternative approaches for dealing with waste heat. When several members of Congress introduced legislation to resolve the issue by explicitly subjecting the agency to the provisions of the Fish and Wildlife Coordination Act, the AEC objected. One reason was that the bills did not grant the AEC any new regulatory authority, so that, in its view, its jurisdiction would still be limited to radiological hazards. A more important consideration was that the agency feared that the proposals, if enacted, would discriminate against nuclear power. Since fossil fuel plants were not licensed by federal agencies, they would not be required to meet the same conditions to control thermal discharges that nuclear plants would.[26]

In hearings held on May 13, 1966, Dingell grilled AEC officials about their views on thermal pollution. He opened the hearings by lamenting the "grossly inadequate protection now being afforded fish and wildlife resources," and the AEC's explanation of its position did not mitigate his anxiety. Harold Price told him that the AEC was "very much in sympathy" with programs intended to protect fish and wildlife but stressed that it opposed measures that would affect nuclear but not fossil fuel plants in doing so. When Dingell asked whether the agency assumed any responsibility for or took any interest in nonradiological environmental problems, Price replied that its authority was restricted to radiation hazards but that it was "very much interested in" preserving fish and wildlife resources. Dingell wondered whether the AEC had proposed any legislative solutions to vest "in your agency power to correct the hazard that is clearly apparent?" Price said no, that he believed the problem was "not peculiar to atomic energy plants, and it ought to be attacked more broadly." Dingell inquired about what the AEC would do if a proposed plant would obviously heat a river enough to be "enormously destructive?" Price responded that "we would be very unhappy" but that the AEC "could not, under the law, deny the license on that ground." Although Dingell was unfailingly polite to Price and other AEC representatives, he did not conceal his annoyance that their expressions of concern about thermal pollution did not convey a willingness to suggest anything they might do about it.[27]

---

[26]Howard K. Shapar to Mr. Trosten, May 9, 1966, John T. Conway to All Committee Members, May 10, 1966, William T. England to John T. Conway, May 17, 1966, Box 512 (Pollution: Thermal Pollution), JCAE Papers; *Nucleonics Week*, May 19, 1966, p. 5; Subcommittee on Fisheries and Wildlife Conservation, *Hearings on Miscellaneous Fisheries Legislation* (n. 22 above), pp. 112–13.

[27]Subcommittee on Fisheries and Wildlife Conservation, *Hearings on Miscellaneous Fisheries Legislation* (n. 22 above), pp. 97, 207–22; William T. England to John T. Conway, May 17, 1966, Box 512 (Pollution: Thermal Pollution), JCAE Papers.

The AEC was aware of the problem but uncertain of how to handle it. Agency officials agreed that thermal pollution required regulatory action, but they opposed any solution that would place nuclear power at a competitive disadvantage with fossil fuel plants. None of the several legislative measures proposed between 1966 and 1969 resolved that dilemma. The AEC did not want to exercise authority over thermal effects of nuclear plants unless fossil facilities had to meet the same conditions. It also objected to granting the secretary of the interior regulatory jurisdiction over thermal discharges from atomic power stations. As an alternative, it continued to consult with the FWS, which, for its part, stopped insisting that the AEC already had the necessary authority to regulate waste heat from nuclear plants. It asked that the AEC urge applicants to take action to control thermal discharges and to cooperate with interested state agencies. The AEC passed on the views of the FWS and, through it, the Federal Water Pollution Control Administration, to nuclear plant applicants as a normal part of the licensing process. But the recommendations were strictly advisory; compliance with them was not mandatory for receiving a construction permit.[28]

Meanwhile, public and congressional concern about thermal pollution continued to grow. The focal point of the enlarging controversy was the proposed Vermont Yankee Generating Station. In November 1966, the Vermont Yankee Nuclear Power Corporation, a consortium of ten utilities, applied for a construction permit for a 514–electrical megawatt plant on the Connecticut River at Vernon, Vermont. The situation in Vermont with regard to energy needs and environmental concerns reflected the national outlook in particularly sharp relief. Vermont had so little generating capacity of its own that it imported about 80 percent of its power, and its out-of-state suppliers were unable to provide for its rapidly increasing demand. At the same time, residents and state officials were committed to protecting Vermont's environmental resources from the threats posed by industrial development and population growth. The Vermont Yankee plant was intended to serve both energy and environmental requirements, but it soon aroused a sharp debate over the issue of thermal pollution.[29]

[28]James T. Ramey to Donald F. Hornig, December 14, 1966, Box 62 (Nuclear Power Reactors), Clarence F. Pautzke to Harold Price, February 8, 1968, James T. Ramey to David Black, February 9, 1968, Draft Memorandum, "Legislation on Thermal Effects," March 12, 1968, Box 64 (Thermal Effects or Pollution), Ramey Office Files, AEC/DOE; R. E. Baker to John F. Newell, March 13, 1967, Legal-4-1 (Federal Water Pollution Agency), Harold L. Price to Commissioner Ramey, October 8, 1969, Legal-4-1 (Memo of Understanding), AEC/NRC.

[29]Richard M. Klein, "Bananas in Vermont," *Natural History* 79 (February 1970): 11–18; John Walsh, "Vermont: A Power Deficit Raises Pressure for New Plants," *Science*

Officials in Vermont and adjacent states were gravely concerned about the threat of thermal pollution. James B. Oakes, attorney general of Vermont, insisted that the plant would need cooling towers to prevent ecological damage from waste heat. New Hampshire, across the Connecticut River from the proposed plant, and Massachusetts, 5 miles south of the site, expressed equally deep apprehensions about the environmental impact of Vermont Yankee. Elliot L. Richardson, attorney general of Massachusetts, complained: "Vermont will receive a million-dollar injection into its economy. Massachusetts will receive hot water." All three states protested the AEC's refusal to regulate thermal effects as a part of its licensing process.[30]

The Vermont Yankee Nuclear Power Corporation initially rebuffed suggestions that it add cooling towers to its plant by maintaining that they were unnecessary and too costly. Within a short time, however, the utility relented in the face of determined opposition from Vermont, New Hampshire, and Massachusetts. The company's concession was not enough to end the controversy. It made plans to use "open cycle" towers, in which the water from the condenser would circulate through the cooling system and then be returned to the river. This would enable the plant to meet Vermont's water standards by raising the temperature of a "mixing zone" in the river by a maximum of 4 degrees. But this was not sufficient to conform with the water standards of New Hampshire and Massachusetts, which required that even at the point of discharge the plant could not heat the river water at all. This could be done only by building a "closed cycle" system, in which the condensate water returned to the condenser after running through the cooling towers. The drawbacks of the closed cycle system were not only that it would be more expensive to build but also that it would reduce plant efficiency substantially. The issue was still unresolved in December 1967 when the AEC

---

173 (September 17, 1971): 1110–15; John Walsh, "Vermont: Forced to Figure in Big Power Picture," *Science* 174 (October 1, 1971): 44–47; Steven Ebbin and Raphael Kasper, *Citizen Groups and the Nuclear Power Controversy* (Cambridge, Mass., 1974), pp. 90–94.

[30]"They Want to 'Cool' Vernon Outflow," *Rutland Herald*, July 25, 1967; "Oakes Convinced Vernon Nuclear Plant Needs Cooling Towers," *Rutland Herald*, July 28, 1967; "Thermal Pollution Issue of A-Plant Still Up in Air," *Burlington Free Press*, October 20, 1967; "Vernon and the AEC," *Boston Globe*, November 10, 1967; *Nucleonics Week*, September 7, 1967, p. 1, September 14, 1967, p. 5; "Thermal Effects: An Acute Issue," *Nuclear Industry* 14 (September 1967): 8–14.

granted Vermont Yankee a construction permit, once again disclaiming responsibility for regulating thermal pollution.[31]

Edmund S. Muskie of Maine observed the Vermont Yankee proceedings with interest and growing impatience with the AEC's position. As chairman of the Subcommittee on Air and Water Pollution of the Senate Committee on Public Works, Muskie had already won recognition as a leading advocate of tough antipollution laws, and he took it on himself to investigate the issues involved in his neighboring states. On September 20, 1967, he wrote to Seaborg, questioning the legal basis for the AEC's refusal to consider thermal effects in its licensing actions. Muskie asserted that an executive order of July 1966, implementing sections of the Federal Water Pollution Control Act of 1965, had instructed all agency heads to combat water pollution from federal government activities. He wondered how the AEC could justify its denial of authority, and he asked for a prompt response to his query. More than a month later, Harold Price replied to Muskie. He pointed out that the executive order did not expand the AEC's regulatory jurisdiction and contended that it applied only to installations operated by federal agencies and not to licensees of the AEC.[32]

Muskie was visibly irritated by Price's letter; one of his staff members commented that the senator thought that the AEC was "thumbing its nose at the intent of Congress." He fired off another letter to Seaborg, reasserting his contention that the executive order and the Federal Water Pollution Control Act required the AEC to regulate thermal pollution. He also noted that his concern over the issue had been further piqued by the application of the Maine Yankee Atomic Power Company to build a plant in his home state. On November 4, ten days after Muskie's letter, Seaborg responded. He reiterated the AEC's standard arguments on why it believed that its authority did not extend to thermal discharges, but he promised that the agency would seek the opinion of the Department of Justice about the legal soundness of its position. In the meantime, Muskie had announced that he would hold hearings to investigate the AEC's

[31]"They Want to 'Cool' Vernon Outflow" (n. 30 above); "Nuclear Pollution Hearings Soon," *Rutland Herald,* October 31, 1967; "Power Plant Wins Federal Board Permit," *Rutland Herald,* December 9, 1967; *Nucleonics Week,* November 23, 1967, p. 6, December 14, 1967, p. 5; "Thermal Effects: An Acute Issue" (n. 30 above), pp. 8–11.

[32]Edmund S. Muskie to Glenn T. Seaborg, September 20, 1967, Harold L. Price to Edmund S. Muskie, October 23, 1967, Box 512 (Pollution: Thermal Pollution), JCAE Papers.

practice of granting licenses "without giving due consideration to the effect of waste heat."[33]

In hearings he conducted in Montpelier, Vermont, on February 14, 1968, Muskie heard representatives of Vermont, New Hampshire, and Massachusetts denounce the AEC for its refusal to exercise jurisdiction over thermal pollution. The governor of Vermont, Philip H. Hoff, after declaring that his state was "blessed with a matchless environment," went on to attack the AEC's position. "We were dismayed during the Vermont Yankee hearings when the AEC decided that thermal pollution was none of its concern," he said. "When it ignored the issue of thermal pollution . . . I think it declared itself to be a promotional agency—in effect, a publicly financed lobby." Officials of the other two states expressed similar opinions in language that was only slightly less blunt. The consensus clearly favored regulatory action by the AEC or some other federal agency. Muskie agreed, observing at one point that the AEC was "about as arbitrary in rejection of responsibility [as] I can recall in [my] experience with federal agencies."[34]

Despite the vocal objections to its denial of authority, the AEC received support for its legal stance from two important sources. The first came from Justice, which the AEC had asked, in response to Muskie's queries, to review the question of whether or not it had statutory jurisdiction over thermal discharges. In April 1968, Justice reported that it concurred with the AEC's view. After examining the provisions of the Atomic Energy Act, the Federal Water Pollution Control Act, and the executive order implementing sections of the latter act, Department of Justice attorneys concluded that the AEC did not have authority to regulate against thermal pollution.[35]

The AEC's legal claims also received support from the U.S. Court of Appeals for the First Circuit in Boston, which sustained the agency's position but viewed its policy implications with an obvious lack of enthusiasm. After the Atomic Safety and Licensing Board, a part of the AEC, granted a construction permit for the Vermont Yankee plant, the state of New Hampshire filed an appeal for a rehearing by the five AEC commissioners. The commission turned

[33]Edmund S. Muskie to Glenn T. Seaborg, October 25, 1967, John T. Conway to All Committee Members, October 31, 1967, Glenn T. Seaborg to Edmund S. Muskie, November 4, 1967, Box 512 (Pollution: Thermal Pollution), JCAE Papers; *Nucleonics Week*, November 2, 1967, p. 2; Bryce Nelson, "Thermal Pollution: Senator Muskie Tells AEC to Cool It," *Science* 158 (November 10, 1967): 755–56.

[34]U.S. Senate, Subcommittee on Air and Water Pollution, *Hearings on Thermal Pollution—1968* (n. 9 above), pp. 311–46.

[35]Joseph F. Hennessey to Frank M. Wozencraft, November 16, 1967, Box 7717, MH&S-11 (Industrial Hygiene, vol. 3), AEC/DOE; Frank M. Wozencraft to Joseph F. Hennessey, April 25, 1968, Box 512 (Pollution: Thermal Pollution), JCAE Papers.

down the request. New Hampshire then took its case to court, arguing, in terms similar to those of Muskie, that the AEC had the statutory obligation to consider thermal pollution in its decision to issue the permit to Vermont Yankee. The court of appeals denied that assertion in a ruling of January 13, 1969. It agreed with the AEC and the Department of Justice that existing legislation did not assign the AEC authority to regulate the thermal effects of licensed plants. But the court also declared: "We confront a serious gap between the dangers of modern technology and the protections afforded by law as the Commission interprets it. We have the utmost sympathy with the appellant and with the sister states of Massachusetts and Vermont." The court expressed its regret that Congress had not resolved the issue by "requiring timely and comprehensive consideration of nonradiological pollution effects." New Hampshire appealed the decision to the U.S. Supreme Court, which allowed the lower court ruling to stand by refusing to hear the case.[36]

Although the AEC won its battle in court, it was left in an uncomfortable position. It had clear judicial support for its argument that it lacked jurisdiction over thermal pollution, but it was under attack from critics who accused it of indifference to the environment. The once widely held assumption that nuclear power would provide both electricity and environmental protection was being questioned because of the emerging debate over thermal pollution. From the AEC's perspective, the best way out of this predicament was to support legislation that would clarify the roles of federal agencies in regulating waste heat discharges. But the agency favored legislation only if it did not discriminate against nuclear power or give the Interior Department final authority to decide thermal issues for nuclear plants. None of the several bills that were introduced during 1968, some granting the AEC and some the Interior Department responsibility over thermal pollution, won enough backing in Congress for passage, and the impasse continued.[37]

[36]AEC-R 141/34 (April 9, 1968), AEC-R 141/36 (April 23, 1968), AEC/NRC; *Nucleonics Week*, July 18, 1968, p. 6; "AEC Holds the Line on Jurisdictional Contention," *Nuclear News* 12 (January 1969): 8–9; "N.H. Challenge to AEC Rejected," *Bennington Banner*, June 16, 1969; State of New Hampshire v. Atomic Energy Commission, 406 F. 2d 170 (1969).

[37]Joseph F. Hennessey to the Commission, April 29, 1968, Glenn T. Seaborg to James F. C. Hyde, Jr., June 12, 1968, Seaborg to Edmund S. Muskie, October 15, 1968, Legal-4-1 (Federal Water Pollution Agency), AEC/NRC; Seaborg to Charles Schultze, December 11, 1967, AEC 783/98 (August 21, 1968), Box 64 (Thermal Effects or Pollution), Ramey Office Files, AEC/DOE; John T. Conway to John O. Pastore, August 27, 1968, Pastore to Muskie, September 5, 1968, General Files—Atomic Energy (Pastore Outgoing Mail), John O. Pastore Papers, Providence College, Providence, R.I.;

While the issue remained unresolved, criticism of the AEC became increasingly more pointed and more frequent. For a time, the attacks were sporadic and localized, largely limited to several members of Congress, a handful of environmentalists, and critics in the specific locations of a few proposed nuclear plants. But the problem of thermal pollution and the AEC's position on it captured expanding national attention after the publication of an article in the high-circulation *Sports Illustrated* in January 1969. The article was written by Robert H. Boyle, a senior editor for the magazine, devout fisherman, conservationist, and author of a book on the natural history and resources of the Hudson River.

Boyle's article, entitled "The Nukes Are in Hot Water," was a scathing attack on the AEC. "What literally may become the 'hottest' conservation fight in the history of the U.S. has begun," it opened. "The opponents are the Atomic Energy Commission and utilities versus aroused fishermen, sailors, swimmers, homeowners, and a growing number of scientists." Boyle went on to describe the threat of thermal pollution to aquatic life and to water quality. He assailed the AEC for refusing to take responsibility for the problem, attributing its inaction to a fear of the "financial investment that power companies would have to make . . . to stop nuclear plants from frying fish or cooking waterways wholesale." He gibed at Seaborg, suggesting that, even though the AEC chairman had won a Nobel Prize for finding plutonium, he had "yet to discover hot water." Boyle predicted that, since "more than 100 nuclear plants are on the drawing boards, . . . almost every major lake and river and stretches of Atlantic, Gulf and Pacific coasts are likely to become battlegrounds." The article was in many ways distorted and unfair; it misrepresented the AEC's position to the point of caricature. Yet Boyle obviously had no intention of writing a balanced scholarly treatise, and his tone of indignation and incredulity was an effective way to advance his own point of view.[38]

Although the precise impact of Boyle's article was impossible to define, it clearly broadened and called attention to the thermal pollution controversy more than any previous discussion had done. Debate over the issue was well under way before the article appeared, but after its publication, and to an appreciable degree because of its publication, thermal pollution became the subject of elevated interest

---

Nucleonics Week, July 4, 1968, p. 1, September 26, 1968, pp. 3–5, October 10, 1968, p. 6; "Thermal Effects Jurisdiction Stirs Further Controversy," *Nuclear Industry* 15 (September 1968): 36–38.

[38]Robert H. Boyle, "The Nukes Are in Hot Water," *Sports Illustrated*, January 20, 1969, pp. 24–28; Talbot, *Power along the Hudson* (n. 12 above), pp. 112–14.

and heightened concern on a national scale. One indication was the reaction and commentary that the article stirred. For three consecutive weeks *Sports Illustrated* ran letters to the editor that both commended and criticized the article. Representative Tim Lee Carter of Kentucky inserted it into the *Congressional Record,* hoping that it would "begin a rational discussion of what might be a tremendous problem in the future." Chet Holifield, worried that some of his colleagues "may have taken Mr. Boyle's utterances at face value," countered the assertions presented in "that esteemed technical journal, *Sports Illustrated.*" He defended the AEC from the charge that it did not care about the effects of waste heat and maintained that nuclear power was essential for achieving the twin goals of producing sufficient electrical power and preserving the environment.[39]

Some industry spokesmen reaffirmed the same view, but the article dismayed many of their colleagues. According to one knowledgeable observer, the story "shocked many in the industry," especially since "many utilities had in fact chosen nuclear power largely *because* of environmental advantages." The AEC's director of public information concluded in March 1969 that, although "public acceptance of nuclear power remains at a high level," the "biggest problem today is the question of thermal effects." He added that "until some positive action is taken to place responsibility for thermal effects this question will continue to give us trouble." One major source of concern was that, even if the environmental effect of a single nuclear plant were relatively inoffensive, the consequences of placing several plants that discharged waste heat into the same body of water might be ruinous. This was a point that Boyle highlighted, and the projections for the rapid growth of nuclear power fed those fears.[40]

The spreading alarm about thermal pollution was evident in protests against a number of proposed nuclear plants. Although the specifics varied widely from place to place, the general patterns of the debate followed similar lines. Like the controversy over the Vermont Yankee reactor, they usually started when state officials or conservationists raised questions about the thermal effects of a plant, became matters of dispute when a utility refused to build cooling towers or take other action to mitigate waste heat discharges, and ended only after considerable acrimony and/or concessions by the power com-

[39]"19th Hole: The Readers Take Over," *Sports Illustrated,* February 3, 1969, p. 62, February 10, 1969, p. 76, February 17, 1969, p. 72; *Congressional Record,* 91st Cong., 1st sess., 1969, pp. E412, H1467–H1469.
[40]"Are the 'Nukes' In Hot Water?" *Nuclear News* 12 (March 1969): 12–15; AEC 688/62 (March 17, 1969), Box 7751 (I&P-4, Public Information), AEC/DOE; Paul Turner, "The Radiation Controversy," *Vital Speeches of the Day* 37 (September 1, 1971): 697.

pany. In several cases, what began as local issues received widespread attention as a part of growing national concern over environmental quality in general and thermal pollution in particular.

One of the first examples of this pattern was a dispute over a reactor that the New York State Electric and Gas Corporation proposed to build on Cayuga Lake, the second largest of the celebrated Finger Lakes. When a group of Cornell University faculty members raised the issue of thermal pollution and urged the utility to add a cooling system to the plant, New York State Electric and Gas refused, citing the high cost of towers. This set off a contentious controversy that ended only when the utility decided to postpone work on the plant indefinitely to study the economic and environmental effect of cooling systems. Thermal discharges also emerged as a major issue in the construction of nuclear plants on Florida's Biscayne Bay. After a series of meetings, hearings, court rulings, and negotiations involving the Florida Power and Light Company, state officials, the Federal Water Pollution Control Administration, and environmental groups over a period of two years, the utility agreed to build a cooling canal system at a cost it had initially deemed to be excessive.[41]

The thermal pollution question generated even more acrimony in the case of the Palisades nuclear plant, located on Lake Michigan in western Michigan. A group of intervenors appealed to the AEC in June 1970 to deny the application of Consumers Power Company for a low-power operating license. They charged that the plant provided insufficient protection against thermal pollution and radiation. The attorney for the intervenors, Myron M. Cherry, argued that the AEC was obligated to regulate waste heat discharges, regardless of the Vermont Yankee decision, and that its radiation regulations were outmoded and inadequate. With construction of the plant complete, Consumers was anxious to secure its operating license, but it resisted making concessions to the intervenors. Finally, in March 1971, after numerous delays, several hearings, and sharp exchanges between the

[41]Luther J. Carter, "Thermal Pollution: A Threat to Cayuga's Waters?" *Science* 162 (November 8, 1968): 649–50; Dorothy Nelkin, *Nuclear Power and Its Critics: The Cayuga Lake Controversy* (Ithaca, N.Y., 1971); Claude R. Kirk, Jr., to Glenn Seaborg, December 12, 1967, Box 180 (Pollution), Seaborg Office Files, and Seaborg to Dante Fascell, February 1, 1968, AEC 544/79 (April 5, 1968), Box 7717 (MH&S-11, Industrial Hygiene, vol. 4), AEC/DOE; Harold L. Price to the Commission, February 27, 1970, MH&S-3-1 (Thermal Effects), AEC/NRC; *Nucleonics Week*, July 10, 1969, p. 3, July 17, 1969, p. 3, February 26, 1970, p. 3, March 5, 1970, pp. 2–3, April 1, 1971, p. 5, July 8, 1971, p. 5, September 2, 1971, p. 4, December 2, 1971, p. 4; "Florida Utility Wins a Round in Thermal Effects Court Action," *Nuclear Industry* 17 (April 1970): 29–30; "Cloudy Sunshine State," *Time*, April 13, 1970, pp. 48–49.

226   *J. Samuel Walker*

attorneys for both sides, the utility decided that it preferred a settlement with its opponents to the prospect of further costly delays. It agreed to build cooling towers and to virtually eliminate the discharge of liquid radioactive wastes into the lake. In return, the intervenors dropped their action against the plant and opened the way for its full-power operation.[42]

Although thermal pollution assumed major proportions as an environmental concern and a regulatory issue, the controversy over it largely died out by the early 1970s. The defusing of the question occurred for a number of reasons. One was that the results of the first meticulous studies of thermal effects, though far from conclusive, were encouraging. An investigation of the Connecticut River in the vicinity of the Connecticut Yankee nuclear plant, which opened in 1967 and did not have cooling towers, demonstrated "no significant deleterious effect on the biology of the river," according to an article published in 1970. Scientists who traced the consequences of thermal discharges from the AEC's plutonium reactors on the Columbia River made a similar assessment, finding "no demonstrable effect" on the salmon or trout in the river. Neither study claimed to evaluate the long-term effects of waste heat or the implications of placing many plants on a single body of water. Their findings, therefore, played only a limited role in alleviating concern over thermal pollution.[43]

A more important influence was that, after years of fruitless efforts, Congress passed legislation that assigned federal agencies a clearly defined role in regulating water quality. Since much of the thermal pollution controversy had centered on the AEC's denial of statutory authority, congressional action removed one of the leading sources of dispute. In January 1969 Muskie introduced a bill that would require applicants for AEC construction permits or other federal licenses to present certification from appropriate state or interstate agencies that the plant could meet the water quality standards of their jurisdiction.

[42]"Cooling Tower Slated for Nuclear Plant," *New York Times*, March 17, 1971, p. 29; *Nucleonics Week*, July 2, 1970, p. 5, February 25, 1971, p. 1, March 18, 1971, p. 3; "In Government," *Nuclear Industry* 17 (July 1970): 33–39; "Cooling Tower Concession Seen as Aim of Palisades Intervenors," *Nuclear Industry* 17 (August 1970): 22–26; Frances Gendlin, "The Palisades Protest: A Pattern of Citizen Intervention," *Bulletin of the Atomic Scientists* 27 (November 1971): 53–56; James B. Graham to Edward J. Bauser, September 29, 1970, Box 512 (Pollution: Thermal Pollution), JCAE Papers; Bauser to All Committee Members, June 30, 1970, Box 181 (Reactors—Palisades), Hosmer Papers.
[43]Daniel Merriman, "The Calefaction of a River," *Scientific American* 222 (May 1970): 2–12; "Burgeoning Atomic Plants Run into Pollution Awareness," *Washington Post*, August 25, 1970, p. 4; *Nucleonics Week*, August 27, 1970, pp. 7–8; USAEC, *Thermal Effects and U.S. Nuclear Power Stations* (n. 10 above), pp. 15–36.

Members of the House proposed similar legislation. Although the measures did not extend the direct authority of the AEC, they required that it formally consider thermal effects as a part of its licensing process. They did not apply only to nuclear plants, or even only to thermal pollution, but to any activity that could lower water quality.[44]

On March 3, 1969, Commissioner James T. Ramey announced that the AEC supported the Muskie bill, a position he reaffirmed three days later when testifying on similar House proposals. He explained that, although the AEC had objected to earlier measures on the grounds that they discriminated against nuclear power, it believed that Muskie's bill addressed the problem satisfactorily, if not completely. The agency had discovered that fossil fuel plants that were at least partially constructed on navigable waters required a permit from the U.S. Army Corps of Engineers and therefore came under the provisions of the bill. In 1967, two-thirds of the large fossil fuel plants licensed would have been included in this category.

There were other reasons that the AEC found Muskie's proposed legislation attractive. Compared to previous bills, it diminished the role of the Department of the Interior, which allayed the AEC's concern that Interior would exert undue influence in its licensing actions. Most important, the AEC was anxious to see a law governing thermal effects passed, because, even though the new proposals were not drastically different than earlier ones, the political atmosphere was. As *Nuclear News* pointed out: "For the AEC, the sooner adequate and appropriate legislative control can be established over thermal effects the better. . . . The rash of adverse public opinion stirred up recently by the national news media (and by the Muskie hearings themselves) has made early and appropriate control mandatory." The AEC's endorsement of the Muskie bill was not enough in itself to ensure its enactment, but it also won the backing of key members of the Joint Committee on Atomic Energy and others who had opposed previous proposals. In March 1970, after the addition of clarifying amendments and more than five months of discussion in conference committee, Congress passed the final version of the legislation as the Water Quality Improvement Act. A broader measure, the National Environmental Policy Act, signed into law on January 1, 1970,

[44]"Muskie Thermal Effects Bill Provides State Certification," *Nuclear Industry* 16 (January 1969): 54–57; "Interior May Seek Own Pollution Plan," *Washington Post*, January 29, 1969, p. A-2.

provided further assurance that federal agencies would treat the problem of thermal pollution.[45]

The most important reason that thermal pollution ceased to be a major focus of environmental concern was that utilities increasingly took action to curb its consequences. Most nuclear plants being built on or planned for inland waterways by 1971 included cooling systems. Although power companies initially resisted the calls for cooling equipment, they soon found that the costs of responding to litigation, enduring postponements in construction or operation of new plants, or suffering loss of public esteem were less tolerable than those of adding towers or ponds. Even though a cooling system added substantially to the expense of a plant, it was still usually a small percentage of the total cost of the facility. Utilities increasingly saw it as a part of the price they had to pay to fulfill their primary objective, which was to meet the growing demand for electricity. Once they reached that conclusion and began to act on it, the issue of thermal pollution lost much of its potency and immediacy.

Even after the thermal pollution question largely faded from view, its legacy lingered on. The most important effect of the debate from the perspective of the AEC and the nuclear industry was that the image of nuclear power as an antidote for the environmental hazards of electrical production was irreversibly tarnished. The controversy played a vital role in transforming the ambivalence that environmentalists had demonstrated toward the technology into strong and vocal opposition. By the end of the 1960s environmental groups spearheaded protests against plans for many nuclear power plants, and thermal pollution was a major element in their arguments. In a similar manner, the issue wakened doubts among the general public about the environmental benefits of nuclear power. Before thermal pollution was featured in a plethora of news stories, public attitudes about the environmental impact of nuclear plants seemed to be at worst uninformed and ill defined, and at best highly favorable. As the

[45]Chet Holifield to Edmund S. Muskie, February 26, 1969, Box 46 (JCAE General Correspondence), Edward J. Bauser to All Committee Members, April 6, 1970, Box 47 (Bauser Memos), Chet Holifield Papers, University of Southern California, Los Angeles; AEC 783/106 (February 13, 1969), AEC 1318/6 (September 12, 1969), AEC/NRC; U.S. Congress, House, Committee on Public Works, *Hearings on Federal Water Pollution Control Act Amendments—1969*, 91st Cong., 1st sess., 1969, pp. 407–23; "In Government," *Nuclear Industry* 16 (March 1969): 37–42; "Muskie Bill for Thermal Effects State Control Gains Vital Support," *Nuclear News* 12 (April 1969): 22; "Conferees Approve Curb on Oil Spills," *New York Times*, March 13, 1970, p. 77; *Nucleonics Week*, April 24, 1969, pp. 4–5, March 19, 1970, p. 2–3.

public became increasingly concerned about environmental problems, however, it increasingly viewed nuclear power as one more threat to environmental integrity. Although no opinion polls on the subject were published in the late 1960s or early 1970s, a survey conducted in 1975, several years after thermal pollution had ceased to be a headline topic, indicated that 47 percent of the public thought that "the discharge of warm water into lakes and rivers" from nuclear plants was a "major problem"; another 28 percent believed it was a "minor problem."[46]

Thermal pollution was not the sole cause for the declining confidence in the environmental advantages of nuclear power that the industry and AEC emphasized. By late 1969, a new controversy was emerging over the health and environmental implications of radioactive effluents released by nuclear plants. Critics alleged that the AEC's regulations for permissible levels of radioactivity discharged to the environment by civilian power plants were inadequate. This set off a bitter debate that received a great deal of attention and eventually displaced thermal pollution as the focus of environmental concern. The thermal pollution issue laid the foundations for the radiation controversy and subsequent disputes over reactor safety. It was the first problem to raise widespread skepticism about the environmental benefits of nuclear power, and the doubts it stirred gradually expanded into other areas. It also undermined the credibility of the AEC. The agency's reluctance to take action against thermal pollution offered support to charges that it was indifferent to the environment. This fueled suspicions about its performance on other environmental issues that were apparent, for example, in the growing radiation debate.

The AEC was convinced that nuclear power offered the means to provide both ample electricity and environmental protection, and it was slow to respond to those who questioned this view. The agency came under increasing attack for failing to weigh the impact of thermal pollution in its licensing procedures, and its protestations that it lacked authority sounded like insensitivity to the environment to its growing legion of critics. In fact, the AEC was concerned with environmental quality; it funded a number of ecological studies on thermal effects and doubled its expenditures for research on the issue between 1969 and 1970. But it was even more concerned with minimizing obstacles to the use of atomic power to meet the nation's escalating energy requirements. As a matter of priorities, the AEC

[46]Louis Harris and Associates, *A Survey of Public and Leadership Attitudes toward Nuclear Power Development in the United States* (New York, 1975), pp. 39, 56.

gave greater attention to the need for power than to the problem of thermal pollution, partly because it believed that the possibility of a shortage of power was a more acute danger, and partly because it had long been inclined to emphasize the development over the regulation of nuclear electricity.[47]

The AEC's commitment to environmental quality would have been more apparent and convincing if it had acted aggressively to combat thermal pollution. It did not oppose regulating against the effects of waste heat, but it insisted that the same standards must apply to fossil plants. Its argument that imposing regulations only on nuclear plants would imperil the technology's growth by placing it at a competitive disadvantage was more of an intuitive assumption than a result of studied analysis. When quizzed about the impact of adding cooling towers on the relative economic advantages of fossil and nuclear plants, Ramey acknowledged in 1968: "I don't know that this would be a significant difference in [their] competitiveness."[48] The AEC made a strong legal case that it lacked the statutory jurisdiction to compel licensees to observe water quality standards, but a growing number of observers wondered why the AEC was so passive in its approach to the thermal pollution problem. The answer was that the agency feared that taking forceful action would discourage the growth of nuclear power. Ironically, in its view, this would lead to greater use of fossil fuels and harm the environment by causing more air pollution. In the thinking of the AEC, it was providing an important benefit to the environment by licensing new plants.

The AEC's reasoning was not clear or persuasive to those whose priorities were different. Critics portrayed it as indifferent to environmental needs and therefore loath to force its licensees to comply with water standards. The complaints were on solid ground in pointing out that the AEC's primary concern was not environmental protection, although they were often oversimplified and sometimes overwrought. Still, they sounded persuasive to many people in a time of growing concern over environmental quality and growing outrage against those who abused it. As a result of the thermal pollution controversy, the AEC and the nuclear industry frequently found themselves included among the ranks of the enemies of the environ-

[47]Walter G. Belter to Milton Shaw and G. M. Kavanagh, July 24, 1969, Box 5626 (Environmental Pollution, 1969), OGM Files, AEC/DOE. For a discussion of the AEC's efforts to balance its developmental and regulatory responsibilities, see George T. Mazuzan and J. Samuel Walker, *Controlling the Atom: The Beginnings of Nuclear Regulation 1946–1962* (Berkeley and Los Angeles, 1984).

[48]JCAE, *Hearings on Participation by Small Electrical Utilities in Nuclear Power* (n. 12 above), p. 43.

ment. In a period of a few years, the image of nuclear power was transformed from being a solution to the dilemma of producing electricity without ravaging the environment to being itself a significant threat to the environment. This perception endured long after the debate over thermal pollution ended, and it played a major role in subsequent controversies over nuclear power and the environment.

2001 to 1994: Political Environment and the Design of NASA's Space Station System

SYLVIA D. FRIES

Not the least of the many questions raised about the U.S. space program in the aftermath of the *Challenger* explosion on January 29, 1986, was whether political pressures impinged on what should have been a purely technical judgment: How reliable were the joint seals on the space shuttle's solid rocket boosters in the then-prevailing temperature of 38° F?[1] The noticeable degree to which the decision to build the space shuttle had been shaped by American politics was, of course, not news; John M. Logsdon and more recently Walter A. McDougall have shown that technology cannot be isolated from politics if our picture of the space program is to be complete.[2] But what did distress many—including the worldly-wise William P. Rogers, chairman of the presidential commission that investigated the *Challenger* accident—was that subsystem engineering decisions appeared to have been affected by politically derived pressures, in this case NASA's ambitious launch schedule intended to sustain an economic justification for the shuttle program itself.[3]

A new automobile design in Detroit or Osaka must run the gauntlet of oil-price predictions, tariffs, changing safety standards, and the ever-elusive market (to name only a few nontechnical considerations). Notwithstanding the complexities of the current regulatory environ-

SYLVIA D. FRIES is director of strategic analysis and the former chief historian of the National Aeronautics and Space Administration. The author thanks Nathaniel B. Cohen, John D. Hodge, Charles J. Donlan, Howard E. McCurdy, A. Michal McMahon, and Russell I. Fries for their helpful comments on earlier versions of this essay, and Lee D. Saegesser of the NASA History Office for invaluable archival assistance.

[1]*Report of the Presidential [Rogers] Commission on the Space Shuttle Challenger Accident* (Washington: U.S. Superintendent of Documents, June 6, 1986).

[2]John M. Logsdon, *The Decision to Go to the Moon: Project Apollo and the National Interest* (Cambridge, Mass., 1970); "The Space Shuttle Program: A Policy Failure," *Science* 232 (May 30, 1986): 1099–1105; Walter A. McDougall, . . . *the Heavens and the Earth: A Political History of the Space Age* (New York, 1985).

[3]*Rogers Commission Report* (n. 1 above), pp. 164–65.

ment, technological development in the private sector must hew to a discipline that imposes the ultimate test of marketability on any new product. The amount of time that any private sector firm can sustain or "push" an unproved product or system on an unreceptive market is limited.

Similarly, the design of a major technological system in the public sector—and not simply the choice of that system itself—is affected by its own highly complex political environment. The public sector, however, imposes no comparable discipline on the bureaucratic proponents of new technological systems. The ongoing uncertainties of congressional and presidential politics, combined with the internecine struggles of federal R&D bureaucracies for influence over the nation's total R&D budget, significantly reduce the likelihood that any new public-sector technology will be the result of systematic planning toward clearly defined technological or utilitarian objectives. Thus historians of technology, in recognizing the role of extrinsic (nontechnical) factors in the shaping of any new technology,[4] must be prepared to distinguish, for explanatory purposes, the *kinds* of extrinsic effects, especially in the public sector, that can alter the logic of a new technological system.

The U.S. civilian space station—a gleam in the eye of numerous NASA engineers since before the agency was founded in 1958 and promoted by NASA as the country's "logical next step" into space—provides an excellent case study of the way public-sector R&D agencies continuously redefine new technologies in the absence of the market discipline that governs private-sector technological development.[5] The number of space station design studies conducted since 1959, both internally by NASA or contracted by the agency to the aerospace industry, easily exceeds a hundred.[6] Because of this, I have selected three clearly distinguishable examples from the almost thirty-year history of space station design in NASA.

---

[4]See, e.g., Thomas P. Hughes, *Networks of Power: Electrification in Western Society, 1880–1930* (Baltimore, 1983); Edward W. Constant II, *The Origins of the Turbojet Revolution* (Baltimore, 1980). For an excellent analysis of the interplay of federal R&D politics and the promotion of science and technology, see W. Henry Lambright, *Governing Science and Technology* (New York, 1976).

[5]The history of the Space Defense Initiative ("Star Wars") to date provides a similar example.

[6]Early space station proposals are summarized in Frederick I. Ordway III, "The History, Evolution, and Benefits of the Space Station Concept," presented to the XIII International Congress of History of Science, August 1971; Barton C. Hacker, "And Rest as on a Natural Station: From Space Station to Orbital Operations in Space-Travel Thought, 1885–1951," unpub. paper, NASA History Office Historical Document (here-

Together these examples illustrate the difficulty of defining a new technological system in the public sector as that system becomes increasingly subject, for its development, to the vagaries of federal R&D politics. Where the market discipline of the private sector differs from the budgetary discipline of the public sector is that the latter, in the ever-changing scene of American politics, is indefinitely negotiable.

The first NASA space station proposal (1959–62) originated as a toroidal or wheel-shaped spacecraft whose rotating image was popularized by Wernher von Braun and Stanley Kubrick; launch constraints eventually turned it into a rotating hexagon. Intended to serve as a technology R&D laboratory in space, its design was partly the product of the enthusiastic first hours of the U.S. manned space program. The second example (1966) made full use of the concept of modularity. Actually a pair of orbiting stations, its design reflected NASA's need, toward the end of the 1960s, to turn to several constituencies for political support—most especially the scientific community. The third and last example is the "power tower" (1981–85; converted in 1985 into the "dual keel" configuration), which anticipates the ability to construct and maintain large structures in orbit. If the first example was conceived as an orbiting R&D lab, and the second as a space station for science, the most recent configuration combines scientific research and industrial processing with a general-purpose space operations base. It, like its predecessors, is as much a product of its political environment as of the engineers who designed it.

As they designed one space station after another, NASA engineers had to adapt not only to the ambiguous and occasionally conflicting desires of NASA's various constituencies but to available launch vehicles as well. Launch vehicles served as technological "givens"; though external to a space station, they had a fundamental influence on its design. The first example, the rotating hexagon, appeared before NASA had successfully developed its big "booster" rocket, the *Saturn V*, which, along with the hardware developed for the Apollo (lunar

---

after NHO); John W. Massey, "Historical Resume of Manned Space Stations," Report no. DSP-TM-9-60, Army Ballistics Missile Agency, Redstone Arsenal, Alabama, June 15, 1960 (NHO); Alex Roland, "The Evolution of Civil Space Station concepts in the United States," unpub. ms., May 1983 (NHO); and John M. Logsdon, "The Evolution of Civilian In-Space Infrastructure, i.e., 'Space Station' Concepts in the United States," in *Civilian Space Stations and the U.S. Future in Space* (Washington: U.S. Congress, Office of Technology Assessment, OTA-STI-241, November 1984). A discussion of space station planning up to the *Skylab* program can be found in W. David Compton and Charles D. Benson, *Living and Working in Space: A History of Skylab*, NASA SP-4208 (Washington, D.C.: National Aeronautics and Space Administration, 1983).

landing) program, provided the technological base for manned space-flight through the 1970s. The twin "cans" of the space station for science, the second example, were based on the availability of the Apollo-Saturn hardware (as well as the orbital maneuvering and docking skills acquired during the Gemini and Apollo programs). NASA's most recent space station concept assumes the use of the Space Transportation System, with its shuttle orbiter as the launch, return, and recovery system.

NASA: In Unsettled Political Waters

The National Aeronautics and Space Administration is, first and foremost, an agency of the federal government. It depends, like all federal agencies, on the good favor of the White House and members of Congress not only for its budgets but for its very survival. Congressional and White House support depends, in turn, on the degree of enthusiasm shown by the general public for what the agency does. However, the general public rarely expresses itself en masse. Instead, it asserts its preferences through an array of constituencies having varying degrees of political clout, depending on the issue or program at stake. *Once in existence,* then, any federal bureaucracy must negotiate its budgets and programs through a political Grand Guignol featuring not only congressional and White House figures but numerous interest groups. Added to them are competing bureaucracies that, having seen the drama before, may cleverly pick out the winning roles. So it is that the one experience shared by every federal manager of an agency serving secondary social purposes—in contrast, say, to the national defense or social security—is anxiety, a state of mind not conducive to the comprehensive and consistent thinking assumed by a rational model of technological systems definition.

NASA's own political situation during the thirty years since it was created in 1958 has been further complicated by the fact that its original mission was technological R&D to advance the exploration of space. The agency's pursuit of its mission has been impeded by the instability and unpredictability of congressional and bureaucratic politics. Moreover, NASA—like the military services—is composed of numerous installations scattered around the country with their own local constituencies who, if the stakes are high enough, will insist that their parochial interests be heard in the Congress and in the White House. And, like any other organization producing more than one "product," any major program decision NASA makes will be affected by an intense internal competition for resources. Charles Lindblom's insight that making (and implementing) federal policy is neither rational nor comprehensive but, instead, a process of "muddling through" applies as well to the evolution of a U.S. space system.[7] That process, too, is messy, and the role played by rational "systems" engineering is limited.

1959–1962: Langley Research Center and the Rotating Hexagon

To an American public affected by Cold War anxieties, the successful orbital flights of the *Vanguard 1, Explorer 1* and *Explorer 6, Discoverer,* and *Pioneer* satellites and probes were but modest consolation in the summer of 1959 for the early space triumphs of the Soviet Union's *Sputnik* satellites. The same assumption of a popular mandate that led to the creation of NASA in 1958, and would later support President Kennedy's manned lunar landing challenge, served as a tacit license for ambitious planning and design work. NASA's top managers, many of whom had risen from the engineering ranks of the National Advisory Committee for Aeronautics (NACA), attempted to define in 1958 a logical sequence of space objectives encompassed by the new agency's charter, and to begin the R&D programs necessary to support them.[8]

That sequence was still being debated in October 1959 at NASA headquarters in Washington when the agency's engineers at Langley Research Center in Hampton, Virginia (the oldest of the former NACA aeronautical research laboratories transferred to the new space agency), formally launched a study of a "manned space laboratory." (The term was then used interchangeably with a manned space station.) While such a laboratory in orbit would serve "as one of the initial steps in the actual landing of a man on the moon in 10–15 years,"[9] its principal

[7]Neither Herbert Simon nor Lindblom would argue that political or bureaucratic decision making is irrational. It is, rather, the classical model of rational behavior that they find inappropriate for explaining administrative or political behavior. Indeed, given that knowledge is imperfect and consequences are often unpredictable, which makes purposeful action to achieve a valued objective impossible, "muddling through" is a thoroughly rational way for public administrators to proceed. See Herbert A. Simon, *Administrative Behavior* (New York, 1945); Charles E. Lindblom, "The Science of 'Muddling Through,'" *Public Administration Review* 19 (1959); and *The Policy-Making Process* (Englewood Cliffs, N.J., 1968). I am indebted to Howard E. McCurdy for many hours of informed and insightful conversation on the effect of political processes and bureaucratic behavior on contemporary R&D programs.

[8]Courtney G. Brooks, James M. Grimwood, and Loyd S. Swenson, Jr., *Chariots for Apollo: A History of Manned Lunar Spacecraft,* NASA SP-4205 (Washington, D.C.: National Aeronautics and Space Administration, 1979), chap. 1, passim.

[9]Memorandum for the Associate Director, Langley Research Laboratory, from Beverly Z. Henry, Jr., October 5, 1959 (NHO).

238   Sylvia D. Fries

function was identical to that of the Langley laboratory itself, namely, a technological R&D center. Joseph A. Shortal of Langley's Applied Mechanics and Physics Division (in which the Langley space station office was located) regarded "the orbiting laboratory as an extension of ground facilities for a broad range of engineering and systems studies."[10] *Developing the technology of long-duration manned space flight was a sufficient purpose unto itself.* A post–World War II policy of fostering technological R&D through federal laboratories, translated in 1958 into a broad mandate for NASA, served as sufficient justification for a space station. That policy was given special urgency by the public's anxieties over apparent Soviet ambitions in space. The station it produced was conceived as an applied research laboratory in the sky, an orbiting replica of the aeronautical research center of the old NACA.

The concept of an orbiting R&D laboratory shaped the design study's guidelines. Two of those guidelines determined in a fundamental way the structure and performance of the conjectured space station. The first of these requirements was artificial gravity, and the second was unitized structure. Together they constituted the principal distinguishing characteristics of the space station design.[11] NASA's former aeronautical engineers took for granted that space-borne laboratories should be manned and assumed that humans, to survive in space, would require simulated gravity; the only known means of achieving this in space was by rotation. At the same time, the station would have to be able to be "carried aloft on a single launch vehicle" and thus consist of a "unitized structure." The only apparent solution to the problem of unitized structure was to divide the station into elements that could be "suitably folded or packaged" to provide a "reasonably compact payload."[12]

Working from these guidelines, Langley's engineers explored six possible space station configurations (fig. 1), each of which posed serious problems either in dynamic properties or in launch and orbital deployment. The dynamic properties and control of large objects in space was totally unknown territory. A doughnut-shaped rotating to-

[10]Ibid.; Edward H. Kolcum, "NASA Explores Space Station Problems," *Aviation Week*, June 26, 1961, pp. 89–93; P. R. Hill and Emanuel Schnitzer, "Space Station Objectives and Research Guidelines," Langley Research Center, *Report on the Research and Technological Problems of Manned Rotating Spacecraft*, NASA TN D-1504 (Washington, D.C.: National Aeronautics and Space Administration, August 1962), pp. 1–4.

[11]Hill and Schnitzer, pp. 4–5. The other requirements were: human factors compatibility, natural and artificial stability, rendevous-dock-abort capability, power generation with variable demand, external environment capability, and reasonable lifetime.

[12]Ibid., pp. 1–4.

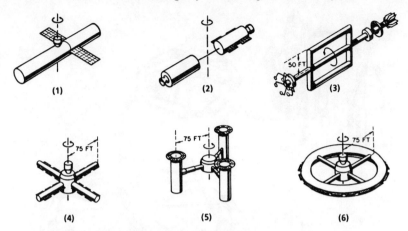

FIG. 1.—Basic space station configurations studied at Langley Research Center, 1959–62. (Langley Research Center, *Report on the Research and Technological Problems of Manned Rotating Spacecraft*, NASA TN D-1504 [Washington, D.C., August 1962].)

rus had the advantage of being dynamically "safe." However, packaging a toroidal structure with a radius of rotation of about 75 feet, which the engineers calculated would be necessary to achieve 1-*g* artificial gravity, challenged their structural and mechanical ingenuity.[13] At first they pondered an inflatable design similar to the rotating torus Wernher von Braun had popularized in his 1952 *Colliers* article and which later turned to the cadences of a Strauss waltz in Stanley Kubrick's 1968 film, *2001: A Space Odyssey.*[14] But Langley's engineers concluded that transferring equipment from a central hub to the periphery of the station, once it had been launched and inflated in orbit, would produce enough motion to jeopardize the station's rotational stability. If the station's living and working areas were rigidly constructed and equipment put into place before launch, the problems posed by the inflatable configuration could be avoided; moreover, a rigid station could be constructed with materials that could provide "adequate protection from the space environment."

Even this solution had the defects of its virtues: a rigidly constructed space station would have to be assembled in space. This defect might be minimized if assembly could be automated. Langley's engineers thus adopted, as the reference configuration for a feasibility study contracted to North American Aviation, an automatically erectable manned orbital space station (fig. 2) that, in their view, combined "the

[13]Ibid., pp. 10–11.
[14]Wernher von Braun, "Crossing the Last Frontier," *Colliers*, March 22, 1952.

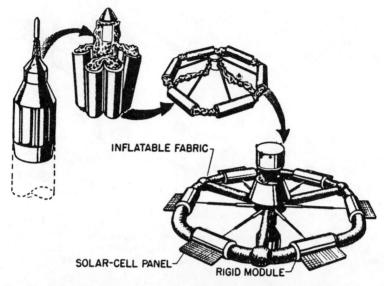

INFLATABLE FABRIC

SOLAR-CELL PANEL

RIGID MODULE

FIG. 2.—Automatically erectable manned orbital space station—Langley Research Center. (See fig. 1 source.)

best features of the inflatable and rigid space-station concepts, that is, the compactness of inflatable designs and the prelaunch equipment installation features of the rigid designs."[15]

North American Aviation narrowed the range of possible configurations for an automatically erectable rotating space station to three: a torus, a hexagon, and a modified hexagon. Of those three, the purely hexagonal configuration offered the least complicated launch package, since its straight-sided modules could be more readily fitted with the launch vehicle (fig. 3). Mechanical screw-jack actuators at the six joints would do the job of deploying the space station from launch configuration into an orbital configuration. The hub of the station would incorporate docking facilities for ferry vehicles.[16]

The need for artificial gravity for human occupants did more than determine the space station's configuration; it significantly influenced two of the most critical variables of space flight technology: weight and power consumption. Environmental control systems, along with lighting, created the largest power demand for a system whose total estimated power requirements exceeded 10 kilowatts (20 kW peak).

---

[15]*Report on the Research and Technological Problems of Manned Rotating Spacecraft* (n. 10 above), p. 11.
[16]Ibid., p. 17.

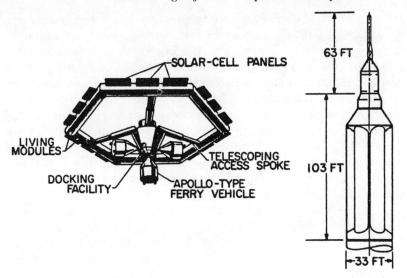

FIG. 3.—Hexagonal configuration automatically erectable rotating space station—
North American Aviation, 1962. (See fig. 1 source.)

A regenerative oxygen supply system added 12 kW to the necessary
power supply. Three possible power systems were investigated: a combination of solar photovoltaic cells and batteries, nuclear space power
systems (then under study by the U.S. Air Force and the Atomic
Energy Commission),[17] and thermionic electrical and thermocouple
power systems. Practical shielding problems made nuclear power systems unattractive, while the development of collectors, conversion
systems, and lightweight engines for solar thermal systems was still
far into the future. The system recommended by North American
Aviation was a solar cell system capable of generating 24 kW of peak
power and 22 kW of average power.[18]

Designing a habitable space station that could be launched with a
single vehicle, and deployed in orbit, was challenge enough in 1962;
but it would also have to be supplied, and crews and cargo returned

[17]The SNAP (Systems for Nuclear Auxiliary Power) program was begun by the
Atomic Energy Commission in 1955 to develop nuclear power systems for space vehicles. SNAP-1, designed by the Martin Company, would generate 500 watts of electrical
power from the heat of the decaying radioisotope cerium-144. The SNAP series involved the use of both radioisotopic fuel and nuclear fission reactors. The first such
reactor power plant launched into space was a 500-watt SNAP 10-A, placed into orbit
from Vandenberg Air Force Base, California, on April 13, 1965. See William R. Corliss,
SNAP Nuclear Space Reactors, U.S. Atomic Energy Commission (September 1966).

[18]Ibid., pp. 59–66, 108–18.

safely to earth. Mastery of the techniques of orbital interception, rendezvous, and docking was one of the most important achievements of the *Gemini* and *Apollo* programs. But in 1962 those techniques were critical unknowns about which, like the behavior of rotating wheels in space, research engineers had no empirical knowledge whatsoever. Vehicle-to-station docking would, for example, require the development of gastight, rotating seals, as well as mastery of the inertial problems inherent in joining two objects—one of them rotating—in space. Finally, the safe orbit-to-earth return of a ferry vehicle would require accurate geometric projections to ensure its return to preselected sites, as well as sufficient on-board power and control to maintain nominal orbits, attitudes, and trajectories.[19]

Events began to overtake Langley's technically logical space station studies when President John F. Kennedy, in May 1961, summoned NASA to place a man on the moon and return him safely to earth by the end of the decade. Doubtful that the agency could soon enough develop the super booster necessary for a direct manned flight to and return from the moon, NASA debated earth orbit and lunar orbit rendevous strategies for a staged ascent to the moon. The lunar-orbit scheme won out in June 1962 because it would allow for use of two separate spacecraft launched by a single *Saturn C-5*. Its carefully deliberated sequence of space projects (which included a space station as an earth-orbit operations base for a manned lunar mission) was interrupted by an ambitious young president's eagerness to rise to the Soviet challenge. NASA's top managers mobilized instead for the Apollo program—and pronounced all space station proposals premature. "The present state of knowledge on the uses for, and requirements of, a space station," commented the Systems Division in the agency's Office of Manned Space Flight, "are so nebulous." Thus arose the question that would dog the footsteps of space station enthusiasts for two decades[20]—what is the purpose of a space station?

A space station program might have been premature in 1962, but Langley's engineers persisted. Between 1962 and 1966 space station system studies continued under contracts to Langley Research Center, centering on the concept of a smaller "Manned Orbiting Research Laboratory" (MORL). Analyses carried out during this period high-

[19]*Report on the Research and Technological Problems of Manned Rotating Spacecraft* (n. 10 above), pp. 95–100.

[20]Memorandum to J. F. Shea and W. A. Lea, from Douglas R. Lord, October 2, 1962; Memorandum for Dr. R. L. Bisplinghoff from William E. Stoney, Jr., October 5, 1962; Memorandum to J. F. Shea from Douglas R. Lord and Emanuel Schnitzer, October 15, 1962 (NHO).

lighted several aspects of space station system design that would reappear in later concepts, for example, an emphasis on common, well-integrated elements in the laboratory's equipment and subsystems to reduce long-term operating costs, and the effect of incompatible research requirements (such as instrumentation, orbit, and station orientation) on the design of the total system.[21]

1966: A Space Station for Science

Of all the political considerations that might have influenced the evolving character of NASA's space station concepts, none was as fraught with ambiguity as the agency's relation with the scientific community. Scientific exploration had been a part of NASA's original mandate, and the agency constantly hoped for the support of the scientific community through such groups as the President's Science Advisory Committee, the National Academy of Sciences' Space Science Board, and the agency's own advisory committees as it defined its programs and tried to sell them on Capitol Hill and Pennsylvania Avenue. But scientists persisted in arguing that the engineering and budgetary demands of *manned* spaceflight would be met only at the expense of funds for basic science.

The necessity of satisfying its scientific constituencies became all the more compelling for NASA in the mid-1960s as the agency began to suffer budget cuts at the hands of a Bureau of the Budget and a Congress hard-pressed to come up with the wherewithal to fund an expanding war in Vietnam as well as the Johnson administration's "Great Society."[22] So it was that, when NASA engineers launched a space station study again in 1966, NASA Associate Administrator for Policy Analysis Breene M. Kerr advised Deputy Administrator Robert C. Seamans, Jr., that his own staff was conducting an independent

---

[21]William N. Gardner, "A Review of Langley Space Station Studies," in *Compilation of Papers Presented at the Space Technology Symposium*, National Aeronautics and Space Administration, Langley Research Center, February 11–13, 1969 (NHO). See also "Report on the Development of the Manned Orbital Research Laboratory (MORL) System Utilization Potential," Douglas Aircraft Co., Report SM-48822 (January 1966).

[22]See Ken Hechler, *Toward the Endless Frontier: History of the Committee on Science and Technology, 1959–79*, U.S. House of Representatives (Washington, 1980); Arnold S. Levine, *Managing NASA in the Apollo Era*, NASA SP-4102 (Washington, D.C.: National Aeronautics and Space Administration, 1982), p. 127; and Sylvia D. Fries, "The Ideology of Science during the Nixon Years: 1970–76," *Social Studies of Science* 14 (1984): 323–41. The subject of NASA's relationship with the scientific community is explored in Homer E. Newell, *Beyond the Atmosphere: Early Years of Space Science*, NASA SP-4211 (Washington, D.C.: National Aeronautics and Space Administration, 1980), chaps. 12, 13.

study "to determine which [space station] benefits would receive the strongest support on a national level. Thus we will know what aspects to stress in discussions with BoB, the President, and the Congress."[23]

It is clear from the results of NASA's space station studies carried out in late 1966 that NASA hoped that the scientific community could be persuaded at least not to oppose the continuation of an agency-wide effort to develop a space station. If no other evidence existed, language would suffice: then (as now) the agency articulated questions of scientific importance less in terms of the merit of any particular investigation as in terms of the *disciplines* (or organized groups of scientists, hence constituencies) likely to find a particular program attractive. When NASA's "space station requirements steering committee," headed by Charles J. Donlan, made its space station study presentation to its top managers, discussion included the importance of emphasizing a space station's value to astronomy. Donlan's committee argued that "Astronomy and the Medical/Biological areas appear to be the most promising application for a Manned Space Station." George M. Low, then deputy director at the Manned Spacecraft Center, "reported that the STAC [Space Technology Advisory Committee] was very negative on a space station; that *support from the scientific disciplines* [emphasis mine] will have to be done" through the Office of Space Science and Applications; the Office of Manned Space Flight "cannot do it."[24]

A direct appeal to the scientific disciplines had been built into the work of the Donlan committee from the start, when Seamans specified that a space station program emphasize "Astronomy, Earth Resources, Meteorology, Biology, Long-term Flight (including aerospace medicine), Research and Development in Advanced Technology, and Orbital Operations and Logistics."[25] Designing a space station to satisfy this broad range of interests proved a tall order. Long-term flight and biological research experiments imposed no particular requirements on station orientation or stabilization, while advanced technology R&D could be carried out with either inertial or earth orientations and 0.1° stabilization accuracy. These three research programs could be accommodated with nominal zero or 10^{-5}-g gravity and a centrifuge for biology and long-term flight experiments.

[23]Memorandum from Breene M. Kerr to Robert C. Seamans, Jr., October 19, 1966 (NHO).

[24]Memorandum for the Record, December 22, 1966. Details action items and "significant discussion" of Manned Space Station Study Presentation to Seamans (NHO).

[25]"The Needs and Requirements for a Manned Space Station," vol. 1: "Summary Report." Prepared by the Space Station Requirements Steering Committee, NASA (Washington, D.C.: National Aeronautics and Space Administration, 1966) (NHO).

Accommodating the projected research programs for astronomy, earth resources, and meteorology, however, was another story. The telescopes required for the astronomy program (gamma-ray, X-ray, optical, and radio) dictated station deployment above the ionosphere, at minimum time in radiation belts and maximum time in darkness. They would have to be maintained in an inertial space orientation with a stabilization accuracy of .001°, gimbal mounted, and rotating 360° along one axis and ± 40° along the other for as long as ten hours, while that portion of the station on which the telescopes were mounted could not be rotated. However, instruments for the earth-resources research and meteorological programs could not be rotated and would have to be operated in continuous alignment with the local earth vertical at orbital altitudes of 200 nautical miles or less and at an orbital inclination of 50° or greater for maximum observations over the entire United States. Keeping the astronomers, meteorologists, and geophysicists happy would fully test the ingenuity of NASA's space station design teams.

Systems support for the station relied on a complex set of requirements involving energy, functional integration, operations and logistics, and continuing advanced technology research in critical areas. The dynamics in space of fluids and large masses would have to be mastered, as would the long-term behavior of various materials and coatings. The station's sophisticated pointing, navigation and guidance, and data transmission requirements all required advanced engineering work in mechanics and electronics. The electrical power required to operate the principal scientific research programs varied from 300 W (astronomy) to 3,676 W (total connect power for biology). Added to this were energy requirements for the long-term flight program, intended to prepare "for manned interplanetary exploration," and the long-term needs of the space station itself. A "closed loop" environmental control and life-support system was essential to the recovery of useful materials from onboard wastes to reduce the volume of onboard supplies and launch weight for resupply missions. This would significantly add to power demands. Donlan's group responded with a large solar-cell power system, to serve until an isotope power system could be developed, in which event solar cells would provide a back-up.[26]

The Donlan committee considered two strategies for resolving the problems of integrating a multidisciplinary research program with varying, and in some instances incompatible, engineering design requirements. One strategy was to attempt to integrate all the projected

[26]Ibid.

research programs "into a single, unified research program, and to equip a space station capable of pursuing an entire program." As the committee explored the "unified approach," however, it identified a number of functional conflicts. For example, the functional requirements for earth resources and meteorological experiments were incompatible with those established for the astronomy research program. Meeting the functional requirements for the entire assemblage of planned research activities would dictate a "big station with both rotational and nonrotational components giving a tendency for the design to be large, and possibly somewhat strained."

Another program-integration strategy, one the committee favored, was the "group approach" in which the entire program was divided "into a sufficient number of parts to separate the conflicting requirement items, and to group together those not in conflict for location in separate modules." Thus NASA arrived at "the *multi-station or group concept,* which offers an alternative means of *resolving the requirements conflict by the expedient of physical separation.*"[27] The concept of physical separation of elements with incompatible requirements was the result of the Donlan committee's effort to identify "natural" groupings that would minimize interdisciplinary conflicts. This concept was thus the technological by-product of NASA's charter to conduct space science as well as its need to diminish the political weight of the scientific community's opposition to costly, large-scale manned programs by combining them with a diverse array of scientific research missions.

If the need to satisfy the scientific disciplines was one critical determinant of NASA's 1966 space station design, the heavy investment being made in the hardware for the *Apollo* and the *Apollo* Applications (*Skylab*) programs—especially the mammoth *Saturn* booster with its 285,000-lb. lifting capability—was another.[28] As the solution to the "group approach" proposed by the Donlan committee for the incompatible requirements of a multipurpose space station, engineers at NASA's George C. Marshall Space Flight Center (MSFC) proposed twin stations, each dedicated to three scientific disciplines with com-

---

[27]Ibid., pp. 68–69. Author's emphasis.

[28]Letter from Edward Z. Gray to Dr. Wernher von Braun, August 8, 1966, App. C (NHO). NASA accumulated eighty-four days of successful manned spaceflight and research experience with its *Skylab* orbital workshop, launched on May 14, 1973, by the giant *Saturn V* rocket. The workshop was contained in the S-IVB stage of the *Saturn,* outfitted with living quarters and work space. Its telescope mount, with ten different kinds of telescopes, provided valuable solar data, while experiments with the melting and solidification of various materials indicated a great potential for microgravity industrial processing in space. See Compton and Benson, *Living and Working in Space* (n. 6 above).

patible functional requirements. Each zero-*g* station, which could be fitted to the top of the Saturn IV-B stage, would contain within it three 22-foot diameter, 7-foot high doughnut-shaped experiment modules (or "cans") dedicated to a single discipline. Similarly configured modules would house each station's subsystems and living quarters for its nine-man crew (figs. 4, 5).

Both stations could orbit at altitudes of 260 nautical miles, as none of the initial experiments required geosynchronous or higher orbits. The dual-station concept would allow each station to be deployed in the orbital inclination best suited to the disciplines being served by it.[29] While earth resources and meteorology would require high-inclination—ideally polar—orbits, the "heavy energy cost" for "initial launch and logistic flights" suggested a reduced inclination of 55°, which would still allow major land masses to be covered. The second station, serving astronomy, could be space fixed and orbited at an inclination of 28½° which, approximating the latitude of the launch site at Cape Canaveral, would enable launch vehicles to take advantage of the earth's natural rotation for orbital placement and thus considerably reduce the energy requirements (and costs) of logistic flights.

Thus two critical aspects of the space station, orientation and orbit—each making serious demands on guidance and propulsion systems—were driven by decisions that were profoundly affected by NASA's political environment. Two of NASA's largest centers—Johnson Space Center and Marshall Space Flight Center—had significant political constituencies in the Congress and among aerospace contractors who would not gladly see an ambitious manned space program die. A strong scientific dimension was necessary to any major manned program in order to win the support of individuals and institutions unaffected by the health of Houston, Huntsville, or the aerospace industry. Rather, the scientific community and its allies wanted NASA to remain true to its charge to lead the nation in the exploration of space.

The tug and pull on NASA's programs from without were reflected in internal bureaucratic tensions between NASA's space science and manned space flight offices. The dual station concept, each with three modules, all six dedicated to an individual research discipline (astronomy, earth resources, meteorology, biology, advanced technology R&D, and long-term flight biomedical and behavioral research) was a veritable judgment of Solomon—wise, perhaps; but it did not save

[29]Marshall Space Flight Center Space Station Working Group, "Response to Requirements for a Manned Space Station and the Evolution of a One-Year Space Station, Part I: Summary Report" (NASA, George C. Marshall Space Flight Center, November 4, 1966), Part I, Sections 3.0–3.0.3 (NHO).

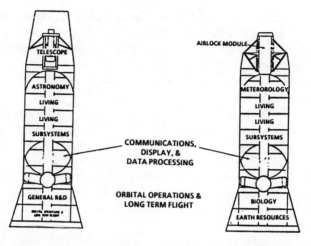

Crew Size: 9
Duration: 5 yrs
Orbit: Low Earth (260 NM)
Inclination: 28 1/2 degrees

COMMUNICATIONS,
DISPLAY, &
DATA PROCESSING

ORBITAL OPERATIONS &
LONG TERM FLIGHT

Crew Size: 9
Duration: 5 yrs
Orbit: Low Earth (260 NM)
Inclination: 55 degrees

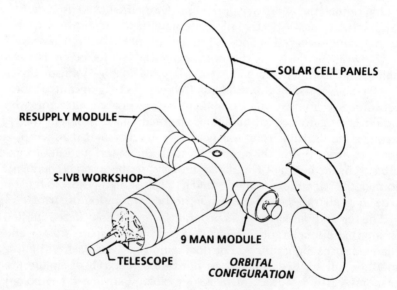

Crew Size: 9
Duration: 5 yrs
Compatible with
Saturn IV-B

Figs. 4, 5.—The 1966 Marshall Space Flight Center dual manned space station concept. ("Response to Requirements for a Manned Space Station and the Evolution of a One-Year Space Station, Part I: Summary Report" [NASA, George C. Marshall Space Flight Center, November 4, 1966].)

the child. NASA had to settle for the *Apollo* Applications Program, renamed *Skylab*, which was launched into orbit in May 1973. Based largely on *Apollo-Saturn* hardware, the orbiting workshop yielded many astronomical data and demonstrated that humans could live and work in space without artificial gravity for about three months; the long-term physiological consequences remain unknown.[30]

With the 1966 space station requirements and systems studies in hand, NASA management included in its FY 67 budget request $100 million for detailed space station definition studies. Its optimism was misplaced.[31] The Bureau of the Budget would have none of any NASA space station, and by early 1968 Lyndon B. Johnson, one-time champion of a vigorous space program, was planning his return to the Pedernales. His successor in the White House, Richard M. Nixon, had numerous presidential preoccupations that are now the well-recorded stuff of history. An ambitious manned venture to Mars—offered as the ultimate objective of NASA's continuing efforts to win White House approval for an ambitious space station program—was not one of them. Not until 1981, after the election of Ronald Reagan, would the White House again be occupied by a president with enthusiasm for highly visible space ventures to demonstrate to the world the nation's vigor and technological prowess.

1969 to 1981: Politics and Space Systems Design

In 1968 NASA management decided to phase out production of the *Saturn V* and to emphasize development of the "shuttle." The space shuttle would be the reusable orbiting component of the proposed Space Transportation System (STS). Originally conceived as a logistics vehicle for a space station, it was soon thought to be the single new program which had a chance of obtaining congressional and White House approval.[32] A political environment now dominated by economic pressures was reflected in Nixon's January 5, 1972, announcement of the decision to proceed with the development of the STS. The many possibilities demonstrated by the U.S. space program

[30]"Preliminary Technical Data for Earth Orbiting Space Station" (NASA, Manned Spacecraft Center, November 7, 1967), vol. 1: "Summary Report," Section 4.1.1.9 (NHO). The medical findings of the Apollo Applications (*Skylab*) Program are described in Compton and Benson, *Living and Working in Space*, pp. 149–50, 339–42.

[31]NASA's budget authority declined from $4.4 billion in FY 1968 to $3.1 billion in 1971. It would go as low as $2.8 billion (in 1974) before returning to 1971–73 levels again in 1976.

[32]John Logsdon, "Space Stations: A Historical Perspective," AIAA/NASA Symposium on the Space Station, Arlington, Va., July 18–20, 1983. AIAA Paper 83–7083, p. 5.

to date, for "learning about our near-earth space environment, the moon . . . the planets . . . the sun and stars" and for "utilizing space to meet needs on earth," observed Nixon, could "never be more than fractionally realized so long as every single trip from earth to orbit remains a matter of special effort and staggering expense." The shuttle, however, would "take the astronomical costs out of astronautics," by providing routine transportation into near space in recoverable, reusable systems.[33]

The president's statement on the STS reflected a deep concern within NASA itself over the growing cost of space exploration. The cost of "doing business in space, coupled with limited and essentially fixed resources available for space exploration," observed NASA's Deputy Administrator George M. Low in May 1972, "places severe limitations on the amount of productive work that NASA can do, unless we can develop means to lower the unit cost of space operations." Low attributed that "high cost" to the "great sophistication" with which most space systems are designed in order to "operate acceptably with low allowable weight" and to the fact that "most systems are individually tailored for their mission, used once or twice, and then never used again. Thus the economies of producing a number of like systems are never attained." Reliance on the shuttle, argued Low, would reduce the cost of space transportation and would enable designers to aim for reliability and low cost, "with weight being a secondary consideration." Of equal importance, however, was the fact that the agency had by now had enough experience to be able to anticipate the range of requirements for most missions and space systems and subsystems; thus it need not continue to develop "individually tailored technologies, but could focus on *multiple-use, standardized* [emphasis mine] systems."[34]

The economic justification for the shuttle program would haunt NASA later as the agency wrestled in 1985 with an ambitious launch schedule, a schedule later alleged by the Rogers Commission to be a contributing factor in the *Challenger* accident. But the economic justification was a reasonable response to the frustration NASA's manager-engineers must have felt as they tried to negotiate the program through the various constituencies they faced in the early 1970s:

[33]NASA estimated costs (through July 31, 1969) for the *Saturn* launch vehicles (I, IB, V) and operations support for the manned lunar landing were $7,940 million and $1,137 million, respectively (NHO). Statement by the President, the White House, January 5, 1972 (NHO).

[34]Memorandum from Deputy Administrator George M. Low to NASA program office administrators, May 16, 1972 (NHO).

the military, the science community, space enthusiasts, the aerospace industry, and the space caucus in Congress. The economy, not national stature vis-à-vis the Soviets, provided the only apparent common political currency. If cost effectiveness was the one test that all new federal programs had to pass, cost-effective the shuttle would be.

The technological effect of the decision to phase out the *Saturn* and develop the STS for subsequent space station designs was substantial, for the *Saturn V* was capable of launching a much larger (285,000 lbs. to 100 nm orbit) payload than the proposed shuttle vehicle, with its 15-by-60-foot payload bay and 65,000-lb. orbital launch capability (fig. 6). (The *Skylab* cluster, by comparison, measured 22 by 133 feet.) Modularity in space station system design—if a future space station were to be truly multipurpose—would be an absolute necessity. NASA's space station design studies carried out between 1970 and 1972 thus focused on a considerably more modest (by earlier standards) "research applications module" that could be launched into orbit by the shuttle.

At the same time, the shuttle introduced an entirely new array of technological possibilities that could be subsumed under the concept of a "space station." To begin with, it would provide a means of routinely replacing crews and expendable supplies between earth and space. No less important for space station designers, the shuttle would enable NASA to ferry into orbit the equipment, structural elements, and astronaut crews necessary to construct a large space structure in near-earth space. Those three possibilities—of a virtually permanent manned presence in space, of routine earth-to-orbit access and return, and of constructing, in space, large-scale multipurpose facilities—provided the framework for the rethinking that NASA's space station concept underwent in the late 1970s.

The same cost-consciousness that underlay the arguments for the shuttle, combined with the technological capabilities promised by the Space Transportation System, forced an additional change in NASA's approach to space station design. The primary cost of NASA's space programs during the agency's first twenty-five years have been a function of two closely interrelated factors: operations—earth-to-orbit launches and ground-based maintenance and servicing of equipment—and weight, the need to "shrink" individual technological subsystems in order to lift them into space. "When we first went into space," observed Richard Carlisle, deputy director for engineering in NASA's current space station program, "the fundamental design approach was to keep all the complication on the ground and put the simplest vehicle in orbit, because we couldn't stand a failure [and] because it was so expensive to get it there." If advanced space missions were to continue, a way had to be found to continue them within

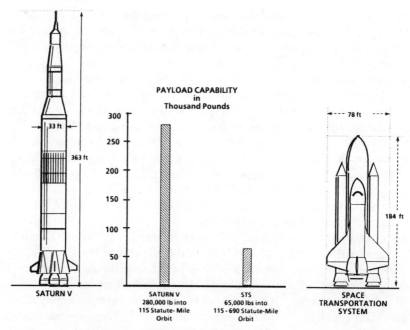

FIG. 6.—Payload capabilities of *Saturn V* booster and Space Transportation System (STS). (See n. 38.)

tolerable economic limits: "we've come to a complete reversal. Now we want to put the simplest thing on the ground . . . and put the most sophisticated thing in orbit, and design it so that it can be maintained and serviced in orbit." And the cost burden is not limited to operations: as NASA's various space missions evolve, so do their technological requirements. A general capability in space becomes as important as any single mission. A space station must be designed so that its capabilities can evolve and grow along with mission requirements that also will change over time.[35]

The agency's commitment to the Space Transportation System thus required a total system design that would achieve the economies necessary to survive in a political environment in which space was enduring diminishing budgets. These constraints underlay NASA's space station studies during the last half of the 1970s. Out of them came the "Space Operations Center" and "Space Operations Base" concepts, which reflected more ambitious ideas of what a space station could

[35] Author's interview with John D. Hodge and Richard F. Carlisle, NASA Office of Space Station, March 4, 1985. Quotation from Richard Carlisle.

or should be. It was not to be simply a laboratory, but would serve as a locus for industrial activity, such as microgravity materials processing, and as a base for space operations, for example, launching satellites and servicing orbital transfer vehicles. Moreover, they extended the functional reach of a space station beyond the limits of a single orbit. The space station was treated not as a single unitary orbiting structure but rather as a number of separate elements—both manned and unmanned platforms tended from an orbiting "operational base." Its uses could then encompass a wide range of missions and supporting operations. Such a design would also distribute the political support for the station over a wider array of constituencies.[36]

1981 to 1994: The "Power Tower"

Since President Ronald Reagan's nominees for NASA administrator and deputy administrator (James M. Beggs and Hans Mark) were both space station advocates, there was reason to believe that a space station program would survive the political and budgetary process better than it had before. Not long after NASA's new top executives were in place, the agency invited the aerospace industry to do background studies for a renewed space station initiative. While each firm's study emphasized particular aspects of possible space station missions, all proposed an incremental, or "evolutionary," approach toward space station development as the best strategy for achieving a truly multipurpose, long-term national capability in space at lowest cost.

Most notable in the industry studies was the shift in emphasis from scientific applications to the economic "payoffs" that might come from space-based operations and industrial research and manufacture. Some envisioned a reduced cost of routine space operations through reliance on a permanent orbiting service and maintenance facility and the ability to move payloads from low earth to geosynchronous orbit with orbiting transfer vehicles serviced by the station. Whether for science, space operations, or space-based manufacture, a space station—according to industry projections—would also provide substantial cost savings through the provision of on-orbit power, data management, thermal control, course pointing, and communications services. Most tantalizing, perhaps, were the long-term industrial

[36]W. Ray Hook, "Historical Review and Current Plans" (1982?), pp. 7–8 (NHO). Statement of John F. Yardley, NASA Associate Administrator for Space Flight, *NASA Authorization for Fiscal Year 1977*, Hearings before the Committee on Aeronautical and Space Sciences, U.S. Senate, 94–2 (January 26, 1976), p. 1046.

growth possibilities for microgravity processing of rare materials and pharmaceuticals—for example, iridium, interferon, and urokinase.[37]

Clearly, no single space structure could provide all of these attributes. Yet they might be achieved by an evolving "architecture" of discrete but technologically compatible elements and subsystems linked for purposes of command, control, and information. This concept provided the "reference configuration"—dubbed the "power tower"—for preliminary design studies contracted to Boeing Aerospace Co., Martin Marietta Aerospace, RCA Astro Electronics, General Electric Company Space Systems Division, Rockwell International Rocketdyne Division, TRW Federal Systems Division, Lockheed Missiles & Space Co., and McDonnell Douglas Astronautics Co.

The term power tower reflects the graceful 450-foot long skeletal truss structure—three times as long as the diameter of Langley's hexagon twenty years earlier—intended to orbit the earth with its main axis and gravity gradient perpendicular to the earth's surface (fig. 7). This configuration called for a common set of modular elements (which could be arranged in various ways to meet different design requirements) to be attached to and serviced by the power tower. These included pressurized modules, articulated solar-inertial power generation devices, and assembly hardware connecting modules, power devices, and externally mounted systems, payloads, and facilities. Equally important to the configuration was that it permitted on-orbit

---

[37]See Beggs's and Mark's confirmation hearings before the Committee on Commerce, Science, and Transportation, U.S. Senate, 97–1 (June 17, 1981). *Space Station Needs, Attributes, and Architectural Options: Final Study Report, Summary Briefing*, McDonnell Douglas Astronautics Company (April 1983), NASA contract no. NASW-3687; *Space Station Needs, Attributes, and Architectural Options Study: Final Review/Executive Summary*, Martin Marietta Aerospace (April 1983), NASA contract no. NASW-3686; *Study of Space Station Needs, Attributes & Architectural Options: Final Briefing*, General Dynamics, Convair Division (April 1983), NASA contract no. NASW-3682; *Space Station Needs, Attributes, and Architectural Options: Final Study Report, Summary Briefing,*, Lockheed Missiles & Space Co., Inc. (April 1983), NASA contract no. NASW-3684; *Space Station Needs, Attributes, and Architectural Options. Summary: Final Briefing*, Grumman Aerospace Corporation (April 1983), NASA contract no. NASW-3685; *Space Station Needs, Attributes and Architectural Options Study: Final Review, Executive Summary Briefing*, TRW Space & Technology Group (April 1983), NASA contract no. NASW-3681; *Space Station Needs, Attributes and Architectural Options Study: Final Executive Summary Briefing*, Rockwell International Corporation (April 1983), NASA contract no. NASW-3683; *Space Station Needs, Attributes, and Architectural Options Study. Final Report, Final Briefing*, Boeing Co. (April 1983), NASA contract no. NASW-3689. A good review of the commercial prospects of space industrialization can be found in David Osborne, "Business in Space," *Atlantic Monthly* 255 (May 1985): 45–53.

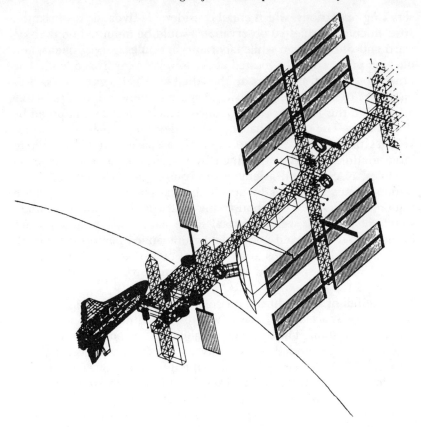

Fig. 7.—NASA space station "power tower" configuration (1984). (See n. 38.)

operations such as remote maintenance, servicing, checkout, and retrieval for co-orbiting unmanned platforms.[38]

The concept offered an elegant solution to the basic problems of
accommodating both astronomy missions—with their sensitive pointing and stability requirements—and manned laboratory and orbital

[38]"Space Station Definition and Preliminary Design: Request for Proposal," National
Aeronautics and Space Administration (Washington, D.C., September 15, 1984), Section C (NHO). A manned core would fly at an altitude of 500 nautical miles and at an
orbital inclination of 28.5° and provide an initial average buss power (electronic information load and transmitting capacity) of 75 kW, with a growth capability of 300 kW.
It should be able to accommodate an initial crew of six (with growth to eighteen) and
five pressurized modules (with eventual growth to ten) consisting of two habitability
modules, two laboratory modules, and one logistics module. Of the two initial habitable
laboratory modules, one would support "materials processing, physics, and chemistry
disciplines for research and development in microgravity." Pressurized and unpres-

256   *Sylvia D. Fries*

servicing operations, which entail considerable dynamic disturbance. Instruments for celestial observations would be mounted on the skyward end of the tower, while laboratory modules, service sheds, and docking ports would be located at the lower, or earthward, end. The power tower (and its successor, the "dual keel") also enabled NASA's engineers to combine modularity in space station design, a principle adopted in the 1960s, with the launch vehicle constraint imposed by the shuttle. The Soviets had opted to develop ever-larger booster vehicles that enabled them to assemble a space station by docking large modules in orbit. Confined by the shuttle to relatively small modules, NASA could assemble the volumetric areas needed for a station's many functions by attaching a larger number of its space station modules to a common frame that would provide a common source of power as well. The total space station system architecture included co-orbiting and polar-orbiting unmanned platforms for earth and celestial observations at altitudes of 500 nautical miles and 700 nautical miles, respectively, and at inclinations of 28.5° and 98.2°.[39] (See fig. 8.)

In the fall of 1986, during one of NASA's periodic design reviews for any new space system, the power tower was modified into a dual keel configuration. The dynamic instability of the power tower's long boom, which depended for stability on gravity gradient, had disturbed NASA engineers who finally opted for the shorter, double- or parallel-truss structure. The dual keel had the added virtue of offering a larger area to which payloads could be attached.[40]

Less visible than the change in the station's configuration in 1981–85 was the addition of a new set of political preoccupations. Following

---

surized payloads, sharing common resources, should be attachable to the exterior of the pressurized modules, and individual customers should have the ability to "remotely command, control, monitor, and process data for their free-flyers and platforms." Both photovoltaic and solar dynamic power generation systems are being suggested as design options. One of the conditions attached to NASA's FY 85 congressional appropriation (PL 98-371) for preliminary space station design work was that the agency and its contractors investigate the alternative of a man-tended space station with automated systems and intermittent manned operations.

[39]The system's "flight mode" illustrates that, while technology can do much, it cannot undo the laws of physics. The dynamics of large structures in space, which so concerned early designers at Langley, remains an important determinant of how the currently suggested space station configuration will appear and move in space. It will be designed to fly in a "torque equilibrium attitude," or "with a small pitch angle in the orbit plane," so that "no momentum, due to aerodynamic and gravity gradient torques, are accumulated over an orbit."

[40]*Defense Daily* 145, no. 31 (April 14, 1986): 241–43; *Marshall Star,* vol. 26, no. 36 (May 21, 1986); *New Scientist,* May 22, 1986, p. 19 (NHO).

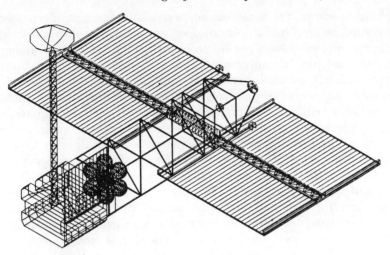

Fig. 8.—NASA space station co-orbiting, low-earth orbit, unmanned platform configuration (1984). (See n. 38.)

the precedent set by the *Spacelab* program, in which the European Space Agency (ESA) flew manned laboratory modules in the payload bay of the space shuttle, NASA tried to interest not only ESA but also Canada and Japan in an international collaboration on the space station. Thus a whole new set of competing political interests has had to be factored into the space station equation. Would all the players agree to develop compatible subsystems? And what would become of the proprietary concerns of international competitors in the high-stakes space technology arena? Could NASA keep any promise that the space station would not be used for military missions?

The space station story is not over, and its future, at this writing, is tangled in the web of the budgetary politics of summer 1987—a future complicated by the uncertain fate of the Space Transportation System. The space station configuration has undergone yet another modification in an effort to accommodate political pressure toward cost reduction. And as NASA confronts the possibility that the United States will return to expendable launch vehicles for routine access to space, the space station may be, once again, fundamentally redesigned.

Conclusion

From the 150-ft.-wide rotating hexagon of 1962 to the "dual keel" of 1986, the attempt by NASA engineers to design a space station has been complicated by the agency's political situation and prior launch vehicle decisions. The result has not been a coherent design evolution governed by an intrinsic technological rationality but rather a series of ingenious contrivances to solve problems that were political in origin.

The need for substantial public-sector technological programs to garner enough public support to sustain themselves during the necessarily long period of time from conception to development introduces a powerful nontechnical factor. Kennedy's decision to go to the moon, the budgetary effect of the Kennedy-Johnson quagmire in Vietnam, the growing political resistance to an inflationary federal budget, the science community's general opposition to manned space flight, the fickleness of the general public's enthusiasm for ambitious manned space projects, the parsimony of the Bureau of the Budget (and later the Office of Management and Budget), the lukewarm interest in space of both presidents Ford and Carter, the sharp divisions over the space program in the Reagan White House—and even the internal struggles between NASA's larger installations and their own constituencies' ability to appeal to Congress—all these combined to form the political shoals that NASA's manager-engineers have had to navigate. But there were no navigational charts to show them how to do so in a predictable and systematic way. Nonetheless, navigate they must. Their counterparts in the private sector have faced analogous uncertainties, and as large-scale private-sector R&D firms become increasingly dependent on federal agencies for revenues, the emergence of all forms of large technological systems will depend more on political, as distinct from market, forces. Historians as well as policymakers will need to become increasingly sensitive to the changing character of the extraneous forces that govern the definition of new technologies. The discipline of the marketplace, however imperfect, means that at some point a system may not work—and it may not sell. But in American politics, there is always the next election.

Part II

Part I

Household Technology and the Social Construction of Housework

CHRISTINE E. BOSE, PHILIP L. BEREANO, AND MARY MALLOY

Historians and social scientists generally agree that the forces of industrialization and the growth of the market economy have progressively absorbed much of the household's economic function. Furthermore, popular belief assumes that the vestiges of old forms of production in the home will surely be eliminated by the application of technological rationality. Put another way, it is thought by the public and many academics that "technology," broadly defined, has "freed" women for other, nonhousework tasks—in particular, employment in the paid labor market. These assumptions are reflected in popular terminology such as "fast foods" (to save time), "convenience foods" (to increase ease of preparation), and "laborsaving devices" (conducive to easing the work load generally). This imagery has such power that much traditional research takes these effects for granted instead of demonstrating or disproving them empirically.

Yet even with the unprecedented growth of the market sector and the almost universal availability of certain items of household equipment and goods, recent studies show that labor in the home still accounts for approximately half of this country's total work time.[1] In this article our goal is to investigate the evidence concerning the effects of technological developments on household work. We believe that popular beliefs about the positive effects are inadequately sub-

CHRISTINE E. BOSE is associate professor in the Department of Sociology, State University of New York at Albany.

PHILIP L. BEREANO is professor of technology and public policy, College of Engineering, University of Washington.

MARY MALLOY is a policy analyst at the New York State Department of Economic Development. She is the coauthor of *Financial Services, Financial Centers, Public Policy, and the Competition for Markets, Firms and Jobs* (New York, 1990). Research for this article was supported, in part, by a grant from the General Electric Foundation to the program in Social Management of Technology, University of Washington.

[1] Ismail Sirageldin, *Non-Market Components of National Income* (Ann Arbor: University of Michigan Survey Research Center, 1969).

This essay originally appeared in *Technology and Culture*, vol. 25, no. 1, January 1984.

stantiated, and we present alternative explanations for the current structure of household work.

Productivity in the home cannot be calculated in the same way productivity in the market sector is computed. The output is not sold for a price or measured against the time spent as expressed in outputs per unit. The increasing dominance of the exchange economy has transformed the home from a center of both production and consumption into one primarily for consumption. Hence, we will define "household production" as work in the home, or household economic work; some activities are literally production, others are consumption and management. This definition includes the provision of both goods and services, although we recognize that the mix of these two components has changed over time: formerly the household produced a lot of goods and a fair amount of services, but today household work largely involves services and consumption. Furthermore, in this discussion we will use the terms "labor" and "work" synonymously.[2]

Technology is widely believed to have increased the convenience or efficiency of performing housework. We understand efficiency in this usage to be a summary indicator for reductions in time, exertion (or ease), and/or cost, and therefore we have divided our investigation of household production into examinations of technology's effects on each of these three factors.[3] Efficiency, along with rationality, is one of the two hallmarks of the ideology of technological development.[4] Although efficiency is often taken as an objective or goal in itself, especially by economists, it more properly represents a statement concerning the ability of particular means to achieve a goal. Thus, to talk about the efficiency of housework—that is, the saving of time or money or the easing of effort—requires that we understand the whole operational nexus and purpose of the household. However, household functions are very decentralized social phenomena.[5] Since the

---

[2]An important distinction between the two is made by Hannah Arendt in *The Human Condition* (Chicago, 1958). Labor is the cyclical, repetitive, and unending satisfaction of life's basic needs, consumption necessities. It produces no permanent products. Work relates to the production of artifacts, objects of some durability, for use rather than consumption. Work has a beginning and an end. In Arendt's terminology, "housework" was once both labor and work but today is almost solely labor. In fact, it probably embodies the clearest examples of labor, such as washing dishes, taking out garbage, and other endless chores.

[3]"Efficiency" is defined in *Webster's Ninth New Collegiate Dictionary* as "effective operation as measured by a comparison of production with cost (as in energy, time, and money)."

[4]Jacques Ellul, *The Technological Society* (New York, 1964).

[5]Scott Burns, *Home, Inc.* (New York, 1975).

degree to which a process is centralized may play a role in determining its efficiency, we must recognize the difficulty of sharing or
coordinating household activities that are carried out by dispersed
units. In addition, household chores occur on a small scale, involve
the servicing of personal needs, and are labor intensive.[6] Even within
the household, then, chores are inherently inefficient.[7]

Yet, internal household efficiency (and certainly equity) might be
affected by technology if it could change the household specialization
of labor or the way in which tasks of household maintenance are
divided among members of that household. The practice in American
households today is for women to do the largest proportion of these
tasks, and there has been relatively little change in this over the last
fifteen years.[8] Furthermore, the total time spent on housework either
increased or remained stable between 1930 and the 1950s.[9] (We know
relatively little about task sharing prior to this time.) Still, we might
ask how changes in the specialization of labor *might* take place. There
are several ways. First, some of the work could be accomplished by
provision of equivalent market services. Options include employment
of domestic help within the home; the use of fast-food and laundry
services outside the home; or participation in communal services such
as the group cooking proposed eighty-five years ago by Charlotte
Perkins Gilman.[10] Second, the allocation of all housework tasks
among household members could be rearranged, with a diminished
proportion done by women. Related to this is the potential alteration
of household labor demands so that housework would absorb a
smaller percentage of women's total available work time. Such a reduction could occur because of smaller family size, lower standards of
cleanliness, or the woman's adoption of other roles, such as that of
paid employee outside the home.

---

[6]Lenore Davidoff, "The Rationalization of Housework," in *Dependence and Exploita-
tion in Work and Marriage*, ed. D. L. Barker and S. Allen (London, 1976), pp. 121–51.

[7]Hildegard Kneeland, "Limitations of Scientific Management in Household Work,"
Journal of Home Economics 20 (May 1928): 311–14.

[8]Catherine W. Berheide, Sarah F. Berk, and Richard A. Berk, "Household Work in
the Suburbs: The Job and Its Participants," *Pacific Sociological Review* 19 (October 1976):
491–518.

[9]Joann Vanek, "Time Spent on Housework," *Scientific American* 231 (November
1974): 116–20; Ruth Cowan, "A Case Study of Technology and Social Change: The
Washing Machine and the Working Wife," in *Clio's Consciousness Raised: New Perspectives
on the History of Women*, ed. Mary Hartman and Lois Banner (New York, 1974), pp.
245–53.

[10]Charlotte Perkins Gilman, *Women and Economics* (Boston, 1898; New York, 1966).
See also Dolores Hayden, *The Grand Domestic Revolution* (Cambridge, Mass., 1981).

In regard to this last possibility, the conventional paradigm holds that adoption of new household technologies leads to an increase in women's labor-force participation by freeing them from housework. Although paid employment is associated with a reduction of the amount of time spent on unpaid work in the home, we must examine the evidence to see if technology caused this employment. Moreover, it is not clear that increased labor-force participation frees women from housework. One needs to ascertain both who performs the housework when a woman works outside the home and the woman's total number of work hours (paid in the labor force and unpaid in the household) under these conditions in order to determine if her labor-force participation actually changes the distribution of household chores. Therefore, we include the household specialization of labor as a fourth dependent variable (along with ease, cost, and time) when a change in the application of technology is considered as the independent variable.

If we ask which technologies can reasonably be said to have changed household work structure, it is clear that different technologies have varying impacts; how should we compare, for example, plumbing, the vacuum cleaner, and the wire whisk? We find it most useful to categorize household technologies by a typology which expands on one used by Heidi Hartmann,[11] distinguishing them on the basis of their form and level of capital investment into four major classifications:

(1) utilities: the technological infrastructure of the household—for example, running water, electricity, gas, sewerage—which functions continuously, is virtually universal, and is provided under special legal and regulatory plans;
(2) appliances: machines used in performing housework;[12]
(3) foods: new forms of packaging and preservation, as well as those subsumed under the rubric of "convenience";
(4) market-sector services: alternatives to household functions, such as garbage collection in lieu of incineration and fast-food restaurants or diaper services in lieu of cooking and laundering.

[11]Heidi Hartmann, "Capitalism and Women's Work in the Home, 1900–1930" (Ph.D. diss., Yale University, 1974).
[12]Appliances can be further disaggregated to distinguish between large ones and small ones involving different analytic elements such as initial cost, frequency of purchase, and frequency of use; or between durables and nondurables; or between hand tools used as direct extensions of manual labor and devices with electrical or other power augmentation. Our discussion will sometimes reflect these distinctions, although they are ignored in much of the previous research.

Our model is one which allows a test of the traditional notion that changes in technologies for the household have yielded benefits previously unavailable, particularly to women. Utilities, appliances, convenience foods, and market-sector services are believed to have reduced the *time* and *cost* of performing housework, to have increased the *ease* with which such tasks are performed, and to have diminished the *share* of these tasks normally allotted to adult women. Our test of this model entails a survey of research in several fields.

Within the realm of housework we have generally focused on food-related tasks—including production or purchase, storage, preparation, and cleanup—an area chosen because of the large amount of research compared with other aspects of housework and because food production continues to change considerably, thus displaying more visible effects. Our study is also delimited by the types of households which have been studied previously. As in much of social science research, the focus of technology studies has been on the "ideal" adult woman–adult man household, usually with children present, of the white middle class. It has rarely examined single-parent households or individuals living alone, for instance, though where possible we will note data on class and race variations.

Hypotheses and General Expectations

The traditional explanation of changes in technologies for the household (as for technologies elsewhere) is that new devices and techniques have been developed because they brought benefits not previously provided. New technologies usually do offer benefits, but any realistic assessment of their effects will show these to be mixed. Benefits are often experienced directly by only a portion of the population. Other sectors may reap ancillary benefits from the technologies, such as increased profits from marketing them. Still other sectors, however, can actually suffer adverse consequences including increased noise, psychological stress, or unemployment.

The idea of unalloyed benefits serves to facilitate initial technological development and subsequent diffusion through the population. Any negative effects are popularly ignored or else seen simplistically by the people adversely affected, believing these effects peculiar to them. For example, our investigations suggest that some "costs" associated with household technology changes have been accommodated by individual families or housewives under the assumption that they are individual—if not unique—burdens. An example is the new stresses associated with selecting specific equipment from a large marketplace array, learning to use it, storing it, cleaning it, and repairing it. More specifically, since much of this stress falls particularly on the housewife, she tends to see these as "her" problems, which amplifies any existing feelings of inadequacy.

Only recently, with the confluence of various movements in consumerism, women's liberation, and technology assessment, has this traditional premise been subjected to a more rigorous analysis. The heightened contradictions in the structure of housework have facilitated this analysis. Adherents to these movements have pointed out that total time spent on housework has not declined in the last fifty years even though the availability of modern "conveniences" has increased. Despite the increasing entry of women into the paid labor force, the impact of new household technology may have made the prescriptive norm that "women's place is in the home" descriptively true both by increasing the number of hours required for household tasks and by (technologically) depriving working-class women of paying jobs as domestics, seamstresses, or laundresses. Clearly several structural trends, and not individual shortcomings, are responsible for this dilemma.

Our hypothesis, then, is that the effects of technological developments on housework have been both positive and adverse. We separate the applications of technology, our independent variable, into four categories—utilities, appliances, foods, and services—and examine their effects on four aspects of household labor, our dependent variable: time, ease, cost, and allocation of tasks among household members. At the same time we keep in mind these questions:

(1) Which individuals or groups actually reap benefits and which groups and individuals bear risks and/or costs? (Whose objectives are accomplished by technological changes?) This is both an economic and an ethical question.
(2) Do the technologies themselves (or some of them) have the results which are claimed for them—saving labor, time, and cost (i.e., "convenience")?
(3) When there are positive effects, what do people (especially women) actually do with the time, money, or personal energy thereby saved? Has the gender specialization of household labor actually changed?
(4) When there are negative results, for what objective or subjective reason are the technologies nevertheless utilized?[13] What are the technological effects on household worker alienation/satisfaction?

[13]For example, a 1968 survey of American housewives found that over half the respondents gave time as the most important reason for buying convenience foods while less than half mentioned the saving of work. Apparently it is more legitimate to save time through the use of convenience foods if that time is to be spent on the family than it is merely to lessen effort. Thus, time saving may be more important than effort saving to housewives. See Rosemary Scott, *The Female Consumer* (New York, 1976).

If technology has had mixed or negative results, new strategies for social structural change and reallocation of household labor will be necessary.

Sources of Evidence

Since no one discipline addresses all of the issues above, we have drawn on information from several fields. A multidisciplinary approach does not guarantee that every question can be answered currently, yet such an approach carries us further than would any one method alone. In this section, we outline the kind of evidence available within the literature of each discipline.

Historical literature documents which technologies have been used over time. Work by Ruth Cowan and Susan Strasser relies primarily on content analysis of women's and business magazines to examine changes in kitchen technologies.[14] Other perspectives are provided by Gwendolyn Wright and by Barbara Ehrenreich and Deirdre English, who look at the rise of the domestic science movement at the end of the 19th century and how this encouraged women's interest in new kitchen technologies.[15] On the whole, few historical works examine the normative or ethical issues involved in technological change.[16] Did women welcome or resist change? Were changes the result of choice or of the social requirements of the exchange economy?

In contrast, work in anthropology helps set the context to explore the interaction between cultural values and particular items in the material environment.[17] Yet most small-scale material innovations

[14]Ruth Cowan, "A Case Study of Technology and Social Change: The Washing Machine and the Working Wife"; "The 'Industrial Revolution' in the Home: Household Technology and Social Change in the 20th Century," *Technology and Culture* 17 (January 1976): 1–23; "Two Washes in the Morning and a Bridge Party at Night: The American Housewife between the Wars," *Women's Studies* 3 (1976): 147–72; "From Virginia Dare to Virginia Slims: Women and Technology in American Life," *Technology and Culture* 20 (January 1979): 51–63; Susan Strasser, *Never Done: A History of American Housework* (New York, 1982).

[15]Gwendolyn Wright, "Sweet and Clean: The Domestic Landscape in the Progressive Era," *Landscape* 20 (October 1975): 38–43; Barbara Ehrenreich and Deirdre English, *For Her Own Good: 150 Years of the Experts' Advice to Women* (Garden City, N.Y., 1978).

[16]For exceptions, see Martha Moore Trescott, ed., *Dynamos and Virgins Revisited: Women and Technological Change in History* (Metuchen, N.J., 1979); Sigfried Giedion, *Mechanization Takes Command* (New York, 1948); Bettina Berch, "Scientific Management in the Home: The Empress's New Clothes," *Journal of American Culture* 3 (Fall 1980): 440–45.

[17]Marvin Harris, *Culture, People, Nature* (New York, 1975); Marvin Harris, *The Rise of Anthropological Theory* (New York, 1968); Marshall Sahlins and Elmer Service, eds., *Evolution and Culture* (Ann Arbor, Mich., 1960); Marshall Sahlins, *Stone Age Economics* (Chicago, 1972); Autumn Stanley, "Daughters of Isis, Daughters of Ceres: Women Inventors in Agriculture" (Paper presented at the annual meeting of the National Women's Studies Association, Bloomington, Ind., 1980).

have been largely ignored by ethnographers, particularly those items associated with women and with kitchen activities.[18]

Within home economics two areas are of interest: research on housework and research on food practices. Studies of housework, although numerous, are unfortunately dominated by the ideas of "household engineering." The pioneering work of Christine Frederick[19] narrowed the problems of housework research to the application of scientific principles of efficiency; subsequent research was limited to how work in the home should be performed, with little attention to why it is done. While Steidl and Bratton have attempted to explore the affective and cognitive dimensions of housework, they too fail to go beyond the problems of efficiency.[20] Consequently, their research, in keeping with the home economics tradition, lacks a broader attempt to situate housework in a social or cultural context.

Unlike housework research, the literature on food practices recognizes the importance of normative questions in the preparation, consumption, and storage of food.[21] But perceiving that behavior is value laden is one thing; explaining what determines these values is another. Both the housework and food-habits research are limited by their purpose and the probable absence of intent to address fully the question of structural changes within the economy or household, which we address here. There is particular difficulty in finding data on ethnic or class differences in the normative mode of carrying out housework. Research by Ehrenreich and English suggests that such differences exist.[22] But no research has been done on the impact of such change on different ethnic or economic groups, either in terms of actual rate of adoption of new kitchen technologies or food types or in the change of prescribed behavior associated with such actual changes.

The "new home economics" differs from the prescriptive approach of the earlier home economics literature in seeking to apply mi-

[18]Support for the existence of this problem in ethnographies is provided by H. R. Bernard and J. Pelto, *Technology and Social Change* (New York, 1972).

[19]Christine Frederick, "The New Housekeeping," serialized in the *Ladies' Home Journal* (September–December 1912); published by Doubleday (Garden City, N.Y., 1913).

[20]Rose Steidl and Esther Bratton, *Work in the Home* (New York, 1968).

[21]W. J. Fewster et al., "Measuring the Connotative Meaning of Food," *Home Economics Research Journal* 2 (September 1973): 44–53; Kathryn Kolasa, "Participant Observation in Nutrition Education Program Development," *Journal of Nutrition Education* 6 (July–September 1974): 89–92; Virginia Steelman, "Attitudes toward Food as Indicators of Subcultural Value Systems," *Home Economics Research Journal* 5 (September 1976): 21–32.

[22]Ehrenreich and English (n. 15 above).

croeconomic theory to household production. Drawing on the early works of Margaret Reid,[23] it views housework as a production function in which the utilities of a household unit are maximized, using differential allocation of individuals' labor, under the constraints of income and working time available.[24] These studies assume that, as income rises, families will usually substitute durable goods for time. Recent research by Myra Strober suggests, however, that this may not be the case for working women.[25] Furthermore, research by Richard and Sarah Berk indicates that the types of labor substitution which should occur within a family that is maximizing its utilities simply do not occur.[26] Finally, the values and tastes which inform consumer choices, as well as the employment status of women, need to be examined.

We have also considered the literature in marketing, particularly the area concerned with consumer choice of household durables and food products. We know that sex roles influence greatly the purchase of certain items. Wife-dominated decisions such as those involving food, small appliances, or medicinal purchases reflect female activity in the home. Larger kitchen appliances appear to entail more joint decision making, perhaps because of cost.[27] Husbands play the major role in the purchase of "brown" appliances (e.g., television, stereo) that do no housework in contrast to "white" ones that do. In more recent research, we find that, where the wife is employed, the husband appears to be moving into the formerly "female" area of food purchase.[28] There is a hypothesis that when income contribution is shared there will be a relative decline in traditional masculine and feminine areas of decision making, although the significance of this for marital equality has been challenged.[29] This information suggests certain trends, but most research available on product choice and decision making measures only gross influence and fails to investigate

[23]Margaret Reid, *Economics of Household Production* (New York, 1934).

[24]Theodore Schultz, ed., *Economics of the Family* (Chicago, 1974).

[25]Myra Strober, "Wives' Labor Force Behavior and Family Consumption Habits," *American Economic Review* 67 (February 1977): 410–17.

[26]Richard A. Berk and Sarah F. Berk, "A Simultaneous Equation Model for the Division of Household Labor" (Paper presented at the annual meeting of the American Association for the Advancement of Science, Boston, 1976).

[27]C. R. Gisler, "Is the Buying Influence of Men Understood?" *Printer's Ink* 224 (September 1948): 39.

[28]F. I. Nye and Lois W. Hoffman, *The Employed Mother in America* (New York, 1963).

[29]See D. M. Wolfe, "Power and Authority in the Family," in *Selected Studies in Marriage and the Family,* ed. R. F. Winsch, R. McGinnis, and H. R. Barringer (London, 1963); and Dair Gillespie, "Who Has the Power?" *Journal of Marriage and the Family* 33 (August 1971): 445–48.

how and why such influence is exerted.[30] Furthermore, knowing who purchased an appliance or tool does not tell us who uses it with the most regularity. Unfortunately, studies of product preference and attitudes are carried out by private marketing firms and generally are not available to the public. Brief summaries of these studies occasionally appear in trade journals, but, with few exceptions, information on education, employment, or ethnic background of the respondents is absent. Overall, marketing literature lacks sensitivity to the complex normative issues surrounding the purchase of kitchen equipment and food products.

Finally, sociological research is of both methodological and substantive interest to us. Much of the research is based on household observations and multi-indicator survey techniques. Many studies look at specialization of labor and types of housework, although few list the actual technologies used to do the work.[31] Research has often focused on the housewife role and more recently on the content of housework.[32] Studies of the job are useful in breaking down tasks of food management into component parts and in examining social class differences in time spent on housework.[33] Examinations of the housewife role have considered levels of personal satisfaction and how these feelings relate to role content.[34]

In sum, there is information on technologies available to the home, on household specialization of labor, on cost/ease/time associated with certain technologies, and on product choice. There is almost no information on variations across ethnic groups and only limited data across economic groups. Only anthropology has dealt with the relevant normative questions, but not primarily in the area of small-scale technologies. In addition, we should note that literature which examines large-scale changes over time in the economy and technology tends to ignore the impact of such changes on household work structure.

[30]Harry L. Davis, "Measurement of Husband-Wife Influence on Consumer Purchase Decision," *Journal of Marketing Research* 8 (August 1971): 105–12.

[31]For an exception, see Charles A. Thrall, "Household Technology and the Division of Labor in Families" (Ph.D. diss., Harvard University, 1970).

[32]Helena Lopata, *Occupation: Housewife* (New York, 1971); Sarah F. Berk, Richard A. Berk, and Catherine W. Berheide, "The Non-Division of Household Labor," mimeographed (Evanston, Ill.: Northwestern University, 1976); Ann Oakley, *The Sociology of Housework* (New York, 1974).

[33]Joann Vanek, "Household Technology and Social Status: Rising Living Standards and Status and Residence Differences in Housework," *Technology and Culture* 19 (July 1978): 361–75.

[34]Berheide et al. (n. 8 above); Oakley; Mirra Komarovsky, *Blue-Collar Marriage* (New York, 1962); Myra Marx Ferree, "Working-Class Jobs: Housework and Paid Work as Sources of Satisfaction," *Social Problems* 23 (April 1976): 431–41.

Understanding these limitations to the evidence available, we will now review four technological systems—utilities, appliances, foods, and market services—in terms of their effects on each of our dependent household production variables: time, ease, cost, and the specialization of labor.

Technological Impacts on Ease of Housework

Ease of housework is a complex cluster of both objective and subjective elements that includes reducing physical fatigue, increasing the pleasantness of performing tasks, adding variety as a means of stimulating interest, guarding against boredom, and enhancing feelings of self-worth. Thus, ease of housework and reduction of time spent on housework are not conceptually identical. Empirically, studies have indicated that, even when a saving of time is demonstrated by the use of new appliances, there is not always evidence that effort or fatigue is reduced.[35] However, many people—houseworkers and researchers alike—make no distinction between time and ease. Where the two are distinguished, Heidi Hartmann has suggested that the easing of effort is more important to consumers than is the saving of time.[36] Other research indicates that reliance on convenience foods to save effort is common but varies with stage in the life cycle.[37] Data on appliance usage are more mixed.

In the light of the complex nature of "ease," we begin by restating the traditional notion that new household technologies are adding interest to tasks and fostering a more cheerful attitude in the houseworker.[38] Unfortunately, this does not distinguish between the set of objective tasks which constitutes housework and the social role of housewife.[39] From advertising in women's magazines and on television, we can infer the assumption that technology will make work easier and more pleasant and therefore will make the housewife happier. But studies of worker alienation in other kinds of jobs note that it is important to distinguish between the task being performed and

[35]M. K. Heiner and N. M. Vedder, "Studies in Dishwashing Methods: An Attempt to Apply Methods of Job Analysis to a Household Process," *Journal of Home Economics* 22 (October 1930): 393–407.

[36]Hartmann (n. 11 above).

[37]Thomas W. Anderson, *The Convenience-oriented Consumer,* University of Texas at Austin, Studies in Marketing no. 14 (Austin, 1971).

[38]For example, Committee on Household Management and Kitchens, President's Conference on Homebuilding and Home Ownership, *Household Management and Kitchens* (Washington, D.C., 1932), pp. 30–44.

[39]A useful distinction made by Nona Glazer-Malbin, "Housework," *Signs* 1 (Summer 1976): 905–22.

the context of the workers' routine. Housework is basically manual, and mechanization of the tasks only means the worker must now tend the machines. Since much of the work in the modern home is socially isolated, involves monitoring several activities at once, and has many emotional burdens which are not subject to rationalization or mechanization,[40] there may be inherent limits on the degree to which technology may actually ease housework.[41]

Increased ease of tasks does not guarantee increased satisfaction with the housewife role. Unfortunately, there are few data to consult here. One study found, however, that ownership of equipment and other amenities may affect the way particular tasks are performed or make them more interesting, but it does not create satisfaction with housework as a whole.[42] Satisfaction or dissatisfaction was unrelated to the number of appliances owned; respondents registered dissatisfaction over the lack of social interaction and the monotony inherent in the housewife role. In other studies we find that middle-class women feel primarily "neutral" about housework—neither interested nor uninterested—but similar to alienated blue-collar workers.[43]

Insofar as household technologies are designed to support the home system, and thereby keep women economically marginal to the larger society, they may actually increase dissatisfaction with housework. Several studies have documented women's preference for paid employment over housework.[44] The debilitating effects of being "just a housewife" are no longer myth or speculation; the National Center for Health Statistics has found that fewer working wives suffered from nervousness, insomnia, trembling and perspiring hands, nightmares, headaches, dizziness, and heart palpitations than did a matched sample of nonemployed wives.[45] The monotony of the home setting, the repetition of menial tasks, and the isolation and lack of stimulation from other adults have been identified as sources of

[40]Allison Ravetz, "Modern Technology and an Ancient Occupation: Housework in Present-Day Society," *Technology and Culture* 6 (Spring 1965): 256–60.
[41]Although women would apparently like this to occur; see "Blue Collar Wives Seek Convenience," *Advertising Age* 44 (October 8, 1973): 33; "How Housewives Would Design Kitchens If They Had the Chance," *Electrical Merchandising*, May 14, 1962, p. 29.
[42]Oakley (n. 32 above).
[43]Berheide et al. (n. 8 above); Phyllis Chesler, *Women and Madness* (New York, 1972).
[44]E. Mostow, "A Comparative Study of Work Satisfaction of Females with Full-Time Employment and Full-Time Housekeeping," *American Journal of Orthopsychiatry* 45 (1975): 538–48; Ferree (n. 34 above); Lillian Breslow Rubin, *Worlds of Pain: Life in the Working-Class Family* (New York, 1976).
[45]National Center for Health Statistics, *Selected Symptoms of Psychological Distress* (Washington, D.C., 1970), pp. 30–31.

chronic fatigue in full-time housewives.[46] And the problem is not confined to middle-class women, for an increased incidence of this "housewife syndrome" has also been found among working-class and native American women.[47]

Thus far, we can see that the traditional assumption that easier work will necessarily increase housewives' role satisfaction is incorrect. Next we turn to question whether specific technologies actually ease the housework itself, independent of their impact on the housewife's role.

Although it is difficult to prove, utilities have probably changed household work more than any other technical improvement because they eliminated several truly burdensome tasks. Hot and cold running water ended the pumping, carrying, and heating of water; electricity and gas eliminated chopping wood, carrying coal, and continual stoking and cleaning of stoves. But precise impact is hard to measure for several reasons. First, prior to 1910, we have few data on total time and effort expended on housework before and after the installation of utility systems. Second, since it is not clear how to define housework for the preindustrial period, it is hard to judge whether the burden of housework was subsequently eased. For example, if housework is anything done in the home, chopping wood for heating might not have previously been considered as such; but if it is defined as unpaid work or work necessary to maintain the home, the installation of centralized heating certainly would have eased housework. Third, some evidence indicates that the total volume of housework has not declined, but this is not inconsistent with utilities having had a profound impact on the allocation of labor within households.

It is likely that effort saved on some tasks was merely transferred to other activities carried on by women. Time-budget studies from later periods which compare rural/urban time allocations all show an increase in time spent on purchasing, management, and child care, and a decrease in time spent on meal preparation.[48] Some of these changes over time may be due to appliances rather than utilities, but it is likely that utilities eliminated certain tasks to make room for others. Furthermore, electrification undoubtedly fostered second-level effects by facilitating the development of many appliances. Rising stan-

[46] Betty Friedan, *The Feminine Mystique* (New York, 1965).

[47] Billye Fogleman, "Housewife Syndrome among Native American Women," *Urban Anthropology* 4 (Summer 1975): 184.

[48] Vanek (n. 9 above); W. F. Ogburn and M. F. Nimkoff, *Technology and the Changing Family* (Cambridge, Mass., 1955); John Robinson and Philip Converse, "Social Change Reflected in the Use of Time," in *Human Meaning of Social Change*, ed. Angus Campbell and Philip E. Converse (New York, 1972).

dards of cleanliness increased housework volume, and the task-extending nature of small- and medium-sized appliances may have offset many of the original gains in ease of effort attributable to utilities. While technologies can both give and take away, it seems safe to conclude that utilities eased some of the effort required for heating homes and providing hot water.

How do small- and medium-sized appliances make tasks more difficult instead of easier? Even *Fortune* magazine has cited the fact that an array of separate appliances requires a great deal of time and work to take out of the cabinet, put together, use, and clean up.[49] Cleaning kitchen appliances can become a major project for the conscientious housewife, since their plastic moldings and ridges, chrome trim, and doodads all seem designed to harbor dirt.[50] Repair of appliances has become more difficult and mysterious, often costing almost as much as purchasing the appliance in the first place. With the increased specialization of household machinery, the difficulty of understanding the actual mechanical and/or electrical operation has increased, so that one who is knowledgeable about how a certain type of appliance operates may not be able to understand another, much less fix it. Furthermore, much of our equipment embodies a planned obsolescence to sustain demand and necessitates repairs or replacement, which certainly requires additional effort.[51] There is also an increased amount of noise in the house due to appliance operation.

These factors all argue against the view that household appliances necessarily ease the performance of housework. "Laborsaving devices" may actually create new forms of labor and increase job fatigue.

We next examine food technologies and their effects on easing housework. Unfortunately, our assessment must be based primarily on speculation for two reasons. First, most studies focus on time saved rather than on effort and ease. Second, comparisons of "starting from scratch" versus convenience foods have not taken into account shopping, planning and management time, or meal types. The entire cooking and eating process has not been studied, only a portion of it. Thus, these studies report (small) time differences regarding only part of the meal-preparation process. To the extent that convenience foods require fewer operations from refrigerator to table and necessitate keeping fewer ingredients on hand, they may save some effort;

[49]"Why Nobody Is Happy about Appliances," *Fortune* 85 (May 1972): 180–83; on storage or retrieval, see "How Housewives Would Design Kitchens If They Had the Chance."

[50]Julia Kiene, "Beware the Bridge Table," *Electrical Merchandising*, July 1958, p. 30.

[51]Vance Packard, *The Wastemakers* (New York, 1960); see also "Why Nobody Is Happy about Appliances."

but to the extent that they impose different planning, shopping, and storage activities, they may require more exertion. However, certain food-related technologies promise to make formerly elegant or exotic experiences readily available to the masses, fostering changing expectations similar to those discussed above for appliances.[52]

The final independent variable that might have an impact on ease of household work is market services, which could move housework outside of the home instead of having each household performing every task. This alternative has never been fully developed. William Baumol suggests that, at least in the post–World War II period, in an economy that primarily produces services for capital and commodities, such commodities combined with women's labor at home prevented the growth of labor market services relevant to housework.[53] As a general pattern this may still hold true, although the number of services provided varies with the household task. Laundry services and home food delivery appear to have declined, while eating out (which became necessary and acceptable during World War II with the mass entry of women into the labor force) appears to be a long-run trend.

This trend is supported by several factors. First, there is a continued increase in the rate of married women's labor-force participation. Second, there is real convenience to eating out. Restaurant sales soared as a result of this ease, combined with the fact that between 1972 and 1975 the cost of eating at home rose faster than that of eating out.[54] Third, although the relative cost advantage of eating out was subsequently reversed, most women do value their own time and ease. When Mrs. Average Housewife tells us on a national commercial that she likes her chicken "finger lickin' good" because her time is valuable, we can suspect that she knows a bargain when she sees one; after fifty years of convenience foods and laborsaving devices, women have come to agree with the rationale for the fast-food industry—that true convenience comes only when someone else does the work.

However, there are also limitations on the potential for market services' replacing home food preparation. There have been massive advertising campaigns by supermarkets and the appliance industry aimed at pointing out that it is now cheaper to eat at home, if the cook's time is not counted. Supermarkets know that they are facing a

---

[52]This was once true even for the prosaic tin can; see Karen de Witt, "The Technology That Revolutionized Eating," *New York Times,* November 7, 1979.

[53]William Baumol, "Macroeconomics of Unbalanced Growth—the Anatomy of Urban Crisis," *American Economic Review* 57 (June 1967): 415–26.

[54]Charles Vaugh, "Growth and Future of the Fast Food Industry," *Cornell Hotel and Restaurant Administration Quarterly* 17 (November 1976): 18.

major threat. (In the next few years there will be over 1.5 fast-food restaurants for every supermarket in America and a total of 30,000 convenience stores offering fast-food takeout service.)[55] And, while one can purchase high-protein meals at fast-food restaurants, overall quality and nutrition remain more controllable with home cooking. But it is cost considerations that set the strongest limits: inflation cuts back on the ability of middle- and lower-income groups to eat out. Among higher-income groups, the trend may be different, with women combining eating in better restaurants with more time spent in gourmet cooking at home.

On the whole, we may summarize by noting that, where available, market services appear to have eased housework. Convenience foods may also help reduce fatigue. As for utilities, we can conjecture that they did reduce fatigue but that their secondary effects created more housework. None of these technologies is likely to have made housework more pleasant or varied. Satisfaction studies also indicate that technology has not affected the housewife's perceptions of self-worth. Evidence about appliances is the most mixed and will be taken up again in the section on time below.

Technological Impacts on Cost of Housework

We have found the least information in the area of cost-effectiveness of household technologies. The majority of data are on appliance and food technologies, and most of this information is on cost changes during the most recent decades. We know little about how utilities relate to cost. Much of the household work now done by running water, electricity, or oil and gas, and paid for in monthly bills, was once done by individuals pumping water, chopping wood, or hauling coal. The cost of this labor is hard to measure and compare with current dollar outlays. We can make better cost measurements and studies of changes over time for the recent period. For example, no one can ignore the increase in cost of home heating in the last few years and the concomitant need for supplementary technologies such as insulation to offset these costs. Undoubtedly some of those costs are being met with the labor of family members who install insulation themselves (or who chop, split, and carry fuel for wood stoves).

More studies have been done of large- and small-scale appliances, though these primarily address saving time rather than cost. The kitchen appliance industry has felt threatened by the trend toward eating meals away from home and has recently been tailoring its wares

---

[55]"Super Markets Competing for Fast Food Dollar," *Santa Barbara News-Press*, October 9, 1977.

to compete with fast-food outlets.[56] Small deep-fat fryers, single and double hamburger makers, and electric hot dog cookers are being marketed in an effort to bring the fast-food taste into the home. For the affluent consumer, the single professional, and the full-time homemaker, another line of goods has been developed with more sophisticated multipurpose food processors, crepe makers, electric cookie and canapé makers, electric woks, and crock pots; apparently higher-income groups are combining eating in expensive restaurants with more elaborate cooking at home. For others who are in the home full time, cooking has become a creative outlet or a chance to improve the nutritional content of meals. As usual, there are few cross-ethnic or racial data; what little evidence exists concerns black families, which have been found to purchase appliances or convenience foods at a slower rate than whites of the same income level,[57] preferring to spend money in other ways.

The next section will indicate that appliances do not appear to save time and are normally quite expensive. Therefore we might ask, Who buys appliances? The discussion above hints at the answer: white households with higher incomes and/or a full-time homemaker. Why are they bought? First, people believe that appliances save time. Second, appliances have symbolic value for men and for women. Women often see the housewife role as a supportive one, performed out of a sense of duty rather than for money. If a woman believes that the latest equipment increases the quality of her work and in turn the quality of home life, she has a powerful incentive to want a well-equipped home. Since work in the home is emotionally charged, its quality is not subject to the same criteria of efficiency and technological rationality as is work in the paid labor force. Male identity is also involved. Within the bounds of traditional sex roles and family power, the domination of males rests on an ability to provide a comfortable standard of living (or even luxury items) for their families. Thus men, too, see value in household technology. Furthermore, we know that much household technology is bought by men for women, sometimes as gifts. The ability to give may be a way of expressing male dominance to a spouse who does not have equal purchasing power. However, to date we have virtually no rigorous data on kitchen appliances as gifts, on who decides to purchase appliances, or on the motivations for such purchases.

Among food technologies, convenience goods have important ef-

[56]"Fast Food Chains," *Consumer Reports* 44 (September 1979): 508–13.

[57]Dorothy Newman and Dawn Day, *The American Energy Consumer: A Report to the Energy Policy Project of the Ford Foundation* (Cambridge, Mass., 1975); Raymond Bauer and Scott Cunningham, *Studies in the Negro Market* (Cambridge, Mass., 1970).

fects on costs of housework. The Department of Agriculture found, for example, that 64 percent of the processed foods it studied were priced higher than the equivalent amount of homemade food.[58] In another Department of Agriculture study, of 158 convenience foods examined, only forty-two cost less than their fresh or home-prepared counterparts. For eighty of those that cost more, the work time saved and its economic value were determined; this amounted to 60¢ or less per hour for 53 percent of the eighty convenience items, 61¢ to $1.20 per hour for 31 percent of the items, and more than $1.20 per hour for the remaining 16 percent. While these may sound like significant savings, making up for the extra purchase price, only 1 percent of the items saved more than ten minutes, and 80 percent saved five minutes or less.[59] In a 1971 book, Sidney Margolius claimed that in cases where time is saved, the time may be valued at approximately $4.30 per hour.[60] The economic worth of this factor would depend on how much time, on the average, is actually saved.

On the whole, convenience foods save some time but cost more than home-prepared foods. Until recently, consumers were willing to pay the extra costs, but now they are more wary. Increases in food prices have led to the replacement of the canned soups, frozen entrées, and prepared desserts in the average market basket with fresh fruits and vegetables, cheeses, and so on. The consumption of canned fruits and vegetables also declined between 1972 and 1977, in spite of efforts to stimulate demand.[61]

To some extent, these changes in consumption patterns may be votes against the nutritional deficiencies of convenience foods, since the average person has been eating several pounds of artificial chemicals a year in prepackaged foods. But there are other reasons that convenience foods may be spurned. Even though there are now ersatz ethnic convenience foods, a mass market tends to eliminate ethnic variety.[62] While anthropological studies have shown the importance of food in maintaining ethnic identity, we do not know how rapidly and in what manner majority-culture American food preferences affect subculture eating patterns or ethnic identification. At the

[58]"More Foods Today Are 'Fresh' from Factories and Quick to Prepare," *Wall Street Journal*, June 21, 1977.

[59]Harry Harp and Denis Dunham, "Comparative Costs to Consumers of Convenience Foods and Home-prepared Foods," U.S. Department of Agriculture Market Research Report 609 (Washington, D.C., 1963).

[60]Sidney Margolius, *The Great American Food Hoax* (New York, 1971).

[61]*Business Week*, January 17, 1977, p. 81.

[62]Waverly Root and Richard de Rochement, *Eating in America* (New York, 1976); Stuart Ewen, *Captains of Consciousness: Advertising and the Social Roots of the Consumer Culture* (New York, 1976).

turn of the century, public school home economics classes were intended to teach nutrition as well as cleanliness and thrift to poor and especially immigrant children. One effect was to change ethnic cooking styles along with the nutritional balance. A recent study of Asian Indian academics in the United States found that many traditional dietary restrictions have been dropped.[63] Husbands, who were in daily contact with Americans, changed their eating patterns faster than did their homebound wives. About other groups we know less. Still, the reemerging sense of cultural heritage among many ethnic and racial groups probably has contributed to the recent trend away from convenience foods. In sum, while time may be saved by convenience foods, they cost extra money, probably are less nutritious, and are more ethnically homogeneous than home-prepared meals.

The final technological impact on cost of housework is that of market support services. Within the food industry we find that in 1965 one meal in four was eaten away from home. A decade later the number was approximately one in three, with some experts predicting it to hit one in two in the near future.[64] Supermarkets are feeling the competition; the food service industry's share of the food dollar is now 42 percent, with fast foods seeing the quickest growth.[65] Eating out appears to be a long-run trend, although it will be affected by inflation and disposable income levels. It certainly seems unlikely that market services will entirely replace home food preparation within our current economic system.

The long-term cost advantage of food services and restaurants probably will depend on how women's time is valued. As women's participation in the paid labor force increases, their time becomes of potentially greater value. This would make home preparation costs increase and might give eating out a cost advantage such as it had in the early 1970s. However, we must expect class variation in response to women's paid work. If working women are primary wage earners, or providing a second income to cope with inflation, family income may not be high enough to allow eating out, and women's "cheaper" labor will be used to cook. But if a wife's paid work more than compensates for inflation and increases the options available to the household, her time at home may be seen as more important. Furthermore, as restaurant prices rise, working-class families will be more likely to eat at home, thereby saving money, while expending women's labor. At the same time, families with greater resources can better

[63]Santosh Gupta, "Changes in Food Habits of Asian Indians in the United States," *Sociology and Social Research* 60 (October 1975): 87–99.

[64]Vaugh (n. 54 above).

[65]Lee Flaherty, "Change in Woman's Status Spurs Battle of Supermarkets vs. Fast Food Chains," *Advertising Age*, May 23, 1977, p. 158.

afford to eat out even as prices rise. The pattern is similar when more labor of other kinds is needed at home: professionally employed women will pay for outside help, while clerically employed women will get unpaid labor from family members.[66]

On the whole, the popular belief that technology makes household work cheaper is not supported sufficiently. There are no clear measures of the impact of utilities. Appliances and convenience foods appear to be more expensive, although the latter may save some time. Only market services seem potentially cheaper than work in the home, but this is contingent on placing an economic value on the homeworker's labor.

Technological Impacts on Time Spent in Housework

There exist some technology-specific studies on the saving of time, and, using the typology previously set forth, we can look at these within each of the categories—utilities, appliances, foods, and market services.

Data on utilities are too slim and contradictory to warrant conclusions, especially regarding food preparation. In one study comparing Eastern European provincial households without running water to urban households having not only running water but mechanical amenities, there was no significant difference in the total time spent in housework.[67] Another study claimed that running water saved between one-and-a-half to two hours per day in pumping and heating functions.[68] A third study considered the daily time differential for dishwashing between fifty homes equipped with running hot and cold water and forty-four homes with no pump or running water in the kitchen, concluding that the amount of time spent in the two types of homes was the same, 1.6 hours per day, and also that running water did not save time in meal preparation.[69] A fourth study supported this conclusion: the acquisition of amenities affects the expenditure of time very little[70]—this despite the contrary beliefs of many people (including many who actually lived through the technological changes).

[66]S. S. Angrist, "Socio-Economic Differences in How Working Mothers Manage Work, Childcare and Household Tasks," *Social Science Quarterly* 56 (March 1976): 631–37.

[67]Alexander Szalai, "The Situation of Women in the Light of Contemporary Time-Budget Research" (Paper presented at the UN World Conference of the International Women's Year, Mexico City, 1975).

[68]Mary Rowe, "The Length of a Housewife's Day in 1917," *Journal of Home Economics* (December 1917, reprinted in October 1973 issue).

[69]Inez Arnquist and Evelyn M. Roberts, *The Present Use of Work Time of Farm Homemakers,* Agricultural Experiment Station Bulletin 234 (Pullman, Wash., 1929).

[70]Committee on Household Management and Kitchens (n. 38 above).

Although these studies suggest that running water has no impact on time spent in housework, we must remember that they were conducted before the diffusion of many modern devices dependent on household utilities and with limited samples of farm households. We assume that utilities *did* save time on tasks predating the introduction of those utilities. The problem in documenting this assumption is that the time saved by the introduction of utilities was applied to other household tasks, many of them newly developed. In other words, while some activities are eliminated with the introduction of utilities, others are added (especially because of concomitant increased urbanization and industrialization). Thus one could argue that, since food service had not previously been widespread, the introduction of utilities was a primary force behind the realized decline in meal preparation time, but in terms of total time urban women were no closer to liberation from housework than their rural sisters.

Turning to appliances, we find that virtually the only machines which have been studied in detail are mechanical and electrical dishwashers. Most studies show a reduction in time spent dishwashing with the use of appliances; however, the figures for the time spent in various modes of dishwashing vary among the studies, which were conducted over a forty-year time span. The most recent found the time expended to be 4.9 hours per week with dishwashers and 6.3 without.[71] The figures from a 1930 study were twenty-six minutes and forty-four seconds per day washing with a portable machine, twenty-two minutes and thirty-one seconds per day washing by stationary machine, and thirty-eight minutes and eight seconds washing by hand; while a 1956 study indicated thirty-six minutes a day with a dishwasher and some hand rinse as compared with one hour and thirteen minutes per day solely by hand.[72] There are a few other studies of individual appliances. One indicates that a gas stove may save a half-hour per day over a coal range because there is no need to clean up coal dust or carry out ashes, another that modern (1929) plumbing, electricity, and equipment saved two hours per day for meal preparation and cleanup and 0.7 hours for routine cleaning and care of fires.[73]

We know that in some middle-class families there is a small positive correlation (.20) between number of appliances and household work

[71]Florence Hall and Marguerite Schroder, "Time Spent on Household Tasks," *Journal of Home Economics* 62 (January 1970): 23–29.

[72]Heiner and Vedder (n. 35 above); Elaine Weaver, Clarice Bloom, and Ilajean Feldmiller, *A Study of Hand vs. Mechanical Dishwashing Methods*, Agricultural Experiment Station Bulletin 772 (Kent, Ohio, 1956).

[73]Rowe; Maude Wilson, *Use of Time by Oregon Farm Homemakers*, Agricultural Experiment Station Bulletin 256 (Corvallis, Oreg., 1929).

time. Apparently either appliances create more work or women use the time saved elsewhere to keep up with rising standards of house-keeping.[74]

In other words, while the time savings in specific tasks which resulted from the introduction of certain technologies were impressive, the time women spent in total housework ironically did not decline. One reason is that utilities fostered the use of not just large appliances but also many single-task, usually small, appliances. The general effect of much of this equipment was part of the raising of standards of living rather than the saving of time. Today, not only have standards risen, but the proliferation of some small appliances has extended rather than eliminated tasks.[75] Thus, the net effect of technological change is not time saving.

As for convenience foods, if preparation for use is the major factor to consider, one could generally conclude that these do save time. Yet the time involved in food producing and/or shopping is usually ignored in time studies of prepared, packaged meal-sized goods. A hundred years ago most Americans produced their own food or relied on local markets for those things they did not grow themselves (consequently there was less variety than today). Moreover, most food was bought in bulk, so that shopping was likely to be a less frequent venture. Today, while prepared foods may save time and effort, this convenience is severely undercut at the supermarket. There we find aisle after aisle of food choices made available by a national marketing system and the wonders of food technologies. The sheer number of choices, together with the need to serve nutritious, attractive, and tasty meals, can increase time for meal planning and food selection. If one shops two or three times a week (each time going to a centralized, i.e., nonlocal, shopping center), makes selections with care, loads the goods into the car, unloads them at home, and puts them away, all of that adds up to considerable time. Although shopping patterns vary—for example, black women tend to shop less frequently than white women and to buy basic ingredients in larger quantities[76]— shopping takes time.

However, we could still make the argument that the smaller meals served today compared with those served fifty years ago have surely decreased the time spent in preparation. Before World War I, the

[74]Berheide et al. (n. 8 above).

[75]Joseph J. Spengler, "Product-Adding vs. Product-Replacing Innovation," *Kyklos* 10 (1957): 249–80; Steffan Lindner, *The Married Leisure Class* (New York, 1972).

[76]Robert F. Dietrich, "Know Your Black Shopper," *Progressive Grocer* 54 (June 1975): 44–46.

average American family ate three large meals a day: breakfast, lunch, and dinner consisted of steak or roast, fried potatoes, cakes or pies, starchy vegetables, hot cakes, and relishes.[77] Today, meals are smaller. Volume alone would seem to suggest less time in the kitchen, irrespective of technologies. However, the larger meals of past eras were made up of similar foods; roast or steak with potatoes was common at all three meals, and probably the breakfast roast was reheated and served at lunch or dinner. Modern meals, in contrast, clearly feature different food types, making three separate preparations common. Urbanization and declining family size may have made meals smaller, but new technologies complicated (and gave variety to) the cooking process.

Unfortunately, our assessment of the time savings due to the technology of convenience foods is necessarily speculative, although not to the same extent as was true for utilities. Since the "scratch" versus convenience studies do not measure and compare shopping, planning, time management, family size, or meal types, their comparisons (that, e.g., a certain convenience food saves a minute and a half over preparing it from basic ingredients) seem meaningless.[78]

Finally, we come to market services. Again, we cannot be definitive, but we believe that market services help save time. A family that eats out often spends less time in meal preparation. Yet much of the use of market services is related not to their technological convenience per se but, rather, to the increase in women's paid employment and the decrease in average family size. Family size and age of children have been found to be extremely significant factors in determining overall time spent in housework and in meal preparation in particular.[79] Furthermore, in the last fifty years the percentage of employed women has more than doubled. This, together with diminishing family size, apparently decreases the time spent on housework. Why? Is it because women have more technological help in the kitchen, or because there is more convenience in market services, or because the volume of housework is less in smaller families or in those with working mothers/wives? The answer is undoubtedly more complex than the existing data can support. We speculate that the availability of market services facilitates a decline in time spent on some forms of household production (e.g., laundry, cooking), a decline that was initially made possible by utilities and some large appliances and by the

[77]Cowan, "Two Washes in the Morning" (n. 14 above).

[78]See, e.g., Harp and Dunham (n. 59 above); and Margolius (n. 60 above).

[79]Kathryn Walker and Margaret Woods, *Time Use: A Measure of Household Production of Family Goods and Services* (Washington, D.C., 1976); Wilson; Vanek (n. 9 above).

lack of availability of a full-time homemaker; however, centralized market services have also meant that an increasing percentage of housework time is spent on consumption tasks.

Technological Impacts on Household Specialization of Labor

Technology began to affect specialization of labor with the long-term trend of industrialization. Prior to the Industrial Revolution, the household had been a center of both production and consumption for all its members. As industrialization began, the household retained its dual character, producing goods for home consumption and for the market economy under the cottage system. The latter function diminished rapidly as centralized factories developed, leaving the home as a center of consumption and socialization. Production for home and market became physically separated. The market economy produced goods for use in the home, rather than developing food, laundry, or child-care services to take these functions from it.[80] Susan Strasser has suggested that this choice was made between 1907 and 1916 when large capital investors found a profitable outlet in the automobile.[81] The concomitant residential dispersion made many group services unprofitable compared with such technologies as appliances and convenience foods which fit the atomized pattern.

As production moved out of the home, the work of household maintenance did not decrease. If anything, standards of output were raised; once the industrial ethic of efficiency and labor saving developed, the home became another site to apply these values. The rationalization of the home was thus dependent on the prior industrialization and rationalization of the outside workplace. The decline in the number of servants early in this century (due in part to immigration restrictions) was seen as a "crisis" given the pressures of efficiency and higher housekeeping standards.

Two social trends in the early 20th century make these connections explicit. The first was the domestic science movement of the 1920s, which attempted to render housework more like industrial management, and the second was the new home economics, which sought to apply microeconomic theory to household production. These movements illustrate how the respective technical and theoretical principles of scientific factory management, as developed by Frederick W. Taylor, were extended to the home by writers such as Christine Fred-

[80]Hartmann (n. 11 above); Gilman (n. 10 above).
[81]Strasser (n. 14 above).

erick and Lillian Gilbreth.[82] Current home economics literature is still full of applications of time- and motion-study techniques.

We argue that, cumulatively, technologies have helped make a reallocation of household labor difficult to accomplish. They have been used to privatize work and thus to increase the work load of many individual women.[83] Housework remains decentralized, conducted inefficiently within many single units. In fact, it may now be difficult to move some housework tasks out of the home.[84] First, the small scale of household work and technologies is labor intensive. Second, the work has become so laden with emotion that attaining a more communalized form may be impossible.[85] Finally, since women's labor at home is unpaid and thus seen as "cheap," it could be indefinitely used for these tasks, retaining the specialization of labor within the home and keeping housework structurally separated from the paid labor market.[86] Bearing these factors in mind, we can now look at the impact of utilities, appliances, foods, and services.

Although it cannot be proved that utilities have had a profound effect on the household specialization of labor, they have reallocated wives' time.[87] This may be owing to appliances as well, but we assume that utilities facilitated at least some of the change. Of course, this trend does not alter the burden of housework but, rather, its content. In household production, as elsewhere, we find a tendency to focus released time on new goods and services rather than more leisure. Utilities undoubtedly made it possible for more women to enter the paid labor force or allowed change in the household separation of labor to occur, but they did not *cause* such changes.

It is also possible that some household appliances have been used as a substitute for more equal allocation of household labor. Husbands do little housework, "spending an average of 1.6 hours a day on all household work, whether or not wives were employed."[88] Studies of

[82]See Christine Frederick, *The New Housekeeping: Efficiency Studies in Home Management* (New York, 1913); Lillian Gilbreth, *The Homemaker and Her Job* (New York, 1927), and *Management in the Home* (New York, 1954). These principles have also been extended to the office, where many women encounter them as clerical workers (see Harry Braverman, *Labor and Monopoly Capital* [New York, 1974]).
[83]Cowan, "Two Washes in the Morning" and "From Virginia Dare to Virginia Slims" (n. 14 above); Gilman (n. 10 above).
[84]Cowan, "From Virginia Dare to Virginia Slims" (n. 14 above); Kneeland (n. 7 above).
[85]Ravetz (n. 40 above).
[86]Davidoff (n. 6 above).
[87]Ogburn and Nimkoff (n. 48 above).
[88]Walker and Woods.

this issue control only for age, class, and number of children, not for equipment. Task-specific technologies may develop so that women can take over tasks previously done by other family members rather than vice versa. When families have garbage disposals, wives are more likely to take care of the garbage; the pattern is similar with dishwashers. In other words, new technologies may reduce the amount of time men engage in housework and increase the time spent by women, a finding which contradicts conventional wisdom.[89] Furthermore, to the extent that appliances are designed for use within the home, they reinforce the separation of women from the paid labor force or increase the reluctance to seek market services.

Convenience foods are often claimed to be a major time-saver and therefore a role-equalizer for the household cook. However, time saved is seen as something to devote to the family, and the ultimate gender-based allocation of household labor does not change. Women's expanded role as consumer[90] has encompassed, of course, the purchasing of the convenience foods that in times past were produced at home. The purchases are also influenced by advertising that indicates which kinds of purchases are appropriate for each sex role.

Services probably had the greatest potential for redefining the household specialization of labor. We know, historically, that households were becoming smaller by 1900 because of the reduction of the extended family and diminishing numbers of boarders and servants. In theory, this change in household composition could have been handled either by applying technological solutions in the home or by bringing household functions into labor-force production modes outside the home. In practice, the former prevailed, and technology was brought into the home where women could now perform all the work previously done by other family members or servants. At this point technology kept women in the home rather than liberating them from it.

More recently, the increasing number of women entering the paid labor force is the trend which has had the largest impact on housework. Studies make it clear that housework time reduction is a function of employment and not of the amount of technology available.[91]

[89]Charles A. Thrall, "The Conservative Use of Modern Household Technology," *Technology and Culture* 23 (April 1982): 175–94; Christine E. Bose, "Technology and Changes in the Division of Labor in the American Home," *Women's Studies International Quarterly* 2 (1979): 295–304.

[90]Batya Weinbaum and Amy Bridges, "The Other Side of the Pay Check: Monopoly Capital and the Structure of Consumption," *Monthly Review* 28 (July–August 1976): 88–103; John Galbraith, "The Economics of the American Housewife," *Atlantic Monthly* 233 (August 1973): 78–83.

[91]Alexander Szalai (n. 67 above); Thrall (n. 31 above); Vanek (n. 33 above).

Employed women substitute nondurable time-savers (e.g., convenience foods, laundries, child care) for their labor, shop at fewer stores on fewer days, and prepare fewer meals at home.[92] They use market services. But married women employed outside the home do not do a significantly smaller proportion of housework than married women who are not so employed,[93] even though less total work is done. Thus women's paid employment changes their own allocation of time but does not change the household specialization of labor. It seems that technological phenomena will not bring about such a change; it will occur only when someone other than the adult woman does the work.

The changes in women's distribution of time between home and work force have not been explained by technology itself as an independent variable, although technology may be an intervening variable which facilitates the change. Rather, the demand for women in the labor force, reduced household size, home monotony, aspects of contemporary feminist thought, and the pressures of inflation have drawn women to paid work, and this has in its turn decreased their time available for housework. The redefinition of housework away from production and toward consumption, transportation, and child care, which technology fostered, has facilitated women's move into the labor force, but it is not likely to have caused the current distribution of women's time between paid and unpaid work. While increased ease of work brought by utilities might have "freed" women, the second-level effects were in the opposite direction. Appliances (like convenience foods) in the home often extend women's role therein. Therefore we predict that ownership of increasing numbers of home appliances is likely to be positively correlated with gender-stereotyped specialization of labor within the household.

More technology is purchased as income increases. Beyond a certain income level, women/wives will be less likely to seek paid employment and be more able to fulfill the mother/wife role prescription, using technologies as means toward such ends. As noted, reallocation of labor among household members has simply not occurred. The content of housework has varied, but women's prime responsibility has gone unmodified by utilities and has probably been extended by appliances. Home technology and specialization of labor by gender, though correlated, are linked by the prior variable of income. (An exception to this trend may be very high-income families where servant labor is used in the home. However, this is not a statisti-

---

[92]Strober (n. 25 above); Vaugh (n. 54 above).
[93]Berheide et al. (n. 8 above).

cally significant number of families, and the outcome is not caused by technology but, rather, by purchased personal services.)

At this juncture, only labor-market solutions to housework offer the prospect of relieving women's burden. The proliferation of fast-food services indicates that some chores are moving out of the home. Others, such as child or laundry care, remain centered in the home. The service sector of the economy is clearly growing. It remains to be seen whether the services are oriented toward housework and who provides them. Women moving into paid work may be providing the same services in the labor force as they do in the home. In the past, nontechnological changes, such as those in labor force or household composition, have had the greatest impact on household special-ization of labor, and we can expect future changes to emanate from this source, too. In other words, if men begin to do more housework, it will likely be the result of social and cultural trends, not new technologies.

Conclusions

We can now ask to what extent popular beliefs about technology and housework are true. First, there is the popular assumption that technology has made housework easier. Certainly market services have eased some elements of work, and convenience foods may also have reduced fatigue. As for utilities, we can only surmise that, while they did reduce fatigue, their secondary effects created more and new forms of housework. None of the technologies increased general pleasantness of housework, made tasks interesting, or improved the sense of self-worth of the housewife.

Second, the popular belief that technology makes housework less expensive is not well supported. The impact of utilities on cost cannot be measured, while appliances and convenience foods are more ex-pensive. Only market services appear to be potentially cheaper than work in the home, but this is contingent on placing an economic value on the homemakers' labor.

Third is the time factor, for which popular belief would lead us to expect a decrease. However, we find that if time is saved by some technological means, the saving is offset by concomitant activities and by maintaining the new technological systems. In the past, the most significant factors contributing to saving time in meal preparation were nontechnological, such as smaller families and the increased labor-force participation of women. Now, real savings can be realized primarily by removal of this activity from the home.

Finally, popular belief has it that technology has made for less housework and thus for a redistribution of household labor among household members. However, the evidence (as opposed to anecdotes) indicates that household specialization of labor probably has not changed over time and may actually have become more burdensome to women. Advertising still shows housework as women's work. Ironically, appliances have often fixed and extended women's traditional household roles. The time and energy saved from tasks previously performed have merely been reallocated to new consumption and family care tasks for women. The content mix of housework has changed, even if the gender specialization of labor has not.

Any changes in women's distribution of time between home and outside work have not been explained by technology itself as an independent variable, although technology may facilitate the process of increasing female labor-force participation. Despite a conventional wisdom which asserts that technological change in the home allowed or directly led to increased female labor-force participation during the period of the most intensive industrialization of the home (the 1920s and 1930s, with the large-scale deployment of utilities and large appliances), middle-class women receiving these new domestic amenities did not, by and large, seek employment outside the home. Rather, reduced household size and increased women's labor-force participation have cut into the time spent on housework. But the proportion of housework tasks done by women remains the same. Actual relief of women's prime responsibility for housework may come only with the development and improvement of further private-market services for the household such as those already available in the fast-food industry.

Thus, when we finally look at who has benefited from household technologies, women do not appear to have been the primary beneficiaries. While technologies may have decreased the physical effort of housework, they have not reduced the time involved, alleviated the psychic burdens, altered the allocation of labor by gender, or released women to enter the paid labor force. The acquisition of household technologies is primarily related to one's stage in the life cycle and to economic means, not to women's entry into paid work. It is likely that purchasers believe that appliances and convenience foods do save time, effort, or costs. Often purchases have symbolic connotations as well. Overall, however, household technologies have led to less satisfaction with the work environment and to the proletarianization of housework. The greatest influences on time spent on housework have come from nontechnological changes, changes in household size and in paid employment of women. In the past, wives' labor has substituted for the loss of household service workers and of other (primarily female) family members' aid. In the future, public and market services have the potential to replace home food production and other work, finally lightening women's burden in the home. But an even more equitable and hence preferable solution would involve men taking increased responsibility for the necessary life-support and sustenance activities that constitute housework.

From Virginia Dare to Virginia Slims: Women and Technology in American Life

RUTH SCHWARTZ COWAN

When this topic—women and technology in American life—was first proposed to me as an appropriate subject for a bicentennial retrospective, I was puzzled by it. Was the female experience of technological change significantly different from the male experience? Did the introduction of the railroads, or the invention of the Bessemer process, or the diffusion of the reaper have a differential impact on the male and female segments of the population? A careful reading of most of the available histories of American technology (or of Western technology in general, for that matter) would not lead one to suspect that important differences had existed. Was my topic perhaps a nonsubject? I mulled over the matter for several months and eventually came to the conclusion that the absence of a female perspective in the available histories of technology was a function of the historians who wrote them and not of historical reality. There are at least four significant senses in which the relation between women and technology has diverged from that between men and technology. I shall consider each of them in turn and ask the reader to understand that what I will say below is intended in much the same spirit that many of bicentennial retrospectives were intended—to be suggestive, but not definitive.

Women as Bearers and Rearers of Children

Women menstruate, parturate, and lactate; men do not. Therefore, any technology which impinges on those processes will affect women more than it will affect men. There are many such technologies, and some of them have had very long histories: pessaries, sanitary napkins, tampons, various intrauterine devices, childbirth anasthesia, artificial nipples, bottle sterilizers, pasteurized and condensed milks, etc. Psychologists suggest that those three processes are fundamentally

RUTH SCHWARTZ COWAN is professor of history at the State University of New York at Stony Brook. She is the author of *More Work for Mother: The Ironies of Household Technology from the Open Hearth to the Microwave* (New York, 1983).

This essay originally appeared in *Technology and Culture*, vol. 20, no. 4, October 1979.

important experiences in the psychosocial development of individuals. Thus, a reasonable student of the history of technology might be led to suppose that the history of technological intervention with those processes would be known in some detail.

That reasonable student would be wrong, of course. The indices to the standard histories of technology—Singer's, Kranzberg and Pursell's, Daumas's, Giedion's, even Ferguson's bibliography—do not contain a single reference, for example, to such a significant cultural artifact as the baby bottle. Here is a simple implement which, along with its attendant delivery systems (!), has revolutionized a basic biological process, transformed a fundamental human experience for vast numbers of infants and mothers, and been one of the more controversial exports of Western technology to underdeveloped countries—yet it finds no place in our histories of technology.

There is a host of questions which scholars might reasonably ask about the baby bottle. For how long has it been part of Western culture? When a mother's milk could not be provided, which classes of people used the bottle and which the wet-nurse, and for what reasons? Which was a more crucial determinant for widespread use of the bottle, changes in milk technology or changes in bottle technology? Who marketed the bottles, at what price, to whom? How did mothers of different social classes and ethnicities react to them? Can the phenomenon of "not enough milk," which was widely reported by American pediatricians and obstetricians in the 1920s and 1930s, be connected with the advent of the safe baby bottle? Which was cause and which effect?[1]

I could go on, using other examples and other questions, but I suspect that my point is clear: the history of the uniquely female technologies is yet to be written, with the single exception of the technologies of contraception.[2] This is also true, incidentally, of the technologies of child rearing, a process which is not anatomically confined to females but which has been more or less effectively limited to them by the terms of many unspoken social contracts. We know a great deal more about the bicycle than we do about the baby carriage, despite the fact that the carriage has had a more lasting impact on the

---

[1] The history of nursing practices in early modern Europe is surveyed in Edward Shorter (*The Making of the Modern Family* [New York, 1975], chap. 5), but developments since the appearance of pasteurized milk and sterile (or sterilizable) bottles are not considered.

[2] Norman E. Hines (*A Medical History of Contraception* [Baltimore, 1936]) does not cover more recent developments. Linda Gordon (*Woman's Body, Woman's Right: A Social History of Birth Control in America* [New York, 1976]) focuses on ideas about birth control, but not on the devices themselves.

transport of infants than the bicycle has had on the transport of adults. Although we recognize the importance of toilet training in personality formation, we have not the faintest idea whether toilet-training practices have been affected by the various technologies that impinge upon them: inexpensive absorbent fabrics, upholstered furniture, diaper services, wall-to-wall carpeting, paper diapers, etc. The crib, the playpen, the teething ring, and the cradle are as much a part of our culture and our sense of ourselves as harvesting machines and power looms, yet we know almost nothing of their history. The history of technology is, of course, a new field, and it is not surprising that its practitioners have ignored many of the female technologies. We do not usually think of women as bearers of technological change, nor do we think of the home as a technological locale (in part because women reside there). Both of these common assumptions are incorrect; Adam knew that, but his descendants have forgotten it.

Women as Workers

Women have been part of the market economy of this country from its earliest days. In the colonial period they tended cows, delivered babies, kept taverns, published newspapers, and stitched fancy clothes, among other things. During industrialization they tended looms, folded paper bags, packed cigars, helped with harvests, washed laundry, and stitched fancy clothes, among other things. With the advent of automation they punch cards, handle switchboards, pack cookies, teach school, tend the sick, and stitch fancy clothes, again among other things. All along they have been paid for their work, sometimes in land, sometimes in produce, sometimes in cash.

But women workers are different from men workers, and the differences are crucial, for the women themselves and for any analysis of the relation between women and the American technological order. The economic facts of life for women are almost on a deterministic par with the anatomic facts of life; they are so pervasive over time and place as to be almost universal truisms. There are three of them: (1) when doing the same work women are almost always paid less than men; (2) considered in the aggregate, women rarely do the same work as men (jobs are sex typed); and (3) women almost always consider themselves, and are considered by others, to be transient participants in the work force.[3]

These characteristics of women as workers predate industrialization; they were economic facts of life even before our economy was

---

[3]On the economics of workers, see Robert W. Smuts, *Women and Work in America* (New York, 1959), and Juanita Kreps, *Sex in the Marketplace: American Women at Work* (Baltimore, 1971).

dominated by cash. Sex typing of jobs occurred in the earliest James-
town settlements, even before the household economy had completely
replaced the communal economy: unmarried or poor women worked
as laundresses in return for a portion from the communal store; men
who were not entitled to grants of land worked as cooks and bakers.[4]
Unequal pay for equal work was also characteristic of the early settlements: adventurers who came to settle in Maryland were allotted
100 acres of land for every manservant they brought with them and
60 acres of land for every woman servant; unmarried free men in
Salem and Plymouth were given allotments of land when they requested them, but, after the first few years of settlement, unmarried
women were not; the first American effort to obtain equal economic
rights for women may well have been the request made in 1619 by the
Virginia House of Burgesses that husbands and wives be granted
equal shares of land on the grounds that the work of each was equally
crucial to the establishment of a plantation.[5] That women were regarded as transitory members of the work force even then is shown by
many things: for example, the fact that when girl children were "put
out" for indenture or apprenticeship the persons who received their
work were rarely required to teach them a trade,[6] or the fact that
women who owned and operated businesses in the colonial period
were almost always widows of the men who had first established the
business, who consciously advertised themselves as worthy of patron-
age on those grounds alone.[7] Parents of daughters did not expect that
their girl children would need to know any occupation other than
housework; young women expected that they might need to support
themselves while unmarried but that gainful employment would become unnecessary and undesirable after marriage; married women
expected not to be gainfully employed unless their husbands died or
were disabled.

So it was, and so it continues to be—despite industrialization,
unionization, and automation. The Equal Pay Act of 1964 attempted
to legislate equal pay for equal work for women, but in 1973 it was still
true that women were earning from 37.8 percent to 63.6 percent of
what men in the same job classifications were earning.[8] Power

[4]Julia Cherry Spruill, *Women's Life and Work in the Southern Colonies* (Chapel Hill, N.C., 1938), p. 6.
[5]Ibid., pp. 9–11; also Edith Abbott, *Women in Industry: A Study in American History* (New York, 1910) p. 11.
[6]Abbott, pp. 30–32.
[7]Spruill, pp. 263–64, 276, 280.
[8]United States Department of Labor, *1975 Handbook on Women Workers*, Bulletin no. 297 (Washington, D.C., 1975), p. 130.

technologies have eased and simplified thousands of jobs, yet the labor market is still dominated by sex-typed occupations, despite the fact that the worker's "strength" is no longer a relevant criterion. In the garment industry in New York, for example, men cut and women sew. Thus, when a manufacturer goes into the labor market to find employees, he or she enters one labor market, with its own price structure and its own supply-demand pattern, if searching for a skilled cutter—and a different labor market, with a price structure and a supply-demand pattern all *its* own, if looking for a skilled sewing-machine operator.[9] A fairly sophisticated statistical analysis of sex typing in the labor market has demonstrated that, although some job classifications shifted from being male dominated to being female dominated between 1900 and 1960 (ironically, none have gone the other way), the total amount of sex typing has not changed appreciably. In 1900, 66 percent of all employed women would have had to shift their jobs into male-dominated fields in order for the distribution of women and men in all fields to resemble chance; in 1960 that figure was 68.4 percent. (The corresponding figure, incidentally, for racial typing of jobs in 1960 was 46.8 percent.)[10]

And of course it is still true, as it was in colonial days, that women are not regarded, by themselves or by others, as permanent members of the work force. Young women do not invest in expensive training for themselves because they anticipate leaving the work force when they marry and have children. Employers are equally unwilling to invest in training women because they anticipate the same thing—and with some statistical basis for their suspicion; the labor force participation rates of females fall off sharply between the ages of 18 and 25, the years when most women marry and begin their families.[11] The cumulative result of these attitudes is that women prefer to place themselves in fairly unskilled, unresponsible, and, therefore, lower-paying positions, and employers are content to have them remain there.

These three characteristics of women as workers—the fact that they work for less, that many jobs are not open to them because of sex typing, and that they are transient members of the work force (and therefore difficult to organize and unionize)—should be of signal importance in any discussion of rates of technological change, although they are rarely considered in that context. We are accustomed to

[9]On sex typing of jobs, see Valerie Kincaid Oppenheimer, *The Female Labor Force in the United States,* Population Monograph Series, no. 5 (Berkeley, 1970).

[10]Edward Gross, "Plus ça change . . . The Sexual Structure of Occupations Over Time," *Social Problems* 16 (Fall 1968): 198–206, esp. p. 202.

[11]Kreps, pp. 28–29.

thinking about the price and availability of labor as one of the key
determinants of rates of change in any given industry or any given
locality, but we are not accustomed to thinking of the price and
availability of labor as determined by the sex of the laborers. The ways
in which the sex of workers interacts with technological change can be
illustrated by two somewhat different cases.

The first is the cigar industry in the second half of the 19th century,
a case in which technological change was accelerated by the availability
of female workers.[12] During the middle decades of the century
cigarmaking was localized in factories, but the product was entirely
handmade by skilled male workers, most of them Spanish, Cuban,
and German. In 1869 the New York cigarmakers went on strike, and
in retaliation several manufacturers arranged for the immigration of
Bohemian women who worked in the cigar trade in their native land.
These women were not as skilled as the men they replaced; they used
a simple molding tool to shape the cigar. They also were accustomed
to working at home, which meant that they were amenable to the
tenement system of manufacture, which was much cheaper for the
employers. The women were effective in breaking the strike. In subsequent years more women cigarmakers immigrated as the cigar trade
in Bohemia was disrupted by the Franco-Prussian War. There were
other male cigarmakers' strikes in New York and elsewhere during
the 1870s and 1880s, the net effect of which was that some manufacturers converted entirely to the tenement system and others were
induced to try some simple pieces of machinery (also of European
origin) which could be operated by women. The women were laborers
of choice because they knew the cigar trade yet were willing to work
for less and had not been organized. As one New York cigar manufacturer put it in 1895: "... the handwork has almost entirely disappeared. The suction tables, which are in reality nothing else than
wrapper cutting machines, are used as price cutters. More so, because
there are only girls employed on them."[13]

A somewhat contrary case is that of the ladies' garment industry in
the 20th century; here technological change seems to have been
slowed by the presence of female workers.[14] Since the time that sewing machines were initially hooked up to central power supplies

[12]Abbott, chap. 9.
[13]Ibid., p. 263. Patricia Cooper, a graduate student in history at the University of
Maryland, College Park, will soon complete a dissertation on tobacco workers which
extends and reinforces these conclusions.
[14]This account is based on Elizabeth Faulkner Baker, *Technology and Women's Work*
(New York, 1954), chap. 15.

(steam or electricity) in the last quarter of the 19th century, there has been little technological change in the sewing process, despite the fact that the industry is highly competitive and despite the fact that there have been substantial changes in the technology of the processes that are auxiliary to sewing—namely, cutting and pressing. The sewing process could potentially be automated, but there appears to be a little incentive for manufacturers to do this, partly because the expense would be very great and many of the companies are very small. Yet another reason stems from the fact that sewers are women, and sewing is work that women from traditional cultures like to do. The ladies' garment industry has been populated by successive waves of fairly skilled immigrant women of various sorts: American farm girls who came to the cities to escape rural life in the middle of the 19th century, then immigrant women from Italy and eastern Europe, then black women from the South, then Puerto Rican women, and now Chinese women. Although these women are skilled, and although their trade has been unionized successfully for many years, the wages paid to sewing-machine operators are, as one would expect, significantly lower than the wages paid to other skilled machine operators. As a consequence of this the technology of sewing has remained fairly static.

There is yet another sense in which the characteristics of women as workers have interacted with the technological order in this country—and here we confront one of the most firmly grounded shibboleths about the relation between women's work and technology. It is true that there has been a vast increase in the number of women in the work force in the past century, and during this time some occupations (such as clerical work) have almost completely changed sex. It is also true that during the same period of time power-driven machinery has entered many fields, requiring much less human energy to do work that was once hard to do. Acknowledging that these facts are true, historians and others have concluded that technological change has drawn women into the work force by opening fields of work that were previously closed because of the physical strength required to do the work. That conclusion appears to be almost entirely unwarranted. Women have replaced men in several occupations in which hard physical labor was not required before industrialization (e.g., cigarmaking); they have replaced men in some occupations in which no significant technological change occurred (e.g., schoolteaching); and they have replaced men in some occupations in which technological change made no difference to the physical labor involved (e.g., bookkeeping). In all of these cases the crucial factor is not physical labor but price; women replaced men because they worked for less.[15]

Alternatively, there are many trades in which work has been transformed by the introduction of new machines but in which women have not replaced men. Typesetting is a perfect example.[16] From the colonial period to the present there have always been a few women typesetters, but they have worked in the smallest shops, often shops that were family owned. Typesetting was generally an apprenticed trade in the 19th century, and women were not set to apprenticeships. In any event, it was widely believed that women could not do the work of typesetting efficiently because they were not able to carry the heavy type cases from the composing tables to the press. Women typesetters were occasionally used to break strikes or to cut wages, a practice which did not endear them to the typesetters' union which were formed during the early decades of the century. In 1887 the linotype machine was introduced, and after that time the work of typesetting was not terribly much more difficult than the work of typewriting. Various modifications of that machine, and the more recent introduction of photographic processes, have made the work easier still—but men dominate the trade. The reasons for this are several: after women were admitted to the typesetters' unions, in the latter part of the 19th century, they had to agree to work for scale, which meant, of course, that employers had little interest in hiring them; following this the advent of protective labor laws meant that night work for women was very carefully regulated, which made it unfeasible for women to become typesetters since so much of the work is on newspapers. Thus technological change has been, at best, a mixed blessing for women. More jobs are open to them that they are fit (either biologically or socially) to perform, but many of those jobs are at the very lowest skill and salary levels and are likely to remain that way as long as women are willing, for whatever reasons, to work for less than men and to let themselves be treated as marginal members of the labor force.[17]

Women as Homemakers

Both men and women live in homes, but only women have their "place" there—and this is another one of those salient facts about

[15]Ibid., chaps. 13 and 17.

[16]Ibid., pp. 170–77; Abbott, chap. 11.

[17]Interest in women workers has revived in the last few years: see Judith A. McGaw, "Technological Change and Women's Work: Mechanization in the Berkshire Paper Industry, 1820–1855" (Ph.D. diss., New York University, 1977); Rosalyn Baxandall, Linda Gordon, and Susan Reverby, eds., *America's Working Women: A Documentary History* (New York, 1976); and Barbara Mayer Wertheimer, *We Were There: American Women Who Worked* (New York, 1977).

women's lives which make their interaction with technology somewhat different from men's. The homes in which we live, the household implements with which we work, and the ways in which that work is organized have changed greatly over the years, but the character of that change and its impact upon the people who work in homes (predominantly women) have proved very difficult to gauge.

Some tasks have disappeared (e.g., beating rugs), but other tasks have replaced them (e.g., waxing linoleum floors). Some tasks are easier (e.g., laundering) but are done much more frequently; it takes less time and effort to wash and iron a sheet than it once did, but there are now vastly more sheets to be washed in each household each week. Some tasks have become demonstrably more time consuming and arduous over the years: shopping, for example.[18] Less work needs to be done at home because so many aspects of home production have been transferred to the marketplace (e.g., canning vegetables), but there are now fewer hands to do the work as there are fewer servants, fewer unmarried females living at home, and fewer children per family. An equivocal picture at best.[19]

But one point is worth making. Despite all the changes that have been wrought in housework, and there have been many, the household has resisted industrialization with greater success than any other productive locale in our culture.[20] The work of men has become centralized, but the work of women remains decentralized. Several million American women cook supper each night in several million separate homes over several million separate stoves—a specter which should be sufficient to drive any rational technocrat into the loony bin, but which does not do so for reasons I will discuss in a moment. Out there in the land of household work there are small industrial plants which sit idle for the better part of every working day; there are expensive pieces of highly mechanized equipment which only get used once or twice a month; there are consumption units which weekly trundle out to their markets to buy 8 ounces of this nonperishable product and 12 ounces of that one. There are also workers who

[18]On time spent in housework, see JoAnn Vanek, "Keeping Busy: Time Spent in Housework, United States, 1920–1970" (Ph.D. diss., University of Michigan, 1973).

[19]For an extended discussion of this topic see my papers, "The 'Industrial Revolution' in the Home: Household Technology and Social Change in the 20th Century," *Technology and Culture* 17 (January 1976): 1–22; and "Two Washes in the Morning, and a Bridge Party at Night: The American Housewife between the Wars," *Women's Studies* 3 (Winter 1976): 147–72.

[20] On this point see Allison Ravetz, "Modern Technology and an Ancient Occupation: Housework in Present-day Society," *Technology and Culture* 6 (Spring 1965): 256–60. Also, for a general history of housework, see Ann Oakley, *Woman's Work, the Housewife Past and Present* (New York, 1974).

do not have job descriptions, time clocks, or even paychecks.[21] Cottage industry is alive and well and living in suburbia.

Why? There is no simple answer to that question, but I would like to attempt a rough list of what some of the components of the answer might be, presenting them in no particular order and with no pretense of knowing the relative weight which should be attached to each, or the relative likelihood that some are causes and others effects. To start with, since the middle of the 19th century Americans have idealized the household as a place where men could retreat from the technological order: a retreat, by definition, should not possess the characteristics that one is trying to escape. Increased efficiency and modernity in the home have occasionally been advocated by domestic reformers, most of whom have been women (Catherine Beecher, Ellen Swallow Richards, Charlotte Perkins Gilman, Christine Frederick, and Lillian Gilbreth immediately come to mind), but the general public has been hostile to certain crucial concomitants of those ideas.[22] The farm kitchen has been the American mythic dream, not the cafeteria. In some households the latest and showiest equipment is purchased in order to demonstrate status, not efficiency; in such cases the housebound housewife is as much proof of status as the microwave oven that she operates. In other households status is not the issue, but modern equipment is used to free the housewife for labor which is not currently technology intensive (stripping furniture, planting vegetable gardens, chauffering children), and the end result is far from an increase in overall efficiency. Except for a very brief period in the 1920s, "Early American" has been, far and away, the most popular decor for American kitchens; our ambivalence on the issue of efficiency in the home is nowhere better symbolized than when a dishwasher is built into a "rustic" cabinet or a refrigerator is faced with plastic "wood" paneling. For long periods of time, on either side of the industrial revolution in housework (which can be roughly said to have occurred in the first three decades of this century), the maintenance of a fundamentally inefficient mode of household operation, requiring the full attention of the housewife for the better part of every single day, has been a crucial part of the symbolic quality of the individual American home.

Connected with this is the fact that, also since the middle of the 19th

[21] For an extended discussion of the sociological meaning of this phenomenon, see Ann Oakley, *The Sociology of Housework* (London, 1974).

[22] See Kathryn Kish Sklar, *Catherine Beecher: A Study in American Domesticity* (New Haven, Conn., 1973); Caroline Hunt, *The Life of Ellen H. Richards* (Boston, 1912); and Waida Gerhardt, "The Pros and Cons of Efficiency in the Household," *Journal of Home Economics* 18 (1928): 337–39.

century, most Americans have regarded communalization of households as socialistic and therefore un-American. There have been repeated attempts at communalizing some of the household functions, especially during the first two decades of the 20th century—communal canneries, laundries, kitchens, and even nursery schools appeared in many communities—but they have all failed for want of a supportive community attitude.[23]

The implements invented or developed for the home have very special features which may set them apart from other implements. Many of them were initially developed, for example, not for home use, but for commercial use: the automatic washing machine, the vacuum cleaner, the small electric motor, and the refrigerator, for example.[24] Most of them were not developed by persons intimately connected with the work involved; inventors tend to be men and homemakers tend to be women. On top of this, many of the implements were marketed through the use of selling techniques that also had little relation to the work performed. These three factors lead to the hypothesis that the implements which have transformed housework may not have been the implements that housewives would have developed had they had control of the processes of innovation.

Thus, for reasons which may have been alternately economic, ideological, and structural, there was very little chance that American homes would become part of the industrial order in the same sense that American businesses have, because very few Americans, powerful or not powerful, have wished it so—and the ones who have wished it so have not been numerous enough or powerful enough to make a difference.

Women as Antitechnocrats

This brings me to a final and somewhat related point. For the better part of its cultural life, the United States has been idealized as the land of practicality, the land of know-how, the land of Yankee ingenuity. No country on earth has been so much in the sway of the technological order or so proud of its involvement in it. Doctors and engineers are central to our culture; poets and artists live on the fringes.

If practicality and know-how and willingness to get your hands dirty down there with the least of them are signatures of the true American, then we have been systematically training slightly more than half of our population to be un-American. I speak, of course, of

[23]Victor Papanek and James Hennessey speculate about how various implements would have to be redesigned for communal ownership in *How Things Don't Work* (New York, 1977), chap. 2.

[24]Siegfried Giedion, *Mechanization Takes Command* (New York, 1948), pp. 556–606.

women. While we socialize our men to aspire to feats of mastery, we socialize our women to aspire to feats of submission. Men are hard; women are soft. Men are meant to conquer nature; women are meant to commune with it. Men are rational, women irrational; men are practical, women impractical. Boys play with blocks; girls play with dolls. Men build; women inhabit. Men are active; women are passive. Men are good at mathematics; women are good at literature. If something is broken, daddy will fix it. If feelings are hurt, mommy will salve them. We have trained our women to opt out of the technological order as much as we have trained our men to opt into it.

This is probably just as much true today as it was in the heyday of the archetypically passive, romantic Victorian female. An interesting survey of American college girls' attitudes toward science and technology in the 1960s revealed that the girls were planning careers, but that they could not assimilate the notion of becoming engineers and—and this is equally revealing—that there was no single occupation that they thought their male contemporaries and their parents would be less pleased to have them pursue.[25]

Thus, women who might wish to become engineers or inventors or mechanics or jackhammer operators would have to suppress some deeply engrained notions about their own sexual identity in order to fulfill their wishes. Very few people have ever had the courage to take up such a fight. It is no wonder that women have played such minor roles in creating technological change; in fact, it is a wonder that there have been any female engineers and inventors at all.

Conversely, it may be true that the recent upsurge in "antiscience" and "antitechnology" attitudes may be correlated very strongly with the concurrent upsurge in women's political consciousness. This is not to say that all of the voices that have been raised against the SST and atomic power plants and experimentation on animals have been female, but only that a surprisingly large number of them have been. Ann Douglas has recently written a complex analysis of the "feminization" of American culture in the 19th century, in which she suggests that the "tough-minded" theological attitudes that had served as cornerstones of American ideology in the 17th and 18th centuries were watered down and whittled away in the 19th century by several generations of educated and literary women working in concert with similar generations of liberal male theologians.[26] Both groups, she argues, realized that they were excluded from the burgeoning capitalist

[25] Alice Rossi, "Barriers to the Career Choice of Engineering, Medicine or Science among American Women," in *Women and the Scientific Professions,* ed. Jacqueline Mattfeld and Carol Van Aken (Cambridge, Mass., 1965).

[26] Ann Douglas, *The Feminization of American Culture* (New York, 1977).

economy that the older theology had produced; they resented this exclusion and so fought against the economy and the theology together. The temptation to push Douglas's analysis into the 20th century is almost irresistible. If we are experiencing a similar feminization of American culture today, it is the tough-minded ideology of the scientific-technocratic state that is the focus of current animus. Women have traditionally operated on the fringes of that state, so it is not surprising that they should resent it and, when given the opportunity, fight against it. Women have experienced science and technology as consumers, not as producers—and consumers, as every marketing expert knows, are an infuriatingly fickle population. Trained to think of themselves as the possessors of subjectivity, women can hardly be expected to show much allegiance to the flag of objectivity. As more and more women begin to play active and powerful roles in our political and economic life, we may be surprised to discover the behavioral concomitants of the unspoken hostility to science and technology that they are carrying with them into the political arena.

The Cathedral and the Bridge: Structure and Symbol

DAVID P. BILLINGTON AND ROBERT MARK

When Montgomery Schuyler wrote in 1883 what was perhaps the first critical essay on a work of modern engineering as a work of art (the Brooklyn Bridge), he recognized the cultural similarity between the Gothic cathedrals of the 13th century and the long-span bridges of his own era.[1] Just as the cathedrals symbolized the medieval world of stone, so did the bridges of the Industrial Revolution symbolize the new technological world of metal. Yet, while most educated persons of the 20th century will know something of medieval cathedrals and perceive such knowledge as essential to a liberal education, few are familiar with the great modern structures or would accord them a central place in higher learning.

Here, we seek to explore two reasons for this cultural neglect. One is related to a misconception about the cathedral itself and the other to a mistaken belief that a deeper understanding of modern engineering is both inaccessible to the non-engineer and without intrinsic cultural value. Our aim is to show how historical study from an engineering perspective can correct such misunderstanding while making the technical questions intelligible to the general public.

Understanding Cathedrals

The major development of the High Gothic cathedral took place in northern France in the remarkably short period of less than a

DAVID P. BILLINGTON is professor in the Department of Civil Engineering and Operations Research at Princeton University.

ROBERT MARK is professor in the School of Architecture and the Department of Civil Engineering and Operations Research at Princeton University. The research on which they drew for this article was supported by grants from the National Endowment for the Humanities, the Ford Foundation, the Rockefeller Foundation, the National Endowment for the Arts, the National Science Foundation, and the Mellon Foundation. The new educational documents described in the conclusion have resulted from a 1979 NEH grant, "Curriculum Materials for Humanistic Studies in Modern Engineering," with additional support from the Sloan Foundation and the Mellon Foundation and from grants to Princeton University from Alfred P. Sloan Foundation for the program "The New Liberal Arts."

[1] Montgomery Schuyler, "The Bridge as a Monument," *American Architecture and Other Writings*, ed. W. H. Jordy and R. Coe (New York, 1964), p. 17.

This essay originally appeared in *Technology and Culture*, vol. 25, no. 1, January 1984.

hundred years. The religious ideal was to create permanent vertical space, filled with light, for the purpose of bringing communities together. And that functional imperative inspired the creation of new structural systems which allowed the Gothic builders to achieve an extreme of light masonry structure with interior elevations as great as that of a sixteen-story building. High walls, appearing to be composed of little but stained glass, were braced by tiers of exposed flying buttresses. Intervening load-bearing walls were not required, and so they were largely supplanted by window openings, creating a giant skeleton of stone. In effect, the new inventions in structure meant that the builders were confronted with an open-ended command to construct a church as high and as light as humanly possible. These limitlessly rising expectations were controlled only by available funding and the structural capacity of unreinforced masonry.

While the modern world has properly viewed these cathedrals as Christian monuments which symbolize religious ideas of the medieval world, it has missed the major and essential ideas which follow the religious ones: one pertinent to the physical basis for the creation of new forms and the other to their social basis. Such ambitions could be realized only by new engineering (the physical basis) and by vastly increased financial support (the social basis). These forms were not primarily the product of decorative and allegorical ideas, nor could they have appeared without new sources of wealth. Indeed, the cathedrals also stand for the commercial expression of urban competition as 13th-century cities vied with each other over church-building height, much as Chicago and New York were to do in office towers seven centuries later. High Gothic architecture seen in this broader context is part of the urban growth that took place in Western Europe following the Crusades. The expansion of trade and the rise of marketing and manufacturing centers in the 12th century created new economic and social classes in the cities: the commercial middle class who created the necessary economy and the specialized professional craftsmen including those who undertook the large-scale building projects. Surviving fragments of building accounts indicate that the great cathedrals were constructed by relatively well-paid, highly skilled teams of masons and carpenters, with supporting staffs that included the apprentices who insured the continuity of skills.[2]

Gothic cathedrals have been consistently misunderstood: first in the Renaissance by those in the south who found them tasteless, even barbarian (hence the name "Gothic," coined by Vasari in the 16th

---

[2]See, e.g., Lynn White, jr., *Dynamo and Virgin Reconsidered* (Cambridge, Mass., 1968), p. viii.

century), and then in the 19th century, when they were thought by many to be the only true religious architecture—and even their forms were incorporated into train stations, banks, and colleges as part of the Gothic revival.[3] In both instances, the misunderstandings resulted from superficial responses to the visual effect of the immense stone monuments rather than from any detailed analysis of their forms. Indeed, the Gothic revival, which began as a literary-romantic movement in the mid-18th century, became by the mid-19th century part of a romanticized reaction against the Industrial Revolution.[4] Much new building throughout that century and into the 20th was greatly influenced by the same incomplete understanding of the Gothic cathedral. And that misunderstanding had serious practical repercussions.

As an example of how pervasive is this view of the Gothic, we quote from a recent review in the *New York Times* entitled "Cathedrals": "Suger [abbot of Saint-Denis and considered the originator of the Gothic style] inaugurated a joyous period of cathedral building that ended when 'the cold syllogism invaded theology,' when problems of statics and dynamics displaced passion."[5] Engineering is thereby credited with the demise of the Gothic and, even worse, with the displacement of passion. This is the essential basis of the superficial view of Gothic form which gives license to the widely held belief that to build with passion is to avoid engineering and that, as a corollary, if one focuses on the statics, the joyous period of building will end. It is up to engineers to show that such ideas not only are nonsense but also make the task of modern building far more costly and difficult than need be. Contrary to romantic wish, the great cathedrals took their glorious forms *because* their builders were forced to learn statics (empirically, of course), and their passion was channeled by that discipline into the creation of unprecedented forms. These new forms ushered in a joyous period just because they do stand for human creativity rather than pallid imitation. Furthermore, they show what the human passion can constructively accomplish when it is both disciplined and

---

[3]G. Vasari, *The Lives of Painters, Sculptors, and Architects* (1550; reprint ed., New York, 1963), 1:12.

[4]This movement found its greatest strength in the most highly industrialized nation of the 19th century, England; see Kenneth Clark, *The Gothic Revival* (New York, 1962). For an account of its influence on the Continent, see George Germann, *Gothic Revival in Europe and Britain: Sources, Influences and Ideas* (Cambridge, Mass., 1972), and for its effect on 19th-century American architecture, see James Early, *Romanticism and American Architecture* (New York, 1965).

[5]Review of Georges Duby, *The Age of Cathedrals: Art and Society 980–1420* (Chicago, 1981) in the *New York Times*, June 14, 1981. The quoted passage is from p. 182 of Duby's text.

fervent. The meaning of Gothic style is that the structural engineering and the visible form became one, that discipline and passion merged.

In part the superficial response of 19th-century culture to the meaning of the cathedrals obscured development of the new building technology. The truth of this statement rests on much detailed engineering study of Gothic form for which several examples will follow. Before recounting these, however, we shall continue to elaborate upon this idea by turning back to Montgomery Schuyler and his critique of the Brooklyn Bridge.

Understanding Bridges

Schuyler recognized in the Brooklyn Bridge a work of passion and of discipline, but he too rebelled at the idea that the two could coexist in the creation of a single form. Influenced by the same romanticism that separated statics from passion in the Gothic, Schuyler criticized John Roebling's design by seeing it as two distinct parts: first the cables, where Roebling merely followed the law of gravity and thereby allowed something natural and hence beautiful to emerge; and second the towers, where Roebling failed to achieve beauty because he did not employ an architect for their design.[6] Thus Schuyler began what was to become the modern tradition of building criticism which would divide structures into two categories: those made beautiful by engineers who merely followed natural laws without aesthetic choice, and those made beautiful by designers who either covered up or contorted the engineering form in the interest of preconceived aesthetic theory. In the first category the engineer appears as a noble savage, creating beauty through a rational application of statics without any aesthetic predisposition; and, in the second category, the designer creates an illusion of form without primary visual reference to the supporting structural form. Rationalism by the noble savage versus illusionism by the sophisticated aesthete became the dominant dichotomy fostered by critics of 20th-century building design. This critical impasse is often presented to the general public as a choice between the supposed irreconcilables of inexpensive engineering design, which might at times be attractive but was more often woefully ugly, and elegant architectural design, which might at times be reasonably priced but was more often wastefully expensive.[7]

There were at least three reasons why Schuyler could not fully comprehend Roebling's ideas. First, he had no technical training and

[6]Schuyler, p. 173.

[7]See, e.g., Sigfried Giedion, *Space, Time and Architecture*, 5th ed. (Cambridge, Mass., 1967), pp. 676–88.

hence had to respond visually only; second, there was almost no writing by engineers which explained structural form in terms accessible to the layman; and third, Schuyler had developed his ideas on buildings out of mid-19th-century studies, mainly of French Gothic cathedrals by the architectural theorist and restorer of medieval buildings, Eugène Viollet-le-Duc.[8] While Viollet-le-Duc emphasized rationalism (i.e., the relation between structural innovation and style—as illustrated, e.g., by the flying buttresses) and tried to explain Gothic form in terms of structure, the principal influence he had on architectural writers was to impart a sense in which Gothic form was a precursor to modern building ideas. Thus, Viollet-le-Duc's work, appropriated by Henry Adams and others, lent authority to a perceptive but nonstructural view of Gothic form.

Writers like Schuyler and Adams could recognize, thanks to Viollet-le-Duc, that metal structure had the same symbolic meaning for modern industrial society that Gothic masonry had for medieval Christian society. But because these writers had little interest in statics or in the commercial context for building, they could not see even in Viollet-le-Duc's ideas the sense in which the Gothic they loved had demanded the same type of disciplined passion as the metal designs of the great 19th-century engineers: Telford, Brunel, Eads, Eiffel, and Roebling. In short, while they saw cathedral and bridge as comparable symbols, they could not see them as comparably joyous. They tended to praise the cathedral and to condemn the bridge. Paradoxically, this view led to the conclusion that the bridge needed one designer for passion (usually an architect) and another designer for discipline (usually an engineer).

Adams held up the cathedral as a symbol of unity in medieval life, whereas Schuyler represented the bridge as a fact of disunity in 19th-century industrial society. Nevertheless the proper understanding of the modern bridge requires the same sort of explanation needed to understand the cathedral, a technical clarification accessible to laymen, along with a description of the passion and joy inherent both in its creation and in its use. Such clarification can show the deep similarity between the two sorts of structure. The modern bridge represents the extreme potentials for industrial metals and for reinforced concrete—the materials that turned the masonry world into the modern world.

[8]Viollet-le-Duc's major writings are his ten-volume encyclopedia, *Dictionnaire raisonné de l'architecture française du XIe au XVIe siècle* (Paris, 1854–68) and his two-volume manifesto, *Entretiens sur l'architecture* (Paris, 1863, 1872). The *Entretiens* were translated into English by the American architect Henry Van Brunt and published under the title, *Discourses on Architecture* (Boston, 1875).

It is easy but inaccurate to say that cathedrals were religious and bridges commercial. The commercial incentives for cathedrals were as great as any civic competitions of the 20th century. The great cathedrals appeared in prosperous trading towns and represented political and economic facts as well as expressing religious aspirations. And for all that we can properly criticize commercial motives in 19th-century industrialization, the bridge did take on the image of a society changing in a direction away from aristocracy and slavery and toward democracy and freedom. The Brooklyn Bridge, especially, symbolized a religious attitude toward society. This work of pure utility became by design both a public park (its central elevated walkway) and a work of art. As Roebling stated, these new bridges were "the material [which] forms the basis for the mental and the spiritual: without it the mind may conceive, but cannot execute."[9] By contrast to earlier times "this present age is emphatically an age of usefulness. The useful goes before the ornamental. . . . No matter what may be charged against the material tendencies of the present age, it is through material advancements alone that a higher spiritual culture of the masses can be attained."[10]

Moreover, the vision of the bridge has evoked strong religious feelings in many first-rate artists, such as the poet Hart Crane[11] and the painter Joseph Stella. Brooklyn Bridge was as spiritual for these men as the cathedral was for Henry Adams. To elevate cathedrals only to religion is as inaccurate as to relegate bridges only to commerce. The fact that both stand for broader aspects of their times is the reason both are enduring symbols. Again, this argument for bridges and passion requires the same type of clarification as does the argument for cathedrals and discipline. Thus we proceed to several specific examples for each to reveal how a modern engineering view of cultural monuments can both enlighten historical study and encourage future building.

Cathedral Experiments

For Viollet-le-Duc, the Gothic cathedral represented the apex of rational structural design, with its characteristic visual elements (the flying buttress, the pinnacle, and the ribbed vault) derived from structural necessity. While many commentators missed the point of

[9]See quotation from *The Bridge* by Hart Crane in Alan Trachtenberg, *Brooklyn Bridge, Fact and Symbol* (New York, 1965), p. 153. Trachtenberg shows how the bridge became a work of art and a religious symbol.

[10]J. A. Roebling, *Report of John A. Roebling Civil Engineer to the President and Board of Directors of the Covington and Cincinnati Bridge Company* (Cincinnati, April 1, 1867), p. 23.

[11]Trachtenberg, p. 64.

his argument, others understood but were disturbed by the idea that architectural style did not derive primarily from aesthetic intuition. They refused to admit this intrusion of technology and argued that, if Viollet-le-Duc's ideas about how Gothic structural elements performed were incorrect, then, too, was his whole concept of structural rationalism. And indeed, in the light of new investigations, carried out particularly by his 20th-century detractors, inconsistencies in Viollet-le-Duc's technical reasoning became apparent. However, these investigations were not based on the modern structural modeling techniques developed to analyze structural forms as complex as the Gothic.

A series of detailed studies using both small-scale physical models and computer-based mathematical models has clarified these controversies and led to certain general conclusions about Gothic form that are applicable to the modern bridge form as well. Indeed, we have concluded that Viollet-le-Duc's insight connecting Gothic to modern design was sound in principle even if flawed in some details. To illustrate these engineering studies, we begin with a brief outline of the cathedral structure and proceed to show how such study can clarify the meaning of form.

The major obstacle to building covered vertical space in masonry is related to the problem of wall bending. As the space rises, the wall becomes higher and thereby more sensitive to horizontal loads. In the High Gothic cathedral, the structure had to carry not only the vertical weight of walls and vaulting but also the horizontal load of wind and vaulting thrust. This horizontal thrust arises because the vaulting acts like an arch. Arches of simple stones can carry vertical loads only when they are supported both vertically and horizontally; the effect of the combined vertical and horizontal support is to produce compression between the arch stones, thereby overcoming the tendency of the vertical loads to cause tension.

These horizontal forces, however, led to visible cracks in walls and even some collapses that evidently provided medieval builders with sufficient experience to realize that extra bracing was essential. In the very tall churches, this bracing developed into the flying buttress, one of the most striking forms of structure ever devised. And, as noted by Viollet-le-Duc, the impact of their use was to redefine the *style* of the High Gothic churches.[12] The flying buttresses in turn required for their support massive, tall pier buttresses on the perimeter of the church. These might well resist the horizontal forces from the flying buttresses, but in some instances cracking was now observed near the

---

[12] Viollet-le-Duc, *Dictionnaire*, 1:60.

tops of the pier buttresses. To close the cracks (technically, to cancel the tension causing the cracking by increasing the deadweight compression), additional stone was added to the pier-buttress tops in the form of pinnacles, and these, in turn, became another distinguishing feature of Gothic structure.

Both of these examples demonstrate three principles of structural design: first, the limits of form were signaled by difficulties that became visually apparent in full-scale completed works; second, these difficulties provided the stimulus to new design thinking which led to new forms; and third, those new forms celebrated as characteristic of their age were just the ones in which the visible structure became the form.

These general ideas are derived from many studies, of which one will illustrate the approach.[13] A model analysis of the buttressing system for the nave of Amiens Cathedral (constructed 1220–33) confirms that the lower tier of flying buttresses did support the light upper walls against horizontal thrust from the high vaults and that the upper tier of flying buttresses provides support against wind loadings. The tests also revealed that the pinnacles, placed on the outer edges of the pier buttresses, helped to maintain integrity of the pier buttresses by overcoming *local* tension caused by the combination of deadweight and high wind loadings (fig. 1). The pinnacle acts as a prestressing element. This finding was startling because the technical function of the pinnacle is masked by its evident decorative role and because overly simplified statical considerations (typical of 19th-century analyses and invoked in the 20th century specifically to debunk Viollet-le-Duc) would have indicated a more logical placement of the pinnacle to be along the inside edge rather than along the outside edge of the pier buttress.

The sophistication of the placement of the Amiens pinnacles to prestress the outside edge of the pier buttresses demanded explanation. Experience with modeling led us to conclude that the medieval builder had an experimental method parallel to our own—one that embraced the actual building. Tensile cracking caused either by high winds or by the removal of temporary construction supports could have been observed in the newly set, weak lime mortar between the ashlar during the relatively long periods of construction. Successive modifications made to the structure to prevent mortar cracking could then have been the source of structural innovation, with the pinnacled

[13]The building studies are reported on in greater detail in Robert Mark, *Experiments in Gothic Structure* (Cambridge, Mass., 1982). See also Robert Mark, James K. Chiu, and John F. Abel, "Stress Analysis of Historic Structures: Maillart's Warehouse at Chiasso," *Technology and Culture* 15 (January 1974): 49–63.

pier buttress of Amiens as an outstanding example of the success of this approach.

Another study, that of the choir of the cathedral at Beauvais (begun in 1225), demonstrated that the collapse of this highest of all Gothic cathedrals in 1284 might well have been prevented if designers could have seen the cracking caused by tension in the mortar of an upright element supporting the center of its oversized flying buttresses (fig.

FIG. 1.—Pinnacles on the pier buttresses of the nave of Amiens Cathedral, constructed 1220–33. (Photo by R. Mark.)

2). In this case, however, the critical region of the structure was enclosed by a timber roof and was not readily accessible for inspection.

As to Viollet-le-Duc's rationalist argument, our studies have generally vindicated his interpretation of the medieval master's approach to
structure. But in the discovery of the probable medieval technique of
mortar-crack observation, the studies provide only a partial explana-

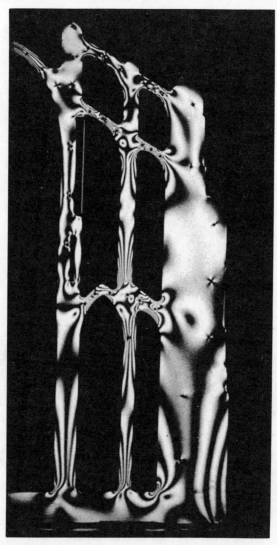

Fɪɢ. 2.—Photoelastic interference pattern, from simulation of high winds, in a model
of the structure of the choir of Beauvais Cathedral, constructed 1225–72. (Photo by R.
Mark.)

tion for the remarkable development in building form that took place during the Gothic era. There were other determinants. In spite of the great changes introduced, each new building retained many of the elements from preceding construction. The system of organization which allowed apprentices to rise through the ranks and even to assume the position of master builder-designer insured familiarity with earlier buildings. In effect, an earlier building acted as an approximate model confirming the stability of the new, larger building. Moreover, the strength of masonry in compression rarely governs structural failure. While the compressive strength of stone is quite variable, in all instances the tensile strength is far less than compression strength. But even more significant, the tensile strength of the mortar used between the imperfectly finished surfaces of the stones is far less than the already low stone tensile strength. Hence, in almost all cases only overall stability (overturning) and the absence or presence of tension within the weak mortar between the stones determine whether a masonry building is sound.

A final observation from a series of computer model studies was that Gothic vaulting is relatively insensitive to small geometric variations. This suggests that it was sufficient to copy existing vaults only in rough detail for use in other buildings, and it also helps to explain the general success of medieval masons with these and other complex structures in a period when design was largely a matter of trial and error.

There were, of course, many variations in detail from building to building. Structural experimentation with full-scale works did not then (or now) lead to a single standard set of details. Rather, inventions such as the flying buttress and the pinnacle liberated designers to refine in countless ways the details once the overall form was recognized as structurally sound. It was the discipline of accepting the observed truth of statics that ushered in the joyous variety of Gothic form.

Bridge Experiments

Just as with the medieval cathedral, the form of the modern bridge arose out of observed, full-scale difficulties. The glory of the Brooklyn Bridge lay predominantly in the visual play of Roebling's diagonal cables with the straight vertical ones (fig. 3). Vertical suspenders were usually used alone to connect deck and main curved cable. The diagonal cables were a direct result of Roebling's observations of the vertical oscillations occurring in suspension bridges under gusting winds; they provided necessary vertical stiffness missing in earlier bridges, many of which had collapsed.

Fig. 3.—View from the elevated walkway of the Brooklyn Bridge, constructed 1869–83 (Photo by R. Mark.)

Roebling knew about these collapses and derived his ideas from substantial, firsthand experience in the field.[14] The history of suspension bridges right up to the present time shows that the major ideas about form came from observations of completed structures, the most famous being the motion pictures of the Tacoma Narrows collapse in 1940. It may surprise the layman to realize that, even in an age of high technology and immense academic research budgets, such apparently needless failures are the main stimuli to new ideas. But in structural engineering the new ideas have always come from the field, and bridge design gives us as clear a picture of this process as any other type of building.

Twentieth-century concrete-arch bridges provide a striking illustration of the similarity between Gothic and modern approaches to design. Here we shall consider two examples of the origins of new form, both from the Swiss structural designer, Robert Maillart (1872–1940).[15] In 1901, Maillart completed, at the little Swiss town of Zuoz, his first major bridge and the first hollow-box concrete bridge built anywhere. The solid vertical walls connecting horizontal deck to curved arch slab exhibited vertical cracks near the abutments shortly after completion. Observing these, Maillart realized the incompleteness of his original idea even though the cracks did not impair the bridge's function (it was in service for two-thirds of a century before being rehabilitated in 1968).

After studying the cracking carefully on the site, Maillart was stimulated in his next bridge design to see a new possibility for form. This appeared in 1905 at Tavanasa as the lense-shaped, three-hinged, hollow-box arch which in the last ten years of his life he refined into his most expressive bridge forms. It was by subjecting himself to the severe discipline of observed behavior that he liberated his imagination from imitative shapes and thereby freed it to conceive of the new forms that have come to characterize 20th-century society.

Maillart's second major new idea in bridge design also arose out of observations of earlier cracking. In 1912 he completed a 60-meter-span solid arch bridge over the Aare River at Aarburg. Several years later, cracks appeared in the deck; and, after the war, when Maillart again began to design bridges, he converted the error (which again did not impair function since the bridge lasted until 1968, when it too was rehabilitated) into a new form, the deck-stiffened arch bridge, which led to a series of masterpieces between 1925 and 1934 (fig. 4).

[14] J. A. Roebling, "Report," *Order of Reference of Supreme Court of the Neutral States* (Saratoga Springs, N.Y., 1851), pp. 457–94.

[15] These examples are given in more detail in David P. Billington, *Robert Maillart's Bridges: The Art of Engineering* (Princeton, N.J., 1979); see esp. chaps. 4 and 7.

As with the flying buttress and pinnacle, the same three-stage process led to the three-hinged and the deck-stiffened forms: first, the limits of form were signaled by difficulties that became visually apparent in completed structures; second, the difficulties led Maillart to the design of new forms; and third, these new forms that were celebrated by the most perceptive art critics as characteristic of our own age were just those in which the structure became the form. It was no coincidence that the first one-man museum show devoted solely to engineering (at the Museum of Modern Art in 1947) displayed the work of Robert Maillart.

Just as in the High Gothic, Roebling, Maillart, and other modern bridge designers stretched materials to their limits to achieve new forms. Thus, their new bridges had to respond to the characteristics of new materials and new forms in society. These new social forms were widely proclaimed in the two major 18th-century revolutions and included such basic ideas as individual freedoms, equality disconnected from hereditary class, and a belief that monarchical society could be restructured for the common welfare by holding out the promise of alleviating oppressive human poverty. It is easy to see today that the grand hopes of Roebling and others were naive, but they were not without benefit. Indeed they are, as Eugene Ferguson

FIG. 4.—Schwandbach Bridge by Robert Maillart, constructed 1933. (Photo courtesy Losinger Co., Switzerland.)

argues, the hallmark of American society[16]—and that argument can be sustained for Swiss society as well.

All of this ferment can be characterized by a new sort of faith, one based on a sharing of natural resources and public money while at the same time expressing new ideas of beauty. These are just the beliefs articulated by Roebling, Maillart, and many other engineers both in their writings and in their works. These beliefs center on minimal waste of natural resources (materials of construction) and of human resources (cost of construction), coupled with the personal expression of style. It is in this sense that the new bridge and the old cathedral are similar symbols and are both expressions of life that includes technology, politics, and art.

Meaning in Structure

Our conclusions about new form in cathedrals and bridges have come from modern engineering studies that are both scientific and historical. The primary objectives of such studies are numerical accessibility, historical accuracy, and design ideas.

By numerical accessibility, we mean that the results of our research are aimed ultimately at educators and hence students. This means that, as engineering specialists, we are still striving to put our arguments in quantitative form because that is the language of engineering, and no one can really understand it without using some numbers. This can be expressed without calculus and without formal mechanics, in the modern academic sense; but it cannot be done without some understanding of stability, loads, internal forces, stresses, and safety. In a series of documents, we have demonstrated this meaning of forms by simple numerical arguments.[17] Engineering without numbers is like history without dates.

Our second major objective, historical accuracy, goes beyond numbers and dates to analyses of the social forces that bear upon all public works at all times in the past. These forces, not so easily quantified as the statics, include the political and economic constraints as well as the ideals and celebrations of people among whom large-scale structures arise. It is particularly crucial for engineers to make the case that bridges and other imposing 20th-century engineering structures are as symbolic of the highest social aspirations in our age as the cathedrals were in theirs. This seemingly impossible parallel can only be drawn convincingly if nonromantic historical accuracy can be focused on medieval life and a correspondingly accurate view shown for

[16]Eugene Ferguson, "The American-ness of American Technology," *Technology and Culture* 20 (January 1979): 3–23.

[17]An example of such a document is David P. Billington and Robert Mark, *Studies in Structural Form* (Princeton University, Department of Civil Engineering, 1983).

20th-century ideals. The sentimental retreat to Gothic revival must be balanced by a renewed realization of the joyous building period in which we now live.

Finally, after numbers and history, our third major objective is to bring to life the individuals who did the best modern design as well as those who wrote most perceptively about how the past, and especially the Gothic past, can be best assimilated into a new tradition for the future. From Viollet-le-Duc and Gustave Eiffel to Robert Maillart and his teacher, Wilhelm Ritter, these were people who approached the modern technological world with vision, enthusiasm, and above all with that combination of passion and discipline which makes their writings and their constructions of enduring value.[18]

What these objectives call forth, in our view, is a new type of educational document—one which presents engineering works in terms of authentic but simplified quantitative analysis; one which details the history of social forces that led finally to the completed structure; and one which includes substantial visual materials to demonstrate the personality of the writers and designers as well as the beauty of their works. These documents consist, therefore, of simplified calculations explaining form, of scholarly texts with bibliographies detailing historical origins and results, and of numerous slides integrated with the calculations and the historical texts. Such documents, we believe, can make both the history and the engineering accessible to engineering and liberal arts students and to the general public and can demonstrate this intrinsic connection between culture and the large-scale structures that symbolize its life.

[18]David P. Billington, *The Tower and the Bridge: The New Art of Structural Engineering* (New York, 1983).

Elegant Inventions: The Artistic Component of Technology

EUGENE S. FERGUSON

If you have a tendency to wonder about the *things* that make up our technological surroundings, as I do, then you have probably had the experience of imaging, or designing, or inventing a new thing or a modification of an existing thing. The earliest invention of mine that I recall was made in 1937 upon seeing a DC-3 passenger airplane land at the Newark, New Jersey, airport. On the spot I invented a landing-wheel spinner to prevent the sudden scuffing action of getting the wheel up to speed, as it touches down, in order to prevent a blowout of its tires. I even wrote to the Douglas Aircraft Company to announce my invention. I received a friendly letter from a vice-president (I suppose he was vice-president in charge of the nut letters). My vice-president told me that many people had tackled the problem, that there were several ways of spinning the wheels to get them up to landing speed, but that all of them required weight that would be better spent in making the treads of the tires heavier. It is interesting to note that the 1937 solution is also the 1977 solution: when an airplane touches down, the tires screech and the airplane bucks as the wheels suddenly, by friction on the runway, are brought up to landing speed.

My invention, clearly not unique, is an example of what I should call low-level inventing: it is mechanical design, the sort of thing most technologists do readily and habitually. It is a kind of technical problem solving that is carried out many millions of times a day by millions of people. The mechanic, engineer, and draftsman designer must respond continually to problems set by their materials, their tools, and their imaginations.

It is pretty well established that design and invention involve visual thinking, although the mechanism is not understood at all.[1] Until Edwin Layton analyzed the nature of technological design and its

EUGENE S. FERGUSON is professor emeritus of history, University of Delaware, and former curator of technology at the Hagley Museum. This article was his 1977 presidential address to the Society for the History of Technology.

This essay originally appeared in *Technology and Culture*, vol. 19, no. 3, July 1978.

relationship to scientific thought, it was difficult to refute the notion held by many scientists and others that the formal sciences were the only sources of knowledge in technology. Layton, in two pioneering papers, has established a fact that scientists and philosophers tend to overlook—that technology has a distinct component of knowledge not derived from science.[2] Nobody denies the contributions of science to technology, but crucial nonscientific decisions are always involved in the designing or shaping of any technological object. Otto Mayr has further recognized a class of abstract ideas in technology that cannot be derived from science—for example, the notion of a feedback control system.[3]

The inscrutability of this nonscientific mode of thought is brought into sharp relief in the case of a totally original invention of the kind I shall call an "elegant invention."

Before the elegant invention occurs, there is no inkling in an ordinary mind (and this includes my mind and most technologists' minds) of a solution to a problem; frequently there is no suggestion even that a problem exists. After an elegant invention comes into being, however, it appears to be a perfectly obvious solution to a particular problem, the sort of thing that elicits the question, "Why didn't I think of that?" Two brief examples must suffice. My first example (fig. 1) is the working or rocking beam, an element of the Newcomen steam engine, which came into use in 1712. This first successful steam engine, designed and built by Thomas Newcomen, an Englishman, pumped water out of mines for over sixty years before James Watt came along; it is, I believe, one of the great synthetic inventions of all time.

In the Newcomen engine, the chain attached to the engine piston (on the left) and the chain attached to the water pumps in the mine (on the right) are constrained by the sectors, or curved ends of the working beam, to move in a vertical line, up and down, as the great beam rocks back and forth, like a see-saw. This working beam, which solves the problem of guiding the chains and rods, on engine and pump, in a straight line as they move up and down, is in my view an elegant invention.

Some years ago, when I spent some considerable time in trying to find out where Newcomen got his idea, I uncovered just one published drawing, in a book of 1696, that made use of the principle (fig.

---

[2]Edwin Layton, "Mirror-Image Twins: The Communities of Science and Technology in 19th-Century America," *Technology and Culture* 12 (October 1971): 562–80, and "Technology as Knowledge," ibid., 15 (January 1974): 31–41.

[3]Otto Mayr stated the concept, until then quite unrecognized, in discussing a paper at the 1973 Burndy Library Conference (see *Technology and Culture* 17 [October 1976]: 663–73).

Dannemora Eld och Luft Machin,
Kongl. Majts och Rikßens Högloflliga Bergs Collegio
Underdän ödmiukaßt Dedicerad af Mårten Triewald.

FIG. 1.—Newcomen steam engine in Dannemora, Sweden, 1734. Engraving, Tekniska Museet, Stockholm. (Courtesy of Hagley Museum.)

2). This drawing, of a horse-driven water pump, would not have led my mind, nor most other minds, to Newcomen's working beam of 1712. Yet in books published after Newcomen's time, it seemed to me that the idea was everywhere, so obvious had it then become after Newcomen's bold, clear statement in the steam engines he built.

As with so many other ideas of the 18th century, the working beam was anticipated in one of Leonardo da Vinci's notebooks, but of course Newcomen had no access to that. Leonardo's notebooks were effectively buried until late in the 19th century. Nevertheless, it is worth a momentary digression to catch a glimpse of Leonardo's original and incisive mind as we follow one of his second thoughts, after he had completed his drawing of a two-cylinder water pump (fig. 3). The sketch at the left substitutes a pair of sectors for the entire circular pulley, or wheel, above the pump cylinders. Beneath the sketch at the

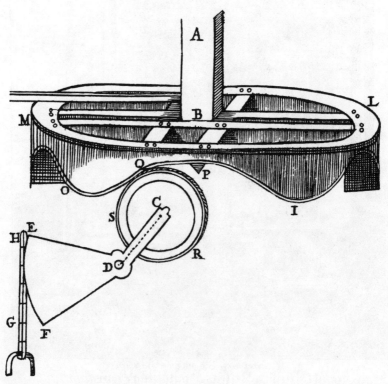

Fig. 2.—Horse-driven pump from V. Mandey & J. Moxon, *Mechanick-Powers* (London, 1696). Arm *CDEF* oscillates about fixed center *D* as scalloped cam turns. Sector *EF* lifts chain *HG*. Note similarity to sectors at ends of working beam in fig. 1. (Courtesy of Iowa State University.)

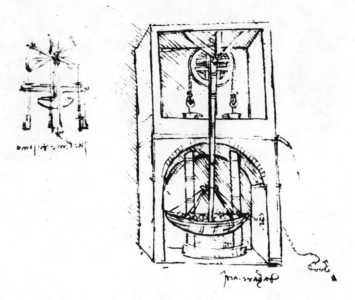

FIG. 3.—Two-cylinder water pump of Leonardo da Vinci. MS. B, f. 54v. (Courtesy of Library of Congress.)

left is Leonardo's notation: "quel medesimo" (the same). With a few strokes of his pen, Leonardo radically simplified the wheel, converting it to a beam while leaving the operation of the pump unchanged.

My second example is of uncertain date (but at least 100 years old),[4] and it has none of the historic importance of the Newcomen steam engine beam. I have chosen it simply because I can recall so vividly my personal response, which was one of wonder and delight, upon learning the solution to a problem whose existence I had never guessed. I have seen many little solid wooden animals, houses, trees, and the like that were clearly sawed off of a long, straight "stick" of an appropriate shape (fig. 4). I have never seen one of the long, unsawed pieces, but I should find it easy to devise a way to give the "stick" its proper shape, using a planelike tool (fig. 5). This is one of those things that pops into my mind when my mind raises the routine question, How was it made? The answer is obvious, and thus of no immediate interest.

In January of 1975 a group of Hagley fellows, under the leadership of my colleague John Beer, traveled in East Germay, Czechoslovakia, and Hungary; in the town of Seiffen, East Germany, they

[4]Mary Hiller, *Pageant of Toys* (New York, 1965), pp. 64–65.

Fig. 4.—Wooden toys animals and trees. (Courtesy of Mrs. E. G. Mobley, Hagley Museum.)

visited a toy museum and watched craftsmen making wooden toys. On a lathe, a craftsman was turning a ring of wood (fig. 6) whose purpose is quite impossible to guess until—the ring is cut apart (fig. 7). Here is my "stick" wrapped up into a ring. How obvious! Yet even though I have a pretty thorough familiarity with lathes and their products, I was not prepared for this, a total surprise and a truly elegant invention.

Let me eliminate from our analysis a red herring that frequently swims into view. I refer to the notion that form follows function, which suggests that the person who produces an elegant invention has somehow found the perfect form for the given function. All he has to do, we are told, is to study the function, and out of that will emerge a form. You may remember that it was Horatio Greenough, the sculptor of the seated figure of George Washington down the hall from us this evening [this address was given in the Flag Hall of the National Museum of History and Technology, Smithsonian Institution], who first tied form to function. That was a full generation before Louis Sullivan gave currency to what has become the simpleminded phrase "form follows function."

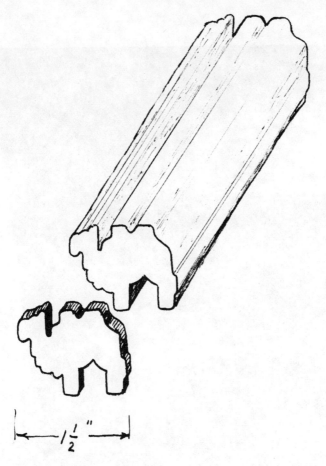

FIG. 5.—Method of producing camel of fig. 4. (Courtesy of Hagley Museum.)

David Pye, one of the wisest men I know, has a way of cutting vague
notions down to size. He points out that the designer, not the function, determines the form.[5] Consider the Newcomen engine. Except
for the specification that water was to be removed from the bottom of
a mine, there was no "function" of a mine pump for form to follow.
There was nothing to tell Thomas Newcomen what his engine should
look like, what the elements should be or how they should be arranged. The fact that his statement of a steam engine, embodied in
wood, metal, and stone, was so obviously correct that it remained

[5]David Pye, *The Nature of Design* (New York, 1964), pp. 10–11. In Pye's first chapter
the notion that form follows function is thoroughly demolished.

FIG. 6.—Lathe in toy museum, Seiffen, East Germany. (Courtesy of Donald R. Hoke, Hagley Museum.)

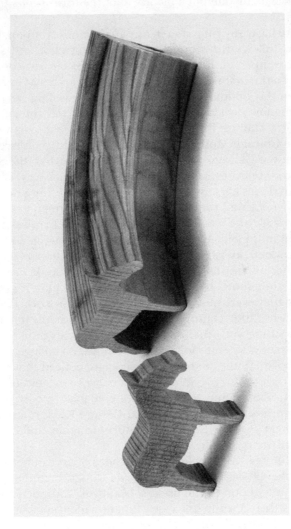

FIG. 7.—Portion of ring shown in fig. 6. Animals are split off as shown. (Courtesy of John Beer, Hagley Museum.)

totally unchanged for two human generations simply points up his genius. The engine certainly did not have to be arranged in the way he chose to build it. I received a letter recently from a designer who said, "To me it always seemed insane to suggest that form follows function, since to anyone but a bloody idiot the form *defines* the possible function."[6]

If we are to have any precision in our analysis of invention, we must reject "form follows function" except in the crudest and sloppiest sense. An example of form defining the possible function exists downstairs, on the first floor, in the direction opposite to Greenough's statue. When this building was being planned, a ceiling height of 14 feet was somehow decided upon. At the time, I was the curator responsible for a Hall of Tools. After construction had commenced, I found in the Chicago Museum of Science and Industry a large steam hammer that the Chicago people were willing to give to the Smithsonian. But I could never put the steam hammer, which was 16 feet tall, in the Hall of Tools because the form of a 14-foot ceiling defined the function and relegated the machine to storage. Fifteen years later, I am pleased to see the steam hammer in the 1876 Exhibition, which was mounted in the old Arts and Industries Building, in a hall whose form (determined in 1879) now follows the function of housing a steam hammer 16 feet tall. In Peter Blake's latest book, *Form Follows Fiasco*, the author shows how much better recycled buildings, applied to purposes they were not designed for, seem to work than those designed in the 20th century in accordance with the dogma that "form follows function." Blake cites, among other examples, the B & O Railroad station in Baltimore that now houses a college of art.

When Brooke Hindle, about four years ago, noticed that there was early in the 19th century a closer affinity between art and technology than between science and technology,[7] he enabled me eventually to grasp the significance of assertions that George Kubler, an art historian, and David Pye, an English furniture designer and craftsman, had made ten years earlier.

"Let us suppose," said Kubler, "that the idea of art can be expanded to embrace the whole range of man-made things, including all tools and writing in addition to the useless, beautiful, and poetic things of the world. By this view the universe of man-made things simply coincides with the history of art."[8] The advantage of Kubler's view is that

[6]Letter from Gary Goodman, Hardinsburg, Ky. (ca. September 1, 1977).

[7]Brooke Hindle, "The Underside of the Learned Society in New York, 1754–1854," in *The Pursuit of Knowledge in the Early American Republic*, ed. Alexandra Oleson and Sanborn C. Brown (Baltimore, 1976), pp. 84–116.

[8]George Kubler, *The Shape of Time* (New Haven, Conn., 1962), p. 1.

we do not have to argue over what is an art object and what is a utilitarian object; we can concentrate on the notion that all objects exist in a continuum from useless to useful, from beautiful to ugly. The ends of the continuum will shift as various people look at it, but the invidious distinction between art and nonart does not have to be made. Thus we begin to see that the nonscientific elements of technology owe a great deal to art. Inscrutability yields to the recognition that the elegant invention is indeed a work of art.

David Pye puts the same idea a little differently and adds a judgment that makes the whole thing plausible. He writes, "The manmade world, our environment, is a work of art, every bit of it. But not all good."[9] Pye observes further, on the basis of his experience in training industrial designers, that one who "is capable of invention as an artist is commonly capable also of useful invention." Leonardo da Vinci, says Pye, is thought to be exceptional in combining artistic and practical talents. Quite the contrary, he concludes, "The combination is usual rather than exceptional, so usual in fact that one is led to suspect that both are really different expressions of one potentiality."[10]

Such is the temper of our age that most technologists would rather be called scientists than artists. Yet necessary as science is to analysis, just as necessary is art to invention. Even in today's scientific technology, the artistic component remains essential in the search for elegant solutions. Science will continue to influence technology, but it is art that will choose the specific shape of the future.

[9]Pye, p. 7.
[10]Ibid., p. 72.

INDEX

Adams, Henry, 309–10
Adapter. *See* Electrical adapter
Adler, George, 131
"Aetna," the, 50–51. *See also* Marine boiler explosions (U.S.)
Agricultural Adjustment Act, 172
Air pollution, 2, 21–42, 204
Alaska Packers Association (APA), 78–79
Alkali Works Regulation Act of 1863 (England), 27, 38
"All-electric" home, 129, 131 n. *See also* Domestic electrification
"All-electric" kitchen, 9, 140
Alternative fuels, 3
American Can Company, 83–84
American City, 144, 147–48
American Engineer, 64
American Journal of Public Health, 146, 151
American Nuclear Society, 193, 205
American Public Health Association, 141, 146–47, 154
American Public Works Association, 141, 147
American Society of Civil Engineers, 141
American Society of Mechanical Engineers, 64
American Telephone and Telegraph (AT&T), 87, 89–91, 93, 95, 98, 104, 111–12, 115. *See also* Bell System
Amiens Cathedral, 312–13
Apollo space program, 235–36, 242, 246, 249
Apollo-Saturn hardware, 236, 249
"Appliance," 119
Arago, 49–50
Arch. *See* Hollow-box arch; Deck-stiffened arch
Arendt, Hannah, 262 n.
Argand furnace, 32, 34–35, 40
Argand lamp, 32–33
Argonne National Laboratory, 181
Art deco, 167
Artificial gravity, 238–42
Aryton, Acton, 26
Astronomy, and the space station, 244–45

Atomic Energy Act, 191, 216, 221
Atomic Energy Commission (AEC). *See* U.S. Atomic Energy Commission
Atomic Industrial Forum, 193
Atomics International, 205
Automatically erectable manned orbital space station, 239–41
"Autonomous technology," 87
Ayer, N. W., 115

Baby bottle, 15, 292
Bache, Alexander Dallas, 54–55
Baekeland, Leo, 166
Baghouses, 38
Bailey, Joseph, 26
Batteries, 134
Baumol, William, 275
Beard, Charles A., 168–69
Beardsley, Robert C., 188
Beche, Sir Henry De la, 25
Beecher, Catherine, 300
Beer, John, 325
Beggs, James M., 253
Bell, Alexander Graham, 7, 89, 98, 103
Bell Laboratories, 171
Bell System, 89–92, 94–97, 100, 104, 107–8 (*see also* American Telephone and Telegraph [AT&T]): Bell Canada, 96–98, 99 n., 101, 102 n.; competition with other vendors, 90–91, 94–95; cultural mind-set of industry leaders, 103–4, 111–13, 116; Pacific Telephone and Telegraph (PT&T), 95, 97–98, 99 n., 102, 105; patent battle with Western Union, 89; Southwestern Bell Telephone Company, 96
Benjamin plug, 123, 127
Benjamin, Reuben, 122–23
Benton, Thomas Hart, 54
Bergmann, Sigmund, 120, 122–23, 126–27.
Berk, Richard, 269
Berk, Sarah, 269
Biot, 49
Black belt, 21
Black Death, 21
"Black fogs," 22
Blackouts, 203